The Myth of Mental Illness

Thomas S. Szasz, M.D.

The Myth of Mental Illness

Foundations

of a

Theory of

Personal

Conduct

A Hoeber-Harper Book

FIFTH PRINTING 1968

THE MYTH OF MENTAL ILLNESS: FOUNDATIONS OF A THEORY
OF PERSONAL CONDUCT

LIBRARY OF CONGRESS CATALOG CARD NUMBER: 61-9714

To my wife, Rosine

"The game must go on: that is Nature's command. But it is up to man to determine the ground rules and the teams. The determination of the rules is principally the responsibility of the specialist in ethics. The delineation of the teams—well, that is a task for which many disciplines are needed."

—GARRETT HARDIN (1959, p. 318)

Contents

I became interested in writing this book approximately ten years ago when, having become established as a psychiatrist, I became increasingly impressed by the vague, capricious, and generally unsatisfactory character of the widely used concept of mental illness and its corollaries, diagnosis, prognosis, and treatment. It seemed to me that although the notion of mental illness made good *historical* sense—stemming as it does from the historical identity of medicine and psychiatry—it made no *rational* sense. Although mental illness might have been a useful concept in the nineteenth century, today it is scientifically worthless and socially harmful.

Although dissatisfaction with the medical basis and conceptual framework of psychiatry is not of recent origin, little has been done to make the problem explicit, and even less to remedy it. In psychiatric circles it is almost indelicate to ask: "What is mental illness?" In nonpsychiatric circles mental illness all too often is considered to be whatever psychiatrists say it is. The answer to the question "Who is mentally ill?" thus becomes: "Those who are confined in mental hospitals or who consult psychiatrists in their private offices."

Perhaps these answers sound silly. If they do, it is because they are silly. However, it is not easy to give better answers without going to a good deal of trouble, first, by asking other questions, such as "Is mental illness an illness?" and second, by resetting one's goals from understanding mental illness to understanding human beings.

The need to re-examine the problem of mental illness is both timely and pressing. There is confusion, dissatisfaction, and tension in our society concerning psychiatric, psychological, and social issues. Mental illness is said to be the nation's number one health problem. The statistics marshaled to prove this contention are impressive: more than a half-million hospital beds for mental patients, and 17 million persons allegedly suffering from some degree of mental illness.

The concept of mental illness is freely used in all the major news media—the newspapers, radio, and television. Sometimes famous persons are said to be mentally ill—for example, Adolf Hitler, Ezra Pound, Earl Long. At other times the label is attached to the most lowly and unfortunate members of society, especially if they are accused of a crime.

The popularity of psychotherapy, and people's alleged need for it, is rapidly increasing. At the same time it is impossible to answer the question "What is psychotherapy?" The term "psychotherapy" encompasses nearly everything that people do in the company of one another. Psychoanalysis, group psychotherapy, religious counseling, rehabilitation of prisoners, and many other activities all are called "psychotherapy."

This book was written in an effort to dispel the perplexities mentioned, and thereby to clarify the psychiatric air. Parts I and II are devoted to laying bare the sociohistorical and epistemological roots of the modern concept of mental illness. The question "What *is* mental illness?" is shown to be inextricably tied to the question "What do psychiatrists *do?*" My first task, accordingly, is to present an essentially "destructive" analysis of the concept of mental illness and of psychiatry as a pseudomedical enterprise. I believe that such "destruction," like tearing down old buildings, is necessary if we are to construct a new, more habitable edifice for the science of man.

Since it is difficult to scrap one conceptual model without having another with which to replace it, I had to search for a new point of view. My second task is to offer a "constructive" synthesis of the knowledge which I have found useful for filling the gap left by the myth of mental illness. Parts III, IV, and V are devoted to the presentation of a systematic theory of personal conduct, based partly on materials culled from psychiatry, psychoanalysis, and other disciplines, and partly on my own observations and ideas. The omission from psychiatric theories of moral issues and normative standards, as explicitly stated goals and rules of conduct, has divorced psychiatry from precisely that reality which it has tried to describe and explain. I have endeavored to correct this defect by means of a game-theory of human living, which enables us to combine ethical, political, religious, and social considerations with the more traditional concerns of medicine and psychiatry.

Although my thesis is that mental illness is a myth, this book is not an attempt to "debunk psychiatry." There are altogether too many books today that attempt either to sell psychiatry and psychotherapy or to unsell them. The former usually set out to show why and how this or that form of behavior *is* "mental illness," and how psychiatrists *can* help a person so afflicted. The latter often employ a two-pronged attack suggesting that psychiatrists themselves are "mentally ill," and that psychotherapy is a poor method for "treating" a sickness that manifests itself in symptoms as serious as those of mental illness.

I should like to make clear, therefore, that although I consider the concept of mental illness to be unserviceable, I believe that psychiatry could be a science. I also believe that psychotherapy is an effective method of helping people—not to recover from an "illness," it is true, but rather to learn about themselves, others, and life.

In sum, then, this is not a book on psychiatry, nor is it a book on the nature of man. It is a book *about* psychiatry—inquiring, as it does, into what people, but particularly psychiatrists and patients, have done with and to one another. It is also a book about human nature, but more narrowly about human conduct—since in it observations and hypotheses are offered concerning how people live.

T. S. SZASZ

Syracuse, New York

Acknowledgments

Many persons have helped in the preparation of this book. First and foremost, I wish to thank Dr. Marc H. Hollender for providing the kind of academic atmosphere necessary for writing such a book. In addition, he read critically the entire manuscript and made many suggestions for improving it.

Dr. Arthur Ecker and Dr. Samuel D. Lipton have also read the entire manuscript and offered discerning criticisms. Dr. Judson Albaugh, Dr. Robert Daly, Dr. Eugene Kaplan, Dr. Ronald Leifer, Professor David Owen, Dr. Louis Patrizio, Dr. Charles Reed, Dr. Julius B. Richmond, Dr. John J. Sandt, and Dr. Edward Sulzer have read parts of the book and contributed valuable suggestions.

I wish to thank the many authors, editors, and publishers for permission to quote from copyrighted material.

I should also like to thank Mrs. Arthur Ecker for improving my grammar and style; Miss Dorothy Donaldson, Assistant Librarian at the State University of New York Upstate Medical Center, for securing many of the references consulted in the preparation of this volume; and Mrs. Margaret Bassett for excellent secretarial services.

Finally, I am deeply grateful to the staff of the publisher, Paul B. Hoeber, Inc., and particularly to Miss Claire Drullard, for the care with which they transformed my manuscript into a finished book.

"Science must begin with myths, and with the criticism of myths."

Karl R. Popper (1957, p. 177)

| Introduction

Sooner or later every scientific enterprise comes to a fork in the road. Scientists must then decide which of two paths to follow. The dilemma that must be faced is: How shall we conceive of what we do? Should we think of what we do in terms of *substantives* and *entities*—for example, elements, compounds, living things, mental illnesses, and so forth? Or should we think of it in terms of *processes* and *activities*—for example, Brownian movement, oxidation, or communication? We need not consider the dilemma in the abstract, other than to note that these two modes of conceptualization represent a developmental sequence in the evolution of scientific thought. Entity-thinking has always preceded process-thinking. Physics, chemistry, and certain branches of biology have long ago supplemented substantive conceptualizations by process-theories. Psychiatry has not.

Scope and Methods of the Study

I submit that the traditional definition of psychiatry, which is still in vogue, places it alongside such things as alchemy and astrology, and commits it to the category of pseudo science. Psychiatry is said to be a medical specialty concerned with the study and treatment of mental illness. Similarly, astrology was the study of the influence of planetary movements and positions on human behavior and destiny. These are typical instances of defining a science by specifying the subject matter of study. These definitions completely disregard method and are based instead on false substantives (Szasz, 1958a, 1959b). The activities of alchemists and astrologers—in contrast to the activities of chemists and astronomers—were not bound by publicly disclosed methods of observation and inference. Psychiatrists, likewise, have persistently avoided disclosing fully and publicly what they do. Indeed, whether as therapists or theorists, they may do virtually anything and still be considered psychiatrists. Thus, the behavior of a particular psychiatrist—as a member of the species "psychiatrist"—may be that of a physician, clergyman, friend, counselor, teacher, psychoanalyst, or all manner of combinations of these. He is a psychiatrist so long as he claims that he is oriented toward the problem of mental illness and health. But suppose, for a moment, that there is no such thing as mental illness and health. Suppose, further, that these words refer to nothing more substantial or real than the astrological conception of planetary influences on human conduct. What then?

METHODS OF OBSERVATION AND ACTION IN PSYCHIATRY

Psychiatry stands at the crossroads. Thus far, thinking in terms of substantives—for example, neurosis, disease, treatment—has been the rule. The question is: Shall we continue along the same road, or branch off in the direction of process-thinking? Viewed in this light, my efforts in this study are directed first *at demolishing some of the major false substantives of contemporary psychiatric thought,* and second *at laying the foundations for a process-theory of personal conduct.*

Discrepancies between what people say they do and what they actually do are encountered in all walks of life, science included. The principle of operationism, made into a systematic philosophy of science by Bridgman (1936), was succinctly formulated by Einstein (1933) in connection with exactly this discrepancy in physics:

> If you want to find out anything from the theoretical physicists
> about the methods they use, I advise you to stick closely to one
> principle: Don't listen to their words, fix your attention on their
> deeds (p. 30).

Surely there is no reason to assume that this principle is any less valid for understanding the methods—and hence the nature and subject—of psychiatry.

Briefly stated, an operational definition of a concept is one that relates it to actual "operations." A physical concept is defined by physical operations, such as measurements of time, temperature, distance, and so forth. In physics, operational definitions may be contrasted with idealistic definitions, the latter being exemplified by the classic, pre-Einsteinian notions of Time, Space, and Mass. Similarly, a psychological or sociological concept, defined operationally, relates to psychological or sociological observations or measurements. In contrast, many psychosocial concepts are defined on the basis of the investigator's self-proclaimed intentions or values. The majority of present-day psychiatric concepts belong in the latter category.

The answer to the question "What do psychiatrists do?" depends, therefore, on the kind of psychiatrist one has in mind. He might be any of the following (the list is not necessarily complete): one who physically examines patients, administers drugs and electric shock treatments, signs commitment papers, examines criminals and testifies concerning them in courts, or, most commonly, perhaps, listens and talks to patients. In this book, I shall be concerned mainly with psychiatry as a special discipline whose method is, rather derisively but nevertheless quite correctly, often spoken of as "only talking." If the word "only" is disregarded as gratuitous condemnation, and if the meaning of "talking" is enlarged to encompass communications of all kinds, we arrive at the formulation of a basic method of psychiatry to which surprisingly few psychiatrists really subscribe. In fact, there is a split, perhaps even an unbridgeable gap, between what most psychotherapists and psychoanalysts do in the course of their work and what they say concerning the nature of it. What they do, of course, is to communicate with patients by means of language, nonverbal signs, and rules. Further, they analyze, by means of verbal symbols, the communicative interactions which they observe and in which they themselves engage. This, I believe, correctly describes the actual operations of psychoanalysis and psychosocially oriented psychiatry. But what do these psychiatrists tell themselves and others concerning their work? They talk as though they were physicians, physiologists, biologists, or even physicists! We hear about sick patients, instincts, and endocrine functions and of course "libido" and "psychic energies," both "free" and "bound." While the need for clarity in regard to scientific method is no longer a new idea among scientists, it requires re-emphasis in our field.

Psychiatry, using the methods of communication analysis, has much in common with the sciences concerned with the study of languages and communicative behavior. In spite of this connection between psychiatry and such disciplines as symbolic logic, semiotic,[1] and sociology, problems of mental health continue to be cast in the traditional framework of medicine. The conceptual scaffolding of medicine, on the other hand, has rested on the principles of physics and chemistry. This is entirely reasonable, for it has been and continues to be the task of medicine to study—and if necessary to alter—the physicochemical structure and function of the human body. Man's sign-using behavior, however, does not seem to lend itself to exploration and understanding in these terms.

The distinction between psychology and physics is, of course, a familiar

[1] The term "semiotic" will be used to designate the *science of signs* (Morris, 1946, 1955).

one. The differences, however, are not usually taken seriously enough. The lack of commitment to psychology as a legitimate science is revealed by some scientists' outspoken expectation that in the end all scientific observations and statements will be phrased in a mathematico-physical idiom. More specifically, in the language of psychiatry and psychoanalysis infidelity to subject and methods is expressed in the persistent imitation of medicine. Thus we continue to speak of and presumably believe in such notions as "psychopathology" and "psychotherapy." This, at least, is the manifest state of our science. At the same time, ideas concerning object relationships and communications have gained greater acceptance, especially in recent decades. But a science can be no better than its linguistic apparatus permits. Hence our continued reliance on such notions as "neurosis," "psychosis," "emotional illness," "psychoanalytic treatment," and so forth cannot be lightly dismissed. We remain shackled to a scientifically outmoded conceptual framework and its terminology. We cannot, however, forever hold fast to and profit from the morally judgmental and socially manipulative character of our traditional psychiatric and psychoanalytic language without paying a price. I believe that we are in danger of purchasing superiority and power over nonpsychiatrists and patients at the cost of scientific self-sterilization and hence ultimate professional self-destruction.

CAUSALITY AND HISTORICISM IN MODERN PSYCHIATRY

The issues of historical constancy and predictability are of the utmost importance for all of psychiatry. Questions such as whether hysteria was "always the same disease" revolve around it, as does also the question of whether a psychotherapist can "predict" whether Mr. X will be happy in marriage with Miss Y. It is implicit in traditional psychoanalytic thought that prediction is a legitimate concern of this science. One often hears, nowadays, about how prediction ought to be used to "validate" psychoanalytic hypotheses. I believe we should have serious reservations concerning such preoccupations with controlling and predicting psychosocial occurrences. Caution and skepticism require that we pay attention to the epistemology of psychiatry, and especially to the implications of deterministic and historic explanations of human behavior.

The psychoanalytic theory of man was fashioned after the causal-deterministic model of classical physics. The errors of this transposition have been amply documented in recent years (for example, Gregory, 1953; Allport, 1955). I wish to call attention here to that application of the principle of physical determinism to human affairs which Popper (1944-1945) aptly termed "historicism." Examination of much of modern psychiatric thought

discloses the fundamental role of antecedent historical events as alleged *determinants* of subsequent behavior. The psychoanalytic theory of behavior is, therefore, a species of historicism. As long as this type of explanation is considered satisfactory, there is no need for other types of explanations, such as will be presented in this book. It should be kept in mind, in this connection, that historicist theories of behavior preclude explanations of valuation, choice, and responsibility in human affairs.

Briefly stated, historicism is a doctrine according to which historical prediction is essentially no different from physical prediction. Historical (e.g., psychological, social) events are viewed as fully determined by their antecedents, in the same manner as physical events are by theirs. The prediction of future events is, therefore, possible in principle. In practice, prediction is considered to be limited by the extent to which past and present conditions can be accurately determined. Insofar as these can be adequately ascertained, successful prediction is assured.

Popper's models of historicist social thinkers were men like Plato, Nietzsche, Marx, and the modern totalitarian dictators and their apologists. According to historicist doctrine the future is determined—in a sense, irrevocably—by the past: "Every version of historicism expresses the feeling of being swept into the future by irresistible forces" (Popper, 1944-1945, p. 160). Compare this with Freud's thesis that human conduct is determined by "unconscious forces" which, in turn, are the results of instinctual drives and early experiences. The crucial similarity between Marxism and classical psychoanalysis lies in the selection of a single type of antecedent cause as sufficient explanation of virtually all subsequent human events. In Marxism, human nature and conduct are determined by economic conditions; in psychoanalysis they are determined by family-historical (genetic-psychological) factors. Paradoxically, therapy is based on the expectation that reason and understanding might help to mitigate the otherwise irresistible forces of historicism. But whether the past is, in fact, so powerful a determinant of future human actions as it is of future physical events is a moot question. It is by no means the established fact that Freud claimed it was. This unsupported—and, I submit, false—theory of personal conduct has become widely accepted in our present day. It even has received legal approval, so to speak, by the American criminal statutes that codify certain types of actions as potentially the results of "mental illnesses."

The principal basis for the failure of historicism is that, in the social sciences, we are faced with a full and complicated interaction between observer and observed. Specifically, the prediction of a social event itself, may cause it to occur or may lead to its prevention. The so-called self-fulfilling prophecy—in which the predictor helps bring about the predicted event—exemplifies the empirical and logical complexities with which prediction in the social sphere is fraught. All this is not intended to deny or minimize the effects and significance of past experiences—that is, of historical antecedents—on subsequent human performances. The past does mold the personality and the human organism, as it may also mold machines (Wiener, 1960). This process, however, must be conceptualized and understood not in terms of antecedent "causes" and subsequent "effects" but rather in terms of modifications in the entire organization and functioning of the object acted upon.

In view of the rather obvious empirical and logical inadequacies of historicist theories, one may ask: What is the value of subscribing to an historicist position? In addition to providing a painstaking refutation of historicism, Popper (1944-1945) suggested an explanation of why many people adhere to it. He stated:

> It really looks as if *historicists were trying to compensate themselves for the loss of an unchanging world* by clinging to the belief that *change can be foreseen* because it is ruled by an *unchanging law* ([ITALICS ADDED] p. 161).

Let us recall in this connection that Freud (1927) proposed a similar explanation for why men believe in religion. He attributed religious belief to man's inability to tolerate the loss of the familiar world of childhood, symbolized by the protective father. Thus, a "father-in-heaven" and a replica of the protective childhood game are created to replace the father and the family lost in the here-and-now. The difference between religion and political historicism, from this point of view, is only in the specific identities of the "protectors." They are God and the theologians in the first instance, while in the second they are the modern totalitarian leaders and their apologists.

It is especially important to emphasize, therefore, that although Freud criticized organized religion for the patent infantilism that it is, he failed to apprehend the social characteristics of the "closed society" and the psychological characteristics of its loyal supporters. The paradox that is psychoanalysis—consisting on the one hand of an historicist theory and on the other of an antihistoricist therapy—thus came into being. Whatever the reasons—and many have been suggested—Freud (1940) adopted and promoted a biopsychological world view embodying the principle of constancy and resting squarely on it. We may assume that historicism had the same function for him, and for those who joined with him in the precarious early psychoanalytic movement, as it had for others: it provided a hidden source of comfort against the threat of unforeseen and unpredictable change. This interpretation is consonant with the current use of psychoanalysis and "dynamic psychiatry" as means for obscuring and disguising moral and political conflicts as mere personal problems (Szasz, 1960c).

In this connection, Rieff (1959) suggested that: "The popularity of psychoanalysis, in an age suffering vertigo from the acceleration of historical events, may be partly ascribed to *Freud's rehabilitation of the constant nature underlying history*" ([ITALICS ADDED] p. 214).

I am in agreement with Popper, however, that there is no such "constant nature underlying history"! Both man and society change, and, as they do, "human nature" changes with them.

In the light of these considerations, what could we say concerning the relationship between psychosocial and physical laws? The two are not similar. Psychosocial antecedents do not "cause" human sign-using behavior in the same manner as physical antecedents "cause" their effects (Ryle, 1949). Furthermore, physical laws are relativistic with respect to physical circumstances, in particular to the size of the mass. The laws governing the behavior of large bodies (Newtonian physics) differ from those that govern the behavior of very small ones (quantum physics). It seems to me that as physical laws are relativistic with respect to mass, so psychological laws are relativistic with respect to social conditions. In other words, *the laws of psychology cannot be formulated independently of the laws of sociology.*

PSYCHIATRY AND ETHICS

From the point of view which will be presented here, *psychiatry, as a theoretical science, consists of the study of personal conduct*—of clarifying and "explaining" the kinds of games that people play with each other; how they learned these games; why they like to play them; and so forth.[2] Actual behavior is the raw data from which the rules of the game are inferred. From among the many different kinds of behavior, the verbal form—or communication by means of conventional language—constitutes one of the central areas of interests for psychiatry. Thus, it is in the structure of language games (Sellars, 1954) that the interests of linguistics, philosophy, psychiatry, and semiotic meet. Each of these disciplines has addressed itself to different aspects of the language game: linguistics to its structure, philosophy

---

[2] A systematic analysis of personal conduct in terms of game-playing behavior will be presented in Part V. The *model of games*, however, is used throughout the book. Unless otherwise specified, by "games" I refer to ordinary card games, board games, or sports. Although it is difficult to give a concise definition of the concept of game, game situations are characterized by a system of set roles and rules considered more or less binding for all of the players.

to its cognitive signification, and psychiatry to its social usage.

It is hoped that this approach will effect a much-needed and long overdue *rapprochement* between psychiatry on the one hand and philosophy and ethics on the other. Questions such as: "How does man live?" and "How ought man to live?" traditionally have been in the domains of philosophy, ethics, and religion. Psychology—and psychiatry, as a branch of it—was closely allied to philosophy and ethics until the latter part of the nineteenth century. Since then, psychologists have considered themselves empirical scientists whose methods and theories are allegedly no different than those of the physicist or biologist. But insofar as psychologists address themselves to the two questions raised above, their methods and theories do differ, to some extent, from those of the natural scientists. If these considerations are valid, psychiatrists cannot expect to solve ethical problems by medical methods.

In sum, then, inasmuch as psychiatric theories seek to explain, and systems of psychotherapy to alter, human behavior, statements concerning goals and values ("ethics") will be considered indispensable parts of theories of personal conduct and psychotherapy.

HYSTERIA AS A PARADIGM OF MENTAL ILLNESS

Modern psychiatry, if dated from Charcot's work on hysteria and hypnosis, is approximately one hundred years old. How did the study of so-called mental illnesses begin and develop? What economic, moral, political, and social forces helped to mold it into its present form? And perhaps most important, what effect did medicine, and particularly the concept of bodily illness, have on the development of the concept of mental illness?

The strategy of this inquiry will be to answer these questions, using conversion hysteria as a paradigm of the sort of phenomena to which the term "mental illness" may refer. Hysteria was selected for the following reasons:

Historically, it is the problem that captured the attention of the pioneer neuropsychiatrists (e.g., Charcot, Janet, Freud) and led to the gradual differentiation of neurology and psychiatry.

Logically, hysteria brings into focus the need to distinguish bodily illness from imitations of such illness. It thus presented the physician with the task of distinguishing the "real" or genuine from the "unreal" or false. The distinction between fact and facsimile—often apprehended as the distinction between object and sign, or between physics and psychology—remains the core-problem of contemporary psychiatric epistemology.

Psychosocially, conversion hysteria provides an excellent example of how so-called mental illness can best be conceptualized in terms of sign-using, rule-following, and game-playing because: (1) Hysteria is a form of nonverbal communication, making use of a special set of signs. (2) It is a system of rule-following behavior, making special use of the rules of helplessness, illness, and coercion. (3) It is a game characterized, among other things, by the end-goals of domination and interpersonal control and by strategies of deceit.

Everything that will be said about hysteria pertains equally, in principle, to all other so-called mental illnesses and to personal conduct generally. The manifest diversity of mental illnesses—for example, the differences between hysteria, obsessions, paranoia, etc.—may be regarded as analogous to the manifest diversity characterizing different languages. Behind the phenomenological differences, we may discover certain similarities. Within a particular family of languages, as for instance the Indo-European, there are significant similarities of both structure and function. Thus, English and French have much in common, whereas both differ greatly from Hungarian. Similarly, hysterical picture language and dream language are closely allied, whereas both differ significantly from a paranoid systematization. To be specific, both hysteria and dreams make extensive use of iconic signs, whereas paranoia makes extensive use of conventional signs (that is, everyday speech). The characteristic impact of paranoid transactions derives not from the peculiarity of the signs used but from the function to which they are put—noncognitive, promotive, object-seeking. To the analysis of personal conduct as communication, similar analyses in terms of rule-following and game-playing will be added. Of the three models, the game is most comprehensive, since it encompasses the other two (i.e., sign-using and rule-following).

Sociohistorical and Epistemological Foundations of Modern Psychiatry

In Part I, our task will be to examine how the modern concepts of hysteria and mental illness arose, developed, and now flourish. The sociohistorical contexts in which medicine, neurology, and later psychiatry were practiced, as well as the logical foundation of basic medical and psychiatric concepts, will be the main targets of interest and critical scrutiny. In the terminology of Gestalt psychology, this means that, at least at the beginning, we shall be more interested in the "ground" than in the "figure." The ground is the historical and sociopsychological context in which hysteria appears as the figure, or problem, to be studied and comprehended. As varying the background in an experiment in visual perception may make an object appear, become intensified, or disappear—so it is with problems of so-called mental illness. When the social background of behavioral phenomena is treated as a variable, the phenomena of mental illness can be seen to appear, become intensified, diminish, or disappear. It has long been known that an hysterical paralysis, for example, may disappear when a person is threatened by an acute danger, say a fire. Similarly, the disappearance of all sorts of neurotic illnesses in people sent to concentration camps is an illustration of how changes in the "ground" affect the perception—or perhaps in this case we may say the very existence—of the "figure."

Inasmuch as psychoanalysis has gradually become identified as the branch of psychology especially concerned with the *intrapersonal* dimensions of human problems, it fell to other branches of the science of man to take cognizance of the *sociohistorical* background in which the phenomena studied are imbedded—first, to so-called dissident schools of psychoanalysis, lately to so-called social psychiatry. I believe that the identification of psychoanalysis with the purely, or even principally, intrapersonal dimension is false. From its inception psychoanalysis has been concerned with man's relationship to his fellow man, and to the group in which he lives. Unfortunately, this concern has been obscured by an ostensibly medical orientation.

Scrutiny of the sociohistorical context in which the modern concept of hysteria arose will necessitate an examination of the problem of imitation. We will thus be led to the logic of the relation between "real" and "false," irrespective of whether this distinction is encountered in medicine, psychiatry, or elsewhere. Since the distinction between "real" and "false" requires human judgment, the criteria on which such judgments in medicine and psychiatry are based, and the persons institutionally authorized to render such judgments, will be of the greatest significance and will be discussed in detail. In medicine, the criteria for distinguishing the genuine from the facsimile—that is, real illness from malingering—were based first on the presence or absence of demonstrable changes in the *structure* of the human body. Such findings may be obtained by means of clinical examination, laboratory tests, or post-mortem studies of the cadaver.

The beginning of modern psychiatry coincided with a new criterion for distinguishing real from false disease, namely, *alteration in function*. Conversion hysteria was the prototype of so-called *functional illness*. As paresis, for example, was considered a structural disease of the brain, so hysteria and mental illnesses generally were considered to be functional diseases of the same organ. So-called functional illnesses were thus placed in the same category as structural illnesses and were distinguished from imitated illnesses by means of the criterion of *voluntary falsification*. Accordingly, hysteria, neurasthenia, obsessive-compulsive neurosis, depression, paranoia, and so forth were regarded as diseases that happened to people. Mentally sick persons did not "will" their pathological behavior and were considered not "responsible" for it. These "mental diseases" were henceforth contrasted with malingering, which was the voluntary imitation of illness. In recent decades psychiatrists have claimed that malingering, too, is a form of mental illness. This poses a logical dilemma—the dilemma of the existence of an alleged entity called "mental illness" which, even when deliberately counterfeited, is still "mental illness."

Beside the empirical criteria for judging illness as real or false, the sociology of the judge officially authorized to render such judgments is of decisive significance. Some of the questions that arise are: What sorts of persons have the social power to make their judgments heard and to implement them? How do social class standing and the political makeup of society affect the roles of the judge and the potentially sick person?

To answer these questions, an inquiry into medical and psychiatric practices in late nineteenth-century Western Europe, contemporary America, and Soviet Russia will be presented.

The conceptual and sociohistorical roots of the notion of mental illness are intertwined. Each root must be clearly identified. This work of clarification will be continued in Part II by (1) re-examining Breuer and Freud's "Studies on Hysteria," (2) surveying contemporary psychiatric attitudes toward hysteria, and (3) critically analyzing the connections between conversion hysteria and modern concepts of psychosomatic medicine.

Foundations of a Theory of Personal Conduct

THE SIGN-USING MODEL OF BEHAVIOR

Although the concept of psychiatry as an analysis of communication is not novel, the full implication of the idea that so-called mental illnesses may be like languages, and not at all like diseases of the body, has not been made sufficiently explicit. Suppose, for instance, that the problem of hysteria is more akin to the problem of a person speaking a foreign tongue than it is to that of a person having a bodily disease. We are accustomed to believe that diseases have "causes," "treatments," and "cures." If, however, a person speaks a language other than our own, we do not usually look for the "cause" of his peculiar linguistic behavior. It would be foolish—and, of course, fruitless—to concern ourselves with the "etiology" of speaking French. To understand such behavior, we must think in terms of *learning* (Hilgard, 1956) and *meaning* (Ogden and Richards, 1930; Ryle, 1957). Accordingly, we might conclude that speaking French is the result of living among people who speak French. The sociohistorical context of the learning experience must not be confused with the history of the subject. The former is the concern of genetic psychology, psychiatry, and psychoanalysis—the latter the concern of philology and the history of languages. It follows, then, that if hysteria is regarded as a special form of communicative behavior, it is meaningless to inquire into its "causes." As with languages, we shall only be able to ask how hysteria was *learned* and what it *means*. This is exactly what Freud (1900) did with dreams. He regarded the dream as a language and proceeded to elucidate its structure and meanings.

If a so-called psychopathological phenomenon is more akin to a language problem than to illness, it follows that we cannot meaningfully talk of "treatment" and "cure." Although it is obvious that under certain circumstances it may be desirable for a person to change from one language to another— for example, to discontinue speaking French and begin speaking English— this change is not usually formulated in terms of "treatment." Speaking about learning rather than about etiology permits one to acknowledge that among a diversity of communicative forms each has its own *raison d'être* and that, because of the particular circumstances of the communicants, each is as valid as any other.

It is my thesis that hysteria—meaning thereby communication by means of bodily signs and complaints—constitutes a special form of sign-using behavior. Let us call this type of communication *protolanguage*. This language has a twofold origin. Its first source is man's bodily make-up. The human body is subject to disease and disability, manifested by means of bodily signs (e.g., paralysis, convulsion, etc.) and bodily feelings (e.g., pain, fatigue, etc.). Its second source resides in cultural factors, especially in the apparently world-wide custom of making life easier, at least temporarily, for those who are ill. These two basic factors account for the development and use of the language of hysteria. *I submit that hysteria is nothing other than the "language of illness," employed either because another language has not been learned well enough, or because this language happens to be especially useful.* There may be, of course, various combinations of these two reasons for using this language.

In sum, then, our task in Part III will be to undertake a semiotical rather than a psychiatric or psychoanalytic analysis of hysteria. First, a detailed examination of the structure and function of protolanguage will be presented. This will be followed by an exposition of the relation of protolanguage to the general class of nondiscursive languages. Considerations of the problem of indirect communication—that is, scrutiny of the structure and function of alluding, hinting, implying, etc.—will conclude the semiotical analysis of hysteria.

THE RULE-FOLLOWING MODEL OF BEHAVIOR

The concepts of rule-following and role-taking both derive from the premise that personal conduct may be studied fruitfully by considering man's "mind" mainly as a product of his social environment. In other words, although there are certain biological invariants in behavior, the precise pattern of human actions is determined largely by roles and rules. Accordingly, anthropology, ethics, and sociology are the basic sciences of human action, since they are concerned with the values, goals, and rules of human behavior (Kroeber, 1954; Kluckhohn, 1949; Sellars and Hospers, 1952).

With the introduction of the rule-following model as a frame of reference for hysteria and mental illness, two questions naturally arise: (1) What kinds of rules are there, and how do they influence behavior? (2) Among a diversity of rules, which are the most relevant for understanding the historical development of the concept of hysteria?

My thesis is that two general types of rules are especially significant in the genesis of behavior which has been variously labeled "witchcraft," "hysteria," and "mental illness." One pertains to the essential helplessness of children and, hence, to the more-or-less biologically required help-giving activity of the parent. This results, especially among human beings, in complicated patterns of paired activities *characterized by the helplessness of one member and the helpfulness of the other*. The second source of rules which will be examined in detail are the teachings and practices of the Judaeo-Christian religions. The New Testament in particular will be surveyed to discern the specific rules of conduct it prescribes. It will be apparent that for centuries Western man has been immersed—or has immersed himself—in an ocean of unserviceable social rules in which he has wallowed and nearly drowned. What I mean by this is that social life—through the combined impact of ubiquitous childhood experiences of dependence and of religious teachings—is so structured that it contains endless exhortations commanding man to behave childishly, stupidly, and irresponsibly. These exhortations to helplessness, although perhaps most powerful in their impact during the Middle Ages, have continued to influence human behavior to the present day.

The thesis that we are surrounded by an unseen ocean of human commands to be incompetent, impoverished, and sick will be illustrated mainly by references to the New Testament. In each person's actual life experiences, however, such influences need not necessarily come from officially organized religious sources. On the contrary, they derive usually from social intercourse with father, mother, husband, wife, employer, employee, and so on. However, the roles of the priestly and medical professions are especially significant in this connection, since their succoring activities rest squarely on the premise that the sinful, the weak, the sick—in brief, the disabled— should be helped. By implication, those who exhibit effective, self-reliant behavior need not be helped. They may even be taxed, burdened, or coerced in various ways. The *rewarding of disability*—although necessary in certain instances—is a potentially dangerous social practice.

THE GAME-PLAYING MODEL OF BEHAVIOR

The communicational frame of reference implies that the communicants are engaged in an activity that is meaningful to them. By "meaningful" I refer to purposeful, goal-directed activity, and to the pursuit of goals in certain predetermined ways. If it appears that human beings are not so engaged, it is useful nevertheless to assume that they are and that we have been unable to comprehend the goals and the rules of their game. This position in regard to human behavior is not novel. It is a reformulation of the classic Shakespearean assertion that there is "method in madness." Similarly, in everyday life when a person acts in an incomprehensible fashion, the observer may ask, in the idiom of American slang, "What is his game?" or "What is his racket?" The basic psychoanalytic attitude toward "neurotic behavior" reflects the same premise. The analyst seeks to uncover and understand conduct in terms of unconscious motives, goals, roles, and the like. In the terms proposed here, the analyst seeks to unravel the game of life that the patient plays. The disposition to regard personal conduct as an expression of game-playing will constitute the theoretical basis of the last portion of this study.

A systematic exposition of the game-playing model of human behavior, based largely on the works of Mead and Piaget, will form the introduction to this subject. This will be supplemented by the construction of a game-hierarchy, with first-level or *object games* distinguished from higher-level or *metagames*.

Hysteria may be regarded as a heterogeneous mixture of metagames. As such, it—and mental illness generally—may be contrasted with uncomplicated cases of bodily illness and its treatment. The latter, being concerned with bodily survival, may be regarded as an object game. The former, being concerned with the problem of how man should live, is an example of a metagame.

Attempts simultaneously to pursue object games and metagames may bring a person into irreconcilable conflicts. Patrick Henry's famous declaration, "Give me liberty or give me death!" illustrates the potential conflict between physical survival and the ethical ideal of liberty. In this example, the end-goal of the metagame—that is, to live as a free man—takes precedence over the end-goal of the object game—that is, to survive at any cost. Conversely, adherence to the object game in this dilemma implies scuttling the metagame.

Games on any logical level may be played well or poorly. This holds true for hysteria, too. However, inasmuch as hysteria is composed of a mixture of several games, and inasmuch as the person trying to play this complex game is unaware of the rules by which he plays and the goals which he has set for himself, the likelihood of serious conflict in pursuing the goals and obeying the rules of the constituent games is great. This type of analysis will help us to see that while so-called psychiatric problems have significant intrapersonal, interpersonal, and social dimensions, they invariably have ethical dimensions as well. Once man rises above the level of playing the simplest sort of object game—the survival game—he is inevitably confronted by ethical choices. The analysis and rational scrutiny of the historical antecedents of "neurotic symptoms" or "character" cannot alone resolve an ethical dilemma. It is obvious that this can be accomplished only by making a human choice and committing one's self to it. This does not negate—on the contrary, it re-emphasizes—the fact that the ability and the wish to make choices are themselves influenced by personal experiences.

The game-analytic description of human behavior unites elements of the sign-using and rule-following models into a coherent pattern. This approach to psychiatry is considered to be especially fitting for an integration of ethical, sociopolitical, and economic considerations with the more traditional concerns of the psychiatrist. Thus, the beginnings of a science and technology of human living, free of the errors of organicism as well as historicism, seem to be within reach.

Book One | **THE MYTH OF MENTAL ILLNESS**

PART I | *Growth and Structure of the Myth*

CHAPTER 1

Charcot's Contribution to the Problem of Hysteria

To do justice to the problem of hysteria, the connections between it and malingering must be fully explored. This task requires us to address ourselves to the historical background of this problem. I shall start with the work of Charcot, with whose contributions modern psychiatry can be said to begin, and shall thence trace the development of this theme to the present day.

To begin with, Charcot was a *neurologist*. This meant that his social role was that of a physician specializing in diseases of the nervous system. But what exactly did this mean in his day? Today, when all of medicine is sharply focused on therapy, it is difficult for most of us to picture the situation as I believe it existed then. We must remember that in Charcot's day neurologists possessed practically no therapeutic agents with which they could appreciably help their patients. Their function, accordingly, was not primarily therapeutic. If the neurologist were a man like Charcot, a professor at a university—for many years he held the chair in pathological anatomy at the Sorbonne—then his primary responsibilities were scientific and educational. His task was to increase our knowledge of diseases of the nervous system without necessarily providing immediate therapeutic benefit to patients. His assignment was, also, to teach students and physicians. Lastly, as a physician in charge of patients at the Salpêtrière, he was involved in the care of patients. While this task had all the appearance of a therapeutic role, it was, I believe, not really therapeutic in the contemporary sense of this word. Most patients, and particularly those with organic neurological ill-nesses, were hospitalized chiefly to segregate them from the more normal, less disabled members of society. In this respect, the patient population of the Salpêtrière was similar to that of some present-day state mental hospitals. Charcot's (nonprivate) patients—like the involuntarily hospitalized mental patients today—were segregated not so much because they were "ill" as because they disturbed others and were too poor and socially un-important to be cared for in private institutions.[1] The patients thus came from and were members of a social class much beneath that of the physicians who worked there. What was Charcot's attitude toward his patients? Freud (1893a) answered this question, and many others as well, in his obituary of his great teacher. He wrote:

> Having at his disposal a considerable number of patients afflicted with chronic nervous disease he was enabled to take full advantage of his peculiar talent. He was not much given to cogitation, was not of the reflective type, but he had an artistically gifted tempera-ment—as he said himself, he was a *"visuel,"* a seer. He himself told us the following about his method of working. He was accustomed to look again and again at things that were incomprehensible to him, to deepen his impression of them day by day until suddenly under-standing of them dawned on him. Before his mind's eye, order then came into the chaos apparently presented by the constant repetition of the same symptoms; the new clinical pictures which were char-acterized by the constant combination of certain syndromes took shape; the complete and extreme cases, the "types," were then dis-tinguishable with the aid of a specific kind of schematic arrange-ment, and with these as a starting point the eye could follow down the long line of the less significant cases, the *"formes frustes,"* showing some one or other peculiar feature of the type and fading into the indefinite. He called this kind of mental work, in which he had no equal, "practising nosography" and he was proud of it (pp. 10-11).

[1] I have discussed elsewhere (Szasz, 1957d, 1958b) the ramified factors that determine whether a person is considered "mentally ill" or "committable" and have emphasized the issues of *power* and *value* in this regard. Thus, today people may be segregated in mental hospitals not only because they are "sick" but also because they are socially unconstructive. This lack of positive contribution to social welfare (however it may be defined) may come about either by default—through stupidity, ineptitude, or lack of human resources—or by rebellion, through the espousal of values and goals too sharply at variance with those dominant in the culture at a given time.

And further on he added:

> But to his pupils, who made the rounds with him through the wards
> of the Salpêtrière—the museum of clinical facts for the greater part
> named and defined by him—he seemed a very Cuvier, as we see him
> in the statue in front of the Jardin des Plantes, surrounded by the
> various types of animal life which he had understood and described;
> or else he reminded them of the myth of Adam, who must have
> experienced in its most perfect form that intellectual delight so
> highly praised by Charcot, when the Lord led before him the crea-
> tures of Paradise to be named and grouped (p. 11).

From our contemporary vantage point, this is a strange, dehumanized view of patients. But then, in some branches of medicine even today,
especially in large charity hospitals, patients often are regarded as so much
"clinical material." The latter expression clearly betrays the nature of the
observer's attitude toward the subject.

I did not, however, cite Charcot's attitude merely to criticize it. As will be
apparent, these observations are important for an historical analysis of the
relationship between malingering and hysteria. For it is clear that if Charcot's
principal interest was to classify neurological diseases, he had to scrutinize
and distinguish all things that looked like diseases of the nervous system,
including those that were, in fact, something else. As the geologist must
differentiate gold from copper, and both from other metals which glitter,
so the neurologist-nosographer must differentiate multiple sclerosis, tabes,
and hysteria. How can he do this?

In Charcot's days the most important tool, besides the clinical examination, was the post-mortem study of the brain. Freud (1893a) provided us
with an interesting glimpse of how Charcot proceeded with his taxonomic
work in his "human zoo." This analogy, although perhaps offensive, was
suggested by Freud himself and fits the situation.

> During his student days chance brought him into contact with a
> char-woman who suffered from a peculiar form of tremor and
> could not get work because of her awkwardness. Charcot recog-
> nized her condition to be "choreiform paralysis," already described
> by Duchenne, of the origin of which, however, nothing was known.
> In spite of her costing him a small fortune in broken plates and
> platters, Charcot kept her for years in his service and, when at last
> she died, could prove in the autopsy that "choreiform paralysis" was
> the clinical expression of multiple cerebro-spinal sclerosis (pp. 12-
> 13).

Freud commented that the patient was not efficient because of her disability, thus implying that Charcot could have procured the services of a more capable servant. The vast changes in social conditions that took place during the past century are well known. Today, both Freud's comment and Charcot's action would strike most of us as rather callous. The very relationship, so patently more advantageous to master than servant and yet allegedly structured for the benefit of the latter, seems repugnant. Clearly, this is a vignette of medical and neuropsychiatric life of a bygone age. Still, it is the human situation in which the modern conception of hysteria arose.

Guillain's (1959) definitive biography of Charcot furnishes considerable additional information consistent with the picture sketched so far. For example, we learn that Charcot moved in the highest social circles. He was a friend of Premier Gambetta and also of the Grand Duke Nicholas of Russia. He is said to have paved the way for the Franco-Russian Alliance. By all accounts, he aspired to the role of aristocratic autocrat. It requires no great feat of the imagination to infer what sort of *personal relationship* must have prevailed between him and his destitute and near-illiterate patients.

A firsthand account, although perhaps somewhat embellished, of the human side of Charcot's work may be obtained from Axel Munthe's beautiful autobiography, *The Story of San Michele* (1930). Of particular interest is Munthe's story of a young peasant girl who took refuge in hysterical symptoms to escape the drudgery of her home life. Munthe felt the "treatment" she was receiving at the Salpêtrière was making her a lifelong invalid, and that Charcot was, in a way, keeping her imprisoned. He tried to "rescue" the girl, took her to his apartment, and hoped to convince her to return home. It appears from Munthe's story, however, that the young woman preferred the social role of hysterical patient at the Salpêtrière to that of peasant girl in her village. Evidently, life in the hospital was more exciting and rewarding than her "normal" existence—a contingency Munthe seriously underrated. What emerges from this account, too, is that the Salpêtrière, under Charcot, was a special type of social institution. In addition to its similarities to present-day state mental hospitals, its function could also be compared to armies and special religious organizations (for example, monasteries). In other words, the Salpêtrière provided its inmates certain comforts and gratifications lacking in their ordinary social environment. Charcot and the other physicians who worked there functioned as rulers vis-à-vis their subjects. Instead of intimacy and trust, we might infer that their relationship to each other was based on fear, awe, and deception.

Charcot on Hysteria

All this is by way of preparing the ground for our initial approach to the relationship between hysteria and malingering. As Charcot's knowledge of neuropathology increased and as his prestige became greater, his interest apparently shifted to disorders which simulated organic neurological conditions. In other words, he turned his attention to patients whose clinical pictures suggested or resembled neurological diseases. Such patients were then called—and, hence, immediately classified—either hysterics or malingerers, depending on the observer's point of view. Those labeled "hysterics" were, by virtue of this designation, declared relatively more respectable and fit objects for serious study. They were regarded as suffering from an illness, rather than as trying to fool the physician or exhibiting merely willful misbehavior. This is the first and perhaps most fundamental connection, although by no means the only one, between the notions of hysteria and malingering. Freud's account (1893a) of Charcot's work is again very illuminating:

> He [i.e., Charcot] explained that the theory of *organic nervous diseases* was for the present fairly complete, and he began to turn his attention almost exclusively to *hysteria*, thus suddenly focusing general attention to this subject. This most enigmatic of all nervous diseases—no workable point of view having yet been found from which physicians could regard it—had just at this time come very much into discredit, and this ill-repute related not only to the patients but was extended to the physicians who treated this neurosis. The general opinion was that anything may happen in hysteria; hysterics found no credit whatsoever. *First of all Charcot's work restored dignity to the subject;* gradually the sneering attitude, which the hysteric could reckon on meeting when she told her story, was given up, *she was no longer a malingerer, since Charcot had thrown the whole weight of his authority on the side of the reality and objectivity of hysterical phenomena* ([ITALICS ADDED] pp. 18-19).

This passage reveals how the study of hysteria was prejudged because of the social importance of its investigator, Charcot. Certain crucial issues, therefore, may have been obscured and must now be re-examined. Even the simple statement that Charcot turned his attention to hysteria rests on the tacit assumption that *this* was the patient's trouble. It was decided, essentially by *fiat*, that in contrast to organic neurological diseases, these people had "functional nervous illnesses." Most of these "illnesses" were called "hysteria." Freud's interesting comment should now be recalled. According to it, so-called hysterics were no longer diagnosed as malingerers because of Charcot's authority. It is significant that Freud offered no empirical evidence or logical reason for preferring the category of "hysteria" to that of "malingering." Instead of evidence or reason for this choice, Freud appealed to ethical considerations, although without explicitly saying so:

> Charcot had repeated on a small scale the act of liberation commemorated in the picture of Pinel which adorned the lecture hall of the Salpêtrière. Now that the blind fear of being fooled by the poor patient which had stood in the way of a serious study of the neurosis was overcome, the question arose which mode of procedure would most speedily lead to the solution of the problem (p. 19).

This situation is historically significant on two counts. First, it marks the beginning of the modern study of so-called mental illnesses. This is well known and widely recognized. Second, it contains what I regard as the *major logical and procedural error in the evolution of modern psychiatry.* Where does this error lie? I shall suggest two more or less distinct answers. They shall be sketched briefly now, since broadly speaking, all of Book One is devoted to an analysis of this question.

Is Every Form of Suffering Illness?

The first error lies in the attempt to elevate the sufferer, socioethically, from the rank of malingerer to that of patient. Freud had compared Charcot's work to Pinel's. But, as I see it, Pinel's liberation of mental patients from the dungeon was not a psychiatric achievement at all, in a scientific-technical sense. He claimed only that the sufferers who had been placed in his charge were human beings, and as such entitled to the human rights and dignities which, in principle at least, motivated the French Revolution. Pinel did not advocate, so far as I know, that the patient should be better treated because he was sick. Indeed, the social role of the sick person was not an enviable one at that time. Hence, an appeal for better treatment on this ground would not have been particularly effective.

I do not, of course, advocate the moral condemnation and social maltreatment of "hysterics." My thesis is simply that humane treatment should not rest on fallacious and misleading grounds. In other words, decency to our fellow man should not be conditional on his "sickness." This form of human decency, much espoused in the Bible and in Christian religious teachings generally, defines the rules of the game of living in such terms as these: "I shall be kindly, benevolent, and helpful, provided you are sick—meaning thereby that you are inferior to me and needful of me." Its implicit corollary is: "If you are healthy (or not sick), I shall give you no quarter. Probably I shall be mean and destructive to you." (This subject will be treated in greater detail in Chapter 11, especially pp. 192-198.)

As I suggested, Pinel's liberation of the mental patient should be viewed as social reform rather than as innovation in medical treatment. This distinction is important. For instance, during the Second World War, the removal of venereal infection from the classification of disciplinary offenses among military personnel was an act of *social reform*. The discovery of penicillin, while bearing on the same general problem—namely, the control of venereal disease—was a medical-scientific act.

What were the social and medical effects which resulted from Charcot's insistence that hysterics were ill and not malingering? Although this diagnosis did not ameliorate the hysteric's disability, it did make it easier for him to be "ill." In my opinion, this type of assistance, like a little knowledge, can be dangerous. It makes it easier for both sufferer and helper to stabilize the situation and rest content with what is still a very unsatisfactory state of affairs. A comparison of Charcot with another famous French physician, Guillotin, may be illuminating in this connection.

Guillotin's highly questionable contribution to human culture consisted of the reinvention and advocacy of the guillotine. This resulted in a relatively painless and, therefore, less cruel form of execution than those previously in vogue. In our day, the guillotine and the rope have been succeeded by the gas chamber and electric chair. Clearly, Guillotin's work is humane or inhuman, depending on which side of the issue we examine. From the point of view of making judicial murder less painful for the executed, it was humane. Since it also made things easier for the executioner and his employers, it was inhuman. Charcot, I submit, acted in a similar manner. To put it succinctly, Guillotin made it easier for the condemned to die, and Charcot made it easier for the sufferer, then commonly called a malingerer, to be sick. It may be argued that as far as dealing with the hopeless and the helpless is concerned, these are real accomplishments. Still, I would maintain that Guillotin's and Charcot's interventions were not acts of liberation; they were rather processes of narcotization or tranquilization. For is it not true that to be killed at someone else's behest, even if in a relatively painless fashion, is not generally listed among the common goods to which mankind aspires? Similarly, to be sick, in the sense of being disabled and malfunctioning, is not regarded as a desirable state. Yet this seemed to be what Charcot achieved.

We might sum up the comparison of Charcot with Guillotin by saying that they made it easier for people (particularly for the socially down-trodden) to be ill and to die. Neither seemed to have made it easier for people to be well and to live![2] They used their medical knowledge and prestige to help society shape itself to an image it found pleasing. Efficient and painless execution fitted well into the self-concept of Guillotin's society. Similarly, late nineteenth-century European society was ripe to see almost any disability, and particularly one, such as hysteria, that looked so much like a disorder of the body, as "illness." Charcot, Kraepelin, Breuer, Freud, and many others lent their authority to the propagation of this socially self-enhancing image concerning what was then "hysteria" and what in our day has become the general problem of "mental illness." The weight of authority of contemporary medical and psychiatric opinion continues, of course, to support this image.

The practical consequences of the events described are pertinent today. As easy methods of execution have *not*, by themselves, led to the abolition of the death penalty but on the contrary have probably delayed social reforms in this regard, so, I believe, labeling people disabled by problems in living as "mentally ill" has in fact delayed recognition of the essential nature of the phenomena. At first glance, to advocate that troubled people are "sick" sounds like a great boon, for it bestows the dignity of suffering from a "real illness." But a hidden weight is attached to this viewpoint which drags the troubled people back to the same sort of disability from which this semantic and social switching was to rescue them.

The second error in decreeing that some malingerers be called hysterics—instead of analyzing the issues—was that it led to obscuring the similarities and differences between organic neurological diseases and phenomena that only looked like them. Since this problem will be discussed in Chapter 2, I shall only mention its outstanding features here. In analyzing hysteria and malingering, there are two basic alternatives. One is to emphasize the similarities between hysteria and neurological illness. The other is to emphasize the differences and thus expose those features of hysteria which might be called malingering in the sense of pseudo illness. Actually, both the similarities and differences are readily apparent (Freud, 1893b). These features

[2] It is important to note, however, that the sick role is socially more acceptable than the role of social outcast (e.g., malingerer, hobo, criminal, etc.). The sick person, although disabled, is regarded as a more-or-less full-fledged member of society (Parsons, 1958a). Thus, to the extent to which Charcot was successful in "promoting" malingerers to hysterics, he did indeed "liberate" the mentally ill.

used to be listed in neuropsychiatric textbooks as guideposts to the "differential diagnosis" of hysteria and organic illness. The similarities between hysteria and illness of the body as a physicochemical machine lie chiefly in the patient's complaints, his clinical appearance, and the fact that he is, in fact, disabled. The differences between the two lie in the empirical findings on physical, laboratory, and post-mortem examination. It is obvious that the similarities and differences do not stand in opposition to one another, for each set refers to different aspects of a larger whole. No logical necessity compels us to believe that every man who complains of being ill or who looks ill or who is disabled—or who manifests all three of these features— must also have a physicochemical disorder of his body. This does not deny the fact that a connection may exist. The nature of this connection, however, is empirical, not logical. Once this much is clear, it becomes a matter of scientific and social choice whether we prefer to emphasize the similarities and, hence, place hysteria in the category of illness, or whether we prefer to emphasize the differences and place hysteria in a category of nonillness. This problem is partly one of epistemology and partly one of scientific utility.

However elusive this problem may have been, in the final analysis it is quite simple, and no different from innumerable problems familiar to scientists. In biology, for instance, one may place men and lower mammals in one class, as mammals or animals, or separate them into two classes, as, say, man versus ape. *The choice should be determined on the basis of the scientific task.* For instance, in the study of the immunology of poliomyelitis, men and apes may be considered members of the same class. It would be ill-advised to use the same system of classification, however, to study the social organization of men and monkeys. Hence, whether or not it is useful to place problems in living under the category of illness depends on the types of questions we wish to ask. By insisting that certain people are mentally ill—rather than merely proposing to *regard* them in this way—we unwittingly limit ourselves to a handful of the possible questions. If this limitation is marked, we may put ourselves out of scientific action, so to speak, perhaps without even knowing it. This, I think, has happened to twentieth-century psychiatry. Advances have been made in spite of the theoretical framework of medicine into which our discipline has been cast, not because of it.

In making this statement, I do not refer to the traditional antagonism between the biological and sociological orientations to psychiatry and psychoanalysis. This is a spurious dichotomy, separating two types of events both of which are determinants of behavior. In speaking of the medical framework of psychiatric theories, I have reference to theoretical models and organizing principles designed to facilitate our understanding of certain events. Biological theory, for instance, is not limited to using biological models. In fact, modern biological thought abounds with physical (e.g., cybernetic) models. Similarly, psychiatry and psychoanalysis have used models other than those based on medicine. The source of the model can never be used to assess its relevance. This always must be done *ad hoc*, by examining the conditions in which it is used and the purposes to which it is put.

Thus far, considerations such as these have received scant attention. In fact, the question of whether so-called behavioral disorders—or, as I prefer to call them, problems in living—should be regarded as and called "illnesses," has always been discussed entirely as though it constituted a problem in ethics or power politics. Undoubtedly, the matter has ethical implications, since the answer to this question may influence or alter existing power structures. Similar problems confront the participants in many scientific disputes. Typical examples are questions about the origin of man or the harnessing of nuclear energy. Inquiries into these problems—like those into the connections between hysteria, malingering, and illness—may result in answers that will carry important ethical and social consequences. This, however, does not mean that the questions themselves are *about* ethics or power politics. Last but not least, even when the inquiry is about a problem in ethics, it may be possible to subject it to both empirical and logical analysis. Since all personal conduct, when analyzed in terms of symbol-systems, communications, and social relations, involves values, it is a prerequisite to its scientific analysis that all the relevant covert value judgments be made explicit (Szasz, 1960b).

The Double Standard in Psychiatry

The aim of this analysis of the problem of hysteria has been to make explicit the *values* which influenced members of the psychiatric profession in the late nineteenth century. Accordingly, I dwelled on Charcot's attitude toward patients to show that: (1) he never considered himself to be the patient's agent; (2) his principal goal and motive was to identify accurately specific diseases. As a corollary of this situation—of the sociology of his work habits, so to speak—he tended to define all the phenomena he studied as neurological disorders. If this accomplished little else, it at least justified the attention he paid to these phenomena and the pronouncements he made about them. In this regard, Charcot and his group had a relationship to hysteria similar to that of the contemporary physicist to nuclear warfare.

War and national defense are matters of politics, sociology, ethics, and so forth. The fact that physical agents of destruction are used in warfare does not make it a problem in physics, just as the use of the brain, or the body, does not make all manner of human activities problems in psychiatry or medicine.

The point is that the prestige of the scientist—whether a Charcot or an Einstein—can be used to lend its possessor social power. He then may be able to achieve social goals that he could not otherwise attain. Once a scientist becomes so engaged, however, he has a powerful incentive to claim that his opinions and recommendations rest on the same grounds as his reputation! In Charcot's case, this meant that he had to base his case about hysteria on the premise that it was an organic neurological illness. Otherwise, if hysteria and hypnosis were problems in human relations and psychology, why should anyone have taken Charcot's opinions as authoritative? He had no special qualifications in these areas. Consequently, if it had been openly acknowledged that he was speaking about such things, he might have encountered serious opposition. Similar considerations prevail today and account for the fact that every physician is officially qualified to do psychotherapy, even though all he has to rely on is, in Zilboorg's (1941) apt words, "his benevolent or not so benevolent ignorance" (p. 370).

These historical developments, I believe, have been the roots of a double standard in psychiatry that still persists. I refer to the dual orientation of physicians and psychiatrists to certain occurrences which they encounter in their practices. Charcot's informal, "off-the-record" comment about hysteria illustrates this phenomenon:

> Some years later, at one of Charcot's evening receptions, I happened to be standing near the great teacher at a moment when he appeared to be telling Brouardel some very interesting story from his day's work. I hardly heard the beginning, but gradually my attention was seized by what he was saying. A young married couple from the Far East: the woman a confirmed invalid: the man either impotent or exceedingly awkward. "*Tachez donc*," I heard Charcot repeating, "*je vous assure, vous y arriverez.*" Brouardel, who spoke less loudly, must have expressed his astonishment that symptoms such as the wife's could have been produced in such circumstances. For Charcot suddenly broke in with great animation, "*Mais, dans des cas pareils c'est toujours la chose genitale, toujours . . . toujours*"; and he crossed his arms over his stomach, hugging himself and jumping up and down on his toes several times in his

own characteristic lively way. I know that for one second I was almost paralyzed with amazement and said to myself, "Well, but if he knows that, why does he never say so?" But the impression was soon forgotten; brain anatomy and the experimental induction of hysterical paralyses absorbed all available interest (Freud, 1893a, p. 295).

Taking this material as our data, we could ask: Why was Charcot so insistent? With whom was he arguing? And we would have to answer: With himself! This would follow if we assumed, as I think we should, that Charcot knew, to some extent, that he was fooling himself in believing that hysteria was a disease of the nervous system. Herein lies the double standard. The organic viewpoint is dictated by social expediency insofar as the rules of the game of medicine are defined so that adherence to this position will be rewarded.[3] Adherence to the psychological viewpoint is required by the physician's identification or empathy with the patient. This dichotomy is reflected in the two basic contemporary scientific methods, namely, the physicochemical and psychosocial. In the days of Charcot and Freud, however, only the former field was recognized as belonging to science. Interest in the latter was synonymous with charlatanry.

Although the problem of malingering will be examined in detail in the next chapter, it is necessary here to say a few words concerning Charcot's views of the relationship between hysteria and malingering. In one of his lectures he said:

> This brings me to say a few words about malingering. It is found in every phase of hysteria and one is surprised at times to admire the ruse, the sagacity, and the unyielding tenacity that especially the women, who are under the influence of a severe neurosis, display in order to deceive . . . especially when the victim of the deceit happens to be a physician (Guillain, 1959, pp. 138-139).

Already during Charcot's lifetime and at the height of his fame, it was suggested, particularly by Bernheim, that the phenomena of hysteria were due to suggestion. It was intimated further that Charcot's demonstrations of hysteria were faked—that is, that they were rather like the rigged tele-

---

[3] Adherence to the organic or physicochemical viewpoint was, and continues to be, dictated also by the difficulty in many cases of differentiating hysteria from, say, multiple sclerosis or brain tumor (especially in their early stages). Conversely, patients with neurological illnesses may also exhibit so-called hysterical behavior or may show signs of other types of "mental illness." This problem of the so-called differential diagnosis between "organic" and "psychological" illness has constituted one of the major stumbling blocks in the way of a systematic theory of personal conduct free of brain-mythological components. I shall repeatedly return to considerations of this problem in the course of developing my thesis.

vision quiz shows of today. This charge appears to have been fully substantiated. Clearly, Charcot's cheating, or his willingness to be duped—whichever it was seems impossible to ascertain now—is a delicate subject. It was called "the slight failing of Charcot" by Pierre Marie. Guillain (1959), more interested in the neurological than in the psychiatric contributions of his hero, minimized Charcot's involvement in and responsibility for faking experiments and demonstrations on hypnotism and hysteria. But he was forced to concede this much:

> Charcot obviously made a mistake in not checking his experiments. Every morning he made rounds on his hospital service with exemplary regularity and a sense of duty, but, like all physicians of his generation, he did not return to his service in the afternoon. Accordingly, his chiefs of clinics, his interns, and other assistants prepared the patients, hypnotized them, and organized the experiments. *Charcot personally never hypnotized a single patient, never checked the experiments* and, as a result, was not aware of their inadequacies or of the reasons of their eventual errors ([ITALICS ADDED] p. 174).

To speak of "inadequacies" and "errors" here is to indulge in euphemisms. What Guillain described, and what others have previously intimated, was that Charcot's assistants had coached the patients on how to act the role of the hypnotized or hysterical person (White, 1941; Sarbin, 1950). Guillain himself tested this hypothesis with the following results:

> In 1899, about six years after Charcot's death, I saw as a young intern at the Salpêtrière the old patients of Charcot who were still hospitalized. Many of the women, who were excellent comedians, when they were offered a slight pecuniary remuneration imitated perfectly the major hysteric crises of former times (p. 174).

Troubled by these facts, Guillain asked himself how this chicanery could come about and how it could have been perpetuated? Why did Charcot fail to discover that the hysterical manifestations he observed and demonstrated were not occurrences of the same type as, say, a gummatous lesion in tertiary syphilis or an elevated temperature in lobar pneumonia? Why did he not realize that they were artificially produced and, hence, rather like theatrical performances? All of the physicians, Guillain hastened to assure us, "possessed high moral integrity" (p. 175). He then suggested the following explanation:

> It seems to me impossible that some of them did not question the unlikelihood of certain contingencies. Why did they not put Charcot on his guard? The only explanation that I can think of, with all

the reservation that it carries, is that they did not dare alert Charcot, fearing the violent reactions of the master, who was called the "Caesar of the Salpêtrière" (pp. 175-176).

The struggle over the "reality" or genuineness of hysterical manifestations continued for many years after Charcot's death. This problem, still not adequately clarified in psychiatric theory, will be analyzed in the next chapter.

We must conclude that Charcot's orientation to the problem of hysteria was neither organic nor psychological. It is often said that he approached hysteria the same way as he approached the neurological syndromes to the understanding of which he contributed so much. According to this view, which certainly is correct, he adhered to the conventional medical thought of his day. I believe it is this attitude, more than anything else—and, of course, its perpetuation in subsequent generations of psychiatrists—that led to an ill-defined conceptualization of psychiatric disease. Zilboorg (1941), although himself an advocate of a vaguely defined (or, more often, an utterly undefined) conception of mental illness, identified this problem well when he wrote:

> One of the most conspicuous features of psychiatric history is that it is totally different from medical history. Psychiatry still lags behind medicine as to the certainty of its task, the sphere of its activity, and the method to be pursued. General medicine, in the narrow sense of the word, never had to ask itself what disease is. It always knew what it meant to be ill, for both the patient and the doctor knew what pain and other forms of physical suffering were. Psychiatry never had such a clear criterion of illness (pp. 519-520).

Although Charcot did not overthrow a narrowly medical conceptualization of hysteria, he did not really fully accept this view. He recognized and clearly stated that problems in human relationships may be expressed in hysterical symptoms. The point is that he maintained the medical view in public, for official purposes, as it were, and espoused the psychological view only in private, where such opinions were safe. Charcot's double standard with respect to hysteria may be illuminated further by the analogy of the citizen's relationship to alcohol in Prohibition-day America. From a legal, official point of view, the drinking of alcohol was prohibited. It was expected that most people would uphold the law and accordingly would abstain from drinking. Looking at the same situation from a sociopsychological viewpoint, one found that drinking was really regarded as an interesting, adventurous, masculine-heroic activity rather than a "sin" or a "crime." In the operation of a double standard, both sets of rules or beliefs are accepted as "right," in the sense that both are implemented in the behavior of the person who holds the double standard.

The Conception of Hysteria as Illness: a Promotive Strategy

Certain interrelations in the notions of hysteria, malingering, and illness as they were used in Charcot's day have been emphasized. My criticism of Charcot was based not so much on his adherence to a conventional medical model of illness for his interpretation of hysteria as on his covert use of scientific prestige to gain certain social ends. What were these ends? They were the acceptance of the phenomena of hypnotism and hysteria by the medical profession in general, and particularly by the French Academy of Sciences. But at what cost was this acceptance won? This question is rarely raised. As a rule, only the conquest over the resistance of the medical profession is celebrated. Zilboorg (1941) described Charcot's victory over the French Academy as follows:

> These were the ideas which Charcot presented to Académie des Sciences on February 13, 1882, in a paper on the diverse nervous states determined by the hypnotization of hysterics. One must not forget that the Académie had already condemned all research on animal magnetism three times and that it was a veritable *tour de force* to make the Académie accept a long description of absolutely analogous phenomena. They believed, and Charcot himself believed, that this study was far removed from animal magnetism and was a definite condemnation of it. That is why the Académie did not revolt and why they accepted with interest a study which brought to a conclusion the interminable controversy over magnetism, about which the members of the Académie could not fail to have some remorse. And remorse they well might have, for, from the standpoint of the actual facts observed, Charcot did nothing more than what Georget had asked the Académie to do fifty-six years previously. *Whether one called the phenomenon animal magnetism, mesmerism, or hypnotism, it stood the test of time.* The scientific integrity of the Académie did not. Like a government reluctant, indecisive, and uncertain of itself, it did nothing whenever it was safe to do nothing and yielded only when the pressure of events forced it to act and the change of formulatory cloak secured its face-saving complacency ([ITALICS ADDED] pp. 362-363).

I have cited these events in detail because I believe that this "change of formulatory cloak," which secured the admittance of hysteria into the French Academy, constitutes an historical paradigm. Like the influence of an early but significant parental attitude on the life of the individual, it continues to exert a malignant effect on the later development of psychiatry. Such "pathogenic" historical events may be counteracted in one of two ways. The first is by reaction-formation. This means an overcompensation opposing the original influence. Hence, in order to correct for an organic bias, the significance of psychogenic factors in so-called mental illness must be overstressed. Much effort in modern psychiatry, psychoanalysis, and psychosomatic medicine seems to have been expended to achieve this end.

The second way to remedy such a "trauma" is exemplified by the psychoanalytic method of treatment. Its essence lies in making the person explicitly aware of the events that influenced his life in the past. In this way their persistent effects on him, influencing not only his past but also his future, can be radically altered. I have depended heavily on historical-reconstructive analyses and interpretations, and these have been based on the same pragmatic rationale. By becoming aware of the historical origins and philosophical foundations of current psychiatric ideas and practices, we may be in a better position to rectify them, if rectification is needed, than we would be without such self-scrutiny.

"In the empirical sciences it is not so much in relation to inference that mathematical logic is useful as in relation to analysis and the apprehension of identity and difference of form. Where identity of form is of the traditional mathematical kind, its importance has long been realized. The kinetic theory of gases has been applied to the stellar universe, which to the non-mathematical mind, appears very different from a gas. — But, where identity of form is not of the sort that can be expressed without logical symbols, men of science have been less quick to recognize it; while the general public, through logical incompetence, has been led into grave practical errors."   Bertrand Russell (1955, p. 39)

CHAPTER 2

The Logic of Classification and the Problem of Malingering

The logic of classification, although of great practical significance to the work of psychiatrists, has received scant attention in their writings. Several psychologists (Piaget, 1953; Bruner, Goodnow, and Austin, 1956; Brown, 1956, 1958) have recently made important contributions to this subject.

Category Formation and Classification

We shall begin with the basic clinical-psychiatric observation that certain people—in particular, the brain-injured and the schizophrenic—employ different methods to classify or group things than do so-called normal persons (Goldstein and Scheerer, 1941; Goldstein, 1948; Kasanin, 1944). More specifically, Von Domarus (1944) interpreted schizophrenic "thought disorder" as a result of the patient's following non-Aristotelian logic. To illustrate: a schizophrenic may equate a stag with an Indian by focusing on a characteristic shared feature—namely, swiftness of movement. On this basis, he classifies both stags and Indians as belonging in the same group.

37

(He also fails to make the basis for his classification explicit—a consideration, however, of lesser interest to us here.) Aristotelian logic, or what is
often loosely called "normal" or "adult" logic, consists of deductive reasoning of the following sort. From the major premise that "All men are mortal"
and the minor premise that "Socrates is a man," we conclude that "Socrates
is mortal." This logical process presupposes an understanding that the class
called "man" consists of specific individuals, bearing proper names.

It will be shown later (in Part III) that the more primitive type of logical
operation, mentioned first, is intimately connected with a simple type of
symbolization, namely, that resting on a similarity between the object
and the sign used to represent it. Such signs are called *iconic*, because
they stand for the object represented much as a photograph stands for
the person photographed. Languages composed of iconic signs lend themselves to and are suited mainly for classification on the basis of *manifest* (e.g.,
structural) *similarities*. On the other hand, logically more complex languages,
for example those using conventional signs (words), permit classifying diverse objects and phenomena on the basis of more *hidden* (functional)
similarities.

Complex language systems, for example those composed of words or
mathematical symbols, lend themselves to the formation of increasingly
higher levels of abstraction. Illustrative is the formation of classes, and of
classes-of-classes, and so on, in such a way that each higher class contains
all the previous classes as members of itself. Thus, John Doe is a member
of the class (called "family") *Doe*. Since all the Does are natives of Vermont,
they may be further said to be members of the class *Vermonters*. The next
superordinate class could be *Americans*, and the next higher *human beings*.

All this is to introduce a logical analysis of the relationship between the
notions of malingering, hysteria, and illness. Clearly, the question of whether
we classify a bit of behavior that looks like a neurological disorder but is
not as "illness," or as something else, has important implications for the
science of human behavior. Yet thus far the basis for classification has been
moral rather than logical.

ON THE NOTIONS OF "REAL" AND "FALSE"

The processes of identification and classification are fundamental to the need
to order the world about us. This activity of ordering, while of special importance to science, is ubiquitous. For instance, we say that some sub-
stances are solid, and others liquid; or, we call certain objects "money,"
others "masterpieces of art," and still others "precious stones." Expressed
logically, we declare that some things are to be grouped in class A, and

others in class non-A. In certain instances it may be difficult to decide if a given item belongs in class A or non-A. This derives from two basic sources. First, in the case of naturally occurring items—for instance, copper and gold—the observer may not possess the knowledge, skill, or tools required to distinguish the two. He may then make the mistake of classifying item non-A (copper) in Class A (gold).

The second source of difficulty in the work of classification derives from man's intelligent, goal-directed participation in the events that shape his life. In other words, not only can two or more naturally occurring objects or events be similar and thus present a problem in differentiation, but it is also possible for man deliberately to imitate item X, making it look, as much as possible, like item Y. Everyday language takes cognizance of this. Many words designate a particular kind of relationship between two items, A and B, so that A stands for the specially designated object or event, and B signifies what may be termed "counterfeit-A." The latter is characterized by looking, more or less, like A, this *similarity in appearance being deliberately created by a human operator* for some purpose. For example, we designate the counterpart of money "counterfeit"; jewelry may be "real" or "costume" (or "paste"); a beautiful painting or sculpture may be a "masterpiece" or a "forgery"; a person may be telling the "truth" or "lying"; a person who complains of bodily symptoms may be a "sick patient" or a "healthy malingerer."

Why this discussion of the logic of classification? What is its relevance to hysteria and the problem of mental illness? My answer is that if we are to have a clear and meaningful concept of illness as a class of phenomena (say, class A), then we must also accept (1) that there are occurrences which look like illness but may turn out to be something else (class B), and (2) that there are occurrences which may properly belong in the class of counterfeit illness (class C). All this is logically inherent in classifying certain forms of behavior as illness. What are the practical implications of the logical relationship between A, non-A, and counterfeit-A? From among several pertinent observations that could be made, I shall select a few and comment on them briefly.

ILLNESS, COUNTERFEIT ILLNESS, AND THE PHYSICIAN'S ROLE

The observer may be fooled because the imitation is very good, because the observer is relatively unskilled in differentiating A from non-A, or because he wants to believe that non-A is A. Translating this into the language of bodily versus mental illness, we may assert that the physician may be fooled because certain hysterical or hypochondriacal bodily symptoms might be exceedingly difficult to distinguish from physicochemical disorders. Or the physician might be unskilled in recognizing manifestations of problems in living and might mistake bodily symptoms for physical illness. Lastly, the physician, committed to the role of expert engineer of the body as a physicochemical machine, may believe that all the human suffering he encounters falls in the class of illness.

The observer may be able to distinguish A from counterfeit-A. Implicit is its converse—namely, that he will believe that he has distinguished A from non-A when in fact he has not. The process of differentiation rests on empirical observations, and culminates in a rendered judgment. In other words, it is *observation*, followed by *arbitration*. The observer's role here is akin to that of umpire, judge, or art expert. For example, a painting may be brought to an art expert, to have him decide if it is a Renaissance masterpiece or a forgery. He may correctly identify the painting as falling into one or the other category. Or he may err either way. (He may, of course, decide that he cannot determine into which class the painting fits.) In medical terms, this corresponds to the well-known "differential diagnosis" between organic and mental disease (or the physician's awareness that he cannot decide). In this role, the physician functions as expert arbiter (Szasz, 1956b). If he limits himself to this role, he will simply classify the item brought to him as either A or non-A (including counterfeit-A)—in other words, the physician will limit himself to telling the patient that the allegedly diseased body which he has brought for examination is sick or is not sick (Szasz, 1958c).

To consider still another step in our analysis of the relationship between A and counterfeit-A: if the observer has distinguished—or thinks he has—two classes of items, so that he can identify some as members of class A and others as imitations of them, he may have certain reactions to his own judgment. His judgment may then be implemented by actions taken toward the items or persons concerned. For example, if money is identified as counterfeit, the police will attempt to arrest the counterfeiters. *What will the physician do when confronted with counterfeit bodily illness?* The physician's action in this situation has varied through the ages. Even today, it varies greatly depending on the personalities and social circumstances of both physician and patient. I shall comment on only a few reactions to this challenge which are significant in connection with this study:

1. Physicians may react like the police confronted by a counterfeiter. This was the usual response before the days of Charcot, Bernheim, and Liébeault. Hysteria was regarded as the patient's attempt to deceive. It was as though the patient had been a counterfeiter who wanted to pass his worthless bills to the physician. Accordingly, the reaction was anger and a wish

to retaliate. For real money—that is, real illness—physicians rewarded people. For fake money—that is, fake illness—they punished them. Many physicians still conduct themselves according to these unwritten rules of the Original Medical Game.

2. A pawnbroker, wishing to avoid loaning money on paste jewelry, behaves as though he assumed that all his customers want to defraud him. He considers it his responsibility to protect himself against this hazard. Similarly, the physician confronted by the hysterical patient may decide that he does not wish to treat him. He sends him away. Such a physician says, in effect: "I deal only with (real) bodily illness." He may or may not be aware that, among the problems with which he must deal, there are certain occurrences that look like illnesses but are not. The analogy of physician with pawnbroker also lends itself to the elucidation of other possible action patterns (e.g., iatrogenic illness).

3. Last, but perhaps most important, is the step that I believe Charcot took and Freud implemented. This step logically complements the rules of the Original Medical Game. Whereas in that situation the observer (physician) felt that he had been deliberately defrauded by the observed (patient), he now alters the situation by *changing the rules of the game*. The patient and his behavior are reclassified. This process may be paraphrased as follows: "Until now, under the old rules, we considered illness as a physicochemical disorder of the body which manifested itself, or was about to manifest itself, in the form of disability. When disabled the patient was to be rewarded in certain ways (e.g., he need not work, he could rest, and he could expect special kindness, etc.). When, however, he merely imitated being disabled, he was to be considered a malingerer and was to be punished." The new rules are: "Persons disabled by phenomena which only look like illnesses of the body (i.e., hysteria) should also be classified as ill. We shall henceforth consider them mentally ill and treat them accordingly, i.e., by the rules applicable to persons who are bodily ill."

I maintain that Freud did not "discover" that hysteria was a mental illness. Rather, he advocated that so-called hysterics be declared "ill." The adjectives "mental," "emotional," and "neurotic" are simply devices to codify—and at the same time obscure—the differences between two classes of disabilities or "problems" in meeting life. One category consists of bodily diseases—say, leprosy, tuberculosis, or cancer—which, by rendering imperfect the functioning of the human body as a machine, produce difficulties in social adaptation. In contrast to the first, the second category is characterized by difficulties in social adaptation not attributable to malfunctioning machinery but "caused" rather by the purposes the machine was made to serve by those who built it (e.g., parents, society), or by those who use it, i.e., individuals (Polanyi, 1958b; Szasz, 1960b).

It is my thesis, therefore, that one of Freud's chief contributions to medicine, psychiatry, and the social order lay in the creation of new rules of human conduct. The creation of these new rules, however, was not made sufficiently explicit. Seemingly, Freud as well as his followers and opponents were all essentially unaware of this reclassification of sufferers. Only the consequences of this change were clearly evident and widely debated. The phenomenon of covert rule-change in regard to sufferers and their reclassification is so significant that I shall discuss it in greater detail.

CHANGES IN THE RULES OF CONDUCT AND THE RECLASSIFICATION OF BEHAVIOR

The physician's role vis-à-vis his undiagnosed patient is often that of expert arbiter. The physician has it in his power to decide whether or not the patient is playing· the medical game—that is, the real-life drama of being ill—according to the rules. If he plays fairly he is rewarded ("treated"); if he is caught cheating, he is punished (sent away, scolded, subjected to unnecessary or sadistic measures, etc.). Beginning with Charcot, the rules of fair play were changed so that certain previously forbidden moves— specifically, the move of being disabled hysterically—were now allowed. This changed the very character of the game called medicine, although its name was retained.

To illustrate the far-reaching implications of this process of reclassification, let us take another look at the art expert as a person engaged in a task somewhat analogous to the physician's. The expert may be commissioned to determine whether, for instance, a beautiful French painting of uncertain origin was painted by Cézanne, as claimed by the art dealer, or whether it is a forgery, as feared by the prospective buyer. If the expert plays the game as he is supposed to, he can reach only one of two answers: He either concludes that the painting is a genuine Cézanne "masterpiece" or states that it is a "forgery."

But suppose that in the process of examining the painting, studying its origin and so on, the art expert becomes increasingly impressed by the craftmanship of the artist, irrespective of who he was, and the loveliness of his work. Might he not conclude that, although the painting is not a genuine Cézanne, it is nevertheless a "real" masterpiece? In fact, if the painting is truly appealing and beautiful, he might even declare that it is a greater masterpiece than a real Cézanne. The artist—let us call him Zeno, hitherto an unknown painter of Greek descent—may then be "discovered" as a "great impressionist painter." But did the expert "discover" Zeno and his masterpiece? Or did he "make" him a famous artist, and his painting a valuable canvas, by the weight of his expert opinion, seconded of course by the weight of many other art experts?

This analogy is intended to show that, strictly speaking, no one discovers or makes a masterpiece. Artists do paint pictures, and people do become, or act, disabled. But the *names*, and hence the *values*, we give to paintings—and to disabilities—depend on the rules of the system of classification that we use. Such rules, however, are not God-given, nor do they occur "naturally." Since all systems of classification are made by people, it is necessary to be aware of who has made the rules and for what purpose. If this precaution is not taken, there is the risk of being unaware of the precise rules, or worse, of mistaking the product of classification for "naturally occurring facts or things." I believe this is exactly what happened in psychiatry during the past sixty or seventy years (Szasz, 1959b). During this period, a vast number of occurrences were reclassified as "illnesses." We have thus come to regard phobias, delinquencies, divorce, homicide, addiction, and so on almost without limit as psychiatric illnesses. This is a colossal and costly mistake.

Immediately, the objection might be raised that this is not a mistake: Does it not benefit addicts, homosexuals, or so-called criminals that they are regarded as "sick?" Of course, such relabeling might benefit certain people. But this happens to be true largely because society as a whole, or people generally, tolerate uncertainty poorly and insist that "misbehavior" be classified either as "sinful" or as "sick." This dichotomy must be rejected. Socially deviant or obnoxious behavior may, in principle, be classified in many different ways. Placing some individuals or groups in the class of sick people may be justified by considerations of social expediency but cannot be supported by scientific observations or logical arguments.

For greater precision, we should ask: For whom, or from what point of view, is it a mistake to classify nonillnesses as illnesses? Clearly, it is a mistake from the point of view of science and intellectual integrity. It is also a mistake if we believe that good ends—say, the social rehabilitation of hysterics or criminals—do not justify the use of morally dubious means; in this case, deliberate, or quasi-deliberate misrepresentation and appeal to falsehood.

The reclassification we are considering has been of special value to doctors and to psychiatry as a profession and social institution. The prestige and power of psychiatrists have been augmented by defining increasingly larger domains as falling within the purview of their special discipline. Mortimer Adler (1937) has correctly noted that psychoanalysts "are trying to swallow everything in psychoanalysis" (p. 122). Is this "good"? It is difficult to see why we should permit, much less encourage, such expansionism in a professional discipline and a science. In international relations, most people no longer treasure the Napoleonic ideal of national expansion at the expense of the integrity of neighboring peoples. On the contrary, expansionism of this kind is widely regarded as an evil (Burckhardt, 1868-1871). Why should not psychiatric expansionism—even though it might be aided and abetted from many sides (by patients, medical organizations, lawyers, etc.)—be considered equally undesirable?

The role of the psychiatric physician as expert arbiter charged with deciding who is or is not ill has not ceased with the renaming of malingering as hysteria and with calling the latter an illness. It has merely made the arbiter's job more intricate and in many ways increasingly nonsensical. All this has contributed to making psychiatric nosology chaotic (Szasz, 1959b). Let us take a closer look at the logic of reclassifying certain non-illnesses as illnesses.

With proper criteria and methods, it is possible to decide that some items are "A's," and all others are "non-A's." At a later time the basis of our classification may be revised and items from the latter group removed and placed in the former. It must be emphasized that the usefulness of class A and the *name* that we give it depend in large measure on the fact that only a few things are included in it. Of all the colors in the visible spectrum, only a few are called green. If we enlarged the range of colors thus designated, which we could certainly do, we would achieve this at the expense of other colors. It is conceivable, for example, that we should become preoccupied with the similarities between green and other-colored lights by focusing on the fact that we can see and read by the light of other-colored lights too. On this basis we may then propose to *call* more and more colors green. If this sort of reasoning were carried to its absurd limits, all colors would be called green. This feat, however, would be accomplished at the cost of obscuring the significant differences between green and blue, red, violet, etc.

Yet something of this sort has, in fact, already happened in contemporary medicine and psychiatry. Starting with such things as syphilis, tuberculosis, typhoid fever, and carcinomas and fractures, we have created the class "illness." At first, this class was composed of only a few items, all of which shared the common feature of reference to a state of disordered structure or function of the human body as a physicochemical machine (Szasz, 1958d). As time went on, additional items were added to this class. They were not added, however, because they were newly discovered bodily disorders. The physician's attention had been deflected from this criterion and had become focused instead on disability and suffering as new criteria for selection. Thus, at first slowly, such things as hysteria, hypochondriasis, obsessive-compulsive neurosis, and depression were added to the category of illness. Then, with increasing zeal, physicians and especially psychiatrists began to call "illness" (that is, of course, "mental illness") anything and everything in which they could detect any sign of malfunctioning, based on no matter what norm. Hence, agoraphobia is illness because one should not be afraid of open spaces. Homosexuality is illness because heterosexuality is the social norm. Divorce is illness because it signals failure of marriage. Crime, art, undesired political leadership, participation in social affairs, or withdrawal from such participation—all these and many more have been said to be signs of mental illness (Szasz, 1958f, 1960b).

Three Interpretations of Malingering

Certain historical transformations in the concept of malingering illustrate my thesis. The concept of malingering can be shown to reflect the particular ideas which the psychiatrist-as-arbiter holds concerning the notion of illness.[1]

MALINGERING AS SIMULATION OF ILLNESS

Prior to the time of Charcot, a person was said to be ill only if his body was physically disordered. Counterfeit illness was called malingering, and the patient so labeled was considered a legitimate object of the physician's hostility. After all, it is our "natural" reaction to feel anger toward someone who tries to fool and trick us. Why should physicians act differently? This, presumably, was the logic that made it acceptable for physicians to act destructively toward such patients. This view of malingering is so well known that it is unnecessary to illustrate or document it. It is probably much less appreciated that this view is by no means extinct today. The following excerpts are from a recent article in the *Journal of the American Medical Association* (Chapman, 1957), which was captioned with this summation for the benefit of the readers:

> Physicians in the United States may be unaware of the patient who spends his time going from place to place, resulting in wide travels, and presenting himself to hospitals, with a fanciful history and extraordinary complaints. It is not uncommon for these patients to have many surgical scars crisscrossing their abdomens, and willingly to allow further surgical procedures to be performed, regardless of

[1] For detailed documentation of this thesis, see "Malingering: 'Diagnosis' or Social Condemnation?" (Szasz, 1956b).

the dangers. Publicizing case histories of such patients seems to be the only way of coping with the problem, which exploits medical services that could be put to better use (p. 927).

The article concluded with the following paragraph:

The case of a 39-year-old merchant seaman is a remarkable example of hospital vagrancy and spurious hemoptysis. Similar patients in Britain have been said to have Münchausen's syndrome because their wide travels and fanciful histories are reminiscent of the travels and adventures of fiction's Baron Münchausen. Such patients constitute an economic threat and an extreme nuisance to the hospital they choose to visit, for their deception invariably results in numerous diagnostic and therapeutic procedures. Publicizing their histories in journals, thereby alerting the medical profession, seems the only effective way of coping with them. *Appropriate disposition would be confinement in a mental hospital.* Such patients have enough social and *mental quirks to merit permanent custodial care*, otherwise their exploitation of medical facilities will go on indefinitely ([ITALICS ADDED] p. 933).

These quotations require little comment. They are offered chiefly to show that a view many consider utterly outmoded is apparently still widely shared. They also illustrate that physicians may often play the medical game without self-reflection, unaware of the rules by which the game is played. Finally, it is interesting to note that the author of the article advocated "permanent custodial care" [sic] as the proper punishment—although he called it "care"—of those persons who try to deceive physicians into believing they are sick. Since physicians often have the social power to make such punishment enforceable, this position is not without serious potential consequences. Indeed, the psychosocial processes underlying the commitment of mental patients to state hospitals have much in common with this attitude toward malingering.

MALINGERING AS CONSCIOUS IMITATION OF ILLNESS

With Freud and psychoanalysis a new system of classification came into being. Bodily illness was class A. Hysteria was still regarded as a form of counterfeit illness, but a very special form indeed. It was asserted that the patient himself did not know that he was simulating. Hysteria was thus viewed as unconscious malingering. This was class B. The concept of malingering was still retained, but the arbiter was instructed, so to speak, to diagnose this condition only when the imitation was *conscious*. This new version of malingering (class C) differed from the previous notion of counterfeit illness (of the body) by virtue of the new dichotomy "conscious-unconscious."

The role and function of the psychiatrist-arbiter has shifted: previously his task was to distinguish bodily illness from all that did not fit into this class; now it includes the differentiation of "unconscious malingering" or "hysteria" from its antonym "conscious malingering." The degree of arbitrariness or error to which this judgment is open is, of course, even greater than was the case previously. This conceptualization and its subsequent developments lent themselves to an increasingly capricious and personalistic usage of the concepts of hysteria, neurosis, and mental illness. The difficulties inherent in these designations and classifications are all around us. For example, Freud (1928) himself made the peculiar statement: "There are people who are complete masochists without being neurotic" (p. 224). Surely this assertion is a monument to the hopelessly capricious and judgmental usage of the terms "masochist" and "neurotic."

Such is the logic of the classical Freudian position concerning the mutual relations of hysteria and malingering. It must be emphasized that Freud omitted any direct discussion of the nature of the relationship between these two alleged entities. This omission, in the "Studies on Hysteria" (1893-1895) and his other writings, is indeed remarkable. In my opinion, it may be interpreted to mean that he wished to avoid the explicit act of judging and condemning any type of suffering as illegitimate (Freud, 1893b). Nevertheless, the concepts of conscious versus unconscious motivation, and those of primary versus secondary gain, compel us to form the "diagnostic" classes "organic illness," "hysteria," and "malingering."

The so-called differential diagnosis between hysteria and malingering has been incorporated into the majority of psychoanalytic textbooks (Glover, 1949; Menninger, 1938). The basis for this was laid by Freud's differentiation of conscious imitation from unconscious copying. In his paper, "General Remarks on Hysterical Attacks," Freud (1909) likened hysterical attacks to *pantomimic representations* (p. 100). In ordinary usage, a pantomime or dumb-show would be regarded as a conscious activity, essentially similar to speech, the difference being that communication is mediated by means of gestural expressions instead of by conventional vocal symbols.

MALINGERING AS MENTAL ILLNESS

The inclination to regard virtually all forms of human conduct as illness—especially if they are unusual or are studied by the psychiatrist (Balint, 1951)—is reflected by the contemporary psychoanalytic view of malingering. According to it, malingering *is* an illness—in fact, an illness "more serious" than hysteria. This is an interesting logical position, for it amounts to nothing less than a complete denial of man's ability to imitate—in this instance, to imitate certain forms of disability. When simulation of mental illness is itself regarded as a form of mental illness, the rules of the medical (or psychiatric) game are so defined as to explicitly exclude the class "counterfeit illness." Only two classes are recognized: A–illness, and non-A–nonillness. *Counterfeit illness, or malingering, is now a species of illness. The good imitation of a masterpiece is redefined as itself a masterpiece.* Since the copy is as pleasing to the eye as the original, this is not an entirely untenable position. Still, this view entails a radical redefinition of the term "forgery." In the case of so-called psychiatric illnesses, such redefinitions apparently occurred without anyone realizing what had happened.

Historically, it was probably Bleuler (1924) who first suggested that simulation of insanity, irrespective of how conscious or unconscious the patient's motives, be regarded as a manifestation of mental illness. He wrote:

"Those who simulate insanity with some cleverness are nearly all psychopaths and some are actually insane. Demonstration of simulation, therefore, does not at all prove that the patient is mentally sound and responsible for his actions" (p. 191).

The view that malingering is a form of mental illness became popular during the Second World War (especially among American psychiatrists). It was believed that only a "crazy" or "sick" person would malinger. A vigorous exposition of this position may be found in Eissler's (1951) essay on malingering. He wrote:

> It can be rightly claimed that *malingering is always the sign of a disease often more severe than a neurotic disorder* because it concerns an arrest of development at an early phase. — *It is a disease* which to *diagnose* requires particularly keen *diagnostic acumen*. The *diagnosis* should never be made but by the *psychiatrist*. It is a great mistake to make a patient suffering from the disease liable to *prosecution*, at least if he falls within the type of personality I have described here ([ITALICS ADDED] pp. 252-253).

This proposition has obvious advantages, for it buttresses the potentially shaky morale of the erstwhile civilian physician conscripted into the military service. It supports—at the patient's expense, of course—the physician's covert endorsement of the aims and values of the war effort. This assertion is based on the fact that although the patient may have been treated more or less kindly as sick, he was, at the same time, deprived of the right and opportunity to rebel, by means of imitating bodily or mental disability, against the demands placed on him. This form of protest was disallowed, and those who resorted to it were demoted and disenfranchised by being labeled "mentally ill," by being given "NP discharges," and by similar techniques of disguised punishment. We touch here on the social implications and consequences of the psychiatrist's participation in social problems (Szasz, 1960c). We need not penetrate more deeply into this difficult area here. Let us remember, however, that whenever the psychiatric situation includes more people than just the psychiatrist and his patient, the effects of the psychiatrist's action on all those involved must be explicitly considered.[2]

Concluding Remarks on Objects and Their Representations

The unifying thread that runs through this chapter is the notion of similarity. An iconic sign—say a photograph—manifests a relationship of similarity to the object it represents. So does a map to the terrain of which it is a two-dimensional model. It should be recalled that the proper use of a photograph or a map implies that they merely represent real things. In our every-day life, it makes a vast practical difference whether objects are clearly recognized as representations or accepted as real—that is, as objects in their own right. This may be illustrated by contrasting stage money with counterfeit money. Although stage money might look like real money, it is at the same time clearly identified as make-believe. Sometimes the clarity or ambiguity of this identification might be a matter of controversy. For in-stance, we could imagine a situation in which stage money was mistaken for real money. The point to be emphasized here is that *the context of a message forms an integral part of the total communicational package.* Thus, whether bills are regarded as stage money or counterfeit may depend not so much on how the objects look as on who passes them to whom, where, and how. The stage setting itself implies that the monies (or daggers, guns, etc.) used are props. The setting of an economic transaction implies that the monies are real, and if they are not real, they must by definition be considered counter-feit.

Let us apply these considerations to the problem of hysteria. In this in-stance, disabled behavior is under scrutiny, but the communicational pack-age must include the situation in which such behavior is presented. If it is presented in a physician's office, we must ask: Should the disabled behavior

---

[2] The following sources on malingering, not specifically referred to in the text, were also consulted in the preparation of this chapter: Cohen (1954), Collie (1913), Freud (1920), Henderson and Gillespie (1950), Jones (1957, p. 23), M'Kendrick (1912), Noyes (1956), Wertham (1949).

be viewed as an object in its own right, or as a representation?[3] If the phenomena presented are regarded and treated as real objects—that is, as a
physicist treats, say, the movements of a planet—then they should be classified as illness or as malingering depending solely on one's definition of what
constitutes illness. If, however, the phenomena are regarded as representations
(models or signs) of other occurrences—that is, as a physicist regards a
laboratory experiment on gravitation employing balls rolling down an in-
cline—then a totally different interpretation becomes possible. We may now
speak of illness-imitative behavior. This, however, can under no circumstances
be called illness unless we are prepared to commit the logically nonsensical
operation of placing an item and its known imitation in the same class.

Agreeing to the proposition that both malingering and hysteria refer to
illness-imitative behavior, we are still left with some uncertainties concerning
the cognitive quality (i.e., the degree of "consciousness") and the intent of
the imitation. Drawing again on the earlier comparison to stage money,
it is known that both actors and spectators are aware that what looks
like money is in fact an imitation—a prop. In contrast, the term "counterfeit" implies that only the counterfeiters know that it is a facsimile, whereas
those who receive it, and who then might even pass it on to others, do not
know this. On the contrary, they believe that they possess the object proper
when they hold merely its imitation. They are deceived.

What is the comparable situation in the case of hysteria? Does the patient
believe that he is ill (object proper), or that he is offering a representation
(facsimile) of illness? Some insist that the patient offers illness in good faith,
as it were; others argue that he knows he is not ill. The two divergent answers
reflect the difference between the diagnoses of hysteria and that of malingering. There is evidence to support both of these positions. The question
raised cannot, therefore, be answered unequivocally. Indeed, the patient's
failure to define his message either as object or as representation constitutes
one of the crucial characteristics of his behavior. (This problem will be
examined further in Part V, especially Chapter 14.)

So much for the patient, in his role as actor or message-sender. What about
the spectators—the recipients of the message? The spectator's reaction to
the drama of hysteria will depend on his personality and relationship to the
actor (patient). Stranger and relative, foe and friend, nonpsychiatric physician and psychoanalyst—each will react differently. I shall comment briefly
on the reactions of the last two only. The nonpsychiatric physician tends to

---

[3] In this connection, see Erving Goffman's *The Presentation of Self in Everyday Life*
(1959), especially his distinction between the signs a person gives, as against those he
gives off (pp. 2, ff.).

treat all forms of disability as objects proper, not as representations. That is, he tends to view all forms of disability as illness or potential illness. The psychoanalyst on the other hand, in his actual work with the patient, will tend to treat all phenomena as representations. But since he has failed to codify this logical distinction clearly he will persist in describing his observations, and in theorizing about them, as though they were objects instead of representations. Representations are no less real, of course, than real objects. Consider here once more the differences between a photograph of John Doe and John Doe in the flesh. These two items occupy different logical levels of conceptualization and discourse.

If we take this distinction seriously, we shall be compelled to regard psychiatry as dealing with communications or sign-using behavior, not with "mental illnesses." Accordingly, psychiatry and neurology are not sister sciences, both belonging to the superordinate class called medicine. Rather, psychiatry stands in a *meta relation* to neurology and to other branches of medicine. Neurology is concerned with certain parts of the human body and its functions *qua* objects in their own rights—*not* as signs of other objects. Psychiatry (as defined here) is expressly concerned with signs *qua* signs—not merely with signs as things pointing to objects more real and interesting than they themselves.

CHAPTER 3 | *Sociology of the Therapeutic Situation*

Psychiatrists have traditionally regarded mental illness as a problem apart from and independent of the social context in which it occurred. The symptomatic manifestations of diseases of the body, for instance diphtheria or syphilis, are indeed independent of the sociopolitical conditions of the country in which they occur. A diphtheritic membrane looked the same whether it occurred in a patient in Czarist Russia or Victorian England.

Since mental illness was considered to be basically like bodily illness, it was logical that no attention was paid to the social conditions in which the alleged disease occurred. This is not to say that the effects of social conditions on the causation of illness were not appreciated. On the contrary, this sort of relationship had been recognized since antiquity. However, although it was known that poverty and malnutrition favored the development of tuberculosis, or sexual promiscuity the spread of syphilis, it was nevertheless held that once these diseases made their appearance, their *manifestations* were the same whether the patient was rich or poor, nobleman or serf. Although the phenomenal features of bodily illnesses are independent of the socioeconomic and political structure of the society in which they occur, this is not true of so-called mental illnesses. The manifestations of psychosocial disabilities vary in accordance with educational, socioeconomic, religious, and political factors.[1]

When persons belonging to different religious and socioeconomic groups become bodily ill—for example, with pneumonia or bronchogenic carcinoma

[1] In this connection, see Freud's discussion of the personality development of two imaginary children, one growing up in a poor, the other in a well-to-do family (1916-1917, pp. 308-312).

—their bodies manifest the same sort of physiological derangements. Hence, in principle, for given diseases all patients should receive the same treatments, irrespective of who they are. This is the scientifically correct position with respect to physicochemical disturbances of the body. There have been attempts to apply this asocial and amoral standard of treatment to so-called mental illnesses, to which, in my opinion, it does not apply. To understand why it does not apply, it is necessary to examine and make explicit how therapeutic attitudes—or, more precisely, physician-patient relationships—vary in accordance with changes in historical and socio-political circumstances. In other words, our task now will be to show how the same sorts of symptoms and illnesses are differently treated in different social situations. To accomplish this, the characteristic therapeutic situations of three different sociocultural settings will be briefly described and analyzed. They are: (1) late nineteenth-century, Western European medicine; (2) medical practice in contemporary Western democracies, especially in the United States; and (3) Soviet medical practice.

The term "therapeutic situation" will be used to refer to medical and psychotherapeutic practice. Since the interrelations of social structure, value, and therapeutic situation are numerous and complex (Sigerist, 1951, 1960), two clearly identifiable aspects of the general problem will be selected for special attention. They may be stated in the form of questions: (1) Whose agent is the therapist (physician, psychotherapist, etc.)? (2) How many persons, or institutions, are directly involved in the therapeutic situation?

Nineteenth-century Liberalism, Capitalism, and Individualism

Nineteenth-century European liberalism and its concurrent economic developments had significant, but probably little understood, effects on the patterns of the physician-patient relationship. Long before this time, medical care was regarded much as other economic goods. It was a commodity that could be purchased by the rich only. To the poor, when given, it had to be given free, as charity. This social arrangement, with its roots in Greco-Roman medicine, was firmly established by the time modern scientific advances in medicine began, during the latter half of the nineteenth century. It should be recalled, too, that this period was characterized by the rapid flowering of liberal thoughts and deeds in Europe, as manifested, for example, by the abolition of serfdom in Austria-Hungary and Russia.

As industrialization and urbanization flourished, the proletariat replaced the unorganized and sociopsychologically less well-defined peasant class. Thus, a self-conscious and class-conscious capitalism developed, and with it recognition of a new form of mass suffering and disability, namely, poverty. The phenomenon of poverty, as such, was of course nothing new. However, the existence of huge numbers of impoverished people, crowded together within the confines of a city, was new. At the same time, and undoubtedly out of the need to do something about mass poverty, there arose "therapists" for this new "disease" of the masses. Among them, Karl Marx (1890) is, of course, the best known. He was no solitary phenomenon, however, but rather exemplified a new social role and function—the revolutionary as "social therapist" (Feuer, 1959). Along with these developments, the ethics of individualism were strongly bolstered. The basic value of the individual—as opposed to the interests of the masses or the nation—was emphasized, especially by the upper social classes. The professions, medicine foremost among them, espoused the ethical value of individualism. This value gradually became pitted against its antonym, collectivism. Although the ethics of individualism and collectivism are polar opposites, their present forms were achieved through a simultaneous development, and they often exist side by side. This was already the case, to some extent, in the days of Charcot, Breuer, and Freud. This contention may be illustrated by some observations concerning the therapeutic situations characteristic of that period.

It should be recalled that the physician in Charcot's Paris (or in his counterpart's Berlin, Moscow, or Vienna) was usually engaged in two diametrically opposite types of therapeutic situations. In one, he was confronted by a private patient of means. This meant that he served, by and large, as the patient's agent, having been hired by him to make a diagnosis and, if possible, achieve a cure. The physician, in turn, demanded payment for services rendered. He thus had an economic incentive, in addition to other incentives, to help his patient. Furthermore, since some bodily illnesses were considered shameful (including not only venereal diseases but tuberculosis and certain dermatological ailments as well), a wealthy person could also avail himself of the social protection of privacy. As a rich man could buy a house large enough to provide several rooms for his sole occupancy, so also he could buy the services of a physician for his sole use. In its extreme form, this amounted to having a personal physician, much as one had a valet, maid, or cook. This custom is by no means extinct. In some parts of the world, wealthy or socially prominent people still have personal physicians whose duty is to care only for them or perhaps their families.

A similar, but less extreme, arrangement is afforded by the private, two-person medical situation. This arrangement insures for the patient the time, effort, and privacy which he considers necessary for his care and still allows the physician to care for other patients within the limits of his available time and energy. The development of privacy as an integral part of the (private) therapeutic situation seems to be closely tied to the capitalistic economic system.[2] The Hippocratic oath commands the physician to respect and safeguard the patient's confidential communications. The Greek physician of antiquity practiced, of course, in a capitalist society, selling his skills to the rich, and helping the poor without recompense.

It is implicit in this discussion that having access to a private therapeutic relationship is desirable. Why is this sort of privacy desired? The answer lies in the connections between illness (or disability) and shame, and between shame and privacy. A few brief comments concerning this subject will have to suffice here. The feeling of shame is intimately related to what other people think of one. Exposure and humiliation are feared both as punishments for shameful acts and as stimuli for increasingly intense feelings of shame (Piers and Singer, 1953). In contrast to public exposure, secrecy or privacy protects the person from being excessively "punished" for his shameful behavior. Irrespective of whether the shameful event is the result of physical disability, psychological conflict, or moral weakness, it is more easily acknowledged if it is communicated to a single person—as in the confessional or in private psychotherapy—than if it has to be made known to many people. Accordingly, privacy in medical or psychotherapeutic relationships is useful because it protects the patient from undue embarrassment and humiliation, and thus facilitates mastery of the problem.

In addition to protecting the patient from embarrassment, privacy and secrecy in the therapeutic situation are desirable and necessary also to protect him from "real"—that is, social rather than intrapersonal—dangers. Social isolation and ostracism, loss of employment, and injury to family and social status are some of the dangers that may threaten a person should his condition or diagnosis become public knowledge. In this connection, such possibilities as syphilis in a schoolteacher, psoriasis in a cook, or schizophrenia in a judge may be considered. These, however, are merely illustrative examples. The possibilities both of rewards and penalties incurred for publicly established diagnoses are virtually limitless. The precise character of the rewards and penalties will vary, once again, with the intellectual-scientific development and moral climate of the society (e.g., Butler, 1872).

---

[2] I do not wish to imply that privacy (in medical or other relationships) is necessarily tied to capitalism as a socioeconomic system. Rather, it appears that the ability to command privacy (or secrecy) depends on social status or power. Money is often the means whereby such power is implemented. Significantly, however, men having high social status in communist societies may have access to privacy without this being dependent on monetary considerations, whereas highly situated persons in capitalist societies, especially if they are in the public eye, often find it virtually impossible to secure privacy in therapeutic relationships.

The second type of therapeutic situation to be considered is charity practice. The differences between it and private practice have often been overlooked as a result of concentrating on the patient's disease and the physician's alleged desire to cure it. In traditional charity practice, the physician was not principally the patient's agent. Sometimes he was not the patient's agent at all. Accordingly, a truly private—in the sense of confidential —relationship between patient and physician could not develop. The physician was technically and legally responsible to his superiors and employers. He was, therefore, bound to orient himself for his rewards, at least to some extent, to his employer, rather than to his patient (and his own conscience). This in no way negates the possibility that the physician may still remain strongly motivated to help his patient. It is often maintained nowadays that removing the financial involvement with the patient enables the physician better to concentrate on the technical task at hand (provided that he is adequately remunerated). While this might well be true in thoracic surgery, it need not be equally true in psychoanalysis. In any case, it is clear that the financial inducement which the private patient offers the physician is absent in charity practice. The main features of these two types of therapeutic situations are summarized in Table 1.

TABLE 1. SOCIOLOGY OF THE THERAPEUTIC SITUATION
PRIVATE VERSUS CHARITY PRACTICE

Characteristics of the Situation	Private Practice	Charity Practice
Number of participants	Two (or few) Two-person situation "Private"	Many Multiperson situation "Public"
Whose agent is the therapist?	Patient's Patient's guardian's (e.g., pediatrics) Patient's family's	Employer's (e.g. institution, state, etc.)
Sources and nature of the therapist's rewards	Patient: money, referrals, etc.	Employer: money, promotion, prestige through status
	Patient's relatives and friends: satisfaction from having helped	Patient's relatives and friends: satisfaction from having helped
	Self: satisfaction from mastery	Self: satisfaction from mastery
	Colleagues: satisfaction from proven competence	Colleagues: satisfaction from proven competence

The contrast between private and public medical care is often pictured as though it were rather like the difference between a palace and a hovel. One is fine and expensive; anyone who could afford to secure it would be a fool if he did not do so, especially if he needed it. The other is inferior and second rate; at best, it makes life livable. Although physicians, politicians, and others have tried to tell the poor that medical care of the indigent was as good as that of the rich, more often than not this message fell on deaf ears. The facts of life are stubborn and difficult to disguise. Thus, instead of accepting this pious message, people have tried to raise their standard of living. In this effort, the people of the United States and some European countries have been the most successful, so far. This has resulted in certain fundamental changes in the patterns of medical care—and hence in the sociology of the therapeutic situation—in these countries. I shall comment on these changes now, and shall then consider medical developments in the Soviet Union.

The Affluent Society and Its Patterns of Health Care

Several contemporary economists (e.g., Drucker, 1949) have called attention to the fact that while traditional economic thought is rooted in the sociology of poverty and want, the socioeconomic problems of modern America, and to a lesser extent those of Western Europe, must be understood in terms of the sociology of excess productivity, wealth, and leisure. In *The Affluent Society*, Galbraith (1958) has presented a masterfully executed economic portrait of the age of opulence. The medical sociology of this era has yet to be written.

Progressive technological and sociocultural sophistication has led to a number of means whereby people may guard themselves against future poverty, want, and helplessness. One of these is insurance. We shall be especially concerned with the effects of health insurance on medical and psychotherapeutic relationships.

INSURED PRACTICE

From our present point of view it matters little whether protection from illness has been guaranteed for the individual by a private insurance company or furnished by the state. Health protection by means of privately purchased insurance is in the tradition of private ownership and capitalism and is, accordingly, popular in the United States. Protection by means of taxation and socialized medicine has been the form chosen in Great Britain. To most Americans, this appears to be more socialistic and hence bad. It is essential to discard these clichés, so that we can address ourselves to the relevant variables in these situations.

Health insurance introduces a completely new phenomenon into the practice of medicine. The most significant feature of insured practice—a name

which I suggest to distinguish it from both private and charity practice—
is that it is neither private nor public. The physician-patient relationship is
so structured that the doctor is neither the patient's nor a charitable institution's sole agent. This arrangement cannot be reduced to the old patterns
of medical care, nor can it be understood in their terms. It is commonly believed that the insured situation does not differ significantly from the private
practice situation. The only difference, it is thought, is that the physician is
paid by the insurance company instead of by the patient. Rarely is insured
medicine regarded as similar to charity practice. Yet I submit that there are
probably more significant similarities between insured and charity practice
than between insured and private practice. The insurance arrangement, like
the charitable one, makes a two-person, confidential relationship between
doctor and patient virtually impossible.

Without penetrating further into the sociological intricacies of insured
medicine, I should like to offer some generalizations which may be useful
for our study of hysteria and the problem of mental illness. It appears to be
a general rule that the more clear-cut, "objective," or socially acceptable a
patient's disease, the more closely insured practice will resemble private practice. For example, if a housewife slips on a banana peel in her kitchen and
fractures her ankle, her treatment may not be significantly influenced by
whether she or an insurance company or the government pays for it.

It is a corollary of this rule that the more an illness deviates from something that happens to a person, and the more it is something that the
person does or makes happen, the greater shall be the differences between the insured situation and the private, two-person situation. For instance, if our patient falls in a factory rather than in her kitchen, she will
then not only receive compensation but also be granted permission to stay
away from work. And if she has a young child with whom she would like
to spend more time at home, she will have a strong incentive to be
disabled for more than a minimum length of time. Obviously, this sort of
situation requires an arbiter or judge to decide whether a person is or is not
disabled ("sick"). The physician is generally regarded as the proper person
for this task. It may be argued that physicians in private practice also play this
role. But this is fallacious argument. The physician in private practice is primarily the patient's agent. Should there be a conflict between his opinion and
the presumed "real facts"—as may occur when the patient is involved with life
insurance companies, draft boards, or industrial concerns—the latter groups
take recourse to employing *their own physicians*. In the case of the draft
board, for example, the examining physician has absolute power to overrule
the private physician's opinion. And if he does not have such power, for

example in the case of an industrial concern, the conflict of interests must be arbitrated by a court of law.

In the case of insured practice, the answer to the question "Whose agent is the physician?" is not clearly spelled out. As a result, it is possible for the physician to shift from one position to another. He may act entirely on behalf of the patient one minute and line up against him the next.[3] In the latter case, the patient can change physicians, if the contract permits. In any case, the entire arrangement precludes a genuine two-person therapeutic relationship.

As a third generalization, I should like to offer the following. So-called mental illnesses share only a single significant characteristic with bodily diseases: the sufferer or "sick person" is more or less disabled from performing certain activities. The two differ in that mental illnesses can be understood only if they are viewed as occurrences that do not merely happen to a person but rather are brought on by him (perhaps unconsciously), and hence may be of some value to him. This assumption is not necessary—indeed, it is unsupportable—in the typical cases of bodily illness.

The premise that the behavior of persons said to be mentally ill is meaningful and goal-directed—provided one is able to understand the patient's behavior from *his* particular point of view—underlies all "rational" psychotherapies. Moreover, if the psychotherapist is to perform his task well, he must not be influenced by socially distracting considerations concerning his patient. This condition can be met best if the relationship is rigidly restricted to the two people involved in it.

On the one hand, therefore, the affluent society brought the widespread adoption of health insurance into being; on the other, it fostered the growth and economic rewards of private medical and psychotherapeutic practice.

THE PRIVATE PRACTICE SITUATION

It is necessary now to refine our conception of private practice. Thus far, this term has been used in its conventional sense, to denote the medical activities of any physician *not employed* by an institution or agency (e.g., a company or labor union). According to this definition, such a physician is engaged in private practice, irrespective of how or by whom he is paid. This common-sense definition will no longer suffice for our purposes. Instead, we

[3] The terms "for" or "against" the patient, and "good" or "bad" for him, are used here solely in accordance with the patient's own definition of his wants and needs. Any other definition, such as attempting to determine whether the therapist is acting on behalf of, or opposed to, the patient in accordance with the therapist's avowed intentions, can lead only to confusion and social exploitation. A good example is the notion that all psychiatrists are "therapists" acting on behalf of the patient's best interests, irrespective of what they in fact do (Szasz, 1957d, 1960d).

shall have to adopt a more limited definition of private practice, based on strict pragmatic criteria. Let us define the Private Practice Situation as a contract between patient and physician: the patient hires the doctor to help him with his own health care, and pays the physician for it. If the physician is hired by someone other than the patient, or is paid by another party, the medical relationship will no longer fall in the category of Private Practice Situation. This definition highlights (1) the *two-person nature of the relationship*, and (2) the fundamental *autonomy and self-determination of the patient* (Szasz, 1957b, 1959g). I shall continue to use the expression "private practice" in its conventional sense, to refer to all types of noncharity, noninstitutional practice. The term Private Practice Situation (with initials capitalized) will be used to designate the two-person therapeutic situation as described above (see Table 2).

TABLE 2. SOCIOLOGY OF THE THERAPEUTIC SITUATION
PRIVATE PRACTICE VERSUS INSURED PRACTICE

Characteristics of the Situation	Private Practice Situation	Insured Practice
Number of participants	Two Two-person situation	Three or more Multiperson situation

Whose agent is the therapist?	Patient's	Therapist's role is poorly defined and ambiguous:
		  Patient's agent, when in agreement with his aspirations
		  Society's agent, when in disagreement with patient's aspirations
		  His own agent, trying to maximize his own gains (e.g., compensation cases)

Sources and nature of therapist's rewards	Patient: money, referrals, etc. Self: satisfaction from mastery Colleagues	Patient: cure, gratitude, etc. Self: satisfaction from mastery Colleagues System or state: money, promotion, etc.

Let us remember that an opulent society fosters not only health insurance but also private practice. In the United States, a considerable proportion of the latter is psychiatric or psychotherapeutic practice. This proportion becomes even more significant if it is considered not in relation to the general category of private practice, but rather in relation to the narrowly defined Private Practice Situation. Indeed, it seems that psychotherapeutic practice is the most important contemporary (American) representative of a truly two-person therapeutic relationship. Deterioration in the privacy of the traditional (nineteenth-century) medical situation may have been one of the stimuli for increasing the demand for psychotherapeutic services. Inasmuch as the physician is no longer the true representative of the patient, the latter has turned to the psychiatrist and to the nonmedical psychotherapist as new representatives of his best interests.

This is not to imply that deterioration in this privacy is mainly responsible for the increasing demand for psychotherapeutic help in contemporary America. The role of affluence itself might be significant in this connection, for as soon as people have more money than is needed to provide the so-called necessities of life (whatever these may be), they will expect to be "happy." They will then use some of their money to seek "happiness." The social function of psychotherapy, from this point of view, must be compared and contrasted not only with that of religion but also with that of alcohol, to-bacco, cosmetics, and various recreational activities.

These considerations touch on the relationship between social class, mental illness, and the type of treatment received for it, a subject recently explored by Hollingshead and Redlich (1958). These authors found, for example, that affluent psychiatric patients tend to receive psychotherapy, while poor patients are treated with physical interventions. Psychological help and physical therapies represent such grossly divergent types of psychiatric actions that no meaningful comparison as to which is "better" can be made between them. Hollingshead and Redlich's findings clearly demonstrate, however, that there are significant connections between economic status, education, and a self-responsible, self-determinate mode of orienting one's self to a help-seeking situation. I emphasize this because I believe that the social impact of the affluent society on psychiatry (and on medicine, generally) is such as to both foster and inhibit the growth of a two-person therapeutic situation. Better education and economic security favor the conditions necessary for a two-person therapeutic contract. At the same time, the spread of insured health protection, whether through private insurance, veterans' benefits, or government-sponsored medical care, creates a new type of therapeutic relationship that tends to preclude a truly two-person arrangement.

Finally, it is worth noting that while the Private Practice Situation is being displaced by insured patterns of care in the democracies, in the Soviet Union it was displaced when physicians became employees of the state. Medical practice in Soviet Russia will now be examined to contrast the role of the physician as agent of the individual (patient) with his role as agent of the state.

Soviet Medicine and the Problem of Malingering

THE SOVIET PHYSICIAN AS AGENT OF THE STATE

The great majority of the Russian population depends on medical services furnished by the state. Private practice exists, but is available only to those occupying the top layers of the Soviet social pyramid. Another crucial feature of the Russian medical scheme is the result of the government's strong emphasis on the production of agricultural, industrial, and other types of goods (Rostow, 1952). The need to work is impressed on the people in every possible way. It follows that for those who wish to avoid working, falling sick and remaining disabled is one of the most important avenues of escape from what they experience as an intolerable demand. Since the presence of sickness is not always obvious to the layman, the physician is chosen as the expert arbiter who must decide which of the persons who claim to be ill are "really ill," and which ones only "malinger." Field (1957) described this as follows:[4]

> It stands to reason that certification of illness cannot be left, under most circumstances, to the person who claims to be sick. This would make abuses too easy. It is the physician, then, as the only person technically qualified to do so, who must "legitimize" or "certify" sickness in the eyes of society. This means, in turn, that abuses of the patient's role will consist in conveying to the physician the impression that one's sickness is independent of one's conscious motivation—whereas it actually is not. This possibility beclouds the *classical assumption* that the person who comes to the physician must *necessarily* be sick (independently of motivation): on the contrary, in certain cases, just the opposite assumption may be held. This has, of course, important implications for both physician and "genuine" patient.
>
> It is held here that a society (or social group) which, for any number of reasons, cannot offer its members sufficient incentives of motivation for the faithful and spontaneous performances of their

[4] Much of the material on the Soviet medical system is based on Mark G. Field's book, *Doctor and Patient in Soviet Russia* (1957). Field's data derive almost entirely from the Stalinist period. It seems clear now that everyday life in Russia was rather tough then, especially during the war years. Since Stalin's death, life apparently has become much easier, the pressure to work and produce less insistent. Hence, the observations cited and the hypotheses proposed, while probably accurate for Stalinist Russia, may not be entirely valid for the current sociomedical situation in that country.

social obligations must rely on coercion to obtain such perform-ances. Because of the presence of coercion such a society will also generate a high incidence of deviant behavior to escape coercion. *Simulation of illness (technically known as malingering) will be one form of such behavior. Malingering can be considered as a medical, a social, and a legal problem.* It is a medical problem only insofar as it is the physician's task to certify who is a *bona fide patient* and who is a *faker*. It is a social problem insofar as the assumption that the per-son who comes to the physician must necessarily be sick (inde-pendently of motivation) is no longer tenable. The opposite as-sumption may sometimes be just as valid. It is often a legal problem because a fraud has been perpetrated.

Malingering may have far-reaching consequences because the "business" of society (or the group) is not done and because ordi-nary social sanctions are inadequate to close this escape valve. This means, in turn, that some provision must be made, some mechanism devised, to control the granting of medical dispensations. The logical point at which to apply this control is the physician ([ITALICS ADDED] pp. 146-148).

According to Field, Russian physicians are afraid to be lenient with pa-tients not demonstrably ill. There is widespread anxiety that every patient is a potential spy or *agent provocateur*.

The social status of the Soviet physician is relatively low. Most of them are women. Their status is similar to that of our social workers or public school teachers. A comparison of American and Soviet medicine raises many questions concerning the merits and shortcomings of public and private sys-tems of education and medical care. I submit that the Soviet physician, the American social worker, and the American public school teacher share a significant common feature: each functions as an agent of society. By this I mean that individuals fulfilling these social roles are hired by society or by large social bodies (e.g., a school system), to minister to the needs of group-members (e.g., schoolchildren, persons on relief, the sick, etc.). *They are not hired by their customers, clients, or patients and, accordingly, do not owe their primary loyalties to them.* This arrangement tends to be beneficial to the group as a whole, but is not always advantageous for the specific individuals served. The clash of interests is greatest when the needs of the group and the individual are widely divergent.

I should now like to call attention to some connections between modern Soviet medicine on the one hand and the social role of the physician in charity practice, say in Charcot's day, on the other hand. The diagnosis of malingering was frequently made in both settings. This was due mainly to two factors. First, the physician was an agent of society (or some part of it), and not of the patient. Second, the physician tacitly espoused as his own the prevalent social values concerning the patient's productive usefulness in the social structure. The Soviet physician, for example, is identified with the value of industrial productivity, just as his nineteenth-century Western counterpart was identified with certain notions concerning the woman's "proper" role as wife and mother in that society (Szasz, 1959a). Escape from both roles—whether that of downtrodden worker or downtrodden woman —was left open along a number of routes, *disability* being one. It seems to me that as the investigators' interest and sympathy turned from the group exerting pressure to the individual on whom pressure was being applied, there was a metamorphosis in the very conception of the problem. The first step, taken in Western countries some time ago, was the change of diagnosis from malingering to hysteria. Perhaps chiefly because of the different patterns of social evolution in Russia, this step has not yet been taken there. One would expect, however, that this change—or one similar to it—may occur in Russia, too, in the near future.

The change in terminology from malingering to hysteria, and through it to the general notion of mental illness as a designation for all sorts of social and interpersonal happenings, is thus regarded as reflecting *social evolution*. The first step, designating the disability malingering, commits the physician squarely to the camp of the oppressor. The second, designating it hysteria, makes him the agent of a "sick" (oppressed) individual. The third step, designating it "mental illness," denotes a stage at which the physician's precise social role and function are ambiguous and officially obscure.

The following quotation from Field (1957) illustrates how strongly the Soviet physician is committed to the role of agent of society, if necessary in opposition to the individualistic needs of any one patient:

> It is perhaps significant to note that the *Hippocratic oath*, which was taken by tsarist doctors (as it is in the West), *was abolished after the revolution because it "symbolized" bourgeois medicine* and was considered incompatible with the spirit of Soviet medicine. "If," continues a Soviet commentator in the *Medical Worker*, "the pre-revolutionary physician was proud of the fact that for him 'medicine' and nothing else existed, the Soviet doctor on the other hand is proud of the fact that he actively participated in the building of socialism. *He is a worker of the state*, a servant of the people . . .

the patient is not only a person, but a member of socialist society" ([ITALICS ADDED] p. 174).

The Hippocratic oath was abolished, I submit, not because it symbolized "bourgeois medicine"—for charity practice is as much a part of bourgeois medicine as private practice—but rather because the oath tends to define the physician as an agent of the patient. It was suggested elsewhere (Szasz, Knoff, and Hollender, 1958) that the Hippocratic oath is, among other things, a Bill of Rights for the patient. Accordingly, the conflict with which the Russian physician struggles is an ancient one—the conflict between individualism and collectivism. (A much abbreviated summary of the contrasting characteristics of Western and Soviet medical systems is presented in Table 3).[5]

TABLE 3. SOCIOLOGY OF THE THERAPEUTIC SITUATION
WESTERN VERSUS SOVIET PRACTICE

Characteristics of the Situation	Western Practice	Soviet Practice
Number of participants	Two or few Private, insured, state-supported	Many State-supported
Whose agent is the therapist?	Patient's Employer's His own *Physician's role is ambiguous*	Society's Patient's (insofar as patient is positively identified with the values of the state) *Physician's role is clearly defined as agent of society*
Ethical basis of therapeutic actions	Individualistic	Collectivistic
Diagnoses encouraged or permitted	Mental illness The sick society	Malingering Psychiatric diagnoses couched in physiologic terms
Diagnoses most avoided or considered nonexistent	Malingering	Mental illness (as problem in living)
Relative social status of physician	High	Low

[5] Considerations of the nature and function of private medical practice in Soviet Russia were deliberately omitted from this discussion. Accordingly, in Table 3, under the heading "Soviet Practice," the salient features of only state-supported medical care are listed.

THE SOCIAL SIGNIFICANCE OF PRIVACY
IN THE PHYSICIAN-PATIENT RELATIONSHIP

Two features of Soviet medicine—first, the Russian physician's fear lest by being sympathetic with an *agent-provocateur*-malingerer he bring ruin on himself, and second, the abolition of the Hippocratic oath—make it necessary to examine further the role of privacy in the therapeutic situation. The first-mentioned observation shows that *the privacy of the physician-patient relationship is not solely for the benefit of the patient.* The belief that it is solely for the patient's benefit stems, in part, from the Hippocratic oath, which explicitly asserts that the physician shall not abuse the patient's trusted communications. The contemporary legal definition of confidential communications (to physicians) lends support to this view, since it gives the patient the power to waive confidentiality. Thus, the patient is the "owner" of his confidential communications. He is in control of when and how this information will be used, or when it shall be withheld.

However, in a psychoanalytic contract—at least as I understand it (Szasz, 1957b, 1959c)—the privacy of the relationship implies that the therapist will not communicate with others, irrespective of whether the patient gives permission for the release of information. Indeed, even the patient's pleading for such action on the part of the analyst must remain frustrated, if the two-person character of the relationship is to be preserved.

The common-sense view that confidentiality serves solely the patient's interests makes it easy to overlook the fact that the privacy of the physician-patient relationship provides indispensable protection for the therapist as well. By making the patient a responsible participant in his own treatment, the therapist is protected, to some extent, against the patient's (and the patient's family's, or society's) accusations of wrongdoing. If at all times the patient is kept fully informed as to the nature of the treatment, it will be his responsibility, at least in part, constantly to assess his therapist's performance, to demand changes whenever they appear necessary, and, finally, to leave his therapist should he feel that he is not receiving the help he needs.

There appears to be an inherent conflict between the benefits which the patient may derive from a private, two-person arrangement and the guarantees of protection afforded him by a measure of therapeutic publicity (the latter providing certain official, socially administered checks on the capabilities and performances of the therapist). In a private situation, the patient himself must protect his interests. Should he feel that his therapist has failed him, his chief weapon is to sever the relationship. Likewise, severing the relationship is the only protection for the (psychoanalytic) therapist, for he cannot coerce the patient into "treatment" by enlisting the help of others, for example, family members. In sharp contrast to the privacy of the psychoanalytic situation, the publicity of the Soviet therapeutic situation—at least in cases not involving top echelon personnel—fosters the use of mutually coercive influences on the parts of both patient and doctor. Thus, physicians can force patients to do various things by certifying or not certifying their illnesses; while patients, in revenge as it were, are provided with wide latitude for denouncing physicians and bringing charges against them (Field, 1957, pp. 176-177).

These observations also help to account for the nonexistence of psychoanalysis, or of any other type of private psychotherapy, in the Soviet Union (Lebensohn, 1958; Lesse, 1958). The incompatibility of communism and psychoanalysis has been attributed to the communist claim that problems in living are due to the inequities of the capitalist social system. It seems to me, however, that the core of the conflict between psychoanalysis and communism is the privacy of the analytic situation. The latter conflicts with too many things in contemporary and near-contemporary Russian life, such as their medical arrangements, housing conditions, etc. As long as this remains the case, the privacy of the psychoanalytic situation must appear alien and unwanted. With provisions for more ample housing, more consumer goods, and perhaps with increasing use of private medical practice, the Russian social scene may be changing. It will be interesting to observe whether private psychotherapy emerges.

MEDICAL CARE AS A FORM OF SOCIAL CONTROL

It is evident that anything that affects large numbers of people, and over which the state (or the government) has control, may be used as a form of *social control*. In the United States, for example, taxation may be used to encourage or inhibit the consumption of certain goods. Since Russian medical services are controlled by the state, they may readily be used for the purpose of molding society (Hayek, 1960).

The frequent use of malingering as a medical diagnosis in the Soviet Union suggests that organized medicine is used as, among other things, a form of social tranquilization (Szasz, 1960c). In this regard, the similarities between Russian medicine and American social work are especially significant. Both are systems of social care. Both fulfill certain basic human needs, while at the same time both may be used—and, I believe, at times are used—to exert a subtle but powerful control on those cared for (Davis, 1938). In Russia, it is the government (or the state) that employs the physicians, and thus may use them to control the population—for example, by means of a diagnosis of malingering. In the United States, state or local governments or private philanthropic agencies (supported by the upper classes) employ social service workers. Without wishing to deny the benefits that often accrue to social work clients, this arrangement clearly empowers the employers to exert a measure of social control—in this case, over members of the lower classes. Both systems—that is, Soviet medicine and American social work— are thus admirably suited for the purpose of keeping "in line" potentially discontented members (or groups) of society.

Employing medical care in the characteristically ambivalent manner sketched above—to care for some of the patient's needs and at the same time to oppress him—is not a new phenomenon encountered first in the So- viet Union. It existed previously in Czarist Russia as well as in Western Europe. The severity of life in Czarist prisons—and perhaps in jails every- where—was mitigated to some extent by the ministrations of relatively benevolent medical personnel, the latter constituting an integral part of the prison-system (Dostoevsky, 1861-1862). Since this social arrangement is widespread, I believe we are justified in placing a far-reaching interpretation on it. It may be regarded as a typical manifestation of an oppressive-coercive tension in the social system, such as occurs, for example, in an autocratic- patriarchal family. In such a family, the father is a tyrant, cruelly punitive toward his children, superior and deprecatory toward his wife. The children's life is made tolerable only by the ministrations of a kind, devoted mother. The social pressures of the Soviet (Stalinist) state, demanding ever-greater productivity, are reminiscent of the role of the harsh father; the citizen is the child; the protective mother is the physician.

In such a system, the mother (physician) not only protects the child (citizen) from the father (state) but by virtue of her intervention is also responsible for the maintenance of a precarious family homeostasis (or social *status quo*). To contribute to the overt breakdown of such a balance may be a constructive—and sometimes even an indispensable—step, provided that social reconstruction is desired.

This type of medical arrangement, like the family life on which it is based, also represents a "living out," in the framework of the existing social struc- ture, of the basic human problem of the need to handle both "good" and "bad" objects. The crudely patriarchal family structure, so well described by Erikson (1950), offers a simple yet highly effective solution for this problem. Instead of fostering the synthesis of love and hate for the same per- sons, with subsequent recognition of the complexities of human relationships, the arrangement permits and even encourages the child—and later the adult —to live in a world of devils and saints. Thus, the father is all-bad, the mother all-good. This leads the (grown) child to feel constantly torn between saintly righteousness and abysmal guilt. Applying this model to the Soviet medical scheme, it is apparent that this problem and its solution appear here in a new edition, so to speak. The Soviet state—or better, the principles of the ideal Communist system—remain the perfect "good object." The state furnishes "free" medical care to everyone who needs it, and of course the care is supposed to be faultless. If it is not, the blame lies with the physicians. Thus, to some extent, the physician fills the role of the "bad object" in the Soviet social scheme.[6] The citizen (patient, child) may be viewed as being sandwiched in between the (bad) doctor and the (good) state. It is consistent with this thesis that the state gives much space to public accusations against doctors (Field, 1957, pp. 176-177). Although these complaints may be loud, one wonders how effective they are. Presumably the patient cannot avail himself of the protection provided for him in Western countries—the right to bring suit for malpractice against the physician. To do this would mean bringing suit against the Soviet government itself. The arrangement, however, serves well as a means to keep both patients and physicians in line. Each possesses enough power to make life difficult for the other, yet neither has sufficient freedom to alter his own status.

In this connection, it is significant that the Russian citizens who have fled the country because of dissatisfaction with the system have expressed a marked preference for Soviet medicine as against the medical care patterns of West Germany and the United States (Inkeles and Bauer, 1959). Here is a striking illustration of how effectively the "good" and "bad" aspects of the Soviet social system have remained isolated in the minds of these people. The Soviet government's official concern for "health" (not specifically defined) is an unquestioned, absolute value. If something in relation to it goes wrong, another part of the system—in this case, the physician—is blamed.

The roots of the physician's role as "social worker" can be traced to antiquity. The fusion of priestly and medical functions made for a strong bond which was split asunder only in recent times—then to be reunited, explicitly in Christian Science, implicitly in some aspects of charity practice, psychotherapy, and Soviet medicine. It is alleged that the great Virchow said: "The physicians are the *natural attorneys of the poor*" (Field, 1957, p. 159).

[6] The famous "doctors' plot" of early 1953 lends support to this hypothesis (Rostow, 1952, pp. 222-226). It was alleged that a group of highly placed physicians murdered several key Soviet officials and were also responsible for Stalin's rapidly declining health. After Stalin's death, the plot was branded a fabrication. In other words, the plot was not "real" but "malingered." My point is that, irrespective of the specific political conflicts and motives that might have triggered this accusation, physicians—the erstwhile co-architects of the Soviet state (Field, 1957, p. 174)—were now accused of destroying the very edifice they had been commissioned to build.

This concept of the physician's role must be scrutinized and challenged. There is nothing natural about it, nor is it at all clear that it is necessarily always desirable that doctors should act as though they were attorneys.

At this point, some connections between the foregoing considerations and the historical narrative concerning Charcot, presented earlier, may be noted. It was suggested that the change from diagnosing some persons as malingerers to diagnosing them as hysterics was not a medical act, in the scientific-technical sense of the word, but rather an act of social promotion. Charcot, too, had acted as an "attorney for the poor." Since that time, however, social developments in Western countries have resulted in the creation of social organizations and social roles whose function is to be "attorneys for the poor" (i.e., to act as representatives of their special interests). The Marxist-socialist movement itself was perhaps the first of these. There were many others, too, such as labor unions, religious organizations (which, incidentally, are the traditional guardians of the "poor"), social work agencies, private philanthropies, and so forth. In the social setting of contemporary democracies, the physician may have a multitude of duties, but being the protector of the poor and oppressed is hardly one of them. The poor and downtrodden have their own—more or less adequate, as the case may be—representatives, at least in contemporary America.[7] There is the National Association for the Advancement of Colored People, the Anti-Defamation League, the Salvation Army, and a legion of other less well-known organizations whose chief purpose is the protection of various minority groups against social injustice. From the point of view of a scientific ethic—that is, from a position that values explicit honesty as against covert misrepresentation—all this is to the good. If an individual or group wishes to act in behalf of the interests of the poor, the Negro, the Jew, the immigrant, etc., it is desirable that this be made explicit. If this is true, by what right and reason do physicians project themselves (as physicians) into the role of protectors of this or that group? Among contemporary physicians, it is the psychiatrist who, more than any any other specialist, has arrogated to himself the role of protector of the downtrodden.

Concurrently with the development of appropriate social roles and institutions for the protection of the poor, the medical profession witnessed the development of many new diagnostic and therapeutic techniques. Hence, for two important reasons, it became unnecessary for the physician to function as an "attorney for the poor." First, the poor now had real attorneys of their own, and therefore no longer needed to "cheat" their way to being

---

[7] In this connection, see for example *Attorney for the Damned*, a selection of Clarence Darrow's addresses (A. Weinberg, 1957).

humanely treated by means of faking illness. Second, as the technical task which the physician had to perform became more difficult—that is, as modern surgery, pharmacotherapy, radiology, psychotherapy, etc., came into being —the physician's role became increasingly better defined by the nature of the technical operations in which he was engaged. For example, radiologists have certain well-defined jobs, as do urologists and neurosurgeons. This being the case, they may have neither time for nor interest in the task of also acting as "attorneys for the poor."

A SUMMING UP

The prevalence of malingering in Russia, and of mental illness in the West, may be regarded as signs of the prevailing social conditions. These diagnostic labels refer only partly to the patients to whom they ostensibly point. They refer also to the labeler as an individual and a member of society (Stevenson, 1959; Wortis, 1950). (To some extent this is true for all diagnoses.) "Malingering" is a manifestation of strain in a collectivistic society. The label also betrays the physician's basic identification with the values of the group. "Mental illness," on the other hand, may be viewed as a manifestation of strain in an individualistic society. Yet mental illness is not the antonym of malingering, for the former diagnosis does not imply that the physician functions as the patient's sole agent. Mental illness is an ambiguous label. Those who use it seem to wish to straddle and evade the conflict of interests between the patient and his social environment (relatives, society, etc.). The significance of interpersonal and social conflicts tends to be obscured by emphasis on conflicts among internal objects (or identifications, roles, etc.) within the patient. I do not wish to minimize the theoretical significance and psychotherapeutic value of the basic psychoanalytic position concerning the function of internal objects. My thesis is simply that it is as possible for a person to use intrapersonal conflicts (or past misfortunes) to avoid facing up to interpersonal and sociopolitical difficulties as it is for him to use the latter difficulties to avoid facing up to the former. It is in this connection that mental illness plays an important role as a concept that claims to explain, whereas it only explains away (Hardin, 1956; Szasz, 1959b).

The evasion of interpersonal and moral conflicts by means of the concept of mental illness is expressed, among other things, in the present "dynamic-psychiatric" view of American life (Szasz, 1960c). According to this view, virtually every human event—from personal unhappiness and marital in-fidelity at one end of the spectrum to political misbehavior and deviant moral conviction at the other—is regarded as a facet of the problem of mental illness. Along with this *panpsychiatric bias*, and probably largely because of it, the psychiatrist has tended to assume—without, however, having made this explicit—that the psychoanalytic two-person contract somehow applies to every other so-called psychiatric situation as well. Thus, the psychiatrist has habitually approached his problem—irrespective of whether he found it in the military service, the state hospital, or the court room—as though he were the patient's personal therapist (i.e., as though he were the patient's agent). He is, therefore, bound to find "psychopathology" or "mental illness," just as the Soviet physician—functioning as an agent of the (suspicious) state—is bound to discover "malingering." Yet neither finds or discovers anything remotely resembling an illness. Rather, the first, speaking in terms of mental illness, bases his prescription on the premise that the physician is the patient's agent; the other, speaking in terms of malingering, bases his prescription on the premise that he is an agent of society.

PART II | *Hysteria:*
An Example
of the Myth

"I have not always been a psychotherapist. Like other neuropathologists, I was trained to employ local diagnoses and electro-prognosis, and it still strikes me myself as strange that the case histories I write should read like short stories and that, as one might say, they lack the serious stamp of science. I must console myself with the reflection that the nature of the subject is evidently responsible for this, rather than any preference of my own."

Sigmund Freud (Breuer and Freud, 1893-1895, p. 160)

CHAPTER 4 | *Breuer and Freud's*
"Studies on Hysteria"

To bring into focus the original *scientific problems* which Freud intended to clarify, we must turn to Breuer and Freud's "Studies on Hysteria" (1893-1895). In it we find the type of clinical "raw material" which made it necessary for contemporary physicians to struggle with the problem of hysteria.

Some Sociohistorical Remarks Concerning Hysteria

Freud's studies under Charcot centered largely on hysteria. When he returned to Vienna in 1886 and settled down to establish a practice in so-called nervous diseases, a large proportion of his clientele consisted of cases of hysteria (Jones, 1953). Then, even as today, the hysterical patient presented a serious challenge to the physician whom she consulted. The comfortable and safe course lay in adhering to traditional medical attitudes and procedures. This meant that the patient as a person, though the object of sympathetic human interest, could not be also the object of rational-scientific interest. Respectable science was interested only in afflictions of the body. Problems of human living—or of existence, as we might say today—were thus treated as though they were manifestations of physical illnesses. The dilemma implicit in the problem of hysteria simply could not be solved within the framework of nineteenth-century thought (Riese, 1953). Breuer and Freud's singular achievement lay in adopting an attitude toward neurotic suffering that was at once humane and inquiring. Accordingly, their observations merit the closest possible attention—bearing in mind, however, that most present-day physicians and psychiatrists practice under entirely different social and technical circumstances.

It is often stated that psychoanalysts no longer encounter the type of "hysterical illness" described by Breuer, Freud, and their contemporaries (e.g., Wheelis, 1958). Usually this is attributed to cultural changes, especially to the lessening of sexual repressions and to changes in the social roles of women. In addition to these factors pertaining to the position of the patient, the social role of the physician who sees hysteria has also changed. Thus, while it is true that psychoanalysts, in their private offices, rarely if ever encounter "classical cases of hysteria," this type of disability still comes to the attention of other physicians—for example, general practitioners and various specialists in large medical centers (Ziegler *et al.*, 1960). I believe that hysteria, as described by Breuer and Freud, is still prevalent in America as well as in Europe. Those who suffer from it, however, do not, as a rule, consult psychiatrists or psychoanalysts. Rather, they consult their family physicians or internists and are then referred to neurologists, neurosurgeons, orthopedic and general surgeons, and other *medical* specialists.

Rarely do medical advisors define such a patient's difficulty as psychiatric. Physicians may dread referring the patient to a psychiatrist, mainly because such referral requires that they redefine the nature of the patient's difficulty. Yet, psychiatry, defined as a medical specialty, partly serves the purpose of abrogating the need for such redefinition. A "functional complaint" is still considered an "illness" and the sufferer is merely sent to "another doctor." Referral to a nonmedical psychotherapist would entail a more radical redefinition of the nature of the patient's ailment. This explains the hierarchical referral system that exists in the United States (especially in the larger metropolitan centers). While physicians refer some of their "mentally ill" patients to psychiatrists, they seldom make referrals to nonmedical psychotherapists (psychologists, social workers, etc.). In contrast, psychiatrists—especially child therapists and psychoanalysts—often refer *their* patients to nonmedical psychotherapists. This practice illustrates my thesis: the need to refer a patient to a psychiatrist confronts the physician with the task of redefining the patient's illness as personal rather than medical. The psychiatrist's patient generally accepts this definition, and is willing therefore to accept a nonmedical expert as psychotherapist.

Physicians also fear missing an "organic diagnosis." They tend to distrust psychiatry and psychiatrists, and find it difficult to understand what psychotherapists do (Bowman and Rose, 1954). These are some of the reasons why hysterical patients have become rather rare in private psychiatric practice. Finally, socioeconomic considerations too are relevant in this connection. For reasons to be discussed later, conversion hysteria tends nowadays to be an affliction of relatively uneducated, lower-class persons. This fact alone may account for the distribution of such cases. They are encountered least often in the private offices of psychoanalysts—and most often in free or low-cost clinics or in state hospitals. The few hysterics who do finally consult a psychotherapist will have had so many medical and surgical experiences that they will no longer communicate in the pure language of "classical hysteria."

The Observational Data

It must be frankly recognized and acknowledged that it is impossible to study a phenomenon scientifically without looking at it through eyes biased by theory (Braithwaite, 1953). The simile between sight and scientific explanation is worth pressing in this connection. Literally to "see something," we must have well-functioning eyes, optic nerves, and occipital cortices. Similarly, to "see something"—in this instance, not literally but rather scientifically—requires that we look at our observations with the aid of more or less well-functioning theories (or hypotheses). If we look with conceptually blind eyes, we shall see nothing of scientific interest. Hence, nothing is really wrong with scientific prejudices provided that observations are so described that even those who do not share our theories can reproduce them. Thus, it should be possible for various workers to agree on an observation and still disagree on the best hypothesis for it. The distinction between observation and theory, although almost self-evident for the physicist and philosopher of science, is insufficiently appreciated in psychiatry and psychoanalysis. Consider, for example, the psychoanalytic concepts, "unconscious," "preconscious," and "conscious." It is rarely clear whether an occurrence qualified by one of these adjectives denotes an observation or an explanatory hypothesis. Dreams are often said to be unconscious material. Of course, this could not mean that the dream report is unconscious. I mention this example only to emphasize the importance of clearly differentiating observation from hypothesis (and various levels of hypotheses from each other). To achieve this goal, it is necessary to avoid using *inexplicit* theoretical or philosophical biases. The authors of *Studies on Hysteria* often fell short of this ideal.

COMPLAINT OR DISEASE?

My basic thesis is that Breuer and Freud cited examples of patients complaining of various bodily feelings (usually of an unpleasant nature) and then seriously complicated the issue by speaking of these symptoms as though they constituted disorders in the physicochemical machinery of the human body. The following excerpt[1] illustrates this contention:

> A highly intelligent man was present while his brother had an ankylosed hip-joint extended under an anaesthetic. At the instant at which the joint gave way with a crack, he felt a violent pain in his own hip-joint, which persisted for nearly a year. Further instances could be quoted. In other cases, the connection is not so simple. It consists only in what might be called a "symbolic" relation between the precipitating cause and the pathological phenomenon—a relation such as healthy people form in dreams. For instance, a *neuralgia* may follow upon *mental pain* or *vomiting* upon a feeling of *moral disgust*. We have studied patients who used to make the most copious use of this sort of symbolization ([ITALICS ADDED] p. 5).

Note the terms "neuralgia," "mental pain," and "moral disgust." Without belaboring the issue of methodology—and whether we are doing and talking physics or psychology (Szasz, 1957a)—it is clear that these expressions refer not to observations but rather to complex inferences at best or philosophical preconceptions at worst. "Neuralgia" implies a neurological, that is, physicochemical, disorder of the body. Presumably, the authors meant to say "neuralgialike," implying that to the contemporary physician such pain suggested "neuralgia."

The concept of "mental pain," like "moral disgust," codifies the Cartesian dualism, according to which the world consists of two sets of realities, one physical, the other mental. Thus "moral disgust" presumably must be contrasted with "physical disgust," such as one might feel when confronted with spoiled food. But, in either case, as affects, there are not discernible differences between the two. In other words, the adjective "moral" refers to a statement on the level of a theoretical construct. "Moral," "gastrointestinal," and other possible types of disgust are, emphatically, not things anyone can observe.[2] Conceptual analyses of these problems, separating observation statements from logical inferences, go far toward putting the matter on a firmer scientific footing.

---

[1] All passages cited in this chapter, unless otherwise noted, are from Breuer and Freud's "Studies on Hysteria" (1893-95).

[2] This problem was discussed in detail in my book, *Pain and Pleasure* (Szasz, 1957a); see especially the analysis of the distinction between "neurotic" and "objective" anxiety, and "mental" and "physical" pain (Chapter 4).

WHAT KIND OF DISEASE DOES THE PATIENT HAVE?

The crux of the difficulty which Freud faced, and to which I am pointing here, was that he was forced to ask himself the question: *What kind of disease* does this patient (who has consulted me) have? Stating the question in this form precludes the answer that he has no disease. Freud solved the problem by making a "differential diagnosis," as behooved a physician. The patient's complaints are viewed as the symptoms of his (or her) particular disease.

By way of illustration, consider the following excerpt from Freud's account of the case of Fräulein Elizabeth von R.:

> In the autumn of 1892, I was asked by a doctor I knew to examine a young lady who had been suffering for more than two years from pains in her legs and who had *difficulties in walking*. *All that was apparent* was that she *complained* of great pain in walking and of being quickly overcome by fatigue both in walking and in standing, and that after a short time she had to rest, which lessened the pains but did not do away with them altogether. . . . I did not find it easy to arrive at a *diagnosis*, but I decided for two reasons to *assent* to the one proposed by my colleague, viz., that it was a *case of hysteria* ([ITALICS ADDED] pp. 135, 136).

It was a hard fact of life that Freud was frequently faced with the need to make a differential diagnosis (Freud, 1900, p. 109). He was very proud when he made a correct neurological diagnosis in a case referred to him as one of hysteria (Freud, 1905a, pp. 16-17).

Although Freud regarded hysteria as a disease, he comprehended far more, even at this early date, than could be fitted into this semantic and epistemological straitjacket. The following statement is significant in this connection:

> Here, then, was the unhappy story of this proud girl with her longing for love. Unreconciled to her fate, embittered by the failure of all her little schemes for reestablishing the family's former glories, with those she loved dead or gone away or estranged, unready to take refuge in the love of some unknown man—she had lived for eighteen months in almost complete seclusion, with *nothing to occupy her but the care of her mother and her own pains"* ([ITALICS ADDED] pp. 143-144).

Is this a *disease* which Freud described here? Perhaps his contemporary critics were correct when they complained that Freud did not concern him-

self with the same sorts of problems as did they. They recognized that Freud
did not really speak about diseases of organisms (or bodies), as was then
customary. Instead, he addressed himself to the problem of people as human
beings, as members of society, or simply as persons.

In the passage cited above Freud spoke of an unhappy young woman and
the *bodily feelings* with which she *communicated* her unhappiness. He asserted that his work was similar to the biographer's rather than to the
physician's (Breuer and Freud, 1893-1895, pp. 160-161). Psychoanalytic
therapy rested on the assumption that the biographee would profit from a
closer acquaintance with his own life history. This was a significant assumption, although by no means a novel one. The roots of this attitude to
life are traceable to the ancient Greeks. The Socratic assertion that "The
unexamined life is not worth living" is the philosophy that underlies psychoanalysis as a general scientific system. The maxim "Know thyself" is the
guiding rule of psychoanalytic treatment.

Briefly, my thesis is that Breuer and Freud's observations on hysteria,
though couched in medical-psychiatric terms, are statements concerning
certain special patterns of human communication. Or, if we wish to categorize
these phenomena as abnormal or pathological, they could be called disturbances or distortions in communication (Ruesch, 1957). Emphasis on disturbance or distortion, however, distracts unnecessarily from the scientific
(cognitive) task and overemphasizes the need for therapeutic interference.
Adhering closely to the observational level of discourse (Braithwaite, 1953),
it can be asserted that the patients described were unhappy or troubled.
Furthermore, they expressed their distress in so-called bodily symptoms
which to the contemporary physician suggested neurological illnesses. In
no case was there any evidence that the (hysterical) patient did, in fact,
suffer from an anatomical or physiological disorder. Unfortunately, this did
not deter Breuer and Freud (1893-1895, pp. xxii, xxiv, xxix) from entertain-
ing a partly "organic" hypothesis for the "cause" of this "disease."

The Theoretical Structure

Despite the novelty of their discoveries, the philosophical orientation—or,
more precisely, the metascientific position—which underlay Breuer and
Freud's scientific thinking was anything but unorthodox. Indeed, both men,
and Freud apparently more than Breuer, were imbued with and committed
to the contemporary scientific *Weltanschauung*. According to it, science was
synonymous with physics and chemistry (mathematics then being regarded
as an auxiliary tool of these sciences). There was a tendency to force

psychology into behaviorism or, that failing, to reduce it to its so-called physical and chemical bases. This goal of reducing psychological observations to physical explanations—or at least to "instincts"—was espoused by Freud from the very beginning of his psychological studies, and he never completely relinquished it (Szasz, 1960a).

WHAT KIND OF DISEASE IS HYSTERIA?

Both Breuer and Freud approached hysteria as though it were a disease, essentially similar to (other) physicochemical disorders of the body (for example, syphilis). The main difference between the two was thought to be that the physicochemical basis of hysteria was more elusive, and hence more difficult to detect with the methods *then* available. They acted (and wrote), at least initially, as though they had to content themselves with "playing second fiddle," so to speak, by working with psychological methods of observation and treatment, while they were waiting for the discovery of a physicochemical test of hysteria and its appropriate organic treatment. It is pertinent to recall that when "Studies on Hysteria" was published (1895), the Wasserman test (1906) had not yet been devised, and proof of the syphilitic etiology of general paresis had not yet been histologically documented (Noguchi and Moore, 1913). The prevalent attitude toward psychopathology was—as it often still is—that the detection of physicochemical disorders in the human bodily machinery is the proper task facing the investigating physician. In effect, this constitutes a definition of the investigator's social role. All else is makeshift or *ersatz*, and is relegated to a second-class position. Thus, psychology and psychoanalysis were given only second-class citizenship in the land of science.

THE PRESTIGE OF PHYSICAL EXPLANATIONS IN MEDICINE
AND ITS EFFECTS ON PSYCHOANALYSIS

It seems to me that the search for the physical causation of many so-called psychological phenomena may be motivated more by the prestige-need of the investigators than by a quest for scientific clarity. We have touched on a related issue when it was suggested that adherence to the medical model of thought enables the psychiatrist to share in the social status inherent in the role of the physician. Here, a similar phenomenon is encountered with respect to the scientific prestige of the investigator. Since investigators in physics enjoy much greater prestige than those in psychology or in the study of human relations, it is advantageous for many psychiatrists and some psychoanalysts to claim that, fundamentally, they too search for physical or physiological causes of bodily illness. This makes them, of course, pseudo physicists and pseudo physicians, and has many regrettable consequences. Yet, this striving for prestige by aping the "natural scientist" has also been successful, at least in a social or opportunistic way. By "success" I refer to the widespread social acceptance of psychiatry and psychoanalysis as allegedly biological (and hence ultimately physicochemical) sciences, and to the prestige of their practitioners based, in part, on this linkage between what they claim they do and what other (physical) scientists do.

There are two consequences implicit in this analysis. The first is that psychological methods of investigation, and theory-constructions appropriate to them, are scientifically legitimate, irrespective of the methods and theories of physics. The second is that we may dispense with considerations of the physicochemical causes or mechanisms of hysteria (and of other mental illnesses, too), since there is neither observational evidence nor logical need for them (Polanyi, 1958a & b).

THE THEORY OF CONVERSION

Freud's original conception of hysterical conversion was stated concisely in the following lines (apropos of the case of Fräulein Elizabeth von R.):

> According to the view suggested by the conversion theory of hysteria, what happened may be described as follows: *She repressed her erotic idea from consciousness and transformed the amount of its affect into physical sensations of pain* ([ITALICS ADDED] p. 164).
>
> This theory calls for closer examination. We may ask: What is it that turns into physical pain here? A cautious reply would be: Something that might have become, and should have become, *mental pain*. If we venture a little further and try to represent the ideational mechanism in a kind of algebraical picture, we may attribute a certain quota of affect to the ideational complex of these erotic feelings which remained unconscious, and say that *this quantity* (the quota of affect) *is what was converted* ([ITALICS ADDED] p. 166).

Here we have the problem of "conversion hysteria" in *statu nascendi*. Freud asked: What is being converted (to physical pain)? Why does the patient have physical pain? Ancillary questions are: What causes it? How does a conflict, or affect, become converted to physical pain?

Freud replied by taking recourse to what Colby (1955) aptly called a "hydraulic metaphor." It seems evident, however, that no such complicated explanation is required. All that is necessary is to frame our questions differently. We may ask: Why does a patient complain of pain? Ancillary questions are: Why does the patient complain about his body when it is physically intact? Why does the patient not complain about personal troubles? If we pose the second set of questions, then the answers must be phrased in terms of the complainant's personal troubles. Indeed, Breuer and Freud's descriptions of their patients go far in answering these questions.

Let us see really how much the idea of hysterical complaints *as symptoms* of physical (bodily) disorders has complicated our problem. Freud wrote:

> The mechanism was that of conversion: i.e., in place of *mental pains* which she avoided, *physical pains* made their appearance. In this way a transformation was effected which had the advantage that the patient escaped from an intolerable *mental condition:* though, it is true, this was at the cost of a *psychical abnormality*—the splitting of consciousness that came about, and of a *physical illness*—her pains, in which an astasia-abasia was built up ([ITALICS ADDED] p. 166).

Throughout this passage (which is illustrative of many others), the words "mental" and "physical" appear as though they described observations, when in fact they are theoretical concepts used to order and "explain" the observations. On the basis of Freud's foregoing definition of conversion, it would be justifiable to assert that the problem is almost entirely epistemological rather than psychiatric. In other words, there is no problem of conversion, unless we insist on so framing our questions that we inquire about physical disorders where, in fact, none exist.

The questions which, we assume, Freud asked might be paraphrased as follows: Why does a psychological problem take physical form? How does a psychological problem become manifest as a physical phenomenon? These questions recodified the classic riddle of the "jump from the psychic into the organic" which psychoanalysis, and especially the theory of conversion, then sought to elucidate (F. Deutsch, 1959). Because of this conceptual framework, so-called psychological phenomena—such as bodily complaints, and so-called physical phenomena—such as anatomical or biochemical alterations, have been juxtaposed as though they constituted two sides of the same coin (Alexander, 1943).

I believe that this view is false. We shall not regard the relationship between the psychological and the physical as a relationship between two different types of events or occurrences, but shall rather consider it to be akin to two different modes of representation or language (Schlick, 1935; Russell, 1948). More will be said about this problem in subsequent chapters.

I submit that the classical models of hysteria and conversion are no longer useful either for nosology or for therapy. Today, however, there may be social and institutional grounds for adhering to this theory. The notion of hysteria as mental illness, and the psychoanalytic theory of hysteria (especially the idea of conversion), have become social symbols for psychoanalysis as a medical technique and guild. The original psychoanalytic theory of hysteria—and of neurosis, following more or less closely on the same scheme —made it possible for physicians (and allied scientists) to retain a fairly homogeneous picture of "diseases." According to this scheme, diseases could be divided into somatic and psychical, the latter retaining a large measure of apparent simplicity, borrowed from the former. In this way, too, psychotherapy could be regarded as an enterprise similar in all essentials to established modes of medical and surgical treatments. The alternative to this familiar and comfortable point of view is to abandon the entire physicalistic-medical approach to mental illness and to substitute novel theoretical viewpoints and models, appropriate to psychological, social, and ethical problems. Explicit recognition of the social (institutional) function of certain present-day psychiatric ideas should prove helpful in keeping an open mind toward a searching analysis of the roots of the notion of mental illness.

"There are powerful special interests which strive in any case to keep science isolated so that the common life may be immune from its influence. Those who have these special interests fear the impact of scientific method upon social issues.—If the schools are used for the purpose of instilling belief in certain dogmas—a use in which something called 'education' becomes simply an organ of propaganda—and this use continues to grow, it will be in some measure because science has not been conceived and practiced as the sole universal method of dealing intellectually with all problems." John Dewey (1938, p. 37)

CHAPTER 5

Contemporary Views
on Hysteria
and Mental Illness

Although a newcomer among the sciences, psychiatry is characterized by a plethora of diverse, competing, and often mutually exclusive theories and practices. In this respect, it must be frankly acknowledged that psychiatry is more similar to religion and politics than to science. Indeed, in religion and politics we expect to find conflicting systems or ideologies. Widespread consensus concerning the practical management of human affairs, and the ethical systems involved to govern and justify particular systems of group-formation, are regarded merely as indices of the political success of the governing ideology. Matters of scientific theory (and, to some extent, also of scientific practice) do not, as a rule, concern entire populations. Hence, large-scale consensus in regard to such matters is not expected. At the same time, it is unusual for scientists widely and persistently to disagree among themselves concerning the explanations and practices appropriate to their special areas of competence. For instance, there is little disagreement among scientists concerning physiological, biochemical, or physical theories—even though individual scientists may profess to different religions (or to no religion) and may be members of different national groups. This is not true for psychiatry.

In studying human behavior, we are confronted by the disconcerting fact that psychiatric theories are nearly as numerous and varied as psychiatric symptoms. This is true not only in historical and international perspectives but also within single nations. Thus, it is especially difficult to describe and compare, say, American and English, or American and Swiss psychiatry, for none of these countries presents a psychiatrically united front. The reasons for this state of affairs, and its important implications for our efforts to build an internationally respectable science of psychiatry, cannot be considered here. I should like to emphasize only that I believe that much of the difficulty in the way of building a coherent theory of human behavior lies in our inability—or, sometimes unwillingness—to separate description from prescription. Such questions as "How *are* men constituted?" "How *do* they act?" "What *are* the relations between society and the individual?" can and must be separated from such questions as "How *should* men act?" or "What *should* be the relations between society and the individual?"

Dewey (1938) has emphasized, as have others, that education may be used not only to impart skills and knowledge but also to engender communal feeling and group cohesion. It is perhaps not an accident that this problem is most acute in disciplines concerned with human behavior, and among them particularly in psychiatry which perforce must address itself to normative aspects of personal conduct.

Psychoanalytic Conceptions

In common with most psychoanalytic authors, Fenichel (1945) distinguished anxiety hysteria from conversion hysteria. Anxiety hysteria, which is also a synonym for phobia, he described as the "simplest compromise between drive and defense" (p. 194); the anxiety motivating the defense becomes manifest, while the "reason for the anxiety" remains repressed. In other words, the person experiences anxiety without knowing why. Fenichel illustrated the dynamism of this process by citing the example of simple childhood phobias: "Small children are afraid of being left alone, which for them means not being loved any more" (p. 196). The crux of the dynamism of anxiety hysteria is laid bare here as simply an equation, on the part of the child, of the experiences of being left alone and unloved. Since it is considered normal for children to feel anxious when they are unloved, this reaction is not defined as a psychological disease entity. However, being left alone, per se, apparently is not considered a sufficient cause for feeling anxious. Hence, if such a reaction occurs, it must be due to something else. The *meaning* of being left alone is then advanced as the cause of the "abnormal reaction."

The child's reaction of anxiety on being left alone may be interpreted in at least two ways. First, it may be considered pathological (or "bad") if it is assumed that the reaction signifies excessive proneness to feeling unloved (perhaps because of many actual experiences of rejection). Second, the reaction may be considered normal (or "good") if it is regarded as an expression of the child's ability to learn and symbolize, and hence make connections between superficially more or less dissimilar situations. According to the latter view, a phobia, and virtually all other "psychological symptoms," are similar to scientific hypotheses. Both types of phenomena—that is, "making mental symptoms" as well as making hypotheses—rest on the fundamental human tendency to construct symbolic representations and use them to guide subsequent behavior.

In his discussion of conversion hysteria, Fenichel (1945) consistently used the mixed physical and psychological language which I have criticized earlier. For example, he spoke of "physical functions" providing unconscious expression for repressed "instinctual impulses" (p. 216). Here, much as was the case in Breuer and Freud's writings, complaints about the body ("hysterical pain") or communications by means of bodily (nonverbal) behavior (gestures, "hysterical paralysis") were erroneously described as alterations in physical functions. I believe that the crux of the matter is simply that in conversion hysteria the symptom refers to the patient's body, whereas in anxiety hysteria it points to a human situation (loneliness in a dark room).

The significance of unrecognized epistemological errors in the concept of hysteria may be illustrated by Fenichel's following analysis of a case of so-called hysterical pain:

> A patient suffered from pain in the lower abdomen. The pain repeated sensations she had felt as a child during an attack of appendicitis. At that time she had been treated with unusual tenderness by her father. *The abdominal pain expressed simultaneously a longing for the father's tenderness and a fear that an even more painful operation might follow a fulfilment of this longing* ([ITALICS ADDED] p. 220).

In contrast, consider an account of the same type of phenomenon as described by Woodger (1956). It concerns the case of a girl who developed abdominal pain and consulted a surgeon.

> He [i.e., the surgeon] recommended an operation for the removal of the appendix and this was accordingly performed. But after recovery and convalescense the girl again complained of abdominal

pain. This time she was advised to consult a surgeon with a view to treatment for adhesions resulting from the first operation. But the second surgeon referred the girl to a psychiatrist from whose inquiries it transpired that the girl's education had been such that she believed it to be possible to become pregnant by being kissed. The first abdominal pain had appeared after the experience of being kissed by an undergraduate during his vacation. After the recovery from the operation this girl was again kissed by the same undergraduate with a similar result (p. 57).

In the psychoanalytic formulation of the *observational datum* (abdominal pain), there is a constant intrusion of abstractions expressing the preformed philosophical attitudes of the observer. Thus, Fenichel spoke (in an earlier passage not quoted) of the "original physical pain," and contrasted it with the current, presumably, "hysterical pain." He then proceeded to translate "abdominal pain" into a "longing for the father's tenderness." Thus, the crucial issue of validation was completely omitted. In other words, could it not happen that a patient's abdominal pain was due to, say, tubal pregnancy, and yet that it also meant that she longed for her father's love?

The problem of whether the "meaning" of pain could also be its "cause," and if so in what way, is far more complicated than the psychoanalytic theory of hysteria would have it. According to the latter, some pains are "organic," others "hysterical." Thus a longing, a wish, a need—broadly speaking, psychological "meanings" of all sorts—are regarded as "causal agents" similar, in all significant respects, to tumors, fractures, and other bodily lesions. Clearly, nothing could be more misleading, since fractures and tumors belong in one logical class, while desires, aspirations, and conflicts belong in another (Ryle, 1949). I am not saying that psychological motives can never be regarded as "causes" of human conduct, for evidently this is often a useful way of describing social behavior. It should be kept in mind, however, that my desire to see a play is the "cause" of my going to the theater in a sense very different from that in which we speak of "causal laws" in physics (Schlick, 1932; Peters, 1958).

Glover (1949), too, followed the usual psychiatric classification in regard to hysteria. He asserted that "two major types of hysteria exist, namely, conversion hysteria and anxiety hysteria" (p. 140). He thus implied that "hysteria" is an entity found in nature rather than an abstraction or theoretical construct made by man. Moreover, he too employed a mixed physical and psychological language—for example, in speaking of "physical symptoms" and "psychic contents." Thus, the above-mentioned criticisms apply to his writings as well.

However, one of Glover's formulations was novel and deserves special comment. It is the notion, today widely accepted by psychoanalysts, that conversion symptoms possess "specific psychic content," whereas so-called psychosomatic symptoms do not (pp. 140-141). This distinction, useful as it is, could be formulated more simply by comparing the former to actions, and the latter to happenings. In other words, conversion symptoms are intentional signs: they are bits of behavior that are intended to convey a message. This is why they must be regarded as communications. In contrast, so-called psychosomatic symptoms—say, peptic ulcer or diarrhea—are in the nature of physical (pathophysiological) occurrences. As such, they are not intended to be communications. Nevertheless, they may be interpreted as signs by certain observers (who may be astute and knowledgeable, mistaken, or even deluded, as the case may be). Accordingly, psychosomatic symptoms (of this type)—much as happenings of all sorts—need not be looked upon as communications. However, since not all communications are intentional, psychosomatic symptoms, too, may validly be interpreted as messages of a certain type.

This point of view is, indeed, implicit in the classic psychoanalytic papers of Freud and Ferenczi. The communicational possibilities of diseases of all types (and not only of a few specially labeled psychosomatic), for both diagnosis and treatment, inspired Groddeck (1927, 1934) to propose far-reaching, and at times fantastic, interpretations of these phenomena. Groddeck's ideas, though scientifically unsystematized and unverified, must be considered forerunners of subsequent developments which led to a better appreciation of the communicational significance of all human behavior.

Beginning in the 1930's, psychoanalysts began to place increasing emphasis on so-called ego-psychology—which meant, among other things, emphasis on communicative, interpersonal behavior rather than on instinctual needs and their vicissitudes. At about the same time, Sullivan provided impetus for an explicitly interpersonal-sociologic and communicational approach to psychiatry and especially to psychotherapy. He thus spearheaded a trend that has become general within the body of psychoanalysis itself. I refer to the increasingly explicit recognition that human experiences and relationships—and especially human communications—are the most significant observables with which psychoanalysts and psychosocially oriented psychiatrists deal.

Although I believe that Sullivan's total contribution to psychiatry was impressive, it seems that many of his early theoretical formulations—especially those concerning so-called psychiatric syndromes—were modifications of, rather than improvements on, Freud's conceptions. For example, in *Conceptions of Modern Psychiatry* (1947), Sullivan proposed this definition of hysteria:

"Hysteria, the mental disorder to which the self-absorbed are peculiarly liable, is the distortion of inter-personal relations which results from extensive amnesias" (p. 54).

Sullivan's description of hysterical interpersonal strategies, though unencumbered by physiologizing about behavior, is open to the same criticisms as were leveled against the traditional psychoanalytic concept. For Sullivan, too, spoke of hysteria as a mental disorder, as though it were a disease entity. Moreover, he believed that amnesias caused this disorder. But how could amnesia "cause" hysteria? Is this not like saying that fever "causes" pneumonia? Moreover, this formulation of Sullivan's was only a modification of Freud's (1910a) classic dictum that "hysterical patients suffer from reminiscences" (p. 16).

There can be no doubt, of course, that both Freud and Sullivan were correct in identifying painful ("traumatic") memories, their repression, and their persistent operation as significant antecedent factors in the personal and social behavior of hysterically disabled individuals. In his later work, Sullivan (1956) has described hysteria as a form of communication and laid the ground for seeing it as a special type of game-playing behavior. Sullivan's views on hysteria will be discussed again in connection with the presentation of a game-model theory of this phenomenon (Chapter 15).

Fairbairn (1952) has been one of the most successful exponents of a consistently psychological formulation of so-called psychiatric problems. Emphasizing that psychoanalysis deals, above all else, with observations of, and statements about, object relationships, he has reformulated much of psychoanalytic theory from the vantage point of this ego-psychological (and by implication, communicational) approach. In his paper, "Observations on the Nature of Hysterical States" (1954), he wrote:

Hysterical conversion is, of course, a defensive technique—one designed to prevent the conscious emergence of emotional conflicts involving object-relationships. Its essential and distinctive feature *is the substitution of a bodily state for a personal problem;* and this substitution enables the personal problem as such to be ignored (p. 117).

I am in agreement with this simple yet precise statement. According to this view, the distinctive phenomenal feature of hysteria is the substitution of a "bodily state" (Fairbairn) for communications by means of ordinary language concerning personal problems. As a result of this transformation ("translation") both the content and the form of the discourse change. The content changes from personal problems to bodily problems, while the form changes from verbal (linguisitic) language to bodily (gestural) language.

Accordingly, hysterical conversion is best regarded as a process of translation—a conception first proposed by Freud. It was Sullivan and Fairbairn, however, who gave impetus to the fuller appreciation of the communicative aspects of all types of occurrences encountered in psychiatric and psychotherapeutic work.

Organic Theories of Hysteria

No attempt will be made to review the principal organic—that is, biochemical, genetic, pathophysiological, etc.—theories of hysteria. I shall only state my position vis-à-vis organic theories of hysteria (and mental illness, generally) and their relation to the present work.

Many physicians, psychiatrists, psychologists, and other scientists believe that mental diseases have organic causes. Let me make clear that I do not, of course, believe that human relations, or mental events, take place in a neurophysiological vacuum. Any form of human activity may, in principle, be describable in terms of chemical or electrical occurrences taking place in the bodies of the participants. Accordingly, it may be maintained that if a person, say an Englishmen, decides to study French, certain chemical (or other) changes will occur in his brain as he learns the language. Nevertheless, I think it would be a mistake to infer from this assumption—even if it were verifiably true (which so far it is not)—that the most significant scientific statements concerning this learning process are expressed in the language of physics. This, however, is exactly what the organicist claims.

Notwithstanding the widespread social acceptance of psychoanalysis in contemporary America, there remains a wide circle of physicians and allied scientists whose basic position concerning the problem of mental illness is essentially that expressed in Carl Wernicke's famous dictum: "Mental diseases are brain diseases." Because, in one sense, this is true of such conditions as paresis (and the psychoses associated with brain tumor or systemic intoxications), it is argued that it is also true for all other things called mental diseases. It follows that it is only a matter of time until the correct physicochemical, including genetic, bases (or "causes") of these disorders will be discovered (e.g., Pauling, 1956). It is conceivable, of course, that significant physicochemical disturbances will be found in some patients (and "conditions") now loosely labeled mental illnesses. This may be especially likely in the general group now diagnosed "schizophrenic." I believe, nevertheless, that the paresis-model is but one among many explanatory models which is useful and necessary in psychiatric work. We know now that not all bodily diseases are caused by microbial agents as was often mistakenly believed during the hey-day of bacteriology. Similarly, there is no reason to believe that all mental illnesses are caused by brain diseases.

Let us sharply distinguish between two epistemological positions. The first, extreme physicalism, asserts that only physics and its branches can be considered sciences (J. R. Weinberg, 1950). It is necessary, therefore, that all possible observations be formulated in the language of physics. The second position—a sort of liberal empiricism—recognizes a variety of legitimate methods and languages within the family of science (Mises, 1951). Indeed, since different types of problems are considered to require different methods of analysis, a diversity of scientific methods and expressions (languages) is not merely tolerated but is rather considered a *sine qua non* of science. According to this position, the value, and hence the scientific legitimacy, of any particular method or language depends on its pragmatic utility (rather than on how closely it approximates the ideal model of theoretical physics).

It is well to recognize that both attitudes toward science rest on certain value judgments. Physicalism (and variations on its theme) asserts that all of the sciences should, as far as possible, be like physics. If we adhere to this view the physical (which, in the case of medicine, includes the chemical, physiological, etc.) bases of human performances will be regarded as most significant. In contrast, the second type of scientific attitude (whether it is called empiricism, pragmatism, operationism, or by some other name) focuses on the value of instrumental utility—that is, the power to explain the observed and to influence it. Since psychosocial theories of human activi-ties are useful for explaining and influencing human behavior, the psycho-social sciences and their theories would have to be accorded a relatively high position in this system of values.

I have stressed these considerations because it seems to me that most of those who adhere to an organicist position in psychiatry espouse a system of values of which they are unaware. Thus, they imply that they recognize as scientific only physics (and its branches), but instead of asserting this clearly and explicitly, they say that they object to psychosocial theories only because they are false. For illustrative examples of this type of work, the reader is referred to the writings of Purtell, Robins, and Cohen (Purtell *et al.*, 1951; Robins *et al.*, 1952). They stated:

> From the results of this investigation, it seems proper to suggest that the *diagnosis* of hysteria might be made by following the *standard procedure* used in the general field of *diagnostic medicine:* that is, determining the facts of the chief complaint, past history, physical

examination and laboratory investigation. If the relevant symptoms of hysteria are known, this method can be applied by *any physician* without the use of special techniques, dream analysis or prolonged investigation of *psychological conflicts*. These studies give no information about the *cause* of hysteria or about the specific mechanisms of symptoms. *It is believed that these are unknown.* Further, it is believed that they will be discovered by *scientific investigation,* rather than by the use of *non-scientific methods,* such as pure discussion, speculation, further reasoning from the dictums of "authorities" or "schools of psychology" or by the use of such pretentious undefined words as "unconscious," "depth psychology," "psychodynamics," "psychosomatic," and "Oedipus complex" and that fundamental investigation must rest on a firm *clinical basis* ([ITALICS ADDED] Purtell *et al.,* 1951, p. 909).

It is to be hoped that the authors' complaints against psychoanalysis will not distract the reader from noting that they have defined science covertly so as to exclude the nonphysical disciplines from it. As a definition, this is legitimate, although it is no longer shared by contemporary students of science.

We are forced to conclude that the psychologically minded psychiatrist and his organicist colleague, though often members of the same professional organizations, do not talk the same language and do not have the same interests. It is not surprising, then, that they have nothing good to say to each other, and that when they do communicate it is only to castigate each other's work and point of view.

European Psychiatric Positions

As in the preceding section, no attempt will be made to survey specific contributions to hysteria or mental illness. All that is intended is a brief commentary on principal European psychiatric positions.

The contemporary European psychiatric scene is characterized, in part, by certain consequences of what we called the double standard in psychiatry. The breaking apart of neuropsychiatry into organic and psychosocial approaches, which occurred at the birth of modern psychiatry, was a divorce, metaphorically speaking, that made for a badly broken home. Some of the children who came from this background have still not recovered from the effects of their traumatic origin. This is especially true of European psychiatry. In the United States, perhaps largely because of the influence of such men as George Herbert Mead, Adolph Meyer, and Harry Stack Sullivan, the idea that psychiatry deals with purely medical-neurological problems was never wholly accepted. In Europe, however, the breach between psychiatry as a medical-physiological and as a humanistic-psychological enterprise has never healed. Thus, both of these views—and various compromises between them—have prevailed and gained acceptance.

In European medical schools, a neuropsychiatric or largely organic orientation to psychiatry is the rule (Laughlin, 1960). Psychoanalysis (Freud) and analytical psychology (Jung) are represented to a small extent or not at all. Stierlin (1958) discussed the contrasting psychiatric attitudes toward the psychoses in Europe and the United States. In Europe, particularly in university circles outside of Great Britain, a physicalistic conception of science has been used as a persistent defense against too close a human contact with the mentally ill patient. The belief that psychotic patients suffer from mental illnesses which are manifestations of brain pathology—whatever its scientific merit—is useful for psychiatrists who wish to deny their patients' personal and social problems. Karl Jaspers, Kurt Schneider, and most other leading contemporary German psychiatrists subscribe to the thesis that paresis is the prototype of all mental illness. "In the course of this development," wrote Stierlin, "psychiatry almost became a branch of neurology. Even now in most German university hospitals, the psychiatric department is fused with the neurological clinic" (p. 142). A recent report by Kinberg (1958) concerning Swedish psychiatry lends support to Stierlin's description of the situation.

Curiously, a view widely held in organicist psychiatric circles—and shared by many psychoanalysts—holds that only (or mainly) the psychoses are due to as yet undiscovered brain diseases. Lesser problems in living—manifested by less flamboyant social disturbances than characterize the classical psychoses—are considered to be psychosocial in nature. This distinction, though perhaps having appeal to common sense, must be recognized as being wholly without empirical or logical foundations. To regard "minor" upheavals in living as problems in human relations, learning, and so forth—and more "major" upheavals as due to brain disease, seems to be a rather simple example of wishful thinking.

In contrast to the organic (neuropsychiatric) approaches, found mostly in medical colleges and university clinics, three other distinct schools of thought deserve special comment. They are (Freudian) psychoanalysis, (Jungian) analytical psychology, and existential analysis (*Daseinsanalyse*). Psychoanalytic societies, affiliated with the International Psycho-Analytical Association as their parent organization, exist in the following European countries: Austria, Belgium, Great Britain, Denmark, France, Germany,

Holland, Italy, Sweden, and Switzerland. Excluding the British group the combined membership of the remaining societies is less than 250. Clearly, this is a very small number not only in absolute terms but even more in proportion to the total population of the countries represented. Whatever the reasons, in continental Europe psychoanalysis has remained a psychotherapeutic specialty of relatively slight general influence. Another difference between European and American (although not between European and British) psychoanalysis is that *only* in the United States has psychoanalysis been defined as a medical specialty. Although physicians seem to be the preferred candidates everywhere, a significant proportion of European psychoanalysts are medically untrained.

While psychoanalysis has developed much more in America than it has in Europe, Jung's influence has been vastly greater in Europe. Analytical psychology, even more than (European) psychoanalysis, has become detached from medicine and has allied itself with psychology, pedagogy, and the humanities. Among Jungian analysts, physicians are a minority. Probably partly for this reason, the role of analytical psychology, much as that of European psychoanalysis, has been to meet the needs for private (office) psychotherapy. Their influence on hospital psychiatry and psychiatric education has been small.

The third major nonorganic school of European psychiatry is existential analysis (Binswanger, 1956; May, Angel, and Ellenberger, 1958). Like Jungian psychology, it has become entirely dissociated from medicine, although some of its practitioners are physicians. This is emphasized to underscore the depth of the gulf that separates the organic and psychosocial approaches to psychiatry in Europe. Although borrowing liberally from Freud, Jung, and Adler, existential analysts and psychiatrists of related orientations (for example, phenomenological psychiatrists) seem to have disavowed even their ties to psychology and sociology. Existential psychology, as I see it, is a sort of reaction-formation to the extreme physicalism of traditional European psychiatry. In opposing this dehumanized view of man (May, 1958), however, the existential psychologists abandoned not only medicine but the psychosocial sciences as well, and embraced, instead, a philosophical movement of dubious scientific and moral value (Niebuhr, 1958).[1] As a result, their view of human life has become somewhat mystical—appealing perhaps more to those with theological than to those with scientific propensities. It seems to me especially significant that existential psychiatry, as the distinctively European humanistically oriented psychiatry, did not attach itself to

---

[1] Jaspers chose to keep silent during the Nazi régime, while Heidegger actually joined the movement (Kaufmann, 1956, pp. 47-48).

the important researches of the two great European psychologists, Jung and Piaget. Instead, it took its inspiration chiefly from Kierkegaard and Heidegger (Kuhn, 1950).

Existential analysis, insofar as it addresses itself to the problem of man's place in the universe, is a ponderous and often pompous way of trying to make scientific sense out of questions concerning the whys and hows of human living (Barrett, 1958). In the light of empiricism and modern philosophy (Feigl and Sellars, 1949) existentialism seems to be merely a new name for an inquiry that has, for some time now, been pursued by anthropologists, ethicists, linguists, philosophers, psychologists, psychiatrists, and sociologists. Insofar as existential analysis is devoted to the study of human experiences and behavior, and insofar as it uses the methods of (psychoanalytic) psychology—that is, verbal communication, empathy, historical reconstruction, and so forth—it is a branch of science, belonging in the subgroup of the psychosocial disciplines. It is thus an empirical science, without, at the same time, being a physical science.[2]

While this is not the place for a critical assessment of the significance of existential analysis for psychiatry, I should like to conclude by saying that the exponents of this school of thought seem to me to ignore the significant contributions of social psychology (e.g., Dewey, 1922; Mead, 1934, 1938; Newcomb, 1951), empiricism (e.g., Bridgman, 1936; Russell, 1945, 1948), and the philosophy of science movement (e.g., Frank, 1941; Kemeny, 1959; Rapoport, 1954). Many of the difficulties with which existential psychiatrists grapple have been recognized and successfully surmounted.

This overview of various attitudes toward and theories of mental illness illustrates some of the difficulties that must be overcome before adequate scientific consensus concerning explanations of human behavior will be possible. To achieve this aim, it will be necessary, first, to clarify the problems, operations, and statements of psychiatry; second, to analyze and elucidate the relations between ethics, religion, and the sciences of human behavior (of which psychiatry is one).

---

[2] For a searching analysis of the methodology and epistemology of social science, and its relation to physical science, see Popper's classic study, *The Poverty of Historicism* (1944-1945).

"The so-called 'psycho-physical problem' arises from the mixed employment of both modes of representation in one and the same sentence. Words are put side by side which, when correctly used, really belong to different languages."

Moritz Schlick (1935, p. 403)

CHAPTER 6 | # Hysteria and Psychosomatic Medicine

The concept of conversion hysteria, which originated in psychiatry and psychoanalysis, has influenced medicine itself by its impact on what has become known as "psychosomatic medicine." This ambiguous borderland area lies, as it were, between psychoanalysis and psychiatry on one side and medicine on the other. Since the notion of conversion has been incorporated into the very basis of the theory of psychosomatic medicine, my criticism of it—if valid and acceptable—should help to clarify problems in psychosomatic medicine resting on or utilizing this concept.

Conversion and "Psychogenesis"

The concept of hysterical conversion was modern psychiatry's first answer to the question: How does the mind influence the body? As I have already stated, I am in agreement with those who do not consider this to be a well-framed question.

To examine the so-called problem of the "psychogenesis of organic symptoms," it must first be asked: What is an "organic symptom"? The meaning of this term can only be inferred from the ways in which psychiatrists (and others) have used it. The term "organic symptom" has been applied to three distinct classes of phenomena. First, it denotes *bodily complaints*—for example, pain, itching, or palpitation. In medicine, these are usually referred to as "symptoms," to distinguish them from "signs," which constitute the second category. To be more precise, the latter should be spoken of as *bodily signs* or *nonverbal communications* (e.g., cough, unsteady gait, tic, and so forth). Third, the term "organic symptom" may refer to the evidence of alteration in the function or structure of the body *obtained by means of special methods of observation*. In this group fall such things as listening to a heart murmur, measuring blood pressure, and making fluoroscopic and other physicochemical observations. Physicians as well as behavioral scientists commonly refer to all of these—and even to a fourth class, the *inference of a bodily disorder*—simply as "organic symptoms." This sort of semantic and logical looseness precludes an accurate scientific analysis of the subject matter with which we are expected to deal. Let us briefly examine how each of these categories differs from the others and how they interrelate.

From the physician's standpoint, bodily complaints (symptoms), bodily signs or nonverbal communications (signs), and the recording of special examinations (tests) share the common feature that each pertains to matters of observation. The first two involve observations made by the so-called unaided ear and eye, whereas the third requires the use of various extensions of our biologically given sense organs. Specifically, bodily complaints are observed by means of hearing: the patient informs the physician of his complaints. Bodily signs are observed chiefly by means of vision: the patient exhibits, so to speak, certain kinds of bodily behaviors, such as a limp, which the physician sees. These two classes, therefore, are essentially alike. They differ only in the sensorial equipment used to perceive the messages.

Symptoms and signs (as these terms are used in medicine) thus stand in the same relationship to each other as do spoken and written words. This relationship appears to be little appreciated. Instead, it is widely held that bodily signs are much more accurate and reliable guides to diagnosis than are complaints. This is true only insofar as most people find it easier to lie than to malinger (that is, mimic illness.) Yet, this need not always be the case, and there is no logical, and little empirical, evidence to support the belief in the superiority (in the sense of truthfulness) of bodily signs over complaints. Both can be falsified. And in both cases, a diagnosis of illness—in the sense of bodily disorder—can be made only by drawing inferences from observations.

The third class, too, consists of observation records (Woodger, 1956, p. 16), these having been obtained by techniques which supplement unaided vision and hearing. Hence, the results of so-called tests do not differ logically from direct observations of the patient. Empirically, they may be much more refined and therefore more secure sources of inference. What characterizes tests (and some bodily signs), is that the observations they present circumvent the patient's ego or mind. This being the case, it can be asserted with certainty that tests do not lie or deliberately misinform. (However, those who administer or record the tests may.) Thus, although the patient's lying or malingering can be eliminated by appropriate tests, the possibility of error cannot be. For example, it may be thought that a shadow on a chest film is a sign of tuberculosis—whereas, in fact, it might be a sign of coccidiomycosis, or could even be an artifact.

Sometimes it is assumed that all three types of observations invariably point to underlying "causes"—to bodily disorders. This assumption is unwarranted. We must recognize that observations concerning body functions on the one hand, and the concept of a bodily disorder or disease, such as essential hypertension or duodenal ulcer, on the other, belong in two entirely different categories. The former are observations, the latter inferences. The relationship here between observation and inference is, of course, the same as it is in the other empirical sciences. As singular events, inferences may be verified or falsified—for example, when a surgeon operates for peptic ulcer. Such concrete events, however, are merely members of a scientifically more interesting class called generalizations (or hypotheses). The statement, "All persons who complain of abdominal pain of a certain type . . . suffer from duodenal ulcers," is an example of a generalization based on many single observations.

All this is well known. It is the next step that is often forgotten or not understood: the essential relation between observations and inferences is that of regularity. Saying this, I have simply stated the modern conception of causality as being nothing but the observation of persistent regularities (Schlick, 1932). Herein lies the distinction between physical (scientific) causation and human volition: the former is a description of recurrent regularities, while the latter refers to making something happen. Thus, duodenal ulcers do not compel that pains be felt; rather, they are simply accompanied, as a rule, by complaints of pain. The point of this discussion is to emphasize that there is no firm, point-to-point correlation between observations of body function and inferences concerning disease.

Still, some observations are evidently more valuable than others. Accordingly, in obscure cases the inference of a bodily disorder is seldom made nowadays when it can be supported only by observations of complaints and signs. In ordinary or obvious cases, on the other hand, such simple direct observations may be entirely sufficient. For instance, when we see a man who has been hit by an automobile lying in the road bleeding profusely, his condition does not require the use of laboratory techniques to tell us that he has been hurt. Even in this case, however, we may be unable to ascertain the exact nature of his injuries without making use of roentgenological and other examinations.

Making a specific diagnosis always involves drawing inferences from observations. Obviously, this can be a difficult and frustrating enterprise, since sufficient evidence for drawing reliable inferences is often lacking. Whatever evidence is practically obtainable must usually be relied upon. An added problem in medical diagnosis, of particular concern to us here, is that the patient may offer misleading or false information to the physician (e.g., pseudocyesis, "malingered" insanity). Accordingly, it may be stated as a general rule that alterations in body function or structure of a type that cannot be produced at will—for example, the typical blood picture of lymphocytic leukemia—are the most trustworthy bases for making a so-called physical diagnosis. If no such alterations—demonstrable by appropriate physicochemical methods, bypassing the patient's mind—can be found, the inference of a bodily (physical) disorder rests on shaky grounds. It is possible, of course, that such diseases exist, but we simply do not have the means to detect them.

In general, the empirical-scientific attitude in medical diagnosis obligates one to assume that anyone might be either (physically) healthy or sick. It is logically false, and practically very unwise, to assume—as patients and physicians often do—that someone who has a bodily complaint is physically sick until proved otherwise. This is rather like postulating the existence of God on the basis of faith in a deity and placing the burden of disproof on others. As skeptics, we must reject this gambit. Instead, our position should be similar to that of Anglo-American law toward criminal guilt: a person is innocent until proved guilty. Proof of guilt, moreover, must be furnished by the accusers. Accordingly, as medical diagnosticians we should assume that a person is physically healthy until it has been proved—if not beyond a shadow of a doubt, which seems hardly possible, at least to a degree of reasonable likelihood—that he is sick (Szasz, 1959e).

In this light, so-called hysterical symptoms are distinguished by the fact that although the patient complains of his (or her) body, no physicochemical alterations can be found in it. It should be recalled in this connection that many of Freud's early cases of hysteria were relabeled by later workers as hypochondriasis and schizophrenia (Reichard, 1956). The nature of the patient's bodily feelings and the specific patterns of his bodily preoccupation were not then the objects of psychological interest, nor could they have been before the basic groundwork of psychoanalysis had been laid.

It might be objected that although the absence of physicochemical bodily alterations may be clear enough in cases of hysteria in which the symptoms center around so-called subjective manifestations such as pains or paresthesias, in hysterical paralyses there are "objective" signs of a bodily disorder. Indeed, this mimicry of neurological illness by (the "signs" of) hysteria is, at least partly, responsible for the traditional linkage of neurology with psychiatry.

The similarity between hysteria and neurological disease, however, rests only on appearances. This was recognized in one common pre-Freudian view which considered hysteria to be a voluntarily produced or malingered disability. This view reflects the recognition that although the body as a machine is intact, it functions as though it were not. The same idea is expressed in speaking of "functional" versus "structural" disorders. However, the problem is not so much whether or not the body functions properly, but rather whether the physician can find the observational basis, by means of physicochemical methods, for a diagnosis of a disorder of the body. Thus, in patients with hysterical paralyses, the reflexes are normal and all available tests and post-mortem techniques for studying the nervous system fail to reveal any physicochemical alteration in the body.

In contrast, we speak of the disease, *essential hypertension*, even in the absence of any "disorder of the body" other than the elevated blood pressure recording and even though the patient has no complaints. Thus, to speak of essential hypertension as an "organic symptom" and to place it in the same logical class as "hysterical pain" lays the ground for an epistemological muddle out of which no amount of psychosomatic research could lead us.

Illustrative of this muddle are attempts to classify various mechanisms responsible for the "psychogenesis of organic symptoms." Felix Deutsch (1922) was probably the first to note that such "symptoms" could arise by a mechanism other than that of hysterical conversion. Saul (1935) later made the same observation:

> Some psychogenic organic symptoms, such as tremor or blushing, are the *direct* expressions of emotions or conflicts, while others are only their *indirect* results. Examples of the latter are (a) the effects of acting out, such as catching cold from throwing off the bedclothes during sleep, (b) the incidental soreness of an arm due to an hysterical tremor (p. 85).

Although the distinction between hysterical conversion and this type of phenomenon is important, and Deutsch and Saul deserve credit for emphasizing it, many important issues remain obscured by the use of such inexact language and by adhering to the simple Cartesian view of twin realities. The term "common cold" denotes an inference. It is a bodily disorder or so-called disease entity, rather than a symptom. Its symptoms are stuffiness of the nose and malaise, and its signs are fever and injection of the mucous membranes of the nose and pharynx. Similarly, although it is true that after a prolonged period of "hysterical" paralysis disuse atrophy of the part will occur, it is absurd to speak of a sore arm caused by hysterical tremor, or of a disuse atrophy caused by hysterical paralysis as "symptoms" or "signs" of hysteria. These are better spoken of as the consequences or *sequelae* of certain antecedent events or acts, much as, say, generalized weakness and the loss of one's job might be the consequences of a prolonged bout of typhoid fever. Surely, no one would suggest that all these be classified as "organic symptoms." Yet Alexander (1950), Deutsch (1939), and Saul (1935) have offered us precisely this type of classification.

I submit that there are no "organic symptoms" in any of the above-mentioned examples. A common cold is, medically speaking, a disease—and, logically, an inference. A sore arm is simply a complaint about the body. It contains no inherent proof, so to speak, of a dysfunction that could be called "organic." Furthermore, it is completely meaningless to speak of "psychogenesis" in the situation mentioned by Saul because any illness that a person develops may be shown to be related to some antecedent bit of conduct. If this is all that is required for an illness to be labeled "psychogenic," then every illness must be said to be psychogenic. But in that case the word "psychogenic" becomes meaningless.

Conversion and "Organ Neurosis"

The next major theoretical construct of psychosomatic medicine to be considered is the notion of "vegetative" or "organ neurosis." The connection between organ neurosis and hysteria is rather similar to the connection between hysteria and neurological illness. Twentieth-century psychiatrists have generally assumed that, until the days of Charcot, Kraepelin, and Freud, many cases of hysteria were mistakenly classified as neurological diseases. Hysteria as a new diagnostic category was thus enthusiastically welcomed. Its value was thought to lie in preventing the confusion of two similar and yet different "diseases."

In a like fashion, until the late 1930's—and especially until Alexander's paper, "Fundamental Concepts of Psychosomatic Research" (1943)—the term "hysteria" was used to describe all sorts of clinical phenomena. Thus pains, paralyses, pseudocyesis, diarrhea, asthma, and many other observations were conceptualized as and labeled "conversion hysteria." In protest against this allegedly loose classification, a separation of two classes was suggested:

some phenomena were to be subsumed under the heading of "hysteria," while others were henceforth to be placed in the class of "organ neurosis." Ostensibly, this innovation was basically a matter of nosology; hence, it required good clinical description on the one hand and accurate logical and epistemological reasoning on the other. Yet, in fact, the distinction was based on neither of these criteria, but rested instead on anatomical and physiological distinctions between cerebrospinal and autonomic systems.

THE PHILOSOPHICAL BASIS OF PSYCHOSOMATIC CLASSIFICATIONS

It might be best, at this point, to reconsider the philosophical roots of the problem of psychosomatic classification. Alexander (1943), recognizing the significance of philosophical considerations for this subject, took the explicit position that "there is no logical distinction between 'mind' and 'body,' mental and physical" (p. 3). He further added that the division of medical disciplines into physiology, medicine, neurology, psychiatry, and so on "may be convenient for academic administration, but biologically and philosophically these divisions have no validity" (p. 3).

Instead of viewing the difference between psychology and physiology as stemming from the hierarchical organization of human beings—as biological *and* social organisms—Alexander postulated that "psychic and somatic phenomena take place in the *same biological system* and are probably *two aspects of the same process*" ([ITALICS ADDED] p. 3). In this approach, Alexander continued to adhere to the traditional Cartesian mind-body dichotomy, no matter how hard he strained to overcome it. The image of mind and body as two aspects of the same coin must be contrasted with the model of hierarchical organization, according to which physical organization is the most basic level, biological organization is superordinate to it, while psychological and social levels constitute increasingly higher orders of systems.

The philosophical position enunciated by Alexander seems unsupportable. To assert that "there is no logical distinction between 'mind' and 'body' " flies in the face of the most basic *logical* concepts regarding classes. I do not wish to belabor this matter. I should only like to say that I adhere to the view of those contemporary philosophers of science who have shown that the relationship between body and mind is better regarded as analogous to that existing between, say, a football team and its team spirit (or *esprit de corps*). The former is an observational datum for physics; it has location in space; it is public. The latter is a datum for psychology and sociology; it has no spatial location; and it is not public in the sense in which physical objects are public.

If we accept this view, however, we shall no longer be able to adhere to what might be called the "philosophy of symmetry" regarding mind and body, so clearly described by Alexander and so much in vogue at the present time. According to this symmetrical view, persons consist of, or can be studied as, two symmetrical halves, bodies and minds. It is maintained, or hoped, that by studying both halves—much like first studying two halves of a cadaver bisected along its axis of symmetry, and then recombining the results—a composite picture of the "whole man" will emerge. Instead of this happy result, the "psychosomatic approach" has led neither to better therapies for patients nor to clearer theoretical insights for investigators. The challenge of the Cartesian dichotomy was not met. It was sidestepped. And so it is still with us, but now it is even more difficult to recognize and root out than it was three decades ago, when modern psychosomatic medicine began.

A CRITIQUE OF ALEXANDER'S DEFINITION OF "VEGETATIVE NEUROSIS"

The distinction between hysterical conversion and so-called vegetative or organ neurosis has been drawn most clearly by Alexander (1943). Interestingly, this is one of the few fundamental theoretical issues in psychoanalysis to be accepted by analysts of otherwise varied theoretical and therapeutic bents. However, consensus provides no guarantee against mistake. In this case, agreement rests on shared philosophical misconceptions concerning the duality of physical and psychological realities, and on a persistent but unacknowledged tendency *to describe diverse human experiences and communications in medical or quasi-medical terms.*

> It seems advisable [wrote Alexander] to differentiate between hysterical conversion and vegetative neurosis. Their similarities are rather superficial: both conditions are *psychogenic*, that is to say, they are caused *ultimately* by a chronic repressed or at least unrelieved tension. The mechanisms involved, however, are fundamentally different both psychodynamically and physiologically. The hysterical conversion symptom is an attempt to relieve an emotional tension in a symbolic way, it is a symbolic expression of a definite emotional content. This *mechanism is restricted to the voluntary neuromuscular or sensory perceptive systems* whose function is to express and relieve emotions. *A vegetative neurosis* consists of a psychogenic dysfunction of a vegetative organ *which is not under control of the voluntary neuromuscular system.* The vegetative symptom is not a substitute expression of the emotion, but its normal physiological concomitant ([ITALICS ADDED] p. 9).

The apparent attractiveness of this formulation—which derives partly from its simplicity, and partly from the fact that it makes use of the familiar distinction between cerebrospinal and autonomic systems—insured wide acceptance for it. Since I have already commented on certain aspects of this formulation, I shall limit myself here to listing, and briefly discussing, the points that I believe deserve special scrutiny.

1. Alexander wrote of the symptoms of the voluntary neuromuscular and sensory perceptive systems, and also used the term "vegetative symptom." It is no mere quibbling to assert that only persons can have symptoms—parts of the body cannot. This medical and psychosomatic usage—which allows one to speak of "organic symptoms" and the like—leads to a hopeless confusion of affects and complaints with body parts and lesions. Losing sight of the fact that both patients and physicians are in the habit of assigning the former to the latter may lead, for example, to the physician's denial of the "reality" of phantom experiences, as one of its typical consequences (Szasz, 1957a).

2. Freud's original idea that conversion symptoms are pathological because "substitutive innervations never bring full relief" (p. 6) was retained intact. This view is an objectionable one because it defines what is "pathological" in terms of the theory of a disorder. It runs counter to the common practice of measuring deviations from a norm by descriptive criteria, whether these be medical, social, or ethical (Szasz, 1960b). Not specifying the criteria of "normality" and "abnormality" in clear, descriptive terms—and instead using complicated and not fully defined theoretical conceptions for this purpose—is, in my opinion, the principal cause of the notorious difficulties in psychiatry and psychoanalysis of distinguishing between "pathological symptoms" and "normal sublimations." The lack of publicly stated and generally agreed upon criteria leaves open the opportunity to interpret observations in accord with one's unspecified personal biases. The psychiatrist's moral preferences may thus be enunciated in the disguise of scientific descriptions or "facts" (Szasz, 1959a).

3. Reference to the notion of "innervations" signified that the models of hydraulic systems and electrical circuits—used originally to explain hysteria—would be used also to explain so-called psychosomatic problems. According to these models, tension-discharge via detours—that is, by "substitutive innervations"—is, by definition, less satisfactory than discharge in the "open circuit." Unless great care is exercised, there is the danger of mixing up the explanatory metaphor with the primary data of observation.

4. We may conclude that the definition of vegetative neurosis is simply a restatement, in physiological language, of the detour-mechanism described above. "A vegetative neurosis," wrote Alexander (1950), "is not an attempt to express an emotion but is the physiological response of the vegetative organs to constant or to periodically returning emotional states" (p. 42).

This theory could be paraphrased as follows: "Dammed up libido, if discharged via the neuromuscular or sensory systems, leads to (causes?) hysteria; if discharged via the autonomic nervous system, to vegetative neurosis." The symmetry is complete. But what does this definition really mean? What does it tell us?

To clarify this problem, we must ask two additional questions: How can we tell whether a person is afflicted with a "vegetative neurosis"? What is the relationship between the patient's symptom (or complaint) and his illness in hysteria and vegetative neurosis respectively?

The first question is best answered by reference to a specific example. Alexander's (1950) paradigm of a vegetative neurosis is chronic gastric hypersecretion which, in time, may lead to the disease, *peptic ulcer:* ". . . emotional conflicts of long duration may lead as a first step to a *stomach neurosis* which in time may result in an ulcer" ([ITALICS ADDED] p. 44). The physical lesion itself is considered to be an "organic disease," and only the antecedent physiological dysfunction is labeled a "vegetative neurosis."

The question remains: How can we tell whether someone has a vegetative neurosis? By no means is the answer clear. For instance, is the measurement of chronic gastric hypersecretion *prima facie* evidence of a vegetative neurosis? Or is it necessary that the person exhibiting this type of physiological activity develop an ulcer? Or must he at least complain of abdominal pain? If a diagnosis of vegetative neurosis can be made only in the latter two instances, of what use is it to us? If, however, chronic gastric hypersecretion per se is an unequivocal sign of a vegetative neurosis, then we have merely created an inferred "entity" which tells us no more than the observation on which it is based. The main point of this discussion is that the relationship between complaint and vegetative neurosis is at once undefined and inconstant. Some persons with chronic gastric hypersecretion complain of intense pain, while others have no complaints at all—yet, as the term is customarily used, both could be said to "have" such a "vegetative (or organ) neurosis."

In the case of conversion hysteria, the relationship of complaint (or symptom) to illness is entirely different. Clearly, it would be absurd to speak of someone who displays neither complaints nor manifestations of disability as suffering from hysteria. In a typical instance of this, a person may complain of, say, numbness and tingling of the right forearm. Physical examination and special tests reveal nothing unusual. The body as a machine appears to be intact. In cases of so-called vegetative neurosis this is not true. In these cases, we deal with bodily malfunctions (which may themselves be the causes of still further bodily malfunctions), while in hysteria we deal with persons with healthy bodies. It is, therefore, a great mistake to place these two groups in one and the same logical class, which is done when both are considered to be "neuroses"—that is, one "conversion," the other "vegetative" or "organ neurosis."

Another difficulty in trying to be clear about what is meant by a vegetative neurosis is that the basic term "neurosis" itself is ill defined. Does the word "neurosis" refer to *observable behavior, reported behavior,* or a *theory of a specific pathogenetic process?* In principle, it is legitimate to call any one of these classes "neurosis." It is important, however, that we know what we are doing. According to standard psychoanalytic usage (e.g., Fenichel, 1945; Freud, 1940; Glover, 1949), *the word "neurosis" refers to the analyst's theory of a psychopathological mechanism.* The latter is conceptualized in terms of dammed-up impulses (or libido), and various types of ego-mechanisms (defenses), the two together giving rise to a variety of overt manifestations (the "symptom picture"). Because of this conceptualization, not only persons but various parts of their bodies may be said to be "neurotic"—depending on where the "dammed-up impulses" are located. In a phobia, for example, they are regarded as contained in the person. In stuttering, they are allegedly converted into an hysterical symptom and reside in the speech organs. Finally, in peptic ulcer, the organ of digestion is thought of as "neurotic."

These examples illustrate how far one can go astray in mistaking explanatory metaphors for the things they are supposed to explain. I believe that we would be better off if we were to drop the whole notion of organ neurosis. Its psychoanalytic relevance is limited to buttressing the hydraulic elements in our understanding of neurosis. This we do not need. It makes no positive contribution to psychoanalytic psychology as theory or as therapy. On the contrary, the explanations it provides only hinder us from seeing the unsolved problems which remain concerning the general subject of how man's mode of life, including his personal and social relationships, affect his bodily functions.

Pushing this logical analysis another step leads to the question: What disorders of the voluntary nervous system correspond to the disorders of the autonomic nervous system which Alexander called vegetative neuroses? There are several disorders that could be so conceptualized. The neurological *sequelae* of pernicious anemia will be used as an illustrative example. A person afflicted with this disease in its early stages may complain of weakness and fatigue. Special laboratory tests will usually lead to the findings characteristic of pernicious anemia. Pernicious anemia as a pathophysiological process—like chronic gastric hypersecretion in our previous example—may be the "cause" of certain organic changes in the central and cerebrospinal nervous systems. This "end-stage"—which, of course, is not really an end-stage either, but rather another step in a long series that could be said to start with birth and end only with death—would correspond to the formation of a demonstrable peptic ulcer. Since the notion of vegetative neurosis implies the presence of demonstrable physicochemical alterations (abnormalities) in certain of the internal organs of the body, a homologous phenomenon in the cerebrospinal nervous system must exhibit the same characteristics. A two-stage sequence is necessary, the first stage consisting of a pathophysiological alteration, the second of the development of a more-or-less fixed, structural disease entity. Examples of this sort of process are pernicious anemia, poliomyelitis, and multiple sclerosis.

It may be objected that this view takes no account of the important observations according to which a person's psychological state (to put it loosely) seems to have a rather striking relationship to some of the bodily disorders subsumed under the category of vegetative neurosis. This objection is valid. The central problem of psychosomatic medicine, if framed this way, is still with us and I do not imply that I have a simple solution for it. It does seem that when people do not express themselves in words and actions (which is not the same thing as "discharging tension"), they are more prone to express themselves in some other ways, bodily illness being one of them. How best to investigate and describe this is a large problem (Szasz, 1958c, 1959d). Its further analysis need not concern us here, since our purpose was only to elucidate the influence of the concept of conversion on psychosomatic theory.

Conversion of Energy Versus Communication and Translation

The notion that neurotic symptoms "discharge tension" is based on the physical model of energy-discharge. According to this scheme, psychological functioning is conceived on the model of a hydraulic system (Colby, 1955; Pumpian-Mindlin, 1959). A column of water, representing potential energy, is dammed up behind a barrier and seeks release. It may be discharged along a number of different pathways: (1) Along the route mapped out for it—that is, "normally," in speech or appropriate overt behavior; (2) Along an alternate route, which represents a "misuse" of the apparatus (e.g., leakage from the hydraulic system, perhaps at the sides of the dam, not via the sluices provided). Dammed-up tension is discharged via "conversion" into "bodily symptoms." This is "conversion hysteria"; (3) Along still other channels (e.g., leakage at other points in the system), leading to bodily disease. This is "vegetative" or "organ neurosis."

The suggestion that we abandon the scheme of energy conversion in psychiatric theory and substitute for it models of communication, language, and translation is no longer novel (Ruesch and Bateson, 1951; Ruesch, 1959; R. Spiegel, 1959).

Translation refers to rendering a message from one idiom into another, say from Hungarian into English. When the process of translating is completed, we say that the two statements "mean the same thing." In such a context, we cannot very well speak of energy-transfers, nor of changes in information content. It is more profitable to focus on the practical, interpersonal (social) situation that makes translation necessary—namely, that people who do not speak the same language cannot communicate with one another by means of language. Translation is the act that makes communication in such a situation possible. It unblocks a previously blocked communicational situation (Bohannan, 1954). Let us consider a hypothetical example.

A patient whose mother tongue is Hungarian comes to the physician (or to the hospital). The physician speaks only English. How is he to understand the patient? The following possibilities exist: (1) The physician learns to speak Hungarian. (2) An interpreter is hired who translates the patient's Hungarian into the physician's English. (3) The patient learns to speak English. (4) The patient not only learns to speak English, but, reflecting upon the problem of communication that exists, becomes explicitly aware of problems of communication and translation and makes their study his object of interest.

To understand hysteria, we must substitute bodily feelings for Hungarian (patient), and demonstrable bodily disorder for English (physician). The patient knows, after all, how to tell others how he feels. This is, as it were, his mother tongue. The physician's special language, on the other hand, is that of medicine, consisting of elevated temperatures, specific pains for various diseases, and so forth; it is the language of organic illness (or of potential organic illness). The task is to *translate from complaint to illness.* The four alternatives for establishing communication in the face of this language barrier are as follows: (1) The physician learns about body-language, and about distinguishing "functional" from "organic" cases. (2) An interpreter is hired. This means that whenever the language of bodily disease does not fit, the patient is referred to a psychiatrist (or some other specialist). The physician sends the patient to someone who can talk to him since he, the physician, cannot. (3) The patient learns to speak the language of "real illness." He seeks out physicians who will take medical or surgical action in the face of slight, or nonexistent, evidences of physical malfunctioning. He may thus obtain vitamins, placebos, "shots," or get his appendix, teeth, or (her) uterus removed. (If he persists too long, or gets into the "wrong hands," however, he may be labeled a "hypochondriac" or "polysurgical addict.") (4) The patient learns that, although it is generally advantageous to speak the language of the "natives," it too, like all other languages, has its limitations. He may then learn about his own communications, their history, aim, scope, malfunction, and general limits. This may be accomplished by undergoing psychoanalytic treatment, or sometimes simply by learning, contemplation, and association with wise friends.

Book Two | **_FOUNDATIONS OF A THEORY OF PERSONAL CONDUCT_**

PART III | *Semiotical*
Analysis
of Behavior

"Non-human beings seldom produce the signs which influence their behavior, while human individuals in their language and post-language symbols character- istically do this and to a surprising degree. Here is a basic difference between men and animals, and until behavioral theory develops a semiotic adequate to this difference it will remain what it is today; a careful study of animals and a pious hope for a science of the human person. Charles W. Morris (1946, p. 198)*

CHAPTER 7

Hysteria
and Language

The symbolic-logical definitions of such terms as "language," "sign," and "symbol" will be indispensable for our further work.[1] The concept of sign is the most basic of the three, and we shall start with it. Signs are, first of all, physical things: for example, chalk marks on a blackboard, pencil or ink marks on paper, sound waves produced in a human throat. "What makes them signs," according to Reichenbach (1947), "is the intermediary position they occupy between an object and a sign user, i.e., a person" (p. 4). For a sign to be a sign, or to function as such, it is necessary that the person take account of the object it designates. Thus, *anything in nature may or may not be a sign, depending on a person's attitude toward it.* A physical thing is a sign when it appears as a substitute for the object (for which it stands) with respect to the sign user. The three-place relation between sign, object, and sign user (person) is called the *sign relation* or *relation of denotation.*

The Structure of Protolanguage

Clearly, the notion of sign encompasses a great deal. According to strict (symbolic-logical) usage, however, to use signs is not the same as to use language. What, then, are nonlinguistic signs? We may distinguish, following Reichenbach, three classes of signs. In the first class may be placed signs that

[1] The reader especially interested in this type of analysis may consult Reichenbach (1947), whose conceptual scheme was adopted as the basis for the present exposition.

acquire their sign function through a *causal connection* between object and sign. Smoke, for example, is a sign of fire. Signs of this type are called *indexical*. The second class is made up of signs that stand in a relation of *similarity* to the objects they designate: for example, the photograph of a man or the map of a terrain. These are called *iconic signs*. In the third class are placed signs whose relation to the object is purely *conventional* or *arbitrary:* for example, words or mathematical symbols. These are called *conventional signs* or *symbols*. *Symbols* usually do not exist in isolation, but are coordinated with each other by a set of rules, called the rules of language. The entire package, consisting of symbols, language rules, and social customs concerning language use, is sometimes referred to as the *language game*. In the technical idiom of the logician, we speak of language *only* when communication is mediated by means of systematically coordinated conventional signs (symbols).

According to this definition, there can be no such thing as a "body language." If we wish to express ourselves precisely, we must speak instead of *communication by means of bodily signs*. This is not mere pedantry. The expression "bodily sign" implies two significant characteristics. First, that we deal here with something other than conventional, linguistic symbols. Second, that the signs in question must be identified further as to their special characteristics. In speaking of bodily signs, I shall always refer (unless otherwise indicated) to phenomena such as so-called hysterical paralyses, blindness, deafness, seizures, and so forth. These occurrences speak for themselves, as it were, and hence communication by means of such signs need not involve speech. In this, they are distinguished from certain other bodily signs, such as pain, which may be communicated either verbally or by pantomime (i.e., by behavior suggesting to the observer that the sufferer is in pain). Finally, since speech itself makes use of bodily organs, it too could loosely be called a "bodily sign." This, however, would be a vague and nontechnical use of this expression. By adhering to a more precise definition, we can readily differentiate between two types of speech: first, ordinary speech, *using socially shared symbols* (called language), and second, the use of *vocal noises that are not symbols* (e.g., regressed schizophrenic vocalizations). The latter, although making use of the so-called speech apparatus, *logically* belongs in the same class as bodily signs. So much for initial definitions. Let us now take up the question posed earlier: What are the characteristic features of the signs employed in so-called body language?

BODY LANGUAGE IS COMPOSED OF ICONIC SIGNS

It is evident that body signs—for example, a so-called hysterical seizure—are not conventional signs. Neither are they indexical signs. Indexical signs stand in a cause-and-effect relationship to the object they signify. Smoke is a sign of fire; fever is a sign of infection; light breaking over the eastern horizon is a sign of sunrise. In all of them a causal—or we might also say associational and temporal—relationship exists between sign (fever) and object (infection). Clearly, body-signs (of the type now being considered) are not of this sort.

The concept of iconic sign fits exactly the observations described as body signs. The relationship of iconic sign to denoted object is one of similarity (Aldrich, 1932). A photograph, for example, is an iconic sign of the person in the picture. Viewed in this light, an *hysterical seizure is an iconic sign of a genuine (organic) epileptic seizure*. Or, an hysterical paralysis or weakness of the lower extremities could be (said to be) an iconic sign of weakness due to multiple sclerosis or tabes dorsalis. In brief, body signs are best conceptualized as iconic signs of bodily illness. This interpretation is consistent with the fact that communications of this type occur chiefly in interactions between a sufferer and his helper. The two participants may be defined specifically as "patient" and "physician"—although many other types of helpless-helpful interactions also exist. The point to re-emphasize is that body signs, as iconic signs of bodily illness, form an integral part of what could properly be called the language of illness. In other words, just as photographs as iconic signs have special usefulness in and relevance to the movie industry and its patrons, so iconic signs pertaining to the body and its functions have special relevance to the "healing industry" and its patrons (e.g., medicine, the ministry, social case work, etc.).

BODY LANGUAGE IS A PROTOLANGUAGE

Having identified the signs of which body language is composed, we can now examine the type of communicational processes made possible by means of these signs. Again, it is necessary to consider briefly the technical classification of languages devised by logicians. Philologists and linguists of traditional schools of thought have classified languages in accordance with their own interests and needs (Sapir, 1921). These classifications distinguish different individual languages, such as English, German, French, Hungarian, Armenian, and so forth. Individual tongues and dialects are then ordered into larger groups called families of languages. Thus, we speak of Indo-European, Finno-Ugric, Indian, and other groups, in each of which many individual languages are subsumed.

Logicians and philosophers, under the impetus of Whitehead and Russell (1910), have developed a completely different kind of language classification. According to this scheme, different languages are divided off from one another depending on the level of complexity of the logical descriptions and operations involved. This method of classification has had far-reaching effects in mathematics, logic, and the philosophy of science. From it we have learned that conversational languages have within them several logically heterogeneous "languages."

According to the logical classification of languages, we distinguish different levels of language. The first, or lowest level, is called object language.[2] The signs of this language denote physical objects, for example, cat, dog, chair, table, and so on. We may next introduce signs referring to signs. The words "word," "sentence," "clause," and "phrase" are signs belonging to (the first-level) metalanguage. This iteration of the coordination of signs and referents may be repeated, in principle at least, *ad infinitum*. Thus, progressively higher levels of metalanguages can be constructed, by forever introducing signs which denote signs at the next lower (logical) level. The distinction between object language and metalanguage (and metalanguages of increasingly higher orders) is undoubtedly the single most significant contribution of symbolic logic to the science of language. Only by means of this distinction did it become apparent that in order for us to speak about any object language, we need a metalanguage. It must be remembered, of course, that on both of these levels of language, the same linguistic stock may be used. Thus, wrote Jakobson (1957), "we may speak in English (as metalanguage) about English (as object language) and interpret English words and sentences by means of English synonyms, circumlocutions, and paraphrases" (p. 163). So-called ordinary language consists of a mixture of object and metalanguages.

For our present purposes, it is especially important to note that, in this scheme, the lowest level of language is object language. There is no room here for what goes in psychiatry by the name of body language. This is because body language is composed of iconic signs. Hence, it constitutes a system logically more primitive than the operations of object language. The question may now be raised: What type of a language is body language?

Inasmuch as conventional signs (or symbols) make up the lowest level of language, and signs of signs the first level of metalanguage, and so on, a communication system employing signs that denote less, so to speak, than do conventional signs themselves may be regarded as forming a level of language below that of object language. I suggest, therefore, that we call this type

[2] The word "object" is used in several different senses in this book, depending on the context in which it appears. It is used in a technically specialized fashion in two situations. In connection with object relationships, "object" usually means a person, less often a thing or idea. In connection with logical hierarchies, say of languages, the term "object" denotes a level of discourse about which one may speak only in a metalanguage. The logical relationship between object and meta levels is always a relative one. Thus, a first-level metalanguage may be considered an object language with respect to a second-level metalanguage.

of (body) language a protolanguage. This seems fitting since the word "metalanguage" denotes that languages of this type are later, beyond, or higher than object languages. The prefix "proto," being the antonym of "meta," refers to something that is earlier or lower than something else (as in "prototype").

Placing certain types of body symptoms—that is, those that are iconic signs—in their proper places in the logical hierarchy of languages will be of considerable help in formulating psychiatric problems. To begin with, the very notion of understanding something hinges on its expressibility, either in conversational or in technical languages. This means that whatever it might be that we try to understand or describe must be expressed in terms of object and metalanguages. What, then, is the function of protolanguage? As we shall see, it is not quite true that intelligible communication is possible only by means of object and metalanguages.

THE NATURE OF PROTOLINGUISTIC COMMUNICATION

An hysterical symptom, say a seizure or paralysis, expresses and transmits a message, usually to a specific person. A paralyzed arm, for instance, may mean: "I have sinned with this arm and have been punished for it." It may also mean "I wanted or needed to obtain some forbidden gratification (erotic, aggressive, etc.) by means of this arm." But what exactly is meant when it is stated that a symptom has such and such a meaning? This problem raises such related questions as: Does the patient—the sender of the message—know that he is communicating? Does the receiver of the message—physician, husband, wife, etc.—know what he or she is being communicated? If they do not know, how can they be said to be communicating?

Although Freud never raised these questions, at least not as I have framed them, he gave some good answers to them. Perhaps precisely because they were so useful, his answers obscured the original questions which stimulated them and which were never explicitly stated. Freud suggested that we distinguish two basically different types of "mentation" and "knowledge," one conscious, the other unconscious. Unconscious activity is directed by so-called primary processes, while conscious mentation is logically organized and is governed by so-called secondary processes (Fenichel, 1945, pp. 14-15, 46-51).

The term "conscious" was never specifically defined in psychoanalysis, but was used rather in a common-sense, phenomenological sense. The concept "unconscious" was much more carefully elaborated by Freud (1915), and was later differentiated from the "preconscious." Several recent workers have presented careful analyses of this concept and its usage (Peters, 1958; Mac-

Intyre, 1958; Bellak, 1959). For our present purpose, it is enough that Freud
spoke of the unconscious partly as though it were a region in the mental
apparatus, and partly as though it were a system of operations. He assumed
the existence of such alleged occurrences as unconscious knowledge, unconscious conflicts, unconscious needs, and so forth, and used these expressions to describe them.

Unfortunately, this terminology obscures some of the logical problems
that must be solved. It is basic to science as a social undertaking that we
recognize as knowledge only that which can be made public. This is why
the scientific idea of knowledge—as contrasted with mystical or religious
versions of it (Burchard, 1960)—is so inextricably tied to the notion of
representation by means of conventional signs. What cannot be expressed in
either object or metalanguage cannot, by definition, be knowledge. For
instance, the message of a painting may be interesting and beautiful, yet its
"meaning" cannot be called knowledge.

If we adhere to this more precise terminology, it will be necessary to
concede that body languages of the type considered *do not*, as such, express
knowledge. This is not the same as to assert that they are devoid of information. We touch here on the distinction between knowledge and information,
which, in our usage, is the same as the distinction between verbal symbol
and iconic sign (Tarski, 1944). Thus, a cloudy sky may be said to "contain"
information, for its "message" could be read by a human as a sign of impend-
ing rain. We may not say, however, that a cloudy sky "contains" knowledge.
Similarly, to obtain the hidden meaning, so to speak, of a message framed in
the idiom of body signs, it is necessary to translate protolanguage into
ordinary language. Freud expressed a similar idea when he spoke of making
the unconscious conscious, or translating the former into the latter. Yet, he
never clearly conceptualized the "unconscious" as *nothing but* a language or
a form of communication. Hence, while the idea of translating protolanguage
into ordinary language *describes* some of the same things that Freud described as rendering the unconscious conscious, the two schemes are not
identical.[3]

A question has been raised concerning the connection between the use of
protolanguage and the sender's "knowledge" of the messages so communicated. This relationship is an inverse one. In other words, while it is usually
impossible to speak about something one does not know, one may readily

---

[3] There are some evident similarities between what I have called *protolanguage* and
Freud's concept of *primary process* thinking, and also between it and the *paleologic* of
Von Domarus and Arieti (Arieti, 1955, 1959). The differences between protolanguage
and the two latter constructs should become clear in the course of subsequent exposition
of my thesis.

express by means of protolanguage that which is not (explicitly) known. The main reason for this is that learning and knowledge on the one hand, and symbolic codification and communication (language, mathematics, etc.) on the other, are interdependent and can grow only together (Szasz, 1957c). Since the use of iconic (body) signs is the simplest communicational device available to man, communication of this type varies inversely with knowledge and learning. The thesis that relatively less sophisticated human beings are more likely to use protolanguage is consistent with our knowledge concerning the historical and social determinants of so-called hysterical symptoms. Consider, for example, the time when human beings tried literally to be *icons* of Christ on the cross, exhibiting so-called hysterical stigmata. Conversations in this protolanguage can occur only if the participants in the communicational process do not readily speak a higher level of language. Once a more naturalistic-scientific attitude toward religion became widespread—and this could occur only with a more widely disseminated education of the masses—this particular form of communication began to disappear.

Symbolization in Hysteria: A Critical Example

My thesis will now be illustrated by means of an excerpt from Breuer and Freud's "Studies on Hysteria" (1893-1895). The following is from Freud's account of his treatment of Frau Cäcilie M.:

> In this phase of the work we came at last to the reproduction of her facial neuralgia, which I myself had treated when it appeared in contemporary attacks. I was curious to discover whether this, too, would turn out to have a psychical cause. When I began to call up the traumatic scene, the patient saw herself back in a period of great mental irritability toward her husband. She described a conversation which she had with him and a remark of his which she had felt as a bitter insult. Suddenly she put her hand to her cheek, gave a loud cry of pain and said: "It was like a slap in the face." With this her pain and her attack were both at an end.
>
> There is no doubt that what had happened had been a *symbolization*. She had felt as though she had actually been given a slap in the face. Everyone will immediately ask how it was that the sensation of a "slap in the face" came to take on the outward forms of a *trigeminal neuralgia*, why it was restricted to the second and third branches, and why it was made worse by opening the mouth and chewing—though, incidentally, not by talking.

> Next day the *neuralgia* was back again. But this time it was
> cleared up by the reproduction of another scene, the content of
> which was once again a supposed *insult*. Things went on like this
> for nine days. It seemed to be the case that *for years insults, and
> particularly spoken ones, had through symbolization, brought on
> fresh attacks of her facial neuralgia* ([ITALICS ADDED] p. 178).

Here, as elsewhere, Freud spoke of a process of "symbolization." By
means of it, an insult was changed into pain. In his theory construction, however, Freud called this "conversion," thus perpetuating the so-called riddle
of the jump from the psychic into the organic. Clearly, all one needs is to
conceptualize in terms of translation and the problems of conversion and
psychogenesis assume novel, more manageable proportions.

I suspect that at least one of the reasons for Freud's failure to carry
through consistently with the model of translation was that he did not
grasp exactly what type of symbolization he had identified. How can a
slap on the face be "converted" to (what looks like) trigeminal neuralgia?
How can one be a symbol for the other? Freud did not answer these questions nor, in fact, did he raise them. Instead, he proceeded as follows. First,
he *assumed* that the symbolization described above is essentially similar to
that obtaining between verbal symbol (conventional sign) and referent (i.e.,
the object symbolized). Then he proceeded with his work as though this
had been a fact, instead of an unverified—and, as it turned out, incorrect—
assumption. Accordingly, he interpreted hysterical symptoms as though the
translation required were no different from, say, rendering ancient Greek
into modern English (Bohannan, 1954). Furthermore, he approached the
why of symbolization through the traditional model of medicine. The
problem thus became: Why does conversion occur? Or, stated more generally: Why does a patient "develop" hysteria? In this way, Freud ended
up with a classical medical problem, so to speak: namely, with the problem
of the "etiology of hysteria." However, if we regard hysteria as a language,
asking and looking for its "etiology" will be about as sensible as it is to
ask for the "etiology" of mathematics. A language has a history, a geographic
distribution, and many other characteristics, but it cannot be said to have
an "etiology."

There remains for us to consider the type of symbol which Freud described in the case history cited. The precise sign-relation, or relation of
denotation, between sign, object, and person must be identified and described. How can a facial pain denote a slap on the face? Why should an
insult be so denoted? In reply to the first question, it appears that this type

of symbolization hinges on a two-fold relation.

First, there is the similarity between pain caused by a slap and pain caused by neuralgia (meaning thereby any sort of physical disorder whose symptom is facial pain). Hence, Frau Cäcilie's facial pain is an iconic sign of (the pain due to) a facial illness. Indeed, to some extent every pain constitutes an iconic sign of every other. Just as in a picture of an egg we recognize every egg we ever saw, so each pain we experience is, in part, built up of all the pains we have ever had.

Second, the pain of a slapped face, or of being insulted and humiliated, is not only an iconic sign of facial neuralgia—it is also an indexical sign. This is because being slapped (or being hurt in any other way) and having a pain stand in a temporal and cause-and-effect relationship to one another. We know, or can infer, "slaps" from "pains," even though this may not be the only way in which such information can be obtained. Hence, a pain can be an indexical sign of being slapped in the face or of having trigeminal neuralgia—in the same way as having a fever can be an indexical sign of harboring an infection. Both types of sign-relations enter into the actual communicational patterns we are considering. For example, a woman communicating facial pain to her husband may "sound" to him—especially if he has hurt her—as though she were saying: "Do you see now how you have hurt me?"[4] This hypothetical woman making the same communication to her physician may, on the other hand, "sound" to him—especially if he is preoccupied with physical disturbances of the body—as though she were saying: "I have trigeminal neuralgia." Although both husband and physician read the pain as a sign at once iconic and indexical, they read it differently depending on their specific position in the three-place relation holding between sign, object, and person (interpreter of sign). It is because of his special position in this three-place relation that the psychoanalyst tends to read the facial pain as an iconic sign (i.e., this "looks like" neuralgia but probably is not).

The second question, namely, "Why should a slap on the face—or being humiliated—be denoted in this particular fashion (by facial pain)?" will be discussed in detail in subsequent chapters (especially Chapter 9). It should suffice here to note that, as a rule, the use of this type of body language is fostered by circumstances that make direct verbal expression difficult or impossible. The time-honored custom of referring to sexual organs and activities by Latin words rather than in terms of one's native tongue affords a typical illustration. Translation from what could be, or had been, ordinary

---

[4] For a beautiful literary portrayal of this sort of communication, see Edith Wharton's novel, *Ethan Frome* (1911).

language into protolanguage serves a similar purpose. It makes communication concerning a significant subject possible, while at the same time it helps the speaker disown the disturbing implications of his message. The specific choice of body signs is generally determined by the unique personal-historical and social circumstances of the sufferer, in accordance with the principles discovered by Freud.

The Concept of Symbol in Psychoanalysis

It was suggested that when Freud referred to the memory of a slap on the face having been "converted" into facial pain, he did not understand the type of symbolization he had identified. The validity of this assumption is supported by the fact that even today, more than seventy years after Breuer and Freud's original work, psychiatrists and psychoanalysts still employ the concept of symbolization in a quite inconsistent and confusing manner. I have commented on this elsewhere (Szasz, 1957c), in connection with the problem of schizophrenia and its treatment (e.g., by means of "symbolic realization"). Let us now see exactly how the concepts of symbol and symbolization are used in psychoanalysis.

Freud used the term "symbol" in its ordinary sense, to refer to a sign-referent relationship. Having distinguished three fundamentally different types of signs, we may now ask: In which type of sign was Freud especially interested? Clearly, whenever Freud (and other psychoanalysts) spoke of "symbols" or "symbolization," they referred to iconic signs. They used these terms to indicate, in general, that item X was used to represent item Y and that this was possible because X resembled Y, or reminded the sign-user (patient) of Y. This is a description of item X functioning as an iconic sign of item Y—say, the umbrella as a symbol for penis, or the purse as symbol for vagina. (In psychoanalysis almost never does the word "symbol" refer to conventional signs.) An immense psychoanalytic superstructure of "symbolism" has been built on the simple, though fundamental, idea of similarity (iconicity). On closer examination, the entire edifice appears to be nothing but a tedious reiteration of relations of similarity.

In his studies of hysterical symptoms, for example, Freud (1910a) emphasized that the symptom is always a symbol of a (repressed) traumatic memory. A "painful" human experience is thus similar to a "painful" illness. Thus, painful afflictions of various parts of the body may be iconic signs of virtually all conceivable unpleasant happenings. Freud was aware that he was using the concept of symbol in this fashion. My point is that he failed to distinguish this type of symbolization from other types. In a footnote to the *Interpretation of Dreams* (1900), added in 1914, he came very close to an explicit definition of "Freudian symbol" as iconic sign. He wrote:

> Aristotle remarked . . . that the best interpreter of dreams was the man who could best grasp *similarities; for dream-pictures, like pictures on water*, are pulled out of shape by movement, and the most successful interpreter is the man who can detect the *truth* from the *misshapen picture* ([ITALICS ADDED] p. 97).

Both Hall (1953) and Morris (1946) have commented upon the psychoanalytic use of the concept of symbol. Hall noted that Freud drew on the law of association, and especially on the law of resemblance, to explain the formation of symbol (sign)-referent connections. Hall listed *resemblance* in shape, function, action, color, value, sound, physical position, and resemblance in several other characteristics as the bases for Freudian symbols. Although psychoanalytic symbols are overwhelmingly iconic in character, a few are based on indexical relationship between sign and referent. Church as a symbol of virtue is a typical example. Morris, too, tried to account for the position of psychoanalytic symbols in the general framework of semiotic and noted that they are "essentially general icons" (p. 276).

Simple as it might seem, the logical character of so-called Freudian symbols was not recognized for a long time. Ferenczi, for example, wrote a series of celebrated papers, first on so-called "hysterical materialization," later on "symbolism," which are nothing but repetitive exercises in establishing iconic relationships between *apparently* unrelated items. Thus, his analysis of hysteria and hypochondriasis (1919, 1923) consists in showing how this or that symptom or complaint "meant" such and such, because for the patient (or sometimes for the analyst) the symptom was an iconic sign of its psychoanalytic "meaning." In his papers on symbolism, he suggested that fresh bed linen, for example, "meant" a sexually unapproachable (clean) woman (1913a); or that a kite might be a symbol of erection (1913b), and so forth (1914, 1921). It is evident that there is potentially no end to such "symbols." Yet even today there still appear articles in psychoanalytic journals purporting to "discover" new symbols (e.g., Altman, 1949). The implication of this kind of work is that psychoanalytic symbols are regarded as things that "exist in nature"—like deposits of ore or petroleum—and are "discovered" by analysts. If this were not the prevailing view—that is, if such symbols were recognized as simply representing relations of similarity that can be constantly manufactured, as it were, both by patients and analysts —there would be little justification for the persistent preoccupation with symbols in psychoanalysis.

The idea that symbols possess an existential character is inherent in many psychoanalytic writings. Jung (1945, 1952), especially, has made it a cardinal point of his psychology explicitly to emphasize the "transcendental meaning" or (alleged) universality of certain symbols (the so-called archetypes). This "naturally given" quality of certain iconic signs was finally seized upon by Fromm (1951, 1957) in his concept of "universal symbol." This concept illustrates the persistent failure in psychoanalysis to recognize the nature and function of iconic signs and sign relationships. Since a sign-referent relationship that is based on similarity is so simple and basic that all human beings, irrespective of vast cultural differences, may share it, it could, in that sense, be considered "universal." But such signs are insufficient to make a "language," in the strict sense of this word.

The most recent psychoanalytic attempt to clarify the nature of symbolization was made by Fliess (1959). He coined the term "picturization" to describe precisely the same type of sign-object relationship logicians call "iconic." The foregoing examples are indicative of the significance of the problem of symbols in psychoanalysis. They also afford illustrations of the tendency to ignore the work of philosophers and students of signs (e.g., Linsky, 1952) and to create idiosyncratic (psychoanalytic) classifications of signs that are variations on the theme of iconicity.

The Function of Protolanguage

Thus far only two aspects of the "body language" characteristic of so-called hysterical symptoms have been considered. First, the elements of this language have been identified as iconic signs. (The occasional occurrence of indexical signs was noted.) It was suggested that this language be called protolanguage to set it apart from, and bring it into relation to, object and metalanguage. Second, the relationship between the iconic signs of body language and the objects they denote was analyzed. This type of inquiry is concerned with the cognitive uses of languages. Its purpose is to clarify the meaning of signs by elucidating the relationship between them and their referents (i.e., the objects to which they refer).

In the science of signs (semiotic), concern with the cognitive uses of language has been designated *semantics*. According to this usage, semantics refers to the study of the relationship between signs and objects (or denotata). Truth and falsehood are semantical indices of the relationship between sign and object. Semantics must be contrasted with pragmatics, which adds the dimension of reference to persons. In pragmatics, one studies the threefold relationship of sign-object-person. The statement "This sentence is a law of physics" illustrates the pragmatic use of language (metalanguage), for it asserts that physicists consider the sentence true (Reichenbach, 1957, pp. 15-16). Although the term "semantics" has a more general, everyday meaning, designating all sorts of studies dealing with verbal communications, I shall use it here in its restricted sense. This will be necessary to distinguish it from other types of linguistic analyses.

Following Reichenbach's classification, we may distinguish three functions, or instrumental uses, of language: the informative, the affective, and the promotive. We shall briefly examine each of these functions of protolanguage.

THE INFORMATIVE USE OF PROTOLANGUAGE

The questions that we have set for ourselves here are: What kind of information is communicated by means of iconic body-signs, and to whom? How effective is this mode of communication? What are its sources of error?

We must keep in mind that in order to undertake this type of analysis—that is, to discuss the *pragmatics of protolanguage*—it is necessary to express our findings in ordinary language or in some logical refinement of it. Thus, we translate our primary data into a symbol-system other (and logically higher) than that in which it is, as it were, given.

The principal *informative* use of a typical hysterical body sign—once again, let us consider an hysterically paralyzed arm as a paradigm—is to communicate and, hence, to convince the recipient (of the message) that the sufferer is disabled. This may be phrased as: "I am disabled," or "I am sick," or "I have been hurt," etc. The "recipient" for whom the message is intended may not be an actual person, but may rather be an internal object or parental image (i.e., the patient's superego).

In everyday usage—and particularly in medical practice—the pragmatic use of "body language" is invariably *confused* with its cognitive use. In other words, when we translate the nonverbal communication of a non-functioning arm into the form "I am sick" or "My body is disordered," we equate and confuse a nonspecific request for help with a request for a specific (in this case, medical) type of assistance. The possibility that the original communication may not have been intended as a means of informing the recipient about any particular wish or need of the sender is thus obscured and ignored. Since the patient's statement is promotive it must be translated as "Do something for me!" This utterance is logically similar to some one's saying "Shut the door!"

A cognitive analysis of such messages is irrelevant and misleading. Nevertheless, when physicians perform a differential diagnosis for an hysterical symptom, they address themselves to body signs as though they constituted cognitive communications. As a result, they come up with the answer "Yes or No," or "True or False." But to say either "Yes, you are ill"—which is what Breuer and Freud did, or "No, you are not ill (you malinger)"—which is what "hardboiled" physicians tend to do, is *equally incorrect*. This is because only semantically can an utterance be said to be true or false. Pragmatically, the issue is whether the recipient of the message believes what he has been told or not. Reichenbach (1947) wrote:

> It should be clearly seen that the instrumental usage of language falls into a category to which the predicates "true" and "false" do not apply. These predicates express a semantical relation, namely, a relation between signs and objects; but since instrumental usage is in pragmatics, i.e., includes the sign user, it cannot be judged as true or false (p. 19).

This explains why, insofar as psychiatry is concerned with the study of sign-users, a purely semantic analysis of communications must, perforce, fail to take account of some of the most significant aspects of the phenomena studied.

From the standpoint of pragmatic analysis, then, the traditional malingering-approach to hysteria is simply one of disbelief and repudiation of the cognitive use of this type of communication. Conversely, the psychoanalytic attitude is characterized by the listener's belief in what the patient says; however, the belief is based on accepting the utterance only as a report and not as a true proposition. It is as though the analyst said to the patient: "Yes, I believe that you believe that you are sick (meaning that your body is disordered). Your belief, however, is probably false. Indeed, you probably believe that you are sick—and want me to believe it—so that we should not have to deal with your 'real troubles.' "

To inquire whether a particular mode of communication serves to inform, or whether it serves some other purpose, is indispensable for sorting out various communicational situations. The purpose of chitchatting is to participate in an easygoing, pleasant human relationship. The imparting of communicatively significant messages is not a necessary part of this situation. This may be contrasted with a teaching situation, in which the teacher must convey a certain amount of novel information to the students.

In regard to medicine and psychiatry (psychoanalysis), a similar distinction seems necessary. Each of these disciplines takes a different interest in and attitude toward body signs. Physicians, concerned as they are with the functioning and breakdown of the human body as a machine, are committed to viewing "body language" as though it spoke in terms of cognitively significant messages. For instance, oppressive chest pain in a middle aged man is conceptualized as a message informing the physician of a coronary occlusion.

In contrast, psychoanalysts are committed—not, however, in the sense of an unalterable belief, but merely in the sense that this position is their characteristic operational attitude—to regard the same phenomena as cognitively insignificant, at least in the form in which they are presented. Thus, while the task of the physician is to diagnose and treat, the task of the psychoanalyst is to foster the self-reflective attitude in the patient toward his own body signs so as to effect their translation into verbal symbols. This process of translation (or sign-transformation), although it can be described in one simple sentence, is in practice a most difficult task. It constitutes, in my opinion, the core of what has been so misleadingly labeled the process of "psychoanalytic treatment" and "cure."

THE AFFECTIVE USE OF PROTOLANGUAGE

The second function to which language may be put is deliberately to arouse certain emotions in the listener and so induce him to undertake certain actions. Reichenbach called this the suggestive and I shall designate it as the affective use of language. Poetry and propaganda, for example, typically serve this function. Few utterances are entirely free of an affective (and promotive) component.

The significance of the affective use of "body language"—or generally, of the "language of illness"—can hardly be exaggerated. The impact of hysterical pantomime, to use Freud's felicitous metaphor, is a matter of everyday knowledge. It is part of our ethical belief system—that is, the rules by which we play the game of life—that we ought to feel sorry for sick people, and should try to be especially kind and helpful to them. Communication by means of body signs, therefore, often has such an instrumental purpose as its chief function. (The third function of language, namely, to induce the listener to take action, is intimately connected with its mood-influencing function.) The purpose of body signs may be simply to induce the following sort of feelings in the recipient: "Aren't you sorry for me now?" "You should be ashamed of yourself for having hurt me so!" "You should be sad (not happy and frivolous) seeing how much I suffer...," and so forth.

In this connection, it is illuminating to consider other situations in which communications are used for a similar purpose. Illustrative are the ceremonials during which the image of the crucified Christ is displayed. This spectacle acts on the recipient as a mood-inducer, commanding him to feel humble, guilty, overawed, and in general mentally constricted—and, hence, ready to be singularly attuned to the messages of those who claim to speak for the man and the deed of which the statuette is an iconic sign. Similarly, *la grande hystérie* seen at the Salpêtrière, or the flamboyant "schizophrenic bodily feelings" encountered today, represent communications in the contexts of specific communicational situations. Their aim is to suggest and induce mood rather than to convey cognitive information. And, in fact, they do induce mood as though the message had read: "Pay attention to me!" "Be impressed by how sick I am! (For I am outstanding at least in the magnitude and terribleness of my illness.)" "Be angry with me (and punish me), for look how angry and annoying I can be!" It is common knowledge that "body language" is very effective for inducing these and similar mood changes (Szasz, 1959f). It is proverbial that by shedding a few tears women can make men do almost anything. A closely related idea is expressed by the saying, "The squeaky wheel gets the grease." Implied in all this is an understanding that a complaint may sometimes be more effective for mobilizing others to action than a simple informative statement.

In general, whenever people feel unable—by means of "normal" mechanisms, such as ordinary speech—to prevail over the significant objects in their environment, they are likely to shift their pleas to the idiom of protolanguage (e.g., weeping, body signs). In other words, when one's love object fails to "listen" to verbal complaints or requests, one will be compelled, or at least tempted, to take recourse in communicating by means of iconic body signs.[5] *We have come to speak of this general phenomenon, which may take a great variety of forms, as "mental illness."* As a result, instead of seeing that people are engaged in various types of communications set in diverse communicational (or social) situations, we construct—and then ourselves come to believe in—various types of mental illnesses, such as "hysteria," "somatization reaction," "hypochondriasis," "schizophrenia," and so forth.

THE PROMOTIVE USE OF PROTOLANGUAGE

The third function of language is to make the listener perform certain actions. This is called the promotive use of language. Such commands as "Thou shalt not steal" or "Turn right" illustrate this usage. Employing the impera-

---

[5] These observations indicate that the informative use of language is most effective in egalitarian or democratic situations. In this type of situation, information will, as a rule, induce the asked-for action. Or it will evoke some sort of counterinformation. On the other hand, when a powerless person seeks aid from a relatively more powerful one, he must usually resort to the affective use of language. Simply asking for something would only expose his own weakness. In contrast, the exhibition of violent suffering might, by making the other party anxious and guilty, bring about the desired action.

tive form makes the promotive use of language explicit. Indicative sentences may also be used promotively, as for example, in the sentence "All men are created equal." Although ostensibly a descriptive-designative assertion, it is clear that the statement was intended to be, and indeed can only be, prescriptive and promotive.

Prescriptive assertions cannot be labeled either "true" or "false." Reichenbach (1947) suggested a simple method for transforming pragmatical relations into statements that may be said to be "true" or "false." This is done by making statements explicitly including the sign-user. "Thus to the imperative 'shut the door' we can coordinate the indicative sentence 'Mr. A. wishes the door to be shut.' This sentence is true or false" (p. 19). The indicative sentence, however, may not have the instrumental (promotive) function which the prescriptive sentence had.

The masquerading of promotive assertions in the guise of indicative sentences is of great practical significance in psychiatry. Statements concerning "psychosis" or "insanity," involving persons other than the psychiatrist and the patient, almost always revolve around unclarified equations of these two linguistic forms. For example, the statement "John Doe is psychotic" is ostensibly indicative and informative. Usually, however, it is promotive rather than informative, and may be translated—by explicitly including the sign-users—as follows: "Mrs. John Doe does not like the way her husband is acting. Dr. James Smith believes that men preoccupied by jealousy are 'crazy' and potentially dangerous. Hence, both Mrs. Doe and Dr. Smith want Mr. Doe to be confined in a hospital." Clearly, the indicative sentences do not have nearly the same promotive impact as does the much shorter assertion concerning "psychosis."

If language is used promotively and cannot be said to express either truth or falsehood, what does one say in response to it? The answer is that in such instances one promotive usage is opposed by another. The words "right" and "wrong," which are themselves imperatives, perform this function. The command "Thou shalt not steal" may thus be countered by saying either "right" or "wrong," depending on whether we want to make this rule our own. By saying "right" we decide to agree, and by saying "wrong" to disagree, with the speaker's value and corresponding emotional attitudes.

The clearest form in which patients (and physicians) have employed "body language" is undoubtedly in its promotive usage. I refer to such symptoms as, for example, headache or dysmenorrhea in a woman who feels overburdened. By communicating in terms of these complaints (symptoms) she may be able to induce her husband to be more attentive and helpful toward her. And if not her husband, her physician. The action-inducing meaning of iconic body signs, in general, may be paraphrased as follows: ("I am sick, therefore . . .) Take care of me!"—"Be good to me!"—"Make my husband do such and such!"—"Tell my draft board to stop bothering me!"—"Tell the court and the judge that I was not responsible!" And so forth.

From the standpoint of our present analysis, the entire change in renaming certain illnesslike forms of behavior from "malingering" to "hysteria" (and "mental illness") can be understood as nothing but a linguistic change employed for the purpose of achieving a new type of action-orientedness in the listener. The verbal change, as first advocated by Charcot, served to command those charged with dealing with "hysterics" to abandon their moral-condemnatory attitude toward them and to adopt instead a solicitous and benevolent attitude, such as befitted the physician vis-à-vis his patient.

"Intelligence is a slippery customer; if one door is closed to it, it finds, or even breaks, another entrance into the world. If one symbolism is inadequate, it seizes another; there is no eternal decree over its means and methods. So I will go with the logicians and linguists as far as they like, but do not promise to go no further. For there is an unexplored possibility of genuine semantic beyond the limits of discursive language."

Susanne K. Langer (1942, pp. 69-70)

CHAPTER 8 | # Hysteria as
Nondiscursive Language

To understand the function or uses of language can be both easy and difficult. It is relatively easy if we limit the task to the function of language in a specialized discipline, such as logic or mathematics. It is rather difficult if we try to account for all of man's uses of communicative behavior.

Two principal functions of language are usually distinguished: (1) to inform and influence, and (2) to vent emotions. The distinction between cognitive-informative and affective-expressive uses of language parallels the traditional division of the "human mind" into cognitive and emotional "parts." Rigid adherence to this classification tends to recodify and foster the misleading dichotomy between pure thought or cognition on the one hand and pure emotion or feeling on the other. Analysis of the function of nondiscursive languages should help us to modify this false image of man and his "mind."

Our knowledge concerning the informative uses of language is the most extensive and complete. Logic, mathematics, and the sciences generally employ language only, or predominantly, in this way. Indeed, probably because science is so intimately associated with the informative use of language, scientists and philosophers have repeatedly suggested that "the essential business of language is to assert or deny facts" (Russell, 1922, p. 8). This is true, however, only for the language of science, mathematics, and logic, and is false for sign-using behavior encountered in many other situations. As Rapoport (1954) aptly observed:

It is not necessary to look into books on philosophy to find words without referents. Any commencement speech, sermon, newspaper editorial, or radio commercial follows the same philosophic tradition of reinforcing the delusion that anything which is talked about is real: success, charity, public opinion, and four-way indigestion relief. Indeed, nothing is easier than to "define" these noises so as to make it appear that they mean something (p. 18).

These "noises" of everyday speech, which have a great deal in common with the "noises" of psychiatric symptoms, require that we consider the second principal function of language. This, according to logicians, consists of the expression of emotions, feelings, or desires. These expressions, in Langer's (1942) words, are "not symbols for thought, but *symptoms of the inner life,* like tears and laughter, crooning, or profanity" ([ITALICS ADDED] p. 67).

Langer, with whose views I am in general agreement, criticized this black-and-white view of language, according to which signs that do not have clearly defined referents outside the speaker are regarded as mere expressions of the speaker's inner life. While the expressive function is not denied, it is held that various sign-systems may have functions that are at once representative-informative and expressive. In *Philosophy in a New Key* (1942), Langer asserted that there was a necessity for a "genuine semantic beyond the limits of discursive language" (p. 70). Although she made some tentative suggestions concerning the directions in which it might be sought, particularly in regard to the language of music and the visual arts, her work in this regard remained mostly programmatic. One of the purposes of this book is to implement this program by providing a *systematic semiotical analysis of a language-form hitherto regarded as purely expressive,* i.e., *the language of certain bodily signs.*

Discursive and Nondiscursive Languages

The distinction between discursive and nondiscursive symbol-systems—or broadly speaking, languages—has proved to be an indispensable polarity for logic and modern philosophy. Let us first see precisely what is meant by these concepts. Then we shall consider their application to our special problem.

In addition to classifying languages according to their logical complexity or "level" as object and metalanguages, philosophers have proposed still another way to order symbol-systems, namely, by the degree of their discursiveness. *Discursiveness is essentially a measure of the degree of arbitariness of symbolization.* Mathematics and the languages of the various sciences serve the sole function of transmitting information. So-called nondiscursive (or, more precisely, relatively slightly discursive) languages, on the other hand, serve mainly the purpose of emotional expression. Art, dance, and the ritual are characteristic examples. In these communications, symbolization is idiosyncratic rather than conventional.

The special significance of the picture as symbol was emphasized by Langer (1942, pp. 76-77). She noted that a picture, say, of a person, does not describe the man who posed for it but rather presents a replica of him. For this reason, nondiscursive symbolism is often called presentational. It is evident, too, that while discursive symbolism has primarily a general reference, a presentational symbol, on the contrary, presents a specific, individual object. The former is thus eminently abstract, the latter exquisitely concrete. The word "apple" refers to every conceivable apple in the universe, but does not, per se, point to any specific apple. The photograph of an apple, in contrast, represents only the specific apple whose picture it is (Ruesch and Kees, 1956).

In the earliest forms of written language, formal representation of communication was achieved by means of iconic signs. Hieroglyphs are a form of picture writing. According to Schlauch (1942), the two simplest elements in written language are pictographs and ideographs. Both express their messages by means of pictures that resemble the object or idea to be conveyed. They could be regarded as the earliest prototypes of what today is called the analogic type of codification.[1] *Kinesics* (Birdwhistell, 1949), therefore, could be regarded as a modern attempt systematically to explore and understand the hieroglyphics that a person writes, not on marble tablets, but on and with his own body.

The advantages of discursive symbolism for transmitting information are known and generally appreciated. The question may be asked: Does nondiscursive symbolism have any function besides that of expressing emotions? Indeed, it has several such functions. First, we shall examine its value for transmitting information of a special kind. Since verbal symbols *describe* the objects they denote in a relatively general, abstract fashion, the identification of a specific object requires much circumlocution (unless it has a *name*, which is a very special kind of discursive sign).

> For this reason [wrote Langer (1942)] the correspondence between a word-picture and a visible object can never be as close as that between the object and its photograph. Given all at once to the intelligent eye, an incredible wealth and detail of information

[1] The distinction between analogic and digital codification corresponds to the distinction between iconic and conventional symbolization (Wiener, 1950, pp. 64-73).

is conveyed by the portrait, where we do not have to stop to construe verbal meanings. That is why we use a photograph rather than a description on a passport or in the Rogue's Gallery (p. 77).

A moment's reflection will tell us that so-called hysterical body signs, *as pictures*, bear a much greater similarity to the objects which they depict than do words describing the same objects.[2] To exhibit, by means of bodily signs—say, by paralyses or convulsions—the idea and message that "I am sick" is at once more striking and more informative than simply saying the words, "I am sick." *Body signs portray—literally, present—in exactly what way the sufferer considers himself sick.* Thus, in the symbolism of his symptom, the patient could be said to present his own (highly condensed) autobiography. This is well appreciated among psychoanalytic practitioners. It is part of the lore of clinical psychoanalysis that the patient's presenting symptom—if he has one—contains, as it were, the entire history and structure of his "neurosis." When psychoanalysts say that even the simplest symptom can be understood fully only in retrospect, looking back on a thorough analysis of the patient, they mean that in order to understand the patient's "symptom" we must be acquainted with all the historically unique features of his personality development and social circumstances.

The situation in regard to cases of typical organic disease is quite different. The patient's symptom—say, angina pectoris (due to coronary insufficiency) —is not autobiographical; in other words, it is not personal and idiosyncratic, at least not characteristically so. Instead, the symptom is anatomically and physiologically determined. The structure of the body sets definite limits on its function. Substernal pain cannot possibly be the sign of, say, a ruptured ovarian cyst. My point is that knowledge of the rules of pathological anatomy and physiology make it possible to infer the "meaning" of the "messages" of certain bodily symptoms. In order to make similar inferences from iconic symbolism, however, it is of no use to be familiar with the logic of the language of medicine. Rather, familiarity with the personality of the sign-user, including his family background, personal history, religion, occupation, and so forth, is required. Accordingly, although so-called psychiatric symptoms are idiosyncratic (in the sense that they are personal), they may be shown to exhibit certain patterns of regularity.

[2] Treating certain forms of behavior as pictures, used to communicate messages, is also useful in comprehending such everyday acts as wearing certain distinctive articles of clothing (e.g., caps, jackets, the use of pipes, etc.). Such "dressing up" behavior is like saying: "I belong to this group," or "I am so and so" (as a means of self-identification, e.g., "I am a Harvard man"). Uniforms, of course, are used deliberately to bestow a specific identity or role on a person, such as "You are in the Navy, now," or "You are an officer," etc. In all these situations we deal with the uses of iconic signs.

These will depend on the patient's personal and social experiences—in brief, on what he has learned as a human being. The experienced (or "intuitive") psychotherapist is one who is familiar with the "meanings" of the predominant patterns of "psychiatric symptoms" or difficulties in a given culture.

It is to be expected that the nondiscursive or presentational form of symbolism should readily lend itself to the expression and communication of so-called psychiatric problems. Such problems pertain to personal difficulties that are, by nature, concrete experiences. Human beings have troubles with their mothers, fathers, brothers, and so forth *as concrete human beings*. They do not suffer from the effects of Oedipal complexes or sexual instincts as abstractions. This is only stating what is obvious. It follows, however, that the use of iconic body signs has the advantage of fitting specifically the references to some individual object. Iconic signs and most "psychiatric symptoms" do not, like the symbols of ordinary language, have a general reference, but point rather to specific individuals or events. The transformation (for it cannot properly be called translation) of presentational symbols into conventional signs (ordinary words), such as occurs in the course of psychoanalysis and some forms of psychotherapy, is thus seen as itself constituting a process of personality change ("treatment"). This should not be construed to mean that verbalization per se is the most significant feature of psychological "treatment." Nor should this idea be confused with the early psychoanalytic notion of "catharsis." On the contrary, a semiotical analysis of psychiatric operations should enable us to see more clearly, and to describe more accurately, the precise mechanisms by which talking often helps people to cope with their problems in living.

THE NONDISCURSIVENESS OF HYSTERIA

To avoid becoming lost in a maze of abstractions insufficiently anchored in empirical observations, let us consider some of Freud's clinical observations, cited earlier. They illustrate that the communicative aspects of hysterical symptoms are incomprehensible in terms of the logic of everyday speech. Discussing the differences between organic and hysterical pains, Freud (Breuer and Freud, 1893-1895) stated:

> I was struck by the indefiniteness of all the descriptions of the
> character of her pains given me by the patient, who was nevertheless a highly intelligent person. A patient suffering from *organic pains* will, unless he is *neurotic in addition*, describe them *definitely* and *calmly*. He will say, for instance, that they are shooting pains,

that they occur at certain intervals, that they extend from this place to that and that they seem to him to be brought on by one thing or another. Again, when a *neurasthenic describes his pains,* he gives an impression of being engaged in a difficult intellectual task to which his strength is quite unequal. He is clearly of the opinion that *language is too poor to find words for his sensations* and that these sensations are something unique and previously unknown, of which it would be quite impossible to give an exhaustive description ([ITALICS ADDED] p. 136).

Freud's excellent clinical description brings out how exceedingly difficult it is for the patient to find words for his so-called "sensations." This is often also true for patients expressing bodily feelings associated with many so-called psychiatric syndromes other than hysteria (e.g., hypochondriasis, schizophrenia, depression) (Szasz, 1957a). This has been generally explained in two ways. Most often, it is attributed to the "fact" that the patient has unusual or peculiar feelings, difficult to put into words (Fenichel, 1945). It has also been ascribed to an over-all impoverishment in the use of verbal language. Without negating the relevance of either of these explanations, let me suggest another. The symptom—say, a pain or bodily feeling—may be part of a symbol system, albeit not of a discursive type. The difficulty in expressing the "feeling" in verbal language is due to the fact that nondiscursive languages do not lend themselves to translation into other idioms, least of all into discursive forms. Rapoport (1954) stated this clearly:

When one deals with nondiscursive languages, translation becomes impossible altogether. For example, music cannot be translated into English. The translation of poetry from one language into another is notoriously difficult, especially if the languages are those of widely dissimilar cultures. A most meticulous description of a dance or ritual will miss the whole point of what it describes.

The reason for this dissimilarity between discursive and non-discursive languages lies in the fact that the nondiscursive symbols are not arbitrary like the discursive ones but are more or less bound up with the meaning to be conveyed. The referents of the nondiscursive symbols (if they can be so called) are not "out there" in the world. The connection between symbol and referent is not arrived at by explicit agreement among the communicants as in the case of discursive symbols. Rather, the referents of nondiscursive symbols are inside the communicants. Hence, they have meaning only if the communicants are somehow attuned to each other (p. 199).

The thesis that the referents of nondiscursive symbols have meaning only if the communicants are attuned to each other is in harmony with the empirical operations of psychoanalysis. Analytic technique rests on the tacit assumption that we cannot know—in fact, must not even expect to know— what troubles our patients until we have become attuned to them.

The Informative Function of Iconic Body Signs

To what extent, and precisely how, may nondiscursive languages be used to transmit information? This question has occupied philosophers and students of signs for some time. Thus far, the weight of opinion has favored those who have maintained that nondiscursive languages cannot be used to transmit information because nondiscursive signs point to their referents too vaguely and ambiguously. At the same time, it has been generally appreciated that some sort of information-transmitting does occur by means of these symbol-systems. The informative function of a special type of nondiscursive language, namely, of so-called hysterical body signs, has long been of interest to psychiatrists. Although hysteria has been approached *as though it were a language,* it has not been systematically codified in this way. Let us therefore consider the *informative uses of iconic body signs as a system of nondiscursive language.*[3]

In general, the informative use of language depends on the referents of its symbols. The radical positivist view, probably rarely held today, maintains that nondiscursive languages have no referents at all. Accordingly, messages framed in this idiom are held to be meaningless (from a cognitive-informative standpoint). A more balanced and, I think, today more widely accepted philosophical position regards the difference between discursive and nondiscursive languages as a matter of degree rather than kind. Hence, nondiscursive languages, too, have referents and "cognitive meaning."

Rapoport (1954), for example, suggested that the referents of nondiscursive symbols are the "inner states" of the communicants. Although Rapoport recognized that nondiscursive languages have referents, he nevertheless adhered to a somewhat dichotomous "out there—in here" classification of them. He thus regarded discursive referents as ideally adapted to the use of conveying information, while nondiscursive referents were assigned the function which I have called *affective.* By this was meant the transmission of a feeling state from one person to another (i.e., pain, joy, sorrow). This is a familiar phenomenon in clinical psychiatry, as it is also in the world

[3] This analysis will apply to phenomena variously labeled "hysteria," "hypochondriasis," "schizophrenia," and so forth. The distinguishing feature is the use of *body signs* and their *iconicity.* The labels of traditional psychiatric nosology are of little use to us in ascertaining where or when to expect to find such signs (Szasz, 1957a).

of art. For example, in psychiatry we speak of the "contagiousness" of anxiety—say, of panic in a burning theater. Although this process may be described as a reproduction of "the referent within one communicant inside the other" (Rapoport, 1954, p. 200), to do so is somewhat misleading, since it would seem that at least in some circumstances a more genuinely cognitive communication takes place.

It is true, of course, that this kind of communication is simple and concrete. Still, it is *not merely* a communication of the sender's inner experience. Consider the example of people fleeing from a burning theater. The panicky behavior of some members of the audience may signify—even to those who saw neither flames nor heard anyone shout "Fire!"—*more* than mere panic. It is true that, first, one may respond to the purely affective function of body language: "People around me are afraid, panicky: I, too, *feel* panicky." Yet, along with this, there is a simultaneous communication of a more informative (cognitive) message: "I am in danger! I must flee to save myself, or otherwise make sure that I shall be safe (e.g., by checking, as best I can, whether there really is a danger present)."

This example is intended to show that the referent *inside* a communicant—say, his affect—can not be detached from the experiencing person's *relationship to the world about him*. In other words, affects are at once private—"inner referents," and public—indices of relationships between ego and object(s) (Szasz, 1957a). Affects (feelings, sensations) are thus the primary link between inner experiences and outer, publicly verifiable occurrences. This is the basis for assigning more than subjective, idosyncratic meanings to referents of nondiscursive languages. Accordingly, the limitation or defect of iconic body signs does not lie only in the subjectiveness of the experience and its expression—that is, in the fact that no one can feel another's pain. Rather, it lies partly in the fact that such signs—say, a person writhing in pain—present a picture that, standing alone, has a very limited cognitive content.

The study of *gestures* is pertinent in this connection. Critchley (1939) has described many striking parallels in the development, use, and pathology of speech and gesture. Gesture is the earliest faculty of communication, the "elder brother of speech" (p. 121). This developmental fact is consistent with the relatively primitive cognitive use to which this form of communication may be put, and with the equally primitive learning (imitation, identification) which it subserves. In semiotical terms, gesture is a sign-system of very high iconicity, verbal speech of very low iconicity, while the notation of mathematics is completely noniconic.

Critchley also commented on the concrete, action-oriented nature of gestural communication as opposed to the relatively more abstract and, therefore, potentially more contemplative character of speech:

> The weakness of the mimic art lies in the difficulty which narration meets as soon as action, or the dialogue of action, is abandoned. It becomes almost impossible to deal intelligibly with such situations as speaking of a person who has not yet appeared upon the scene or who is off stage, or of an object not on the stage, or retailing a past action or outlining a future one (p. 102).

Concrete, action-oriented gestures are manifestations of an early stage in the maturational history of the human being as a *social animal*. The ability to wait, to defer action, to inhibit impulses, to learn by abstraction rather than by imitation, and, finally, to learn about learning itself are features of increasing psychosocial maturation. Collectively, as they are manifested in diverse and increasingly complex uses of symbols, they constitute the differences between adult and child.

HYSTERIA, TRANSLATION, AND MISINFORMATION

When hysterical body signs are used to transmit information, they suffer the same weakness as do nondiscursive languages generally. Weakly discursive languages cannot be readily translated into more strongly discursive ones. When such translation is attempted, the possibilities for error are vast, since virtually any discursive rendition of the original "message" will, in a sense, be false! Hence, there are two basic reasons why hysterical symptoms so often *misinform*. One reason, as just noted, is the linguistic difficulty of rendering nondiscursive symbolism into discursive form. The other reason is that the message may be intended for an archaic internal object—and, therefore, may not be intended at all for the recipient who actually interprets it *here* and *now*.

Misinformation is bound to be generated whenever a communication, framed in the idiom of iconic body signs, is interpreted in (i.e., translated into) the scientific-cognitive language of medicine. Illustrative is the case of the patient who "says" that he is sick by means of hysterical pantomime, and whose communication is interpreted by the physician in terms of the language of medicine. Since according to this special scientific idiom "sickness" means a disorder of the physical body, the patient's original message will constitute a bit of misinformation (for the physician).

Of course, misinformation—whether it be a mistake or a lie—may be communicated by means of ordinary language as well as by iconic body signs. We speak of a lie when the misinformation is considered to serve the speaker's interests and when it is believed that he has sent the false message deliberately. A mistake, by contrast, is an error made indifferently. Hence, a "deliberate mistake" is a logical impossibility. But mistakes out of ignorance or lack of skill (conditions which could be the results of deliberate planning) are possible.

The concepts of *lie* and *mistake*, as two categories of error, closely parallel the twin concepts of *malingering* and *hysteria*. When physicians (or others) speak of malingering, they assume that the patient is lying in order to gain an advantage for himself. In contrast, a mistake is an error from which the person who committed it does not usually benefit—although, since it was made indifferently, he might. It is often assumed, quite erroneously, that mistakes—as opposed to lies—are always injurious to those who make them. In this respect, too, there is a parallel between being mistaken and being sick. Both are obviously unpleasant and potentially harmful, yet both may be turned to advantage. As malingering with body signs corresponds to lying with words, so "hysteria" and "mental illness" correspond to making a mistake. In describing this contrast between lying and erring, I have deliberately avoided the concept of consciousness. It seems to me that when the adjectives "consciously" and "unconsciously" are used as explanations, they complicate and obscure the problem. The traditional psychoanalytic idea that so-called conscious imitation of illness is "malingering" and hence "not illness," whereas its allegedly unconscious simulation is itself "illness" ("hysteria"), creates more problems than it solves. It would seem more useful to *distinguish between goal-directed and rule-following behavior on the one hand, and indifferent mistakes on the other.* Psychoanalytic theory has tended to exclude indifferent mistakes from the realm of human behavior. This was the result of having tacitly assumed that all actions are goal-directed. It then followed that a person's failure to perform adequately would not be due to his ignorance of the rules of the game or to lack of skill in the task. Rather, the failure itself was regarded as a goal, albeit an unconscious one. This hypothesis and the therapeutic attitude it inspired are exceedingly useful. But it is self-evident that not all human error is of this purposive kind. To insist on this view is to negate the very possibility of genuine error.

By reintroducing the distinction between goal-directed misinformation and indifferent error into psychiatry and psychoanalysis, I believe we shall be able to clarify many problems in human behavior. In the case of hysteria, for example, Freud himself emphasized the quasi-rational, goal-directed nature of the process. And so did Shakespeare when he spoke of there being *method* in madness. In brief, *it is more accurate to regard hysteria as a lie than as a mistake.* People caught in a lie usually maintain that they were merely mistaken. The difference between mistakes and lies, when discovered, is chiefly pragmatic.[4] From a purely cognitive point of view, both are simply falsehoods.

Language as a Means of Making Contact with Objects

Thus far, the structure and function of iconic body signs have been examined in the light of the concepts and principles of semiotic. Accordingly, we have considered the informative, affective, and promotive uses of hysteria as a language. However, there remains another function of this language—and of languages generally—which has not hitherto been formally identified, and to the analysis of which we shall now turn.

The study of hysteria, and of psychiatric problems generally, places Donne's famous utterance, "No man is an island, entire of itself," in a new scientific perspective (Szasz, 1959f). Human beings *need* other human beings. This need cannot be reduced to other, more elementary, needs. Freud himself went far in elucidating the young child's vast need for and hence dependence on his parents, especially his mother. Indeed, *regression* was one of Freud's key concepts. By this it was meant that, generally speaking, man finds psychosocial maturation burdensome. Thus, he has a tendency to return to earlier, psychosocially less complex modes of functioning. Implicit in this concept is the idea that when human contact at the current (adult) level proves unendurable, contact is sought at an earlier, more easily masterable level.

The psychology of object relationships—which I hold to be the quintessence of present-day psychoanalysis—presupposes the need for objects. If so viewed, *the task of psychoanalysis as a science is to study and elucidate the kinds of objects people need, and the exact ways in which they need them.* Some generalizations may be formulated. For example, children have a relatively greater need for supportive external objects, whereas adults often turn to internal objects for such help. A large part of recent psychoanalytic literature is devoted to discussions of the various mechanisms for seeking and maintaining object relationships. Emphasis on an object-relationship point of view has made it possible to interpret such phenomena as touching, caressing, cuddling and, of course, sexual intercourse itself as means of *making contact* with objects.

---

[4] What is meant by this is that we hold people responsible for lies but not, as a rule, for mistakes. This leads to the vast problem of the observer's *attitude* toward various forms of personal conduct. For it depends largely on how behavior is *judged* whether it will be rewarded, ignored, punished, treated as illness, etc.

We have no reason to assume that what is true for gestural (nonverbal) communications is not also true for verbal language. In other words, I submit that, since all communicative behavior, by definition, is addressed to someone, it has, among other functions, also the aim of making contact with another human being. We may call this *the object-seeking and relationship-maintaining function of language*. The significance and success of this function varies with the discursiveness of the particular idiom. It seems to be a general rule that if the main aim of the communication is to establish human contact, the language used to achieve it will be relatively nondiscursive (e.g., chitchat, dancing, schizophrenic bodily symptoms). Because of this, we are justified in treating relatively slightly discursive communications mainly as techniques for making contact with objects (people) rather than as techniques for symbolic learning.

This viewpoint lends special poignancy to the interpretation of such things as the dance, music, religious ritual, and the representative arts (painting, sculpture). In all of these, the participant or viewer can enter into a significant—that is, emotionally charged or cathected—relationship with an object by means of the nondiscursive sign-system employed. Using a pharmaceutical analogy, it might be said that the language (i.e., the dance, art, etc.) is the vehicle in which the active ingredient—human contact—is suspended and contained. Many things that people do together have this predominant function, whether it be playing bridge or tennis, going hunting with a friend, or attending a scientific meeting. I do not mean to imply that these situations serve no other functions. Surely, the hunter, though sharing his experience with a friend, may have to feed his family; or a person may attend a scientific meeting to learn from lectures. These instrumental tasks may be overshadowed, however, by the human relationship component of the situation.

Traditionally, language has been viewed as serving the purpose of transmitting "facts" or "truth" from one person to another. This assumption has seriously obscured the object-seeking and relationship-maintaining function of language. Consider, for example, the Biblical account of God speaking to Moses. Their communication was in *dead earnest*. In other words, they did not chitchat to satisfy their (or, in this case Moses's) need for companionship. Instead, God gave Moses the *Law*. The Divine Law is regarded, of course, as a piece of suprahuman "truth," or, in philosophical terms, the quintessence of the positivist's concept of a "logical assertion." But surely nowadays communications in a formally religious setting serve chiefly the function of seeking and maintaining object relationships. Hence, irrespective of how nonsensical, from a cognitive point of view, religious beliefs may be, this does not detract from their satisfying the believer's needs for objects.

Herein lies the main reason for the relative ineffectiveness of logical or scientific arguments alone against religious, national, and professional myths.

The foregoing illustration affords a striking instance of the general intellectual tendency to assume that the important thing in verbal communication is the (logical) content of the message. Thus we look for all sorts of meanings in language, and rightly so. This very meaningfulness, however, distracts attention from the nonspecific object-seeking function of language.[5] Accordingly, people are most apt to recognize this function when the meaning of the communication is blatantly unimportant or absent. This is the case in what we call chitchat. The object-seeking function of verbal language is significant also in many everyday situations. In the small child, it is manifested by incessant questions: "Daddy, what is this, where does it come from, can we have some, can we do this?" Intelligence, curiosity, or the wish to explore one's environment may all have something to do with this type of behavior. In addition, I believe that the child has learned that the *exchange* of verbal communications is a most effective and gratifying technique for being with another person. In this sense, speaking is simply another, more sophisticated, form of seeing, touching, or cuddling. A few words in the dark, or the parents' quiet conversation in another room, tend to have a reassuring effect on children for the same reason.

In general, the object-seeking function of language is most important during the early years of life. As psychological maturation progresses its place is gradually taken over by the informative function of communication. This transformation is represented in condensed form in Table 4. The child's earliest communications often have as their chief aim to seek objects and to maintain contact with them. This does not deny the expressive and informative aspects of early communications, with which we are not concerned here. As maturation progresses, the grasping-function, as it were, of communication diminishes. Gradually, situations of mutual interest arise. Slowly but steadily, children learn to use language abstractly. Major psychological commitment to reading and writing implies an orientation to persons not physically present. While verbal language, as well as the special languages of science, retain an object-seeking quality, this feature becomes increasingly less personal.

Abstract symbol-systems, such as mathematics, become especially valuable for object-seeking for schizoid personalities, precisely because of this feature. Object contact may be sought and obtained by means of abstract symbol-

[5] A logically perfect language, according to Russell (1922), is one that avoids contradictions. Mathematics comes closest to this ideal. Of course, there is no ordinary language that even approximates logical perfection, nor indeed is there any reason to believe that this would be a desirable or feasible aim for it (Black, 1951, pp. 251-255).

TABLE 4. MATURATION OF THE OBJECT-SEEKING FUNCTION OF LANGUAGE

Developmental Stage	Typical Communications and Their Effects on the Recipient	Linguistic Characteristics	What Is Gained and/or Learned?
The baby's cry	Crying, weeping, bodily manifestations of suffering and discomfort: "Feel like me!" "Come to me!"	Nonverbal, nondiscursive, high degree of iconicity	Early identifications; maintenance of the organism
The child's verbal complaint	"It hurts!" "I can't sleep!" "Take care of me!" "Don't leave me!"	Verbal, nondiscursive, reduced degree of iconicity	Internalization of objects and building of the self
The child's questioning	"What is it called?" "Where does it come from?" "Can we have some?"	Verbal, increasingly discursive, noniconic (conventional) signs	Internalization of objects; acquisition of information or knowledge
The adolescent's intelligent conversation	Intellectual curiosity: "Talk to me." "Be interested in me (my mind)." "Respect me for my thoughts and knowledge."	Verbal, increasingly discursive	Same as above; identification as adult by relating to adult objects; increasing emphasis on knowledge as a source of self-esteem
The (young) adult student's communicative attitude toward his teacher	The wish for personal instruction: "Teach me!"	Verbal or special discursive symbol systems	Symbols, skills, and knowledge. (Gradually diminishing interest in teacher as person)
Communication with books	The wish to learn impersonally: "Teach me!" as a message addressed to a physically absent person	Same as above	Same as above in a context of individual achievement
Communication with others in a cooperative situation	The wish to learn in a cooperative enterprise; not "Teach me!" but rather "We shall participate together, exchange ideas and skills, and learn from each other."	Same as above	Same as above in a context of cooperative achievement

systems while at the same time a distance may be maintained between self and object. It is virtually impossible to have a relationship and yet maintain such distance with concrete external objects (people). The fascination with and value of abstractions—whether as "addiction" to books or as religious or scientific systems—lie precisely in this. Yet, for persons employing such schizoid strategies, the lack of concreteness of the object and the ego's persistent lack of contact with people contribute further to an already troublesome alienation from the world of human beings and hence remains a constant source of danger for them.

The object-seeking function of hysteria is of special significance to the work of psychotherapy. Freud's essential thesis was that hysteria constituted a behavioral technique invoked by patients, especially women, when they could reach their love-objects in no other way. When verbal communications, such as pleading and explanations failed, hysteria was tried in the hope that it might succeed. Thus, a woman unable to enlist her husband's sympathy, attention, and interest under so-called normal circumstances, was able to do so when she "fell ill with hysteria." This important social fact has as much to do with the psychology of the receiver of messages as with the psychology of the sender. The early modes of communication—such as crying or temper tantrums—make a much more massive assault on the receiver than do communications framed in the idiom of polite conversation. While the latter can be ignored, the former can not. Hysterical pantomime, much like the demands of children, exerts a powerful effect on the person toward whom it is directed. Confronted with so-called hysterical symptoms (i.e., iconic body signs) therapists as well as marriage partners find it extremely difficult to not respond. And since a response per se is what is sought, at least partly, since it indicates interest and affection, *the value* of hysteria (and of many other so-called mental illnesses) as a technique for making contact with an object is very real indeed. This, however, must not be confused either with "primary" or "secondary gain." The object-seeking value of iconic body signs contains elements of both primary and secondary gain in that both of these refer to attaining ends which themselves presuppose a relationship with an object.

The main difference between the idea set forth here and the traditional psychoanalytic one is that while the latter rests heavily on the distinction between conscious and unconscious motives, and the parallel dichotomy of gaining advantage in a current life situation versus satisfying an infantile need, the former is able to dispense with them. I submit that both sets of constructs are valid and indispensable for the work of psychoanalysis. In the psychoanalytic treatment situation, the object-seeking aspects of hysteria as a language must be adequately explored and made conscious before attempting the actual working out of conflicts.

"We have gathered an impression that the formation of obscure dreams occurs as though one person who was dependent upon a second person had to make a remark which was bound to be disagreeable in the ears of this second one; and it is on the basis of this simile that we have arrived at the concepts of dream-distortion and censorship, and have endeavoured to translate our impression into a psychological theory which is no doubt crude but is at least lucid."

Sigmund Freud (1901, p. 677)

CHAPTER 9 | # Hysteria as
Indirect Communication

Another general characteristic of communications, singularly pertinent to the problem of hysteria, remains to be discussed. It is the relative directness or indirectness of language. This distinction, which is old, rests on the empirical criteria of ambiguity and misunderstanding.

Direct and Indirect Communications

The notions of directness (of communications) and discursiveness are closely related. Highly discursive languages, such as mathematical symbolism, permit only direct communications. Mathematical signs have clearly defined referents, accepted by the mutual agreement of all who engage in "conversation" in this idiom. Ambiguity and misunderstanding are thus reduced to a minimum.

The principal cause of linguistic misunderstanding is that signs may be used in more than one way. In ordinary language, for example, certain signs are employed in several different senses—a circumstance that allows for much ambiguity and hence misunderstanding. By the same token, referential ambiguity allows one to make indirect communications intentionally, by employing expressions known to be interpretable in more than one way. The *multiplicity of meanings* that may be attached to a communication is the specific quality that allows it to be used as an indirect communication.

148

The difference between indirectness and nondiscursiveness now becomes apparent. A language is called nondiscursive not because its signs have a multiplicity of well-defined referents, but rather because the referents are idiosyncratic and, hence, poorly defined from everyone's viewpoint but the sign-user's (and sometimes even from his, too). Directness and discursiveness overlap at one end, in that highly discursive expressions are also direct. They do not overlap at the other end, for nondiscursiveness per se is no guarantee that the language is useful for indirect communications. For this purpose a language of considerable discursiveness (as for example ordinary language) is required. In addition, a certain laxity of language rules is necessary, enabling specific signs to carry multiple references. (The important distinction between denotative and connotative meanings will not concern us here.)

The deliberate use of indirect communications is called hinting, alluding, or speaking in metaphor. The English language is very rich in expressions for indirect communications. In addition to the terms listed, double talk, innuendo, insinuation, implication, and punning are terms used to identify and describe indirect communications of different types. While hinting is neutral in regard to what is being alluded to, innuendo and insinuation refer only to depreciatory allusions. Significantly, innuendo and insinuation have no antonyms. In other words, there are no expressions in the English language (or in any other language, to my knowledge) to describe insinuating something "good" about someone. Although flattery might at times be communicated by allusion, the fact that no special word exists for it provides linguistic support for the thesis that hinting serves mainly to protect the speaker who is afraid to offend.

The general psychological function of allusions will be considered first. Then hysteria, as a typical metaphorical communication, will be discussed.

The Psychology of Hinting

Although seldom explicitly entertained, educated persons generally understand the psychological function of hinting. Accordingly, our concern here will be chiefly to make certain covert ideas explicit. At the same time, it should be possible to add to our understanding of the conditions that foster direct communications and allusions, respectively.

It seems to be a general rule that whenever information-seeking is a primary concern, direct communications will predominate. So-called statements of facts—for example, "snow is white"—and scientific documents generally consist of direct communications. Their aim is to communicate by means of maximally concise and unambiguous messages. The relationship between the communicants—for instance, whether or not they like each other —is not relevant in such circumstances.

In contrast, whenever the relationship between two people is uncertain— and hence when either or both of the communicants feels threatened and inhibited—the stage is set for the exchange of relatively indirect messages. This is because indirect messages serve a dual function—first, to transmit information, and second, to explore and modify the nature of the relationship. The exploratory function of indirect communications may include the utilitarian aim of attempting, however subtly, to change another person's attitude so as to make him receptive toward our needs.

Courtship affords many excellent illustrations of indirect communications. Consider, for example, the "dating game" as played by college students (Gorer, 1948). The boy may desire uncomplicated sex play and perhaps sexual intercourse. The girl, too, may more or less share this interest. In the initial stages of the dating game, however, neither knows how the other wants to play. In fact, they usually do not even know precisely what kind of game they are going to play. It should be recalled that our cultural setting is one in which direct communications about sexual interests and activities are discouraged or even prohibited. Hinting and alluding thus become indispensable.

Indirect communications permit communicative contacts when, without them, the alternatives would be total inhibition, silence, and solitude on the one hand or communicative behavior that is direct and hence forbidden on the other hand. Both of these alternatives are painful. In actual practice, neither is likely to result in the gratification of the needs motivating the behavior. In this dilemma, indirect communications provide a much-needed compromise. As one of the early moves in the dating game, the boy might invite the girl to dinner or to the movies. These communications are polyvalent: the boy's suggestion, and the girl's response to it have several "levels" of meaning. One is the level of the overt message—that is, will they have dinner together, go to a movie, and so forth. Another, covert level pertains to the question of sexual activity. On this level, acceptance of the dinner invitation means that sexual overtures may perhaps be made. Conversely, rejection means not only refusal of companionship for dinner but also that further exploration of sexual activity is rejected. There may be still other levels of meaning. For instance, acceptance of the offer may be interpreted as a sign of personal (sexual) worth and hence be cause for increased self-approval, whereas rejection may mean the opposite and stimulate feelings of worthlessness.

Freud was a master at elucidating the psychological function of indirect communications. Speaking of the patient's associations to neurotic symptoms, he wrote: "The idea occurring to the patient must be in the nature of an *allusion* to the repressed element, like a representation of it in indirect speech" (Freud, 1910a, p. 30). The concept of indirect communication occupies a central position in Freud's theory of dream work and neurotic symptom formation. He compared dream formation to the difficulty which confronts "the political writer who has disagreeable truths to tell those in authority" (Freud, 1900, p. 141). The political writer, much as the dreamer, cannot communicate directly. The censor will not allow it. Hence, they must avail themselves of "indirect representations" (pp. 141-142).

Metaphorical communication is also a frequent source of jokes, cartoons, and humor of all sorts. Why is the story of the rich playboy asking the aspiring actress to come to his apartment to view his etchings funny? It is evident (to an adult audience) that the man is not interested in showing his etchings, nor the woman in looking at them, but that both are interested in sex. The man is interested because it will give him pleasure, the woman because she will be rewarded in some material way. The same message conveyed in direct language—that is, telling of a man offering a woman, say, fifty dollars to go to bed with him—would not be funny, although it might be considered a realistic narrative if it were described with artistic skill.

Freud (1905c) attributed the pleasurable quality of humor to the saving of psychic energy. This explanation was based on a hypothetical scheme according to which man is a self-contained psychological machine, as it were, designed to minimize energy output and maximize available (stored) energy (libido). Yet it is apparent that Freud was well aware of the linguistic finesses involved in humor. He did not, however, offer an explicitly linguistic —or better, semiotical—analysis of humor, dreams, and various psychological "symptoms."[1] A semiotical analysis of humor will have much in common with modern psychoanalytic ego-psychological interpretations of this phenomenon. Both would attribute the pleasurable affects of humor to the successful mastery of a communicative task. For instance, in the girl-being-asked-to-see-an-etching situation, the scene is humorous only if the message is simultaneously interpreted in more than one way. If a metaphor, proverb, or joke is taken literally—as they often are by children, the unsophisticated,

---

[1] It is not to be denied, of course, that, from an operational point of view, much of psychoanalysis revolves around the analysis of language. That psychoanalysis is in a sense a study of communications has been accepted as a matter of course by many analysts. These considerations notwithstanding, it must be emphasized that Freud's work was cast in the explicit framework of medicine and psychiatry (medical psychology). The terms "neurosis," "psychosis," "neurotic symptom," "psychoanalytic treatment"—to name but a few—are eloquent testimony to the medical heritage Freud acquired and from which he freed himself only to a limited extent.

persons who do not speak the language well, or schizophrenic patients—they are neither funny nor interesting. Their psychologically rewarding character derives entirely from the challenge and mastery of an ambiguous or polyvalent message.

THE PROTECTIVE FUNCTION OF INDIRECT COMMUNICATIONS

The protective function of hinting is especially important whenever communications are motivated by relatively ego-alien or socially alien wishes, or by needs that are not apt to be satisfied. In our culture, recourse to indirect communications is most often taken in regard to sexual and dependency needs and problems regarding money. Faced with such "delicate" matters, indirect communications permit the expression of a need and its simultaneous denial or repudiation. A classic example from medical practice is the physician's reluctance to discuss fees with patients and to handle money. Usually a secretary or nurse is delegated to handle this matter. The physician communicating through his employee is (1) asking for money and (2) not asking for money. The first message is contained *explicitly* in the secretary's request; the second is contained *implicitly* in the doctor's attitude. Since the secretary is acting as the physician's agent, in a practical economic sense the physician is asking for money. From a psychological, or human relationship point of view, however, by not discussing financial matters, the physician is "saying" that money is of no significance in his transaction with the patient. As illustrated by this example, much of what is called hypocrisy may be understood as indirect communication, serving, as a rule, the (selfish) interests of the speaker and infringing correspondingly on the well-being of the listener.

In the example cited, the indirect communication permits the physician to enhance his self-esteem by claiming that he is "above" certain ubiquitous human needs (in this case, the need for money and all that it may buy and imply). This phenomenon derives from the premise, widely held in our culture, that the existence and open expression of needs is a childish characteristic, undesirable for "normal" or socially admirable human relationships. The main basis for this notion—a detailed consideration of which is beyond the scope of this presentation—seems to be (1) that children possess large needs and little ability to regulate and satisfy them, and (2) that the socialization of the child is the product of requiring him to deny, alter, regulate, and otherwise modify his needs. At the same time, the child is taught to be increasingly self-reliant rather than dependent. Hence, by contrast with childish "dependence," adults have convinced themselves that they are "independent." Although adults differ appreciably from children, they can hardly be said to be independent. They too possess needs which require other people for their satisfaction. The differences lie mainly in the nature of the needs and the techniques available for satisfying them. To maintain the illusion of independence—which is one of man's self-aggrandizements—it is necessary to use indirect communications.

A person's values will determine whether he considers bodily illness and difficulties in living to be ego-acceptable or ego-alien. In today's health-conscious mood, bodily illnesses are acceptable, but problems in living—lip-service to the contrary notwithstanding—are not (at least in a medical setting). Hence, people are prone to deny personal problems and to communicate in terms of bodily illness. This occurs when, for instance, a man worried about his job and life-goals seeks medical attention for hyper-acidity and insomnia. It is almost the hallmark of contemporary American literary works that they suggest the problems people struggle with and deny by hiding behind chronic invalidism, alcoholism, or so-called mental illness.

In psychoanalytic terms, indirect communications for self-protection are regarded as mechanisms of defense. This connection, though obvious, deserves emphasis because it marks a major area in which the interests of psychoanalysis and the psychology of communicative behavior meet (Ruesch, 1957, pp. 17-18).

HINTING AS INSURANCE AGAINST DISAPPOINTMENT

Indirect communications provide insurance against disappointment and object loss. How is this accomplished?

Let us take the example of a person in dire need of money. A direct request by begging can evoke only one of two responses. The request is either granted or rejected. The fact that the communication is direct means that the message "Please give me money!" can be interpreted in only one way. This form of communication is clear and cannot be misunderstood. Its disadvantage is that it leaves the speaker open to the rejection of his demand. Obviously, if direct repudiation of a request is feared, the forthright expression of wishes or needs will be inhibited. Indirect communication then becomes useful. For instance, in Central Europe between the two World Wars, many veterans, some of them disabled, were utterly destitute. They were forced to become beggars. However, they did not actually beg, but instead stood at street corners in their faded uniforms, silently offering something— a few pencils or outdated magazines—for sale. Similarly, in the United States during the early 1930's, unemployed men stood at street corners "selling" apples.

In these examples, indirectness of communication is achieved by the fact that the needy person does not verbally request money or assistance. Ostensibly, he proclaims that he is selling something that might conceivably be needed. In fact, however, these "vendors" sold things nobody wanted. If someone had wanted a pencil or an apple, he could have purchased it in the appropriate store. Moreover, the poor veterans would accept money without necessarily exchanging merchandise for it. Viewing the situation as a totality, or as a complex behavorial Gestalt, it is apparent that the "beggar" or "street vendor" was offering an indirect (or covert) communication having the following structure:

1. Overtly, he was selling pencils or apples.

2. Covertly, he was begging.

3. As a veteran, displaying his uniform and perhaps also injuries and mutilations, he communicated—at once overtly and covertly—the wish to arouse sympathy and guilt in the passers-by. The injured veteran role implies that *(a)* as vendor he was to be favored over other vendors without this patriotic qualification, and *(b)* he was not to be identified with other non-veteran beggars.

The communicational *functions* of this situation were as follows:

1. The indigent person was enabled to *deny* or *obscure* the full magnitude of his unhappy socioeconomic condition.

2. He could ask and be refused without the rejection being overtly codified. Hence, his pride and self-esteem were protected from further debasement. This consideration can hardly be overemphasized for someone whose self-image has already sustained a devastating blow. It might seem that such deception of one's self and others would hardly be necessary. But necessary it was, just as similar self-deceptions continue to be widely practiced. The point to remember is that the more injured (and vulnerable) a person's self-image is, the greater the need to protect and bolster it. The observer's common-sense appraisal that self-protection by means of hinting is unnecessary is meaningless. What is necessary depends entirely on the experiencing person's perception of himself and the world about him.

3. Last but not least, the *communicational effectiveness*—or, in technical terms, the *promotive power*—of the indirect message was far greater than its direct equivalent (i.e., undisguised begging) would have been. This social fact owed its existence to the low opinion placed on begging and the high value placed on working and "sacrificing for one's country." Moreover, a poor man asking for money directly, without offering work or merchandise in return for it, is generally regarded as aggressive. An indirect demand is experienced as more modest. Hence, it does not generate the angry resistance and rejection which an overt demand might and often does.

Keeping in mind the basic structure and function of this begging-vendorship situation, let us compare it with malingering and hysteria. Malingering, as has been suggested, may be regarded as a type of impersonation.[2] A man who is not sick acts as though he were. This is also true of the indirect communications cited. In the latter instances, it could be said that a man who was not a vendor acted as though he were one. In the first case, illness or the *sick role* is impersonated; in the second, the act of selling or the *vendor role*.

In the frame of reference of communications, the phenomena which, in the tradition of medicine and psychiatry, have been called malingering and hysteria, constitute messages of a special type. These messages imitate a form of communication (i.e., the language of bodily illness) which, in accordance with the prevalent rules of social living, may be expected to promote the need-satisfactions of the speaker. These messages are further characterized by being *allusions* to the speaker's needs, hopes, and expectations.

So long as we are willing to take care of and be especially kind toward those who are sick or disabled, impersonating the sick role will be useful to some people in certain circumstances. Hence, it is logically absurd to expect that hysteria could be eradicated as though it were a disease like malaria or smallpox. What are we to infer from this line of thought?

It seems to me that given a multiplicity of (more or less) conflicting values in a society—and this is inherent in a democracy—needs codified as negative values, accompanied by negative sanctions, will tend to be disguised and expressed as something "better" than they are. Thus, a poor war veteran may have to disguise begging as selling; or a Roman Catholic woman may have to disguise conflicts concerning pregnancy as vaginismus. Thus, *civilization does seem to be inextricably interlinked with "neurosis"*—not however, in terms of the former being a cause of the latter, as Freud (1930) suggested—but rather because all rules of conduct point implicitly to deviations from them. The deviations have meaning only in relation to the rules. Hence, rules and deviations—mental health and mental illness—must be regarded as a single behavioral package or Gestalt.

Dreaming and Hysteria as Hinting

The main advantage of hinting over more direct modes of communication is the protection it affords the speaker by enabling him to communicate without committing himself to what he says. Should the message be ill received, hinting leaves an escape route open. Indirect communications insure the

[2] The problem of impersonation will be examined in detail in Chapter 14.

speaker that he will be held responsible only for the overt meaning of his messages. The overt, ostensible message thus serves as an envelope within which is contained the dangerous, hidden message—the covert communication.

DREAMING AS HINTING

One of the best examples of hinting is the recounting of dreams in the psychotherapeutic situation. In general, any reported dream may be regarded as an indirect communication or a hint. The manifest dream story is the ostensible, overt message, while the latent dream thoughts constitute the covert message to which the dreamer alludes. This function of dreaming—and of dream-communication—is best observed in the psychoanalytic situation, since in it recounting dreams is a fully acceptable form of social behavior. Analytic patients often produce dreams that refer to the analyst. Frequently, such dreams reveal that the analysand possesses knowledge concerning the analyst which he finds distressing and is afraid to mention lest the analyst become angry for being reproached. For example, the analyst may have been late or may have greeted the patient absentmindedly. The patient now finds himself in the difficult position of wanting to talk about this, mainly to restore a more harmonious relationship with the analyst, yet being afraid to do so, lest by accusing the analyst he alienate him still more. In this dilemma, the patient may resort to a dream communication. He will then report a dream in which allusion is made to the distressing occurrence, omitting perhaps the person of the analyst from it. This makes it possible to make the dangerous communication while at the same time the patient is protected, since the analyst can interpret the dream in a number of different ways.

If the analyst is able and willing to accept the charges against him, he can so interpret the dream. Its covert communicative aim will then have been achieved: The important message had been dispatched, the relationship to the analyst has not been further endangered, and a relative communicative harmony (a "good relationship") between patient and analyst has been reestablished. On the other hand, if the analyst is upset, defensive, or otherwise unresponsive to the hidden message of the dream, he might—and indeed often does—interpret the communication in another way. Although this is clearly less desirable for the patient and the course of the analysis, for the patient it is clearly preferable to making an overt charge and being reprimanded for it (which is what he fears). The miscommunication at least does not place an additional burden on an already disharmonious relationship.

The thesis that dreaming may be a form of hinting—that is, a method whereby one person may indirectly communicate with another concerning something disturbing in the relationship between them—apparently is known to children and artists and is intuitively understood by them. A childhood memory of a patient of mine affords a striking illustration of this view of dream-communication. It is significant that the experience to be related pertains not to a genuine dream but rather to what should be called a "counterfeit dream." A person reported certain events saying he dreamt them, although he knew that they occurred in waking life. Like all copying—whether counterfeiting currency or imitating great works of art—this "counterfeit dream" affords an excellent opportunity to study and disclose the most characteristic features of the object under scrutiny.

The patient, a young man, had come for help because of the problem of sexual exhibitionism.[3] In one of his analytic hours, he spoke of the memory of his first ejaculation, which occurred when he was about ten years old. He was masturbating, had an orgasm, and saw, for the first time, some milky fluid exuding from his penis. He felt scared and bewildered. Following this sexual act, he went into his parents' bedroom and told his father that he was awakened by a bad dream. He said he dreamed that he was urinating, but instead of urine, "something else" came out. His father correctly understood the message—that is, as it was intended—and reassured the boy that, "it was all right, and we'll talk about it in the morning." Recalling this episode, the patient wondered why he had *lied,* as he put it, to his father. Why did he say that he dreamed this, when he knew perfectly well he had not. I should add that confessing his "bad" sexual impulses to father (or father-substitutes) was one of this patient's most important symptoms.

A dream reported by this patient will be cited as another illustration of my thesis. It was an anxiety dream from which he awakened in the morning feeling as though he had been "through a wringer." The dream was simply this: "A crime has been committed." The patient added that he did not know what the crime was or who committed it. The patient had previously reported very few dreams, and none at all for several months. Why did he dream now? This dream occurred the night preceding the patient's last appointment with me, before my summer vacation was to interrupt the treatment for a considerable length of time. He began this hour by musing about the fact that he had had no difficulty with exhibitionistic impulses since he started in therapy, but wondered whether he was "really cured." Then he related the dream.

Two important facts must be added. The first is that immediately prior

---

[3] The psychotherapy of this patient was described in detail in my essay: "Recollections of a Psychoanalytic Psychotherapy: The Case of the 'Prisoner K'" (Szasz, 1959c).

to first consulting me, this man had been in legal difficulties because of exhibitionism. Second, at the time of this interruption, treatment was not sufficiently advanced for the patient to feel that he knew the causes of his sexual difficulties or that he had mastered them. He believed that the disappearance of this symptom depended largely on the therapeutic relationship and did not, as yet, lie within himself. In my opinion, too, this was a correct appraisal of the situation.

This dream clearly shows that dreaming occurred in response to a severely threatening disturbance in the analytic situation. The therapist's departure threatened to leave the patient alone, perhaps unable to cope with sexual impulses that were ego-alien, antisocial, and potentially self-damaging. In the dream, and by reporting it, the patient told the analyst something like this: "What will happen when you leave? A crime (exhibitionism) is what might happen. Please do not leave!" This had to be communicated in *dream form,* rather than directly, because the patient's conscious ego could not endure the thought (1) that he might still be so vulnerable to his own unconscious "impulses" or internal objects, and (2) that he was so dependent on the therapist for help. Thus, the dream was an indirect communication *both* to himself and to me. To himself, the patient spoke—indirectly (what crime? by whom?)—of the danger which now faced him. To me, the patient spoke of his vulnerability, and hence, of my responsibility. In this context, "What crime and by whom?" referred to my leaving him.

The idea that dreams are allusions is not new. Freud (1900, 1901) himself said this. However, he paid less attention to dream-communications as interpersonal (or even social) events than he did to the intrapsychic aspects of dreaming. In a short paper provocatively titled "To Whom Does One Relate One's Dreams?" Ferenczi (1912) dealt with dreams as indirect interpersonal communications. More recently, Gitelson (1952), Kanzer (1955), and Tauber and Green (1959) called attention to the communicative function of dreams. Gitelson, for example, reported several dreams which occurrred in response to the patient's perception of the analyst's disturbing countertransference. He tacitly assumed, as I believe many analysts do, that some dreams are "transference-communications." But he did not examine why the patient communicated in this instead of in some other way.

HYSTERIA AS HINTING

As has been emphasized, any message expressed in a relatively nondiscursive idiom may be used for hinting. Hence, communication by iconic body signs, as in hysteria, is well suited for hinting. Freud attributed the multiplicity of meanings characteristic of hysterical and other psychiatric symptoms to a "motivational overdetermination." In other words, he interpreted the multiple meanings of dreams and symptoms—each meaning or interpretation having something to recommend it—to the multiplicity of (instinctual) motives which, he assumed, the final act (symptom) satisfied. In the present study, the same phenomena are examined from a semiotical rather than a motivational point of view. Accordingly, instead of "overdetermination of symptoms," I speak of diversity of communicational meanings.

The hinting function of hysterical symptoms may be illustrated by the following example. Freud's patient Frau Cäcilie M., suffered from hysterical facial pain, which had at least two distinct meanings.

1. Its *overt meaning*, directed to the self, significant objects, physician, and others, was something like this: "I am sick. You must help me! You must be good to me!" (The physician may have interpreted the message more specifically as: "This is facial neuralgia, possibly tic douloureux.")

2. Its *covert meaning*, directed principally to a specific person (who may have been either an actual person, or an internal object, or both), may be paraphrased as follows: "You hurt me as though you slapped my face. You should be sorry and make amends."

Such communicational interactions are common between husbands and wives and between parents and children. Disregarding individual psychological factors, this type of communication is fostered by social conditions rendering people closely interdependent for mutual need-satisfactions. Such arrangements require everyone to curb his needs, for only then can he satisfy at least some of them. Having curbed his needs, moreover, he is in a better position to demand that his partner(s) do likewise. Thus, the open, undistorted expression of needs is inhibited and various types of indirect communications and need-satisfactions are fostered.

In contrast to the above, relatively open-ended social situations, for example those encountered in many phases of modern business life, foster relatively impersonal kinds of interdependence, based on *functional-instrumental factors*. A supplies B's needs because of his *special know-how*, rather *than because of the special personal relationship between them*. Historically based, restrictive relationships of families, groups, and institutions must be contrasted with the instrumentally based, nonrestrictive relationships subserving the aims of practical (technologic, scientific, economic, etc.) pursuits. In instrumentally structured situations it is not especially necessary for the participants to curb their needs. This is mainly because the mere expression of needs does not compel others to gratify them, as it tends to do in the family (Szasz, 1959f). Hence, the open expression of needs is not inhibited. Indeed, it is often encouraged, since it helps to identify a "problem" for which someone might have a "solution."

Two antithetical proverbs underscore these principles. One is the Anglo-

American maxim: "Honesty is the best policy." The other is a Hungarian proverb which freely translated, means: "Tell the truth and you will have your head bashed in." At first glance, these two proverbs express contrasting and mutually conflicting exhortations. If treated simply as logical assertions, they are indeed contradictory. The conflict between them, however, is more apparent than real, because each maxim refers to a different social context. Honesty *is*, indeed, the best policy in instrumentally oriented human relationships and in the "open" groups in which such activities flourish. Conversely, one's head will be bashed in for telling the truth, if he operates in an institutional setting or a "closed" group (Popper, 1945). These general principles may be illustrated by the fates of Galileo and Einstein. The former, operating in the institutional setting of the Roman Catholic Church, was punished for "telling the truth." To save himself, he was forced to recant. In our terms, this meant that he proclaimed that what he had previously believed to be the truth was "in reality" a lie. He might as well have said that his discovery was "only a dream." Or, in a somewhat hypothetical present-day setting he might have saved himself by pleading "insanity," attributing his discovery (crime) to a "diseased state of mind" for which (by definition) one cannot be held responsible. Lies, mistakes, dreams, and the products of alleged mental diseases have one thing in common—namely, they do not offend those to whom they are directed (or at least not as much as does the "unmitigated truth"). In contrast, Einstein's ideas concerning relativity—and hence, his "attack" on Newtonian physics—were received with acclamations of praise. The scientific community, governed by instrumental values, conducts itself according to the rule that "honesty (truth) is the best policy."

It might be added here that Freud, by persistently claiming—and perhaps also inviting—nonrecognition of his ideas, seemed to orient himself to the ethics of institutional groups, such as those of organized religion or organized medicine, rather than to the ethics of the scientific community (Szasz, 1956c). His work was well recognized and eagerly accepted by contemporary scientists interested in the problems with which he dealt. (This, of course, excluded most European physicians and psychiatrists). But surely, this is all that anyone who sets forth a new idea can expect. *Freud's nonscientific orientation in regard to the psychoanalytic movement*—in marked contrast to his scientific orientation to the subject matter of this discipline—undoubtedly contributed to the rapid institutionalization of psychoanalytic thought (Freud, 1914; Jones, 1953, 1955). Psychoanalysis as a profession thus became a closed system, family-type of organization (Szasz, 1958e) in which honesty was no longer the best policy. The honest, *forthright assertion* of differences from Freudian thought (for example in Jung, Adler, Rank, Horney) were punishable by "expulsion" from the group; at the same time, broadly hinting at differences continued to be well tolerated. This assertion is borne out not only by the works of certain well-known psychoanalysts, but also by the fact that exceedingly wide differences—in regard to both theory and practice—now prevail among psychoanalysts (and psychoanalytic institutes) within the American and International Psychoanalytic Associations. The existence of these differences is widely recognized—much as problems concerning sex were widely recognized in Vienna in Freud's day. However, since it is feared that clearly facing certain issues will disturb and damage the integrity of the group, focusing attention on them is considered to be in bad taste and is avoided.

Primary and Secondary Gain, Object Relationships, and Indirect Communications

Traditionally, the socially communicative aspects of neurosis were subordinated to the intrapsychic (intrapersonal) and unconscious aspects of it. Perhaps in an effort to give a kind of conceptual superiority to the latter, its achievements—for example, the satisfaction of sexual or pregenital impulses by means of a symptom—were called *primary gain*. This was contrasted with the *secondary* use (hence the name) to which the symptom might have been put. "The secondary gain is merely a special case of the ceaseless efforts of the ego to exploit the possibilities for pleasurable gratification which are available to it. Once a symptom has been formed, the ego may discover that there are advantages which the symptom brings with it" (Brenner, 1955, p. 207). This distinction seems to me to be unnecessarily sharp. It fails to do justice to the exquisite intermingling of intrapersonal, interpersonal, and social levels of communication that characterize most actual human situations. Approaching our problems more operationally, with a focus on communications—and this will include the viewpoints of modern psychoanalytic ego-psychology and of object relations—the distinction between primary and secondary gain becomes increasingly unimportant. In place of these concepts we speak of different levels or hierarchies of object relationships (from entirely unconscious to partly and then wholly conscious), communications, and meanings.

Some brief comments concerning a clinical case will illustrate the differences among the conceptual frameworks of primary and secondary gain, object relationships, and hinting. Let us select as our example what may be considered a typical case of conversion hysteria. The history and psychotherapy of a young woman, whose presenting complaint was abdominal pain, were described in detail elsewhere (Szasz, 1957a, pp. 93-99). A recapitulation of this narrative is not necessary for our present purpose. It should suffice to note that the patient's mother died following an hysterectomy. Within a year, she also lost her father. Shortly afterward, the patient broke down with her "neurotic illness." Depending on one's frame of reference, the following constructions and interpretations may be placed on the symptom of abdominal pain.

1. According to the traditional model of hysteria, the patient had unconsciously identified herself with the ambivalently loved mother. The primary gains of the symptom thus lay in: (*a*) successful displacement of the mother and union with the father in the Oedipal situation; (*b*) punishment, through pain and suffering, for the guilt over "killing" mother. Its secondary gains were: (*a*) gratification of dependency needs from remaining family members and physicians; (*b*) evasion of new problems attendant on growing up and forming new object relationships.

2. In an *object relationship* frame of reference, the situation might be interpreted as follows: (*a*) The patient was unable successfully to complete the work of mourning. She continued to hold on and relate to her mother, as an internal object. (*b*) Illness and suffering provided new means for needed relationship with objects (family members, physicians, etc.). (*c*) By substituting the body for the mother (and other people), the patient oriented herself to a new, maximally safe, object (her own body). The painful illness then served as a constant reminder that the needed object (body = mother) was not lost, but was still present.

3. From the point of view of hinting, or indirect communication by means of symptoms, the following features would have to be emphasized:

a) As an intrapersonal communication the patient was hinting to herself that something was wrong. However, she did not express or experience this directly, for example, by being preoccupied with her mother and mourning her death. Instead, she made allusions to her mother's illness and death by means of the iconic image of her own symptoms.

b) A similar communication was directed to those around her, to whom she turned in her need (interpersonal communication). She could express herself no more directly to them than she could to her own self. In this context, the bodily illness might be interpreted as an allusion to personal object loss, as in (*a*) above.

c) The persistent painfull illness also had an aggressive communicative meaning. It was directed toward her family, who, she felt, had let her down. This message—paraphrased as "You are no good! You see, you still have not helped me!"—too, is clothed in the mantle of an allusion. It was not stated simply and directly in everyday language, but was communicated indirectly by means of the intense annoyance engendered in people entrusted with the care of sufferers whose misery remains persistently unrelieved.

In the actual work of psychotherapy and psychoanalysis, I usually make use of all three types of interpretations and explanations. As a rule, it is most effective to proceed in an inverse order. In other words, I begin by considering the patient's productions as indirect communications, seeking and providing needed object relationships. Only after this, do I turn to interpretations in terms of specific object relationships, and finally to reconstructions of childhood relationships and instinctual conflicts. Of course, this need not be a sharply divided sequence. It is merely a general scheme, resting on the premise that meaningful communication with the patient is most readily made on a level of discourse not grossly unfamiliar to him (or her). The sequence of therapy is then towards increasingly new (for the patient) kinds and levels of communication between patient and therapist. Not all levels of discourse are suitable for all patients. Ideally, as the work of the analysis progresses, a multidimensional perspective of the patient's human situation—past and present, transference as well as extratransference—comes into view and gains increasing definition. In terms of this metaphor, the adequate "development" of this "picture" is the end-goal of the analysis.

PART IV | *Rule-Following*
Analysis
of Behavior

"Man is a rule-following animal. *His actions are not simply directed towards ends; they also conform to social standards and conventions. For instance, we ascribe to people* traits *of character like honesty, punctuality, considerateness and meanness. Such terms do not, like ambition or hunger or sexual desire, indicate the sorts of goals that a man tends to pursue; rather they indicate the type of rule which a man follows in their pursuit—the ways in which he tends to treat others, and the type of regulation that he imposes on his conduct whatever his goals may be. A man who is ruthless, selfish, punctual, considerate, persistent, and honest, does not have any particular goals, rather he pursues whatever goals he has in particular sorts of ways."* R. S. Peters (1958, p. 5)

CHAPTER 10

The Rule-Following
Model
of Human Behavior

To assert that people tend to behave in certain habitual ways is to state explicitly what is probably obvious. This simple empirical observation, however, may serve as the basis of increasingly complex sociopsychological constructs and theories. The notion of social role, as originally conceived by Mead (1934)—and later so fruitfully elaborated by Parsons (1952, 1958b), Merton (1957a & b), and others (e.g., Nieman and Hughes, 1951; Sarbin, 1943, 1954)—rests on and embodies the empirical fact that in given situations people tend to behave in certain set ways.

Psychoanalytic explanations of human behavior have been traditionally of a different character. Psychoanalysis has been correctly described as a motivational psychology, which means simply that it offers explanations couched in terms of motives. According to Freud's earliest hypotheses concerning hysteria and other "mental symptoms," a new motive, hitherto unrecognized by both patient and physician, was alleged to explain the patient's behavior. For example, an obsessional symptom attributed by the patient to solicitude over his loved ones was interpreted as due to death wishes. Thus, one motive or goal, namely "to do good" for someone, was replaced by another, namely "to do harm." It is clear today that although analysis and explanation in terms of motives is useful, it is insufficient for both psychological theory and psychoanalytic therapy. This is because motives tend to explain actions in a general or abstract sort of way. They do not really tell us why Mr. Jones acted in a particular manner at a certain moment. To explain specific, concrete human actions, we must know other things besides what motivates the actor. The somewhat overlapping concepts of role and rule are most useful in this connection.

Motives and Rules

In his essay, *The Concept of Motivation*, Peters (1958) presented a useful analysis of the distinction between psychological explanations couched in terms of motives as against those couched in terms of rule-following or purposive behavior.[1] Crucial to Peters's inquiry was his distinction between *action* and *happening*.

As I have emphasized earlier (Chapter 6), this distinction is inherent in the psychoanalytic theory of "mental illness" and is indispensable for differentiating—at least as regards therapeutic attitude—between physicochemical disorders of the body and "mental symptoms." The former are happenings or occurrences; developing carcinoma of the head of the pancreas is an example. In contrast, so-called mental symptoms are "doings" or actions. They do not happen to one, but are (unconsciously) willed.

Peters noted that to foresee what a person will do, it often is not necessary to know much about him as an individual. It is enough to know the role he is playing:

We know what the parson will do when he begins to walk toward the pulpit in the middle of the penultimate hymn or what the traveller will do when he enters the doors of the hotel because we know the *conventions* regulating church services and staying at hotels. *And we can make such predictions without knowing anything about the causes of people's behaviour. Man in society is like a chess-player writ large* ([ITALICS ADDED] p. 7).

From this, Peters concluded that the first things that we must know about human actions are the norms and goals that regulate the conduct of man. Accordingly, anthropology and sociology must be considered the basic sciences of human action, for these disciplines are concerned with exhibiting,

---

[1] In the exposition of the rule-following model of human behavior which follows, I have relied heavily on Peters's excellent study.

in a systematic manner, the "framework of norms and goals which are necessary to classify actions as being of a certain sort" (p. 7). Psychiatry and psychoanalysis, too, address themselves to these problems, although they may sometimes do so unwittingly. For example, in the psychoanalytic study of perversions or so-called antisocial acts, the observer is perforce concerned with norms and goals. By tacitly subscribing to the socially prevalent norms —as did Freud, for instance, in *Three Essays on the Theory of Sexuality* (1905b)—it may appear as though the author was *not* concerned with norms at all but only with "psychosexual functions" (Szasz, 1959a).

ON CAUSAL AND CONVENTIONAL EXPLANATIONS

What is the basis for distinguishing *causal* from *conventional* (e.g., *rule-following*) *types of explanation in psychology?* We encounter here, in a new and more manageable form, the classical dichotomy between mechanistic causality and vitalistic teleology. In terms of the present inquiry, the distinction is between "hidden-factor" explanations of behavior as against "convention" theories of it. The libido theory is a typical example of the former, while role theories exemplify the latter. Hidden-factor theories, in common with the classic theories of physics, frame their explanatory statements in terms of antecedently acting events or factors (e.g., instincts, drives, libido, etc.). By definition, they must explain the present and the future by what happened in the past. In contrast, rule-following explanations of behavior are framed in terms of (behavior-regulating) conventions. The relation of conventions to time must be explicitly specified. Obviously, many rules that governed conduct in the past no longer do so today. Others may have been active in the past, may still be active in the present, and may be expected to remain active in the foreseeable future. Still others may be projected only into the future (e.g., novel legislative regulations, "Utopias").

There is no logical reason why future events or conditions could not be the "causes" of present ones. Even machines can now be built to behave in a goal-directed manner (Wiener, 1948, 1960). The goal, of course, must be selected by the persons who build the machine. Such machines take account of the future and, in a sense, are regulated by future events. Man's ability to build so-called teleological behavior into nonbiological systems has liquidated whatever meaning the old concept of vitalism might still have had.

What, then, is the difference between a causal and a rule-following type of explanation for a given bit of behavior? According to Peters (1958), Freud was principally concerned with a general class of activities—composed of such things as dreams, obsessions, phobias, perversions, hallucinations, and so forth—characterized by the fact that they seemed "to have no point or a very odd point" (p. 10). Freud reclaimed these phenomena for psychology "by extending the model of purposive rule-following behaviour to cover the unconscious" (p. 11). Hence, it is correct to consider Freud's work a successful extension of the principle of rule-following to so-called unconsciously determined behavior. This position is expressed most clearly in the psychoanalytic attitude toward personality change, for symptoms are treated *as though* they adhered to a rule-following pattern. It is an odd but rather important corollary of this position that nowhere in psychoanalysis is there sufficient allowance made for a person who acts in a self-damaging way because he is stupid or ill-informed. Thus, not only are rule-following explanations accepted in psychoanalysis, but they are overemphasized and applied in situations in which they either cannot fit or are unlikely to do so.

The contrasting thesis—namely, that Freud proposed a mechanical-causal type of explanation for "unconsciously determined" acts—is supported by the fact that he attributed "neurotic" behavior to such things as the repetition compulsion, the persistent operation of a repressed Oedipus complex, infantile fixations, the excessive strength of instincts or part-instincts, and so forth. From a logical point of view, each of these constructs occupies a position similar to an antecedent physical occurrence. Many of the original psychoanalytic explanations of behavior (but certainly not all contemporary ones) have this cause-and-effect type of logical structure. The main reason for this probably was that Freud was ensnared in a moral dilemma from which he tried to extricate himself by means of ostensibly nonmoral arguments. In common with his social milieu, Freud equated "conscious" rule-following behavior with the notions of responsibility and punishability. Thus, because he wished to treat hysteria (and mental illnesses generally) in a nonjudgmental and scientific fashion, he had no choice but to deny and obscure the very discovery he had made—namely, that peculiar or symptomatic behavior also obeys the principles of rule-following actions. His famous therapeutic dictum, "Where id was, ego shall be," could be translated into our present idiom to mean that "obscure and inexplicit rule-following shall be replaced by clear and deliberate rule-following." In the following chapters the precise rules which "hysterical" behavior follows will be described and examined. How this behavior originates and why it may persist will also be discussed.

NATURE AND CONVENTION—BIOLOGY AND SOCIOLOGY

A fundamental principle of modern science is that a *logical gulf* exists between nature and convention (Popper 1944-1945).[2] Adhering to this im-

---

[2] This distinction is completely obscured—or perhaps one should say successfully denied—in the religious conception of "natural law." According to Catholic doctrine, sexual behavior *is* (*should be?*) regulated by "natural law" (Sulloway, 1959).

portant distinction, Peters (1958) re-emphasized that "movements *qua* movements are neither intelligent, efficient, nor correct. They only become so in the context of action" (p. 14). Movements *qua* movements, therefore, are problems for neurology (biology), whereas, movements *qua* signs—that is, actions—are problems for what I have called metaneurology (psychiatry, sociology, behavioral science, etc.). It follows, too, that whether a given phenomenon involving human participation is regarded as *action* or *happening* will have the most far-reaching consequences, because happenings "cannot be characterized as intelligent or unintelligent, correct or incorrect, efficient or inefficient. Prima facie they are just occurrences" (p. 15). For occurrences or happenings, causal explanations are appropriate and conventional ones are not.

Several different conceptualizations may be brought together here. The distinction between *occurrence* and *action* is rather similar to the distinction between *object* and *sign*, and between *genuine* and *facsimile*. It is usually possible to shift back and forth between the two members of these pairs. We then witness shifting emphases between biology and sociology (psychology), between nature and convention. Thus, whether a bit of "disabled," "unhappy," or "deviant" behavior is regarded as "illness" or as something else (malingering, problem in living, communication, etc.) depends on and reflects which of these (opposing) viewpoints is adopted. Behavior viewed as occurrence implies that it is taken at face value and considered the "real thing." Contrariwise, behavior viewed as action implies that it is treated as a sign and considered a representative or carrier of some other thing (a message or "meaning").

Finally, Peters noted that when a person is asked to state the motives for his actions, it is sometimes implied that he might be up to no good. And when it is said that his motives are unconscious, it is often implied further that he is up to no good and does not even know it. Accordingly, there is an important difference between giving a reason for one's action and giving a justification for it. Reasons and causes operate, so to speak, in an ethically neutral field, whereas motives and justifications are used in a context in which ethical considerations are explicitly or implicitly entertained. This is consistent with the earlier analysis of the sociology of hysteria in Freud's day, and lends support to it.

A motive-analysis of mental illness thus functioned not merely as a scientific explanation but also, or perhaps primarily, as a justification both for the patient's behavior and for the physician's interest in the patient and his humane efforts to help him.

Rules, Morals, and the Superego

The psychoanalytic concept of the superego must now be brought into connection with the notion of rule-following and what is usually meant by the terms "ethics" and "morals." By ethics and morals we refer to the rules that men follow in the conduct of their lives, and sometimes also to the study of these rules (e.g., ethics as a science of moral conduct). The psychoanalytic concept superego refers essentially to the same things. We are confronted here with several words, some technical and others in common usage, all of which mean more or less the same thing. For scientific purposes, it is most serviceable to speak simply of rule-following and of the consciousness of rules (to be discussed further in Chapter 13). By so doing, we can avoid several problems. For example, the word morality, as Peters (1958) noted, is not usually used to designate everyday, habitual acts or obsessive behavior. It refers, rather, to the "intelligent following of rules the point of which is understood" (p. 87). On the whole, Freud (1940) failed to deal explicitly with rule-following behavior, except that based on the principle that men (children) obey feared and respected persons (adults). He had little to say concerning cooperative, mutually adjustive behavior among equal adults.

This basic weakness of psychoanalytic theory stems from the fact that Freud was much more interested in pointing up the defects inherent in the "morality of infantilism" than he was in defining what sort of morality is appropriate for the adult, fully socialized human being (Rieff, 1959).

Still, it would be erroneous to believe that psychoanalytic theory makes no contribution to describing and assessing different types of ethical conduct. The crucial notion in this connection is the relative rigidity or flexibility of the superego. The childish, immature, or "neurotic" superego is rigid; it is characterized by slavish adherence to rules which, moreover, may not be clearly understood. The mature or "normal" superego, on the other hand, is flexible; it can evaluate the situation at hand and modify the rules accordingly. According to an early, classic formulation (Strachey, 1934), the effectiveness of psychoanalysis as treatment depends upon the analyst's interventions (mutative interpretations) when these result in changing the patient's superego in the direction of greater flexibility. As far as it goes, I believe that this is a sound conception. However, like the psychoanalytic theory of the superego, it is severely limited by the fact that it is silent on what sort of rigidity is considered "bad" and what sort of flexibility "good." In other words, Freud and other psychoanalysts have persistently dallied with normative systems without ever committing themselves on normative standards.

Indeed, when it came to confronting openly the issue of normative standards, Freud closed his eyes. He went so far as to reiterate the simple, common-sense belief that many people hold—namely, that "right" is what they do:

> Many years ago he [Freud] conducted a private correspondence with Putnam on the subject of ethics. Putnam showed it to me and I remember these two sentences: Ich betrachte das Moralische als etwas Selbstverständliches. . . . Ich habe eigentlich nie etwas Gemeines getan (Jones, 1957; p. 247).

Jones supplied the following translation: "*I consider ethics to be taken for granted. Actually I have never done a mean thing*" ([ITALICS ADDED] p. 247). The German word *selbstverständlich*, as an adjective, might better be translated here as "self-evident." Now, to say that morality is self-evident and to believe that one had never done a mean thing are peculiar statements to come from the lips of a scientist whose object of study was man, himself included. It reflects, I believe, Freud's determination to exclude this area from critical examination. It is instructive, moreover, to correlate this assumption concerning Freud's personal attitude toward ethical problems (including values and rules) with his theory of the superego.

Since psychoanalysis deals predominantly with learned behavior, considerations of norms or standards are always pertinent to the adequate formulation and explanation of its observations. In this connection, Peters (1958) reminded us that: "Social life is never, like the jungle life popularized by evolutionary theorists, a matter of mere survival; *it is a matter of surviving in a certain sort of way* ([ITALICS ADDED] p. 127).

The significance of the fact that virtually all behavior with which the psychotherapist (or social psychologist) deals is learned cannot be overemphasized. The concept of learning is operationally tied to the concept of performance. One learns how to act in order to measure up to norms or achieve goals. Both learning and performance presuppose standards of correctness. "A man who learns something is a man who comes to get something *right*" (pp. 114–115). Accordingly, the notion of performance is fundamental in the sociologist's view of human behavior. Sociological and anthropological studies of how people act usually revolve around the performances which they put on, as it were, for themselves and those about them (Goffman, 1959).

RULES, ROLES, AND PERSONAL COMMITMENT

The notions of rule-following and role-playing are closely related. The concept of role implies rule-following. Conversely, a system of coherent rules constitutes a role (in the abstract). An analysis of behavior based on the game-playing model will be presented in Part V. Here, I wish to emphasize only that the notion of social role—or that of "playing a role" (whether on stage or in real life)—implies a measure of personal participation in or commitment to whatever one is engaged in doing. Thus, we speak of the social roles of, say, doctor, nurse, patient, teacher, policeman, and so forth. These roles refer to action patterns, not happenings. Happenings, as such, are not roles and cannot be subsumed under the role-playing category any more than they can under the category of rule-following.

Often, the line of demarcation between happening and action is not clear. The point at which a passively incurred event becomes transformed into a role-playing situation, provided that the person involved is neurologically intact, may depend on his attitude toward his human condition. By "attitude" I refer to such things as whether he is hopeful or dejected, whether he is oriented toward patterns of active mastery or passive endurance, and so forth. Consider, for example, the hypothetical case of a man who is involved in a train collision on his way to work. Injured and rendered temporarily unconscious, he is taken to a hospital. All this happens to him. On regaining consciousness, he finds himself in the patient role. From this moment on, his behavior—or at least some aspects of it—can and must be analyzed in terms of rule-following and role-playing. Indeed, no other analysis could adequately account for his personal conduct once his total passivity due to unconsciousness is replaced by a measure of awareness. While this may be obvious, it is emphasized because people in quandaries so often regard themselves as utterly helpless, the "victims of circumstances."

Of course, people may or may not be victims of circumstances. Usually, unfavorable circumstances and personal "styles of life" (A. Adler, 1931) both play a role in determining the fates of men. The point is that if a person experiences and defines his situation as though he played no part in bringing it about, this may not in fact be true. On the contrary, this position often serves defensive purposes. In other words, when choices are made—either by specific action, or more often by inaction—and when these lead to unhappy consequences, people often feel that "it was not their fault" that things turned out as they did. In a purely conventional moral sense they might be correct. But this is simply because common sense assigns guilt or blame only to the specific commission of acts—much less often to omissions—and even among these usually only to acts whose deleterious effects are immediate or short range. It is necessary, however, to distinguish between a common-sense or legal-dispositional analysis and a scientific analysis of human relationships. From the point of view of scientific analysis, insofar as people participate in certain antecedent bits of action they contribute their share to the final outcome. How large or small this share is can be evaluated only by examining the circumstances of each individual situation. But in any case, it is an inevitable conclusion, from this point of view, that people do shape their destiny, no matter how much they might bewail the superior forces of alien wills and powers.

Rules and Antirules

To assert that man is a rule-following animal implies more than that he is prone to act on the basis of rules which he has been furnished. He is also prone to act in diametrical opposition to these rules.

In this connection, Freud's (1910b) observations concerning the antithetical meanings of so-called primal words are pertinent. Commenting on a philological essay by Karl Abel, Freud noted that certain basic words of a language may be used to express contrary meanings. In Latin, for example, *sacer* means holy and accursed. This antithetical meaning of symbolism is a major characteristic of dream psychology. In a dream, a symbol (or image) may stand for itself or for its opposite—for example, tall may signify short or young may stand for old. I have suggested (Szasz, 1957a, pp. 162-163) that this principle also applies to affects. Illustrative examples are feeling afraid, which may signify that one is vigilant and prepared for danger; or feeling guilty, which may signify that one is conscientious. This bivalent, antithetical signification seems to be inherent in the nature of man's capacity to form and use symbols of all types. It applies to affects, iconic signs, words, rules, and systems of rules (games)—each of which may signify or, more often, suggest both the referent and its opposite.

Antirules are especially significant in the behavior of psychosocially simple ("immature") persons. Thus, children and simple, poorly educated persons tend to structure and see their world mainly in terms of the rules they have been given plus their opposites. Although it is possible to modify rules or to make new rules, to do so requires a measure of psychosocial sophistication. Hence, these alternatives are not available to young children or, unfortunately, to many adults. It must be emphasized, too, that while positive rule-following tends to assure interpersonal and social harmony, it alone often fails to satisfy human needs in regard to personal autonomy and integrity. To satisfy these needs, it is necessary to follow one's own rules. The simplest rules which we tend to experience as our own are antirules. Thus, as early as during the first year of life, when babies are urged to eat, they learn to protest by not eating. The so-called negativism of young children should probably be looked upon as the following of negative or antirules. This is well understood by common-sense psychologists and is expressed by such sayings as "If I want him to do something, I must ask him to do the opposite." The proverbially stubborn mule can best be made to move forward if his master acts as though he were trying to make him back up. This touches on the entire subject of doing something because it is forbidden, the significance of which in delinquent or antisocial behavior has already received much attention from psychiatrists and psychologists. The notion of antirules delineated here, however, is of somewhat wider scope since it pertains equally to prescriptive and prohibitive rules.

Consider, for instance, the simple rules given in the Ten Commandments. Some are prohibitions—for example, of murder and theft. Others are prescriptions—for example, the injunction to honor one's father and mother. Clearly, each of these implies and suggests its opposite. To be told not to kill creates the idea that one might kill. It might be objected that people had this and similar ideas before the Ten Commandments were promulgated, and that in general laws are aimed at curbing propensities that exist prior to legislation. This is often true. Still, it does not preclude the possibility that laws also create and suggest propensities toward certain forms of behavior. Given the common human inclination to disobey laws—"Forbidden fruit tastes sweeter," as the proverb has it—any particular law will be likely to create a tendency for men to act in opposition to it. The extent to which rules foster negative rule-following behavior depends on many circumstances which need not concern us here. Let us only bear in mind that irrespective of what might be in the minds of men, we cannot make rules without at least implying their opposites.

A Classification of Rules

Having considered rule-following as a general theoretical conception, we are ready to examine the function and transmission of rules.[3] Children growing up in contemporary Western cultures must learn a large variety of rules. These may be conveniently divided into the following three classes: (1) natural laws or biological rules; (2) prescriptive laws or social (religious, moral) rules; and (3) imitative or interpersonal rules.

BIOLOGICAL RULES
Biological rules form a special part of the larger category commonly called the Laws of Nature. In this group belong such things as the necessity to eat

[3] No attempt to present a detailed account of how rules originate and how they are learned by the child will be made here. The interested reader is referred to the works of Jean Piaget (1928, 1932, 1951).

to insure survival. In brief, these rules are concerned with the physics and chemistry of the human body in relationship with its material or nonhuman environment. These rules, which are impersonally fixed and are thus called the Laws of Nature, often are contrasted with man-made, or allegedly God-made, rules. The implicit aim of biological rules—made explicit by man—is survival of the individual as a body or physical machine and survival of the species as a biological system. Many basic biological rules are learned by direct experience, but some, at least in a rudimentary form, may be said to be inborn. More sophisticated knowledge concerning biological rules must be learned by the methods of science. Indeed, the basic medical sciences could be said to be devoted to this end.

In this connection, the question arises as to whether animals "know" certain basic biological rules. In one sense, the answer is "Yes," for without "obeying" them they would perish. It is important, however, to be clear about the sense in which animals "know" such rules. This "knowledge" consists of the appropriate responses to objects (in their environment); it is automatic, conditioned, and nonself-reflective. In a hierarchy of learning and knowing, this type of knowledge would have to be considered the simplest and most basic. It consists of responding to objects as objects, not as signs, and may be called object-learning.

Usually, animals do not know any other types of rules (metarules). Although some species of monkeys play games, and many animals can readily be taught to follow rules by imitation and practice (dancing bears, ball-balancing seals, etc.), it appears that the animal's limited capacity for symbolization restricts his use of rules to those which are nonreflective. In other words, animals cannot use rules intelligently, meaning thereby possessing the awareness or knowledge that they are using rules. This may be inferred from the fact that animals cannot readily modify rules in accordance with the exigencies of a particular situation, nor can they usually create new patterns of rules (new games). Thus animals cannot learn metarules and cannot play metagames.[4]

SOCIAL, RELIGIOUS, OR MORAL RULES

In the group of social, religious, and moral rules belong all prescriptive laws governing social relationships, whether these are said to originate from a single God, a multiplicity of deities, fate, or culture and society. These laws differ from so-called natural laws in regard to geographical scope or distribution and also in the nature of the sanctions. Natural laws hold for all parts of the world, although, as it is now realized, they may not apply in situations

---

[4] A systematic discussion of rule-and game-hierarchies will be presented in Chapter 13.

outside of it, for example on another planet. The fact that basic biological rules obtain consistently throughout all of experiential space-time makes them appear to be universal. These rules say, in effect, that human life as it is now known can exist only under such and such conditions. The expression "human life" is meant here to refer to a certain type of biological organization.

The concept of religious or moral law is in some respects analogous to the concept of biological law. Religious laws are usually proscriptions of certain acts. The analogy between these and so-called natural laws may be made more vivid by phrasing examples of the latter in the typical form of the former, that is, as prohibitive injunctions. They might then read as follows:

"Thou shalt avoid falling off precipices . . . (if you desire to live a long and happy life)."

"Thou shalt avoid jumping into deep rivers . . . (if you desire to avoid drowning)."

The oldest religious injunctions of Western man, the Ten Commandments, were phrased in this form, as in, "Thou shalt not . . . kill, steal, and so forth." They were enforced by sanctions which were believed to be natural occurrences. As water or fire will destroy man, so God in his wrath will punish him if he transgresses. It would seem that in the early epochs of man's social organization, people gave a helping hand to their deities (as they still do in political matters), and yet managed to believe that the sanctions for transgressions were just as automatic and impersonal as those that followed the breaking of the rules of biological survival. Or perhaps it would be more accurate to reverse the equation between natural and moral laws and to assert that primitive man confuses the two because he can conceive of natural law only in the form of willed action. Rather than recognizing the impersonal nature of physical laws, he personalizes the world. This is what is meant by the "animistic spirit" in which the child and primitive man apprehend the world. The religious cosmology presented in the Bible is a classic illustration of animistic "science" and the resultant equation of natural and moral law. For example, the Jews persecuted by the Egyptian Pharaoh do not rise in revolt—like their latter-day successors, who contributed their efforts to making an atomic bomb with which to destroy their enemy—but, instead, their revenge is carried out by God via the "natural occurrence" of a "fatal illness" which strikes at each parent's most beloved possession, his first-born son.

Contemporary (Western) man's most crucial dilemma is perhaps his inability to accept a theological view of nature while at the same time being unprepared to commit himself to a scientific-pragmatic view of it. Thus, many people are caught between one system of thought which is too primitive for them and another which is too complicated (Bridgman, 1959).

The need to equate, and hence to obscure, natural and religious rules forms the basic underpinning of the prescientific world view. Yet even thousands of years ago men must have perceived that it was possible to distinguish between these two types of rules. The notion of miracles was then invoked to undermine man's budding rationalism which threatened to destroy the theological (mystical) conception of the world and man's place in it. In this light, the epistemological function of miracles is to re-establish the identity between physical and religious rules by asserting the verity of observations known to run counter to biological and physical laws. The separation of the waters of the Red Sea, allowing the Israelites to pass through unharmed, but engulfing the pursuing Egyptians, is a typical example. The story of Bernadette, the Saint of Lourdes, affords a relatively recent illustration of the same phenomenon—namely, of the wish to conceive of finding a well, or of recovery from disability or illness, as a mysterious, God-inspired act rather than as an occurrence in conformity with physical laws. This interpretation is consistent with the bitter enmity that has characterized the relations of organized religion to science during the past several centuries.

Today, the term "social rules" designates all the rules that originate from the prevailing practices of a social group (Hollingshead, 1955). If social rules are significantly disobeyed or disregarded, the person will be unable to survive. Emphasis here is on the word "person," for our focus has shifted from biological to social survival. Social survival depends on either adapting to the social rules or changing them to suit one's needs, much as biological survival depends on adapting to biological rules.

In earlier historical epochs, the source of social rules was thought to be God, deities, Moses, Jesus Christ, and other lofty personages. It must be recalled in this connection that according to a deistic conception of the world God is a kind of universal causal theory. His being and activity "explain" everything. Although the educated man of today has completely relinquished this conception in regard to, say, bodily illness—for example, he no longer ascribes measles or peptic ulcer to God—he still adheres to a deistic conception of moral conduct. In view of the current technological situation, both here and abroad, it seems doubtful that we could long afford a cultural lag of this dimension.

The existence and durability of social rules—irrespective of the sources to which man may have attributed them—is evidence of the immense power of the human need to follow rules. Indeed, man's need for rules and his propensity to follow them is equaled only by his burning ambition to be free of rules. As I will try to show later, this antithetical attitude is a special instance of a more general human proclivity—namely, the need for objects and the simultaneous need for aloneness and individuality. Oscillating attitudes of submission to and rebellion against people and rules may be best viewed as manifestations of this fundamental human problem. In our efforts to resolve this dilemma, one of the most potent forces at our disposal seems to be the human capacity for abstraction. This makes it possible to construct increasingly higher levels of symbolization; these constructs, in turn, lead to a lessening of the feeling of compulsion attached to all rules not explicitly understood *as* rules. Thus, for each set of rules we can, in principle, construct a set of metarules. The latter are made up of the specifications governing the formation of the rules at the next lower (logical) level. Explicit awareness of metarules implies an understanding of the origin, function, and scope of the (next lower-level) rules. The acquisition of such understanding represents a form of *mastery*. Only by practicing what may be called the metarule attitude—which, of course is but a special case of the scientific attitude applied to the domain of rules—can a secure yet flexible integration of rules as behavior-regulating agencies be achieved. Finally, the metarule attitude makes it possible to increase the range of choices concerning when and how to comply with rules, when and how to change them, and the limits and consequences of our decisions in regard to these matters.

IMITATIVE OR INTERPERSONAL RULES

Imitative or interpersonal rules are learned, principally in childhood, by imitating someone else's example. Illustrative are the innumerable instances in which *children look*, literally as well as metaphorically, to their parents, siblings, or peers, *to see how they should act*. Their conduct is thus based on example, much as a mock-up model in engineering serves as an example after which the products to be manufactured are fashioned.

The line of demarcation between imitative and social rules may not always be sharp or clear. Some social rules are acquired by imitation. Moreover, since imitative rules are acquired chiefly in the family, they really form a subgroup or special subdivision of the larger class called "social rules." Nevertheless, it is useful—especially for our present purpose in regard to hysteria and mental illness—to draw as sharp a distinction as possible between these two types of rules. Let us therefore pay special attention to the differences between social and interpersonal rules.

Imitative rules usually refer to trivial, everyday matters, such as how to dress, how to eat, how to use certain toys, and so forth. These rules are

TABLE 5. THREE TYPES OF RULES: BIOLOGICAL, SOCIAL, AND INTERPERSONAL

	Biological Rules	Social Rules	Interpersonal Rules
Example	"You must eat to live; otherwise you will starve to death."	"You must worship God to live; otherwise you will be expelled from the group."	"If you are a male, you must grow up to be self-reliant, so that you can provide for your wife and children; otherwise you will not be able to consider yourself a grown man."
Subject matter studied by	Biological sciences	Sociology, anthropology	Psychology, psychoanalysis
Aims of the rules	Survival of physical body and/or species. Biological identity	Survival of (large) group as a social organization. Social (group) identity	Survival of small group (family) or individual, as social being. Individual identity
Sanctions for breaking the rules	1. Illness or disability of the body 2. Dissolution of the physical body: "biological death"	1. Socially deviant behavior and "punishment": "crime," "sin" 2. Expulsion from the group; loss of social identity; "social death"	Interpersonally conflictful behavior; personal defeat, frustration, and unhappiness; "mental illness"; "human failure"
Sanctions codified as	Natural laws	Legal (or religious) "laws"	Customs, standards of personal behavior
Rewards for successfully modifying the rules	Extension of life span and increase in physical effectiveness and health	Enlarged scope of human fraternity and cooperation (e.g., supranational versus national interests and identity)	Creative self-determination; enhanced sense of identity and freedom
Rate of change	Nil or very slow	Gradual	Most rapid

usually not spelled out in verbal form. Instead of their being explicitly stated, they are exhibited in the actual daily behavior of the older members of the family or group. Children acquire these rules by "blind imitation." The "blind" quality of this learning process must be emphasized, for in contrast to, say, attempting to forge another person's signature, this type of imitation is unconscious or unreflective. In learning one's mother tongue, for instance, one is not aware of imitating other people.

In contrast to the trivial nature of many of the acts learned by imitative rule-following, and to the inexplicit nature of these rules, social rules refer to relatively more important behavioral situations regulated by explicitly stated rules (usually in the forms of commands or prohibitions or combinations of these). In other words, while imitative rules refer to customs, social rules codify moral-religious prescriptions or secular laws. The sanctions for each vary correspondingly. Failure to learn or comply with imitative rules leads merely to being thought of as eccentric, stupid, foolish, or naughty. Deviance from social rules, however, brings serious consequences upon the offender, ranging from being labeled bad or guilty to expulsion from family (or group), or even to loss of life. For our present purpose there is no need to expand this discussion of the characteristics of various types of rules. Sociologists, by and large, have concentrated on what we have called social rules. Imitative or interpersonal rules, on the other hand, have been singled out for special consideration by psychologists, and especially by psychoanalysts. Anthropologists have often been attentive to the role and significance of both sets of rules. (A condensed summary of the salient characteristics of the three types of rules is presented in Table 5.)

"The power of reason must be sought not in rules that reason dictates to our imagination, but in the ability to free ourselves from any kind of rules to which we have been conditioned through experience and tradition."

Hans Reichenbach (1951, p. 141)

CHAPTER 11 | # The Ethics of Helplessness and Helpfulness

Let us recall that "hysteria" refers to the expression and communication—chiefly by means of nonverbal, bodily signs—of a state of disability or "illness." The implicit aim of the communication is to secure help. If the problem of hysteria is framed in this way, it becomes logical to inquire: Where did the idea originate that the rules of the game of life ought to be so defined that those who are weak, disabled, or ill should be helped? The first answer is that this is the game usually played in childhood. In other words, every one of us as a weak and helpless child was cared for by adults. Without such help we would not have survived to adulthood.[1]

The second general answer to the question raised above is that the rules prescribing a help-giving attitude toward the weak—that is, the rules characteristic of the child-parent interaction or of the family game—derive from the dominant religions of Western man. Judaism, and especially Christianity, teach these rules. They do so by means of myth, example, exhortation, and whenever possible by the use of appropriate negative sanctions.

This chapter will be devoted to an exposition of the nature and actual psychosocial operation of these two general systems of rules. The first could be regarded as the rules of the family game; the second, as those of the religious game. These rules are singled out for consideration because they provide, in part, the psychosocial basis and continuing rationale for so-called

---

[1] The fact that all child-adult relationships may be subsumed under the category of help-seeking–help-giving does not mean that there are not considerable variations in these relationships. A vast anthropological and sociological literature on child-rearing practices is devoted to the elucidation of precisely these differences (e.g., Linton, 1945, 1957).

hysterical behavior as well as for certain other "mental illnesses." In other words, men learn how to be "mentally ill" by following (mainly) the rules of these two games.[2] Since ethical systems consist basically of rules of social conduct that men are enjoined to follow, the two systems which will be considered may properly be regarded as constituting the ethics of helplessness and helpfulness.

Childhood and the Rules of Helplessness

Freud repeatedly stressed (for example, 1916-1917, 1927) that man's prolonged childhood was responsible for his proneness to develop what he called "neurosis." In its general form, the idea that childishness is somehow related to "mental illness" (as well as to misbehaviors of all sorts) is obviously very old. It would be impossible to credit any one person with this important insight. The main shortcomings of this notion are its generality and vagueness. To be useful, whether for scientific theory-building or psychotherapy, the precise details of the common human tendency to remain childish, or to reassume childish patterns of behavior ("regression"), must be elucidated.

REGRESSION VERSUS INFANTILIZATION

Freud's basic thesis was that man *wanted* to remain a child and was driven forward, as it were, only by forces generated by instinctual (sexual) frustration. This frustration, in turn, he saw as coming from "culture." He thus postulated an irreconcilable conflict between the interests of instinctual and especially sexual satisfaction on the one hand and cultural, including social, needs and development on the other (Freud, 1927, 1930). An inherent part of this scientific-philosophical position is to regard man's tendency toward immaturity as "biologically given." Regression is thus considered to satisfy a "need" similar to the biologically determined needs for water, food, or sexual activity. This view, which provides an "explanation" of the tendency to regress, makes it unnecessary to search for social factors which might contribute to this type of behavior.

In recent decades, numerous students of man have taken issue with this basic theory concerning "human nature." One of the most coherent formulations of the notion that man's tendency toward childishness is not a biologi-

[2] The basic premise which underlies my attempt to formulate a coherent theory of personal conduct is that it is always, at least in part, an expression of *learning and human creativity*. This approach to psychiatry is anything but novel. It received its initial impetus from Freud and Pavlov and was subsequently carried forward by A. Adler (1907-1937), Dollard and Miller (1941, 1950), Fromm (1941, 1947), Goldstein (1951), Horney (1939, 1950), Jung (1940), Sullivan (1947, 1953), and others.

cally determined phenomenon counteracted by civilization, but rather that man is "inherently" capable of developing in a direction of increasing psychosocial complexity, expressed by increasingly rich patterns of symbolization, we owe to Susanne Langer (1942).

Stated generally, one may explain childish behavior in terms of biological causation, in terms of learning, or in terms of a combination of the two. The psychoanalytic concept of regression is biologically anchored but also makes use of learning experiences as determinants of later behavior. The relation of the two components to one another, and their exact proportion, are usually unclear. In my treatment of this problem, biological considerations will be left out of account. Thus, our task is to contribute to the understanding of the psychosocial factors that foster learning on the one hand, and those that foster ignorance on the other.

My thesis is that there are no good grounds for accepting the view that man desires the *status quo* and is driven forward only by privation, culture, or what not. In fact, this formulation seems to be merely a new, more scientific sounding version, of the ancient Biblical story of man's fall from divine grace—of Adam and Eve's expulsion from the Garden of Eden. The very fact that God forbade these two "original sinners" ever to return to the Garden of Eden implied that they wanted to return. For if Adam and Eve did not wish to return to Paradise, how would they have been punished? The traditional psychoanalytic theory of human growth likewise postulates that *regressive goals are primary*. Sublimation is considered a poor substitute; one, it is implied, that would be relinquished instantly if the original regressive goals were rendered (unconflictfully) attainable.

I submit that "Paradise Lost" is a myth. The pleasurable qualities of childhood experiences and of regressive goals generally have been vastly overrated. Dispensing with the whole vexing problem of precisely how happy or satisfying childhood gratifications are, I shall adhere, instead, to a position concerning human psychosocial maturation essentially similar to Langer's. However, I wish to supplement her basic thesis, that man has a need for symbolization and symbolic expression, by adding two complementary notions to it: first, that man has a primary (further irreducible) need for object contact or human relationships;[3] second, that the notions of objects, symbols, rules, and roles are intimately tied together, so that man's growth toward personal identity and integrity on the one hand, and toward social tolerance and decreasing need for group narcissism on the other, go hand

---

[3] For some interesting recent work on object relationships in monkeys, see Harlow and Zimmermann (1959). *The need for object contact* is especially dramatically illustrated by these significant experimental observations. In this connection, see also Fairbairn (1952) and Szasz (1957a).

in hand with increasing sophistication in regard to the understanding and use of symbols, rules, roles, and games (Szasz, 1957c). It seems to me, therefore, that the apparently basic human tendency to remain childish and to strive for so-called regressive goals is not necessarily biologically given but may be better explained along the following lines.

Learning *is* difficult. It requires effort, application to a task, self-discipline, perseverance, and so forth. Persistence in habitual patterns of behavior is, therefore, at the very least, labor-saving. However valid this principle may appear to be—and I do not mean to minimize its significance—its relevance depends on a scarcity of zest and interest in the learner. Should a person have an abundance of these psychological ingredients, that is to say, should he be psychologically affluent—as healthy children, for instance, surely are—the principle that saving labor is a "good thing" will no longer apply. Such a person, much as an economically productive and affluent society, will need to produce and consume rather than to conserve. Hence, the need to save psychological "labor" cannot be considered a general law. Its validity depends on the presence of certain conditions, for example, fatigue, poor endowment for learning (stupidity or feeble-mindedness), or human relationships which discourage or prohibit learning.

It seems to me that the significance of religious, social, and personal prohibitions placed on knowledge and learning have been surprisingly underestimated in most scientific theories of man. It is, indeed, impressive how much human beings learn. Nevertheless, pressures in the opposite direction have been present and active in all historical periods (see, for example, Muller, 1959; Yarnell, 1957). By way of illustration, consider the following examples:

1. Jewish and Christian religions attribute man's fall from divine grace to Adam's having partaken of the fruit of the tree of knowledge.

2. The Roman Catholic Church provides a list of books (and other materials, such as films) which are prohibited for members of this faith.[4]

3. There are many more subtle, but equally powerful, social forces that prevent people from learning the facts of human biology or of other people's religious beliefs or national customs. Many rules of group-conduct (national narcissisms, racial prejudice, etc.), no less than religious beliefs and teachings, foster and reward various forms of covert individual infantilism.

[4] In addition to Freud's *Collected Papers,* works by the following authors have been placed on (and sometimes subsequently removed from) the Roman Catholic *Index of Prohibited Books:* Havelock Ellis, Aldous Huxley, James Joyce, Alfred C. Kinsey, Thomas Mann, Margaret Mead, Bertrand Russell, H. G. Wells, etc. (Blanshard, 1953, pp. 80-87). Despite the significance of these works to the study of behavioral science— and of similar, though perhaps less clear-cut conflicts between science and other aspects of religious belief—at the present time neither psychoanalytic nor religious organizations seem to regard the roles of psychoanalyst and religious believer as being in conflict with each other.

4. Finally, it must be recalled that many persons, acting in specific relationships, foster nonlearning behavior—e.g., the parent who rewards his child's persistent helplessness and dependency in order to enhance his own importance and self-esteem. I believe that this type of occurrence is extremely common (Butler, 1903). If so, it constitutes a significant part of the grand total of human tendencies that press toward childishness, helplessness, incompetence, and "mental illness."

THE RULE: "THE SICK AND THE SUFFERER MUST BE HELPED!"

Like the infant's cry, the message "I am sick" is exceedingly effective in mobilizing others to some kind of helpful action. In accordance with this communicative impact of sickness, physicians—following in the footsteps of their predecessors, the clergy—have tended to define their occupation as a "calling." This implied that it was not only the sick and helpless who were calling them, as indeed they were, but God as well. The helpers would thus hasten to the side of the helpless (the sick or disabled), and would minister to him to restore him to "health." This sort of therapeutic attitude tends to define the role of the helpless or sick person in a complementary manner, that is, as entitled to help, merely by virtue of being disabled. Hence, if we do not help him (particularly if we could), we incur moral blame for our failure.

It frequently happens that this "game of helpfulness" is played so that those who are on the help-giving team have unknowingly obligated themselves to caring for the help-seekers. They no longer choose to offer or withhold help, depending on circumstances, but instead are committed to an unwritten social contract that may be quite burdensome for them. It is no wonder, then, that if a sufferer is found to malinger, his behavior is usually experienced by those at whom his message is directed (the help-giving team) as though it were a form of blackmail. Physicians react to such persons in much the same way as we all would if confronted by an individual holding a contract extremely injurious to us which he was trying to enforce with all the (legal) power at his command. Although Freud did not deal with this problem in these terms, he was aware of it and was prepared to face it in the tradition of scientific rationalism. This may be inferred from his insistence that the financial aspects of the patient-physician relationship be openly discussed (Freud, 1913, p. 346). Until then—and even today in many quarters—physicians had not been in the habit of speaking of money matters with patients. This behavior undoubtedly served several purposes, among them the wish to avoid interfering with the image of the sick-helper relationship sketched above. To preserve the belief that the sick receive medical help because they *need it*, it is necessary to deny or obscure the fact that they pay for it. The possibility that attitudes of "kindness" and "sweetness" toward "poor patients" serve, by and large, the purpose of enhancing the doctor's self-esteem should always be kept in mind.

By the same token, therapeutic attitudes traditionaly ascribed to "kindness" should be scrutinized as potential maneuvers on the part of the therapist to depreciate and subjugate the patient. Recall, in this connection, the relationship between the well-to-do Southern white man and his Negro slave. The master treated his servant with "kindness" and "consideration"—indeed, often with much more kindness than the Negro received in a Northern industrial jungle (as white supremacists are still apt to remind us)—but this very "kindness" formed a part of the code of slavery.

Similarly, much of what passes for "medical ethics" is a set of rules the net effect of which is the persistent infantilization and subjugation of the patient. A shift toward positions of greater dignity and self-responsibility for the disenfranchised—whether "slave," "sinner," or "patient"—can be secured only by honestly and seriously subscribing to a democratic (egalitarian) ethic. This implies that persons are treated with respect, consideration, and dignity under all circumstances. While being accorded the opportunities for more decent human relationships, the formerly disenfranchised must, at the same time, be expected to shoulder certain responsibilities. Among the responsibilities incident to such a realignment of human relationships is the requirement to be self-reliant and responsible even in cases of disability and illness—except, of course, when the disability reaches extreme proportions.[5]

Summing up: The traditional sick-helper relationship rests on unacknowledged rules of the game according to which the sick person is entitled to treatment or help by virtue of his very disability. Although seemingly advantageous for the patient, this arrangement has serious drawbacks for him. It may be changed by altering the helpless-helper relationship so that both the power of the sick to demand and the power of the physician to dominate will be abridged. As a result, the sick person will gain in his ability to help himself, both directly (by becoming more skillful and resourceful) and indirectly (by increasing his range of choice for securing help). The physician, too, will gain, for he will be able to limit and structure his work so that it will be unnecessary for him to engage in sadomasochistic aggression with patients whom he would prefer, for whatever reason, not to treat. Finally, maximal choice in regard to his work activity will enable the physician to enhance his scientific-technical competence (Oppenheimer, 1957).

[5] For an incisive criticism of the ethics of helplessness, and a proclamation in its stead of what might be called the *ethics of self-reliance and competence*, see *The Way Things Are* by Percy W. Bridgman (1959).

HERBERT SPENCER ON HELPING THE HELPLESS

Herbert Spencer (1820-1903), who is often considered one of the fore-fathers of modern sociology, was profoundly interested in the problem of helping the helpless. Strongly influenced by Darwin's evolutionary conceptions of biology, he tried to base sociological principles on biological observations. Although this method contains many possibilities for error, Spencer's views deserve serious consideration.

Spencer's basic thesis that "conformity . . . to two radically opposed principles" on which "the continuance of every higher species of creature depends" (p. 78) was presented in detail in his essay *The Man Versus The State* (1884). In the case of every higher species of animal, Spencer noted, "the early lives of its members and the adult lives of its members, have to be dealt with in contrary ways" (p. 78). I shall briefly summarize what he meant.

Spencer began his argument by mentioning the familiar fact that animals of "superior types" are comparatively slow in reaching maturity. Having matured, however, they are able "to give more aid to their offspring than animals of inferior types" (p. 78). In these species, moreover, "the maintenance of the species can be secured only by a *parental care adjusted to the need consequent to imperfection*" ([ITALICS ADDED] p. 79). On the basis of these observations, he formulated the general law that "during immaturity, benefits received must be inversely as the power or ability of the receiver. Clearly, if during his first part of life benefits were proportioned to merits, or rewards to deserts, the species would disappear in a generation" (p. 79).

Spencer then proceeded to compare and contrast what he called the "*régime* of the family group" with the "*régime* of that larger group formed by the adult members of the species" (p. 79). At some point in their lives, mature individuals (that is, animals) are left to themselves. Henceforth they must fulfill the requirements of life, or else they will perish.

Now there comes into play a principle just the reverse of that above described. *Throughout the rest of its life, each adult gets benefit in proportion to merit, reward in proportion to desert*: merit and desert in each case being understood as ability to fulfill all the requirements of life—to get food, to secure shelter, or to escape enemies. Placed in competition with members of its own species and in antagonism with members of other species, it dwindles and gets killed off or thrives and propagates, according as it is ill-endowed or well-endowed. Manifestly an opposite *régime*, could it be maintained, would in course of time, be fatal to the species. If the benefits received by each individual were proportionate to its inferiority—if, as a consequence, multiplication of the inferior was furthered and multiplication of the superior hindered, progressive degradation would result; and eventually the degenerate species would fail to hold its ground in presence of antagonistic species and competing species. The broad fact then, here to be noted, is that *Nature's modes of treatment inside the family-group and outside the family-group are diametrically opposed to one another;* and that the intrusion of either mode into the sphere of the other, would be fatal to the species either immediately or remotely ([ITALICS ADDED] pp. 79-80).

Spencer applied these observations to the human species and suggested that men can no more afford to flout this Law of Nature than can animals. In other words, while he thought it inevitable and, hence, proper that children should be sheltered by their families, he felt strongly that such an arrangement with respect to adults will bring disaster on the human species. In the true spirit of rugged individualism, so characteristic of the nineteenth-century liberal, Spencer pleaded for the self-reliant responsibility of man as opposed to the ministrations of the paternalistic State.

Surely none can fail to see that were the principle of family life to be adopted and fully carried out in social life—were reward always great in proportion as desert was small, fatal results to the society would quickly follow; and if so, then even a partial intrusion of the family *régime* into the *régime* of the State, will be slowly followed by fatal results. *Society, in its corporate capacity, cannot without immediate or remoter disaster interfere with the play of these opposed principles under which every species has reached such fitness for its mode of life as it possesses, and under which it maintains that fitness* ([ITALICS ADDED] p. 80).

I do not believe that such a direct application of biological or evolutionary principles to the social—and hence inherently ethical—affairs of man is ever justified. I cite Spencer's views on this subject, however, not for their political implications, but rather because of their historical significance. Spencer was a senior contemporary of Freud's. His thesis concerning the significance, especially for social organization, of the basic biological relationship between parent and young offspring became a cornerstone of psychoanalytic theory. Roheim (1943) even created an entire anthropological theory of man based on essentially nothing more than this notion of prolonged fetalization.

Although this argument is plausible and undoubtedly of some value, it is necessary to be cautious lest it be used to "explain" too much. Emphasizing the human infant's biologically determined dependence on its parents in order to explain "neurosis" may be a reversal of cause and effect. It seems probable that the human child remains dependent for so long not because his prolonged childhood is biologically given, but rather because it takes him *this long to learn all the necessary symbols, rules, roles, and games which he must master before he can be considered a "human being"* (and not merely a biologically mature organism).

This line of thought leads to a reconsideration of the problem of the similarities, from a sociopsychological point of view, between being young (or immature) and being disabled (by illness or otherwise). For practical tasks, such as gathering food, fighting off enemies, and so forth, children are useless. In fact, they are liabilities. The physically disabled, or those who, for whatever reason, refuse to play the game (e.g., refuse to work) are similarly useless to society, and in fact constitute a liability for it. If this is true, why do human societies tolerate such disabilities? Evidently, human societies have concerns other than just the "practical" tasks for which disabled individuals are useless. Since disabled adults are functionally similar to children, they fall readily into the same type of relationship to the able as children do to their parents. The disabled need help and will not survive without it. The able are capable of providing help and are motivated to do so. Besides the biologically built-in tendencies which parent organisms may have to provide for their children (and for others in need), there are socially given incentives fostering succoring behavior. In primitive social groups, for example, children could be counted on to help out, as soon as they were strong enough, with the physical toils necessary for survival, and also to assist in fighting off enemies. Thus, to care for them when they were helpless meant to gain later allies.

The weakest link in Spencer's argument is that he failed to make any allowance for the fundamental change from man as *biological organism* to man as *social being*. In regard to the rule of helping those in need, this transformation means a change from acting automatically—that is, in conformity with biologically built-in mechanisms, triggered perhaps by environmental conditions (Ostow, 1958)—to becoming self-reflective, that is, aware of the rules themselves. Rules may be "followed" regardless of which of these attitudes is maintained toward them. In the first instance, they are followed in an obligatory manner, for the person or animal has no opportunity to deviate from them. In contrast, self-reflective rule-following provides an opportunity to make choices. Only then can one truly speak of following and breaking rules. Moreover, awareness of the rules leads to another condition—namely, the (deliberate) imitation of occurrences designed to bring the operation of the desired rules into play. Thus, as soon as men became intelligent, sign-using animals and hence aware of, say, the kinds of relationships that invariably obtain between children and parents, the stage was set to imitate childishness to gain certain ends. The stage for the genesis of hysteria, too, was set at this early phase of human social development. The causes of, or the necessary conditions for, the development of hysteria are first, the biologically determined but socially implemented rule that parents (or well-functioning individuals) care for their children (or for ill-functioning individuals); second, man's growth to self-reflection and awareness, made possible by the development of speech and symbolization. In this light, hysteria appears to be a creative—in a sense, progressive—act, rather than a disability or "regression."

Biblical Rules Fostering Disability and Illness

Jewish and Christian religious teachings abound in rules that reward sickness, malingering, poverty, fearfulness—in brief, disabilities of all sorts. Moreover, these rules, or their corollaries, invoke penalties for self-reliance, competence, effectiveness, and pride in health and well-being. This is a bold assertion, although not a particularly novel one. I shall try to support it by adequate evidence. I wish to emphasize that it is *not* my thesis that prescriptions fostering disability constitute the whole or the essence of the Bible. Taken in its entirety, the Bible is a complex and heterogeneous work, from which many diverse rules of conduct may be inferred. Indeed, the history of Western religions and morals illustrates how, by taking one or another part of this work, it is possible to support a wide variety of social or moral courses of action (Lecky, 1894; Brinton, 1950). It is important to bear this in mind, since our present concern is not to argue for one value and against another.

Personally, I espouse the values of a self-conscious rationality and science. This implies that in matters of human conduct responsibility based on intelligent appraisal of the consequences of one's actions is considered a positive value. Other positive values are those of respect for the autonomy and integrity of one's self and others, and self-determination. No attempt to justify or support these values will be made here. I believe that in a work of this kind it is necessary to make one's point of view toward such matters clear, to enable the reader to make allowances for or to correct the author's bias.

My approach to religious rules and behavior is sociopsychological, not theological. Thus, whether my interpretations of religious rules are "theologically accurate" is largely irrelevant. What is relevant is whether I have inferred correctly or falsely from the actual behavior of persons professing to be religious the rules that govern and explain their conduct.

In addressing myself to scriptural passages as written statements, my position is that of a logically critical interpreter. I shall be critical of certain Biblical rules, but in doing so shall be concerned less with condemning them—this has been done often enough throughout the ages (e.g., Paine, 1794; Lewis, 1926) and hardly merits repetition—than with making explicit the values upheld as worth striving for. Naturally, my interpretations of what certain Biblical passages might mean to contemporary man will conflict with the interpretation of the modern clergyman, who is trying to make scriptural texts fit for present-day consumption. It seems to me that so-called liberal interpretations of religious documents (whether Christian or Jewish) serve the aim of selling religion to modern man. It should not surprise us if vendors wrap up their merchandise so as to make it most attractive for the buyer—in this case, so that it will conflict as little as possible with the scientific and democratic aspects of Western civilization (Raven, 1959).

Fundamentalist interpretations, on the other hand, also serve a promotive aim—to turn back the clock of civilization by returning to an uncompromisingly deistic-mystical (antiscientific) view of the world. The conflict between religion and science, particularly as it affects personal and social behavior, is thus best demonstrated among those people who profess to fundamentalistic versions of the Christian and Jewish religions, e.g., Jehovah's Witnesses, ultra-orthodox Jews (Fellows, 1960).

THE RELATIONSHIP BETWEEN MAN AND GOD

The motif that God loves the humble, the meek, the needy, or those who fear Him is a thread running through both the Old and New Testaments. The idea that man should not be too well off lest he offend God is deeply ingrained in the Jewish religion. It was also present in classical Greek pantheism. Indeed, this element seems to be a part of most primitive religions, according to which man conceives of God in his own image: God is like man, except more so. God, then, is a kind of superman with his own needs for self-esteem and status and it is these privileges that mortal men are enjoined to respect. The Greek legend of Polycrates, the overly lucky king of Samos, illustrates this theme (Schiller, 1798).

This attitude, which amounts to nothing less than a dread of happiness or contentment, is fundamental to the psychology of the person who participates in the Judaeo-Christian ethic. The defensive, self-protective character of this "masochistic" maneuver is evident. For such a technique to be effective, it is necessary to assume the presence of (1) another person (or persons), and (2) the operation of certain rules by which this person (one's opponent) conducts himself.

Two questions may now be raised. First: Who is man's opponent in this game of I-am-not-happy? Second: What are the specific rules of this game that make this defense possible? As to the identity of the opponent, we may say, without going into unnecessary details, that it is God and a succession of other powerful figures vis-à-vis whom the player occupies a slavelike, subservient position. The power differential between the two players, as it were, is crucial, for it alone can account for the fear of envy (Schachtel, 1959, p. 42). In a strong-weak relationship, only the weak member of the pair needs to fear arousing the envy of his partner. The strong has no such fears, because he knows that the weak is powerless to act destructively toward him.

In general, then, the open acknowledgment of satisfaction is feared only in situations of relative oppression (e.g., all-suffering wife vis-à-vis domineering husband). *The experience and expression of satisfaction (joy, contentment) are inhibited lest they lead to an augmentation of one's burden.* This dilemma must be faced, for example, by persons who come from large, poor families and who do moderately well financially while the other family members remain poor. If such a person manages to become very wealthy, he will be able to take care of all the other family members who want to be dependent on him. However, should he be only moderately well off, he will be faced with the threat that, irrespective of how hard he works, the demands of his poor relatives will not let him get ahead. Their needs will always be greater than his assets. (Progressive taxation may create similar feelings in people.) If our hypothetical man wishes to prevent antagonizing his poor, needy relatives, he will be prompted to malinger in regard to his financial situation. Such "malingering," that is, misrepresenting his economic affairs, will protect him from the experience—and, perhaps, the reality—of being robbed of his possessions.

This example demonstrates the close correspondence between misrepresenting health as illness on the one hand, and misrepresenting wealth as poverty on the other. Although, on the surface, both maneuvers seem painful and self-damaging, a more complete inspection of the total human situation in which they occur discloses that they are defensive operations. Their purpose is to sacrifice a part to save the whole. For example, bodily survival may be safeguarded by simulating ill-health (e.g., in wartime). Financial possessions may be safeguarded by pretending to be poor, thus averting aggressive demands upon one's resources.

The fear of acknowledging satisfaction is a characteristic feature of slave psychology. The "properly exploited" slave is forced to labor until he shows signs of fatigue or exhaustion. Completion of his task does not signify that his work is finished and that he may rest. At the same time, even though his task in unfinished, he may be able to influence his master to stop driving him—and to let him rest—if he exhibits signs of imminent collapse. Such signs may be genuine or contrived. Exhibiting signs of fatigue or exhaustion—irrespective of whether they are genuine or contrived (e.g., "being on strike" against one's boss)—is likely to induce a feeling of fatigue or exhaustion in the actor. I believe that this is the mechanism responsible for the great majority of so-called chronic fatigue states. Most of these were formerly called "neurasthenia," a term rarely used nowadays. Chronic fatigue or a feeling of lifelessness and exhaustion are still frequently encountered in clinical practice.

Psychoanalytically, they are considered "character symptoms." Many of these patients are unconsciously "on strike" against persons (actual or internal) to whom they relate with subservience and against whom they wage an unending and unsuccessful covert rebellion. In contrast to the slave, a free man sets his own limits and works, at least sometimes, until he has achieved the satisfying completion of a task. He can then stop, before becoming fatigued, and enjoy the fruits of his labors.

The answer to the second question, concerning the specific rules that make disability or illness potential assets, may be briefly stated as follows. In certain situations, the rules of the game prescribe that when man (subject, son, patient, etc.) is healthy, self-reliant, rich, and proud, God (king, father, physician, etc.) shall be strict, demanding, even punitive. But should man be sick, help-seeking, poor, and humble, then God will treat him with special consideration. He will be forgiven, helped, loved, and permitted to be passive and incompetent. It might seem that I have exaggerated this rule. I do not believe that I have. Rather, this impression probably reflects our spontaneous antagonism to such a rule when it is forcefully stated.

Many Biblical passages could be cited to support this thesis. In Psalms (147:10-11), it is stated:

> He delighteth not in the strength of the horse: he taketh not pleasure in the legs of a man. The Lord taketh pleasure in them that fear him, in those that hope in his mercy.

And in Luke (18:22-25) we read:

> Now when Jesus heard these things, he said unto him, Yet lackest thou one thing: sell all that thou hast, and distribute unto the poor, and thou shalt have treasure in heaven: and come, follow me. And

when he heard this, he was very sorrowful: for he was very rich. And when Jesus saw that he was very sorrowful, He said, How hardly shall they that have riches enter into the kingdom of God! For it is easier for a camel to go through a needle's eye, than for a rich man to enter into the kingdom of God.

The Sermon on the Mount (Matthew 5:1-12) is probably the best-known illustration of the rules fostering dependency and disability. Here, Christ blesses the poor in spirit, the meek, the mourner, and so forth. This passage most clearly enunciates the basic rules by which the Christian God may be said to play His game with Man. What does God pledge Himself to do? And what type of behavior is demanded of man? To formulate my answers, I have transformed and paraphrased the Beatitudes. First, the Biblical phrasing "blessed are" has been translated into "should." Second, each positive injunction so obtained was supplemented by its corollary, framed in the form of a prohibition. The Beatitudes then read (in part) as follows:

The Biblical text (Matthew 5:3, 5, 8)	*Its logical corollary* (Author's interpretation)
Blessed *are* the poor in spirit: for theirs is the kingdom of heaven.	Man should be "poor in spirit"—i.e., stupid, submissive: Do not be smart, well-informed, or assertive!
Blessed *are* the meek: for they shall inherit the earth.	Man should be "meek"—i.e., passive, weak, submissive: Do not be self-assertive!
Blessed *are* the pure in heart: for they shall see God.	Man should be "pure in heart"—i.e., naive, unquestioningly loyal: Do not entertain doubt (about God) and do not be critical!

Stated in this form, it is evident that these rules constitute a simple reversal of rules governing human rewards and punishments in life on earth. In this process of rule reversal, deficiencies in endowment, skill, and knowledge—or, in general, incompetence—have become codified as positive values. Elsewhere (Matthew 6:34), man is explicitly enjoined to "take no thought for the morrow." In other words, man should not plan for the future. He should not try to provide for himself and for those who depend on him. Instead, he should cultivate trust and faith in God. This is, of course, a good rational rule for children, since in fact they cannot—and, if they have a father or a mother, need not—provide for themselves.

But what are the implications of these rules when espoused for and by adult men and women? These are the rules of irresponsibility and childish dependency. It is difficult to exaggerate the conflict between these rules and the demands of living according to the rules of rationality, science, and a democratic or humanitarian conception of adult responsibility. It remains a matter of conjecture, however, to what extent this conflict between religious rules and the demands for adult responsibility continues to contribute to the development of interpersonal incompetence and diminished self-reliance in adult men and women.

Not only do some Biblical rules foster dependency; they also lay the groundwork for using lack of foresight and incompetence as weapons to coerce others to provide for one's needs. We may recall in this connection that the "practical" uselessness of the clergy has been rationalized and made possible by the notion that it is the parishioner's duty to support them. Only in ancient Jewish tradition was this not true. The rabbi had to have a trade so that he would not be forced to accept money for teaching the law of God. This principle is no longer adhered to today. Thus, the significant feature shared by clergymen of all faiths—including the Oriental religions (Narayan, 1959)—seems to be the contractual relationship between priest and parishioner. According to this unwritten agreement, the parishioners must take care of the worldly needs of the priests—while, in return, the priesthood will take care of the spiritual (or otherworldly) needs of the toilers, who are engaged in work useful here and now.

Since so-called mentally ill behavior—and especially conversion hysteria —is intimately linked with inability or unwillingness to perform in the game that is life, it may be instructive to call special attention to Biblical rules that command man to be passive and incompetent. In *The Sermon on the Mount* (Matthew 6:24-34), Christ drew a comparison between man on the one hand and fowls and lilies on the other. Man is enjoined to emulate the passivity of lower biological forms. Since animals and plants do not plan for the future, why should man? Self-help and mastery are explicitly discouraged and condemned. Indeed, wanting to help oneself is interpreted as having "little faith." Of course, such heedlessness for the future can be practiced only to a limited extent. If it were practiced in earnest, it would undoubtedly result in the dying out of its practitioners, as Herbert Spencer predicted. Yet it remains a fact that a certain measure—perhaps sometimes a very large measure—of social irresponsibility is encouraged by such a code. Heedlessness for the future promotes incurring disabilities in living that often do not become socially manifest until much later.

It is implicit in the Biblical rules of helplessness that the disabled may regard their weakened status as *prima facie* evidence of merit, which must be rewarded by the appropriate theological, medical, or psychiatric treatment. In the hysterical transaction, disability is used as a coercive maneuver to force others to provide for one's needs. It is as though the patient were saying: "You have told me to be disabled—that is, to act stupid, weak, fearful, etc. You have promised that you would then take care of me, love me, etc. Here I am now, acting just as you have told me—it is your turn now to fulfill your promise!" Much of psychoanalyic psychotherapy may revolve around the theme of uncovering exactly who taught the patient to behave in this way, and why he listened to such teachings. In the course of this work it may be significant that religion, society, and parents may have conspired, so to speak, to uphold and promote this code of behavior, even though it is so singularly ill-suited to the requirements of our present social conditions.[6]

Historical Context of the New Testament

Since the function of codes of conduct can be analyzed only in reference to specific social conditions and institutions, the social function of Biblical rules must be related to specific historical periods.

At the dawn of Christianity, the Roman Empire was characterized by, among other things, vast inequalities among peoples. Moreover, the inequalities, which pertained to economic possessions, power, and privilege, were openly codified by contemporary laws as the just order. The institution of slavery was an integral feature of all contemporary cultures. Both Greek and Roman societies were dependent on a slave class. The Jews themselves, among whom Christianity arose, had been slaves. My thesis, which in its broad outlines is hardly novel, is that Biblical rules (and especially those of Christianity) reflect the psychology of oppression and slavery.

Karl Marx was among the first to remark on the connections between religion and oppression. In an "Introduction to a Critique of the Hegelian

---

[6] The rules whereby rewards are offered for *negative possessions*—for example, for *not having* wisdom, foresight, happiness, etc.—pervade the whole of the Christian ethic. Being poor is praised in Matthew 19:23-30; being hungry in Luke 6:20-26; being emasculated in Matthew 19:12. The last mentioned might be worth quoting, because the state of being unsexed, extolled in this passage, will be important for us also in Chapter 12. The relevant lines are:

"For there are some eunuchs, which were so born from *their* mother's womb: and there are some eunuchs, which were made eunuchs of men: and there be eunuchs, which have made themselves eunuchs for the kingdom of heaven's sake."

Man's emasculation is here codified as one of the ways of courting God's love. The themes of self-castration and impotence—or more generally, lust and its vicissitudes—are the *leitmotifs* of (1) large parts of the Bible, (2) witchcraft, witch-hunts, and documents dealing with witches, e.g., the *Malleus Malleficarum* (Krämer and Sprenger, 1486), and (3) the early theory of psychoanalysis.

Philosophy of Right" (1844), he made his now-famous observation:

> Religion is the moan of the oppressed creature, the sentiment of
> a heartless world, as it is the spirit of spiritless conditions. It is the
> opium of the people.
>
> The abolition of religion, as the illusory happiness of the people,
> is the demand for their real happiness. The demand to abandon
> the illusions about their condition *is a demand to abandon a con-
> dition which requires illusions* (p. 12).

Marx based his opinions chiefly on the role that organized Christian
religions played in the European politics of his day. He did not consider
religious teachings in their diverse historical contexts. Later on, Engels
(1877) expressed a similar opinion on the relations between religion and
social oppression, emphasizing especially that the Christian notion of "being
one in Christ" may serve as substitute for redressing social inequities. More
recently, Bridgman (1959) noted that "Christian ethics is primarily the
ethics of partners in misery. A society like a modern democracy would have
been unthinkable to Saint Paul" (p. 263).

I concur that the beliefs and practices of Christianity—and especially
those of Roman Catholicism—are best suited for slaves. They are also
serviceable for those who want to be masters, although somewhat less so
than for the oppressed. The religious history of the last two thousand years
is consistent with this general view (Brinton, 1959). In strongly Catholic
countries—as for example, Italy, Portugal, Spain, or pre-World War II
Hungary and Poland—the religious rules were taken much more seriously by
the lower classes (the oppressed) than by the ruling classes (the oppressors).

The ethics and psychology of oppression must be contrasted with the
ethics and psychology of democracy and equality (Abernethy, 1959). Lincoln (1858) said: "As I would not be a slave, so I would not be a master.
This expresses my idea of democracy. Whatever differs from this, to the
extent of the difference, is not democracy." If we define a free, self-govern-
ing, democratic man as did Abraham Lincoln—that is, as one who rejects
the roles of both master and slave—then we have the picture of a man into
whose scheme of life the Biblical rules fit poorly or not at all.

Taken in their entirety and removed from any particular historical context, the following generalization may be made concerning Biblical rules:
*Although some of the rules aim at mitigation of oppression, the over-all
thesis nevertheless fosters the same oppressive spirit from which these rules
arose and with which their creators must inevitably have been imbued.*
Since oppressed and oppressor form a functional pair, their psychology—

that is, their respective orientations to human relationships—tend to be similar (A. Freud, 1936). This is also fostered by the basic human tendency for persons to identify with those with whom they interact. Hence, each slave is a potential master and each master a potential slave. This must be emphasized because it is inaccurate and misleading to contrast the psychology of the oppressed with the psychology of the oppressor. Instead, the common orientation of each should be contrasted with the psychology of the person who feels *equal* to his fellow man.

Given the social inequalities which characterized the social milieu in which Christianity arose and flourished, we may raise this question: By what means could oppressed people improve their lot, at that time? Today education and improved skills are the principal means by which people improve their social conditions. But these techniques were not available two thousand years ago. In fact, they are still missing from those societies in which major social inequalities are codified on the basis of birth or other institutional criteria.

Since the oppressed peoples of the Roman Empire could not hope to ameliorate their lot by means of self-improvement, they had to look for other methods to achieve this end. The simplest way to accomplish this was by changing the rules of the game of life, making new rules more favorable to the formerly oppressed. In other words, an attempt was made to change the rules and to recruit people to espouse the new rules. This may be done either by coercion or by teaching—convincing the "convert" that the new rules will be more profitable for him than were the old rules.

Warfare and forceful subjugation are the traditional methods for enforcing new rules. These methods, however, are useful only for the strong. The weak must rely on more subtle techniques of persuasion. The early versus the later histories of many groups—Christianity and psychoanalysis among them—illustrate this principle (Burckhardt, 1868-1871). When Christianity arose, it and its supporters were weak, in the sense that they possessed little or no social or political power. Hence, they had to depend on noncoercive methods to spread their views. Later, after their followers had gained considerable power (social, political, military), they did not hesitate to adopt coercive measures (the Crusades and the Inquisition).

Rule-changing was, in my opinion, one of the most significant features of early Christianity. In substituting New Rules for old—that is, offering a *New Deal* as Franklin D. Roosevelt called it—Christ was following in the footsteps of Moses (or perhaps of the Jews generally). The essence of the New Rules lay in reversing the old rules, so that "the first shall be last, and the last shall be first" (Matthew, 19:30, 20:16; Mark, 10:31; Luke, 13:30).

THE OLD RULES: THE JEWS AS CHOSEN PEOPLE

The historical prototype of the rule-reversals advocated by Christ seems to be that originated by Moses (or the Jews). Dissatisfied with their real-life situation, the Jews apparently seized upon the inspired idea that, although they were having a poor time of it in their social relations, they were, in fact, God's Chosen People. Now, to be a chosen or preferred person implies that something especially good will happen to one, even if it is only to receive the love of an unseen God. It is undeniable that, from the psychosocial point of view, this is a most useful maneuver. It helps to restore the believer's dangerously weakened self-esteem. And so, he may manage gradually to rise above the hopeless position of the oppressed slave and gain a more dignified human stature.

However useful this maneuver may have been—and its usefulness can probably hardly be overestimated—its general availability was seriously hampered by one simple fact. Judaism was not, especially in the early days of Christianity, a proselytizing religion. In some respects the Jews imitated the slaveholder group, in that they formed what was essentially a new exclusive club. Admittance to this club could not easily be gained. Since there were many more slaves than Jews, this technique of attempted emancipation remained limited to a small band of men and could not gain a general following.

Resting on this historical base—that is, on the lesson of the Jewish technique of freeing oneself from slavery—Christ introduced the spirit of science and democracy into the business of emancipation from slavery. Social status based on instrumental criteria (e.g., personal accomplishment), rather than on institutional role (e.g., parentage), characterizes modern democratic social organizations. Early Christianity represents a significant forerunner of this contemporary trend—for it was Christ who opened the game, as it were, to all comers and who stated that the New Rules shall apply to all who wish to endorse them. Anyone could become a Christian, irrespective of nationality, race, or social status and thus could share in the rewards promised the followers of the New Rules. This far-reaching democratization of Judaism, together with the appealing rewards it promised, must have accounted—or so it may be assumed—for the vast social success of Christianity.

THE NEW RULES: THEIR ORIGIN AND FUNCTION

By New Rules I refer to some of the social rules set forth in the New Testament. The New Testament, however, must not be contrasted with the Old Testament, for the New Rules reversed not those of Judaism but rather those of the social order which prevailed at that time.

What were the prevailing social rules in Christ's day? In general, it was advantageous to be a free citizen of Rome and a believer in Roman polytheism. Given this base-line, it was further advantageous to be healthy rather than sick, wealthy rather than poor, admired and beloved rather than persecuted and hated, and so forth. The New Rules, as set forth by Christ and Saint Paul, consisted of a radical reversal of these basic principles. It was asserted that henceforth the "last" shall be "first"—the "loser" shall be the "winner." The rules of the New Game reverse the rules of the Old Game. Faithful Christians will now be the winners, pagan Romans the losers. Similarly, healthy, wealthy, and admired people will be punished, while the sick, poor, and persecuted will be rewarded.

The New Rules possessed several features that helped to ensure them great success. In the early days of Christianity, there were, of course, many more slaves, sick, poor, and unhappy people than free, healthy, and satisfied ones. This remains true even today. Accordingly, while the rules of the earthly game, as practiced in Roman society, held out a promise of opportunity to only a few men, the New Rules of Christianity held out the promise of bountiful rewards to many. In this sense, too, Christianity represented a move toward democracy. It pitched its appeal toward the needs of the numerical majority. It is significant, in this connection, that in classical Rome, and in similar cultures of past ages,[7] it was the order of things that a numerically large oppressed group took care of the needs of a much smaller oppressing group. The former group included not only slaves, but also the poor, the sick, the stupid, and so forth—in brief, all who were disabled in comparison to their more adequately functioning fellow men. This arrangement, whereby the "disabled" took care of the "able," has undergone profound changes in the course of history.

THE NEW RULES TWO THOUSAND YEARS LATER

Today we know that a specific social role or scientific method, useful and appropriate at one time and for one purpose, may be useless and inappropriate at another time and for another purpose. In regard to Biblical rules, my thesis is that although they once had a largely liberating influence, their effect has long since become oppressive and psychosocially inhibiting. Alas, this transformation has characterized the course of most revolutions, the initial phase of liberation being quickly succeeded by a new phase of oppression (Nietzsche, 1888; Russell, 1954).

The general principle that a liberating rule may, in due time, become an-

---

[7] The social structure of the Union of South Africa represents a contemporary remnant of this scheme.

other method of oppression, has broad validity for rule-changing maneuvers of all types. This is the main reason why it is so difficult today whole-heartedly to espouse new social schemes which offer merely another set of new rules. Although new rules are constantly needed, if social life is to continue as a dynamic process tending toward ever-increasing human com-plexity and self-determination, much more is needed than mere rule-chang-ing. In addition to exchanging new rules for old, it is necessary to be aware of the rationale of the old rules and to guard against their persistent effects. One such effect is to form new rules that are, at least partly, covert reaction-formations against the old rules. Christianity, the French Revolution, Marx-ism, and even psychoanalysis itself—as a revolution in medicine against the so-called organic tradition—all succumbed to the inescapable fate of all revolutions—the setting up of new tyrannies.

The effects of religious teachings on contemporary Western man is still considered to be a delicate subject. Psychiatrists, psychologists, and social scientists tend to avoid it. I have tried to reopen this subject by re-examin-ing some of the values and rules of the Judaeo-Christian religions. If we sincerely desire a scientifically respectable psychosocial theory of man, we shall have to pay far more attention to religious—and also to nationalistic and professional—rules and values than has been our custom.

It should be kept in mind, finally, that when we speak about the effects of religious rules on contemporary man, we speak about a composite picture. For today, in the United States, the term "religion" denotes a wide spectrum of activities and beliefs, ranging from a vague, nondenominational religion-ism that is no more than a kind of patriotic anticommunism, to fanatical beliefs in fundamentalistic versions of Christianity and Judaism (Blanshard, 1960). Clearly, different types and intensities of belief will have different effects.

To what extent democratic institutions and scientific practices are com-patible with particular religious beliefs and conducts is by no means easily established. That fundamentalistic types of religiosity—whether Catholic, Protestant, or Jewish—conflict with the values of the scientific enterprise, there can be little doubt. The conflict between religion and science dimin-ishes in proportion as religion is "liberally" administered and interpreted. The scientific enterprise is the paradigm of the "open society" (Popper, 1945). Religious rules postulating supernatural forces impose some measure of closure on this system. How much closure can science tolerate and still grow? It seems evident that the psychosocial sciences are less viable than their physical siblings. The former will not even be "born" unless the conditions for their survival are favorable. They will not survive if their freedom is seriously curtailed.

"By paying so much attention to the devil and by treating witchcraft as the most heinous of crimes, the theologians and the inquisitors actually spread the beliefs and fostered the practices which they were trying so hard to repress."

Aldous Huxley (1952, p. 127)

CHAPTER 12

Theology, Witchcraft, and Hysteria

Educators, especially those concerned with inculcating religious teachings, traditionally have been concerned with getting hold of their pupils in early childhood. The thesis that religious indoctrination during this period will have a lasting effect on the child's personality antedates psychoanalysis by many centuries. Freud reasserted this widely held opinion when he claimed that psychoanalytic research led him to discover that a person's character is firmly fixed during the first five or six years of life. Although personally I do not share this estimate concerning the significance of the early years of life, it is undoubtedly true that the rules on which a human being is fed, as it were, in the early years of life, profoundly affect his later behavior. This is especially true if a person's rule "diet" in later years does not differ markedly from that of his childhood. It seems to me that a great deal of a person's later education—say, between the ages of six and early adulthood—is composed of an educational pabulum containing many of the same nonsensical rules he had been fed earlier. If this is indeed the case, we shall be ill advised to draw far-reaching conclusions concerning the effects of early learning experiences, since these are often reinforced, rather than modified or corrected, by later influences. I refer here specifically to the values and rules inherent in *religious, national, and professional myths, most of which foster the perpetuation of childish game models and mutually destructive patterns of human behavior.*

What I have called "religious, national, and professional myths," are simply games the main purpose of which is to glorify the group to which the individual belongs (or to membership in which he aspires). All such clannish games must be contrasted with games in which all who are capable of adhering to the rules can participate. The rules of the game based on such a suprareligious and supranational morality would seriously conflict with many of our current habits in living. Nevertheless, I firmly believe that the social trend toward worldwide human equality (of rights and obligations, i.e., to participate in all games according to one's abilities) need not be a threat to men. On the contrary, it represents one of the few values worthy of contemporary man's admiration and support.

In our widespread espousal of clannish myths, we tend to forget their undesirable effects. The currently operating causes of human disharmony thus are constantly de-emphasized, while at the same time the pathogenic significance of past events is exaggerated. I do not wish to detract from the psychological significance of past events, but wish to underscore the significance of major contemporary world views as determinants of human behavior. In this connection, it is significant that although everyone's past life seems to be full of "pathogenic" occurrences, few persons seriously entertain the possibility that their behavior may continue to provide such harmful experiences for themselves and those about them at present and in the immediate future. Perhaps this pushing of "pathogenic" experiences from the present into the past is one of the mechanisms which enables contemporary "psychological man" (Rieff, 1959) to behave as badly in his everyday life as he often does.

In this chapter, I shall try to show that the notion of mental illness is used today chiefly to obscure and "explain away" problems in personal and social relationships, just as the notion of witchcraft was used for the same purpose from the early Middle Ages until well past the Renaissance. Today, we seek and achieve the denial of social, moral, and personal controversies by hastily retreating to playing the medical game. This game constitutes one of the principal contemporary models for understanding the world around us. For over a thousand years, from the beginning of Christianity until past the Middle Ages, European man sought to forge another model of the world for himself—namely, the theological model. This model refers to what could also be called the religious game of life and the rules governing it. An examination of the religious rules and their effects on medieval man will be of interest for several reasons. First, because it illustrates the principles of rule-following behavior; second, because it discloses witchcraft in a new form, as an historical antecedent of the modern notions of malingering and hysteria; and third, because the religious rules surveyed not only are of historical interest but also constitute active social forces in our present day. Hence, they remain of paramount importance in regard to contemporary issues of "mental health and illness."

The Medical Theory of Witchcraft

It is often asserted that the medieval women who were accused of witchcraft "really" suffered from what we now *know* to be hysteria. Numerous contemporary medical and psychiatric authors—Zilboorg (1935, 1941) among them being probably the best known and most eloquent—advocate such a medical-psychiatric view of witchcraft.

THE WITCH AS A MENTAL PATIENT

Zilboorg's thesis that witches were misdiagnosed mental patients was based largely on an interpretation of Krämer and Sprenger's *Malleus Malleficarum* (1486). It seems to me, however, that Zilboorg was determined to prove that witches were mentally sick persons, and that he disregarded all evidence suggesting other interpretations. He disregarded the fact that the *Malleus Maleficarum* shows a much greater resemblance to a legal than to a medical document. The ferreting out and proving of witchcraft were preliminary to *sentencing*. Hence, witch-hunts could be better compared to contemporary anti-Communist witch-hunts than to tracking down, say, cases of diabetes. Although Zilboorg (1935) noted that a large part of the *Malleus* dealt with the legalistic examination and sentencing of witches, he did not draw the logical inference that witches were criminals, or to put it more neutrally, offenders against the prevailing social (theological) order. On the contrary, he suggested that "The *Malleus Maleficarum* might, with a little editing, serve as an excellent modern textbook of descriptive clinical psychiatry of the fifteenth century, if the word *witch* were substituted by the word *patient*, and the devil eliminated" (p. 58).

This interpretation must have seemed too sweeping even for Zilboorg, for later on he offered another opinion which partly contradicts his former generalization: "Not all accused of being witches and sorcerers were mentally sick, but almost all mentally sick were considered witches, or sorcerers, or bewitched" (p. 153).

As is often true of historical documents, the same facts may allow several divergent interpretations. In such cases, logical consistency and psychological plausibility must not be overrated. Evidence that cannot be fitted into such a theory is far more significant than evidence that can (Popper, 1957). Although Zilboorg (1941) emphasized that medieval man was engaged in playing a game quite different from that we now play, he proceeded to cast Krämer and Sprenger's observations into a medical and psychiatric mold. He wrote:

> This passage from the *Malleus* is perhaps the most significant statement to come out of the fifteenth century. Here, in a concise and succinct paragraph, *two monks brush aside the whole mass of psychiatric knowledge which had been so carefully collected and preserved by almost two thousand years of medical and philosophic investigation;* they brush it aside almost casually and with such stunning simplicity that no room is left for argument. How can one raise objections to the assertion, "but this is contrary to true faith?" The fusion of insanity, witchcraft and heresy into one concept and the exclusion of even the suspicion that *the problem is a medical one* are now complete ([ITALICS ADDED] p. 155).

Further on, he added:

> The belief in the free will of man is here brought to its most terrifying, although most preposterous, conclusion. Man, whatever *he does, even if he succumbs to an illness* which perverts his perceptions, imagination, and intellectual functions, does it of his own free will; he voluntarily bows to the wishes of the Evil One. The devil does not lure and trap man; man chooses to succumb to the devil and he must be held responsible for this free choice. He must be punished; he must be eliminated from the community ([ITALICS ADDED] p. 156).

Following Zilboorg, it has become popular for psychiatrists to assume—indeed, to take for granted—that most witches were simply unfortunate persons who "fell ill" with "mental illness." This interpretation deserves to be challenged. The notion that so-called witches were mentally ill people fulfills two distinct purposes. First, it discredits the theory of witchcraft and the entire theological world view in back of it. This is scientifically creditable. To discredit the theory of witchcraft, however, no alternative theory of mental illness is needed. The second purpose of this interpretation appears to be to enthrone the concept of mental illness as an explanatory theory of wide scope and unchallenged power.

CRITIQUE OF THE MEDICAL THEORY OF WITCHCRAFT

When Zilboorg said the authors of the *Malleus* had brushed aside two thousand years of medical and psychiatric knowledge, what did he have in mind? What medical and psychiatric knowledge—worthy of this name

—was then available which would have been relevant to the problems to which the *theologians* addressed themselves? Surely, the ideas of Galenic medicine would have been irrelevant. I submit that medieval man, whether physician, theologian, or layman, possessed no medical (and much less any "psychiatric") knowledge relevant to the problem of witchcraft. In fact, no such knowledge was needed, for there was an abundance of evidence, for those who wished to avail themselves of it, that charges of witchcraft were commonly trumped up for the purpose of eliminating certain people, and that confessions were extorted by means of cruel tortures (Parrinder, 1958). Finally, if the belief in witchcraft was a "medical mistake"—codifying the misdiagnosis of "hysterics" as "witches"—why was this mistake not made more often prior to the twelfth century?

To explain witchcraft, Zilboorg offered a medical explanation without specifying how it was to be used. To what sort of illness do people said to be "mentally ill" succumb? Is it, perchance, to such diseases as paresis or brain tumor? Or, do they succumb to problems in living, arising from—or at the very least precipitated by—family and social pressures, conflicting goals, and so forth? None of these questions is raised, much less answered, by the proponents of the medical theory of witchcraft. Zilboorg's interpretation that the imputation of witchcraft signified a fanatical belief in free will is simply false. It contradicts the most obvious empirical fact—namely, that the majority of witches were women, and especially old, poor, and socially readily expendable women. Moreover, when people were considered to be possessed by the devil, it was generally not attributed to their free will, but was viewed rather as occurring against their "better judgment." Accordingly, the witch-hunters were regarded as the agents of their unfortunate clients —and executing witches was defined as "therapeutic." This perverted, anti-humanitarian definition of what constitutes "therapy" and of who is a "therapist" has persisted to our day in regard to the so-called treatment of major psychiatric illnesses (Szasz, 1957d).

The medical theory of witchcraft ignores two manifest social determinants of the belief in witches and its corollary, witch-hunts. First, a preoccupation with God, Christ, and Christian theology cannot be entirely separated from a belief in bad deities and their cohorts (devils, witches, sorcerers). Second, concern with the sexual activities of witches and devils is a counterpart of the officially antisexual attitude of the Catholic Church. Burning witches and emphasizing the destruction of their bodies must be viewed in the light of medieval man's theological world view. According to it, the body is weak and sinful; the soul's eternal salvation is the only goal worthy of man (Huizinga, 1927). Thus, burning human bodies at the stake must have been a symbolic act—expressing adherence to the official rules of the game (such as: body is bad, soul is good; torturing the body is the surest way to ennoble the soul; etc.)—the main purpose of which was to insure the continued existence of an important social fiction or myth (Vaihinger, 1911). In this regard, burning witches may be compared to destroying confiscated whiskey during Prohibition. Both acts gave official recognition to a rule which few people followed in their actual conduct, During the Middle Ages, sexual conduct was, in fact, exceedingly promiscuous, if measured by our current standards (Lewinsohn, 1958). In both instances, the laws expressed high ethical ideals which most people had no intention of following. Their goal became, instead, cleverly to evade the laws, to appear as though they had been law-abiding, and to make sure that there were appropriate others who were caught and punished. For this *scapegoats* were needed. In situations of this type, it is the scapegoat's social function to play the role of the person who violates the rules, is caught, and is duly punished (Nadel, 1954, pp. 205-206). Bootleggers and the entire class of so-called organized gangsters—both of whom came into being while Prohibition was the law of the land in the United States—could be regarded as the scapegoats to be sacrificed at the altar of the false god of abstinence. The greater the actual discrepancy between prescribed rules of conduct and actual social behavior, the greater the need for scapegoat-sacrifices as a means of maintaining the social myth that man lives according to his officially declared ethical beliefs.

The Scapegoat Theory of Witchcraft

According to this theory, witchcraft represents the expression of a particular method by means of which men have sought to explain and master various ills of nature. Unable to admit ignorance and relative helplessness, yet equally unable to achieve scientific understanding and mastery of diverse physical, biological, and social problems, men have sought refuge in scapegoat explanations. The specific identities of scapegoats are legion: lepers, witches, women, Jews, Negroes, Communists, the mentally ill, and so forth. All scapegoat theories postulate that if only the offending person, race, illness, or what-not could be dominated, subjugated, mastered, or eliminated, all manner of problems would be solved.[1]

While medical men enthusiastically subscribed to the idea that witches were hysterical women who had been misdiagnosed, social scientists leaned

---

[1] Explanations making use of scapegoats have thus much in common with explanations based on what Hardin (1956) called *panchresta* or "explain-alls." Scapegoats could be said to be a special type of *panchreston*.

toward the view that they were society's scapegoats. Parrinder's definitive work, *Witchcraft* (1958), is an excellent presentation of this thesis. I am in substantial agreement with his interpretation, and shall try to show exactly in what ways the scapegoat theory is superior to the medical one. In addition, I shall argue that not only is it misleading to consider "witches" misdiagnosed "hysterics" but it is also misleading to regard people currently "ill" with "hysteria" (or other "mental illnesses") as belonging in the same category as those ill with bodily ailments. Thus, clarification of the sociopsychology of witchcraft should be illuminating not only for its own sake but also in terms of the contemporary problem of hysteria and mental illness.

In connection with the scapegoat theory of witchcraft the following questions may be raised: Who were considered to be witches? How were they tried and who profited from their conviction? What did those people who did not believe in the reality of witches think of witchcraft? Did they think that witches were ill? Or did they believe that the problem was not one of witchcraft at all, but was a matter of trumped-up charges? In discussing these questions, the similarities between the medieval belief in witchcraft on the one hand and the contemporary belief in mental illness on the other will be emphasized. I shall try to show that both are poor explanations which distract attention from the scientific task at hand. Both serve the interests of a special group—one the clergy, the other the medical profession. Finally, both fulfill their function by sacrificing a special group of persons on the altar of social expediency. In the Middle Ages the scapegoats were "witches"; today they are the involuntary "mental patients" or the "mentally ill" (Szasz, 1960d).

WITCHCRAFT AND SOCIAL CLASS

The first question to be considered is: Who were regarded as witches? In comparing witchcraft on the one hand and the notions of illness and especially hysteria and mental illness on the other hand, it is important to bear in mind that the traditional conception of illness rests on the simple facts of pain, suffering, and disability. These imply that the sufferer, the patient himself, considers himself ill. In sociological terms, *the sick role is self-defined* (Parsons, 1952). Illustrative of this kind of self-definition of the sick role are such occurrences as fractures, infectious diseases manifested by high fever and prostration, externally visible tumors, and other similar phenomena.

The distinction between being a mental patient by one own's definition or choice or being so defined against one's will is very important in this connection. The mentally sick role is self-defined usually in the hope and expectation that this maneuver will help to secure certain types of help, for example private psychotherapy. In contrast, when this role is foisted on a person against his will, the maneuver—although not necessarily harmful to all of his interests—primarily serves the interests of those who define him as mentally ill.

During the Middle Ages and immediately afterwards, witch-hunts and witch-trials were frequent occurrences in Europe, and to a lesser extent in England. How did people ascertain, at that time, that someone was a witch? Of course, people virtually never discovered that they themselves were witches. Rather, they claimed and subsequently ascertained—by the methods prescribed—that someone else was a witch. In other words, the witch role, in contrast to the sick role, was characteristically other-defined. In this respect, the role of witch was similar to the contemporary roles of criminal and involuntarily hospitalized mentally sick patient (Aubert and Messinger, 1958).

Although no studies comparable, say, to Hollingshead and Redlich's *Social Class and Mental Illness* (1958) exist concerning the incidence of witchcraft, there is a wealth of empirical data on this subject. Only a brief summary of the salient facts will be presented. Most of the people accused of witchcraft were women. The word "witch" implies "woman," just as the word "hysteric" did formerly. Janet and Freud, as is well known, were pioneers in asserting that there were "male hysterics."[2] In this respect, the parallel between being a witch and being a hysteric is very striking. According to Parrinder (1958), for example, out of two hundred convicted witches in England, only fifteen were men (p. 54). He interpreted this as a sign that women were a persecuted minority in a world ruled by men.

In addition to the very high incidence of women, most persons accused of witchcraft were members of the lower classes. They were poor, stupid, socially helpless, and often old and feeble. Making a "diagnosis" of witchcraft then—much as calling someone mentally ill today—was an insult and an accusation. Obviously, it is safer to accuse socially low-ranking persons than those who are socially prominent (Parrinder, 1958, pp. 31-32). When highly placed persons were accused of witchcraft, as happened occasionally, it was safer as well as more effective if the charge was made by large groups, as for instance a whole nunnery, rather than by single persons. Then, as now,

[2] The discovery of "male hysteria," like Charcot's conversion of malingerers to hysterics (see Chapter 1), was another step in the *democratization of misery*. Freud (1932) was apparently more ready to acknowledge equality between the sexes in regard to suffering (i.e., proneness to "neurosis") than in regard to potentialities for creative performance. His assertion that men, too, may suffer from hysteria must be contrasted with his equally firm conviction that women (and the "masses") were incapable of the same types of work, "sublimations," and "mental development" as men (and members of the upper classes).

there was safety in numbers—the assumption being that if many people saw or felt something, it had to be true! Nevertheless, the educated and the well-to-do could protect themselves from the danger of being branded witches and being "treated" for it—usually by burning at the stake—much as well-informed and wealthy persons today have little difficulty avoiding being diagnosed "mentally ill" by anyone other than themselves. They are thus able to avoid commitment, loss of civil liberties, and "treatment" by means of electric shocks, lobotomies, and the like, which are the fates of those less fortunate.

MISOGYNY, WITCHCRAFT, AND HYSTERIA

Apparently, medieval inquisitors themselves were impressed by the discrepancy between the patently feeble and harmless character of the women accused of witchcraft and their allegedly diabolical and potent actions. Parrinder (1958) commented:

> The explanation was given that their evil deeds had been performed by the help of the devil, but that, like the deceiver he is, he had abandoned his disciples in their moment of need. One of the inquisitors quotes this explanation. "There are those who believe that, once witches are made prisoners and are fallen into the hands of Justice, the Devil deserts them and assists them no more." This was very convenient for the inquisitors, for it meant that they could handle these dangerous women without risk to themselves (p. 58).

Although Parrinder called these antifeminine attitudes, beliefs, and actions "ridiculous," this should not divert our attention from the fact that essentially similar attitudes were prevalent in Europe well into the twentieth century. In fact, such prejudices are by no means extinct today, even in so-called civilized countries. In the economically underdeveloped areas of the world, the systematic oppression and exploitation of women—much like slavery and the exploitation of alien races—remain the dominant customs and rules of life.

While these social facts are of momentous importance insofar as any progress toward an internationally meaningful science of human behavior is contemplated, what is even more significant, especially in relation to hysteria, is the cultural attitude toward women in Central Europe at the turn of the century. This was the time and place of the origin of psychoanalysis, and through it, of the entire body of what is now known as "dynamic psychiatry." That the status of women in this social context was still one of relatively profound oppression, while well known, is easily forgotten or relegated to a position of unimportance. On the whole, women were economically dependent on their parents or spouses, had few educational and occupational opportunities, and were regarded—perhaps not quite explicitly—as the mere bearers of uteri. Their "proper" role and function were marriage and motherhood. Accordingly, they were considered biologically inferior to men in regard to such traits as intellectual ability and finer ethical feelings. Some of Freud's opinions about women were not too unlike those of Krämer and Sprenger.

The following is an illustrative quotation from Freud (1932) concerning what he called "the psychology of women":

> It must be admitted that women have but little sense of justice, and this is no doubt connected with the preponderance of envy in their mental life; for the demands of justice *are* a modification of envy; they lay down the conditions under which one is willing to part with it. We also say of women that their *social interests are weaker* than those of men, and that their capacity for the *sublimation of their instincts is less* ([ITALICS ADDED] p. 183).

Freud's views on feminine psychology have been quoted not so much to criticize them—this has been adequately done by others (A. Adler, 1907-1937; Horney, 1939; Fromm, 1959)—but rather to highlight the significance of social oppression as a determinant of the phenomena called witchcraft, hysteria, and mental illness. As noted earlier (Chapter 9), certain psychosocial conditions strongly foster the disposition to use indirect communications. Social oppression in any form—and its manifestations are varied, among them being the helplessness of childhood, stupidity, lack of education, poverty, bodily illness and infirmity, and racial, religious, or sexual discrimination—must, therefore, be regarded as prime determinants of indirect communications of all kinds (e.g., hysteria, lying, cheating, etc.). This view of hysteria and mental illness is distinguished from purely medical or psychiatric theories by its emphasis on economic, political, and ethical considerations, *in addition* to the usual medical and psychosocial ones.

THE CONFLICT OF INTERESTS IN WITCH-TRIALS

The belief in witches, devils, and their cohorts was, of course, more than just a matter of metaphysics or theological theory. It affected public behavior—most glaringly in the form of witch-hunts and witch-trials. In a way, these were the opposites or mirror images of saintly miracles. Alleged acts of witchcraft or miracle-working could be officially recognized only after they had been passed on and approved as valid by the holders of appropriate social power—in this case, the high-ranking clergy of the Roman

Catholic church. The genuineness of acts of miracle-working, witchcraft, sorcery, and so forth were established by what was basically a legal procedure, set in a theological context. Hence the expression "witch-trials." Obviously, a trial is neither a medical nor a scientific institution.

The distinction between legal and scientific disputes was recognized by medieval man, no less than by the ancients. Yet, this important distinction was obscured by the medical theory of hysteria. It is common knowledge that legal contests serve to settle disputes of conflicting interests. Medical procedures, insofar as they are based on scientific considerations, are designed to settle problems of *fact*—such as the nature of the patient's illness and the measures that might restore him to health. In this situation, there are no obvious conflicts of interest between opposing parties. The patient is ill, wants to recover, and his family and society, too, desire this outcome. Finally, the healer also shares this goal.

This is not so in a legal dispute. Here the crux of the matter is a conflict of interests between two or more parties. What is good (therapeutic) for one, is likely to be bad (pathogenic) for the other. Instead of a healer, or physician, a judge is now empowered to conciliate between conflicting parties or to settle the argument in favor of one of the contestants. This was precisely the case in medieval witch-trials. It is also the case today in many instances of "mental illness." If the conflicts of interests in these situations are not recognized, the opportunity to deal scientifically with the pertinent phenomena is forfeited.

Let us now scrutinize the witch-trial. To begin with, in European witch-trials, it was customary for the judge to receive a portion of the convicted heretic's worldly possessions (Parrinder, 1958, p. 79). Today, we take it for granted in democratic societies that judges are "impartial." Their task is to uphold the law. Typically, the judge occupies a position outside of the immediate socioeconomic orbit of the litigants. While all this may seem dreadfully obvious, it needs to be said because all too often, even today, the impartiality of the judge toward the litigants is an unrealized ideal. In totalitarian countries, for example, so-called crimes against the state fall in the same class as witch-trials: the judge is a biased employee of one of the contesting parties. Even in democratic societies, in acts violating cardinal moral and social beliefs—for instance, treason or subversion—the value of impartially balancing the interests between the contestants is scuttled in preference to *a priori* decisions in favor of whichever side holds power. This is why "political criminals" may become "revolutionary heroes," and should the revolution fail, revert once more to the status of "criminals."

In witch-trials the conflict was officially defined as between the accused and God, or perhaps between the accused and the Catholic (later Protestant)

Church, as God's and Christ's earthly representative. There was no attempt to make this an even match. The distribution of power between accuser and accused mirrored the relations between king and serf—one had all the power and the other none of it. Once again, we encounter the theme of oppression. Significantly, only in England—where, beginning in the thirteenth century with the granting of the Magna Charta, there gradually developed an appreciation of the rights and dignities of those less powerful than the king— was the fury of witch-hunting mitigated by legal safeguards and social sensibilities.

Behind the ostensible conflict of the witch-trial lay the usual conflicts of social class, values, and human relationships. Furthermore, there was strife within the Catholic Church itself which later became accentuated by the antagonisms between Catholics and Protestants. It was in this context, then, that witches and sorcerers, recruited from the ranks of the poor and oppressed, played the role of scapegoats. They thus fulfilled the socially useful function of acting as social tranquilizers (Szasz, 1960c). By participating in an important public drama, they contributed to the stability (such as it was) of the existing social order (Parrinder, 1958, pp. 83-84).

Finally, there was the ever-present motive of revenge on the part of the poor and the weak against the rich and the powerful. The story of such a case is narrated by Aldous Huxley in *The Devils of Loudon* (1952). Here we are shown from the inside, as it were, the human conflicts, passions, and frustrations that made up the brick and mortar of a witch-hunt and witch-trial. Curiously, although Huxley paid consistent lip-service to the medical theory of witchcraft in that he repeatedly referred to the allegedly possessed nuns as "hysterics," he described the case simply as a well-conceived and well-executed plot on the part of a nun whose aim was to torture and kill a sexually alluring and promiscuous priest by whom she felt excited and rejected. The story shows the accumulation of power-groups by the nun in preparation for her assault on the lofty figure who was to be humiliated and legally murdered.

Witchcraft, Hysteria, and Values

It is an explicit assumption in this study that man is a symbolizing and rule-following animal. Clearly, then, the goals that are valued as worth pursuing and the means considered effective and proper for their attainment will in large part determine and "explain" what man does. In this connection, Myrdal's (1944) warning must constantly be kept in mind: "There is no other device for excluding biases in social sciences than to face the valuations and to introduce them as explicitly stated, specific premises" (p. 1042).

The following questions must be raised and answered: What values under-lie the social system in which the "diagnosis" of witchcraft can be made, or in which such a "diagnosis" is fostered? Similarly, what are the values of the social system that fosters the "diagnosis" of hysteria (or mental illness)? Various aspects of this problem were discussed in Part I. We may expand on what was said there by considering specifically the relations between the *dominant values of a society* and *the terms in which interpersonal and social discomforts occurring in it are perceived and defined. The precise nature of values (goals) and the means for their attainment (rules) are most readily inferred from scrutinizing the kinds of games that people play with their lives.*[3]

THE THEOLOGICAL GAME OF LIFE

Life in the Middle Ages, in these terms, was a colossal religious game. The dominant value was salvation in a life hereafter. Much has been written on this subject (for example, Huizinga, 1927; Zilboorg, 1935, 1943). I shall only touch on some highlights. Gallinek (1942) emphasized that "to divorce medieval hysteria from its time and place is not possible" (p. 42). He sum-marized medieval man's purpose in life as follows:

> It was the aim of man to leave all things worldly as far behind as possible, and already during lifetime to approach the kingdom of heaven. The aim was salvation. Salvation was the Christian master motive.—The ideal man of the Middle Ages was free of all fear because he was sure of salvation, certain of eternal bliss. He was the saint, and the saint, not the knight nor the troubadour, is the veritable ideal of the Middle Ages (p. 47).

It followed, however, that if sainthood and salvation formed one part of the Christian game of life, witchcraft and damnation formed another. The two belong together in a single system of beliefs and rules, just as, say, military decorations for bravery and punishments for desertion belong to-gether. Positive and negative sanctions, or rewards and penalties, form a complementary pair and share equally in giving form and substance to the game. A game is composed of the totality of its rules. If any of the rules is changed, the game itself is changed. It is important to keep this clearly in mind to avoid the erroneous belief that the essential identity of a game may be preserved by retaining only its desirable features (rewards), and eliminat-ing all that is undesirable (penalties).

On the contrary, if preservation of the game—that is, maintenance of the

[3] Some aspects of the game-playing model of human behavior, which will be presented in detail in Part V, will be anticipated in this discussion.

social (religious) *status quo*—is desired, this can be best achieved by enthusiastically playing the game as it is given. Thus, searching for and finding witches constituted an important mechanism for playing the religious game of life (as conceived by medieval man), much as looking for and finding mental illness is a convenient technique for keeping the contemporary medical-therapeutic game alive and vigorous. The extent to which belief in and preoccupation with witchcraft constituted a part of the theological game of life may be gleaned from Parrinder's (1958) description of "Pacts with the Devil" (p. 68).

It is significant that the criteria for "diagnosing" witchcraft and heresy were of the same type as the criteria for establishing the possession of genuine belief. Both were inferred from what the person said. Thus the emphasis on private data (Szasz, 1957a) can be traced to medieval Catholic theology. I wish to emphasize the relatively great importance which was placed at this time, and henceforth, on what people verbalized concerning their beliefs, feelings, and experiences. Verbal utterances concerning devotion to God or claims of having seen the Holy Virgin were thus elevated to a rank higher than deeds. Honest service and decent behavior, as such, went for naught. At the same time, extravagant claims were sometimes magnificently rewarded.

Similar methods were used to establish a person's "badness." Empirical occurrences were de-emphasized in favor of self-revelations obtained, if necessary, under torture. All this took place, moreover, in a social setting in which sadistic behavior—especially on the part of noblemen toward serfs, men toward women, adults toward children—was an everyday matter. Its very ubiquity must have dulled men's sensibilities and turned their attention from it. It is not easy to remain interested in what is commonplace—such as man's everyday brutality vis-à-vis his fellow man. Oh, but the dastardly behavior of persons in the grips of the devil. That was another, more interesting matter! Since this could not be directly observed, the diagnosticians of sorcery and witchcraft had to rely heavily on verbal communications. These were of two kinds: first, accusations against persons concerning the commission of evil deeds or peculiar acts, and second, and more important, confessions.[4]

[4] These observations suggest that there is a precise antithesis between operationism (Bridgman, 1936) and the classic Christian principles concerning the proper methods of ascertaining "truth" (or "reality"). The religious techniques mentioned consisted of rendering private experiences into public data by "revelation" (i.e., self-revelation) or by brute force (e.g., confession under torture). In contrast, modern science seeks to develop, elucidate, and make generally available the public aspects of all human experiences (Russell, 1948). The use of force—that is, one person coercing or even cajoling another— is emphatically excluded from this enterprise. Scientific behavior is motivated by the prospects of intellectual, emotional, technological, and other forms of mastery and the enjoyment inherent in such mastery.

There is an obvious link between the private Catholic confessional and the public self-incriminations of the witch-hunts. The publicity of the latter must be placed alongside the equally public claims of saints concerning beatific visions and other experiences.

THE MEDICAL GAME OF LIFE

What are the values of the social system that fosters the "diagnosis" of hysteria? This question touches on the unacknowledged values and, in a broader sense, world views, of our contemporary Western civilization. Clearly, one of the principal values of our culture is science. Medicine, as a part of science, enters this value system. The notions of health, illness, and treatment are the cornerstones of an all-embracing modern medical-therapeutic world view (Szasz, 1958b).

In speaking of science as a widely shared social value, I do not refer to any particular scientific method, nor have I in mind such things as the search for "truth," "understanding," or "explanation." I refer rather to science as an institutional force, akin to organized theology in past ages. It is to this version of "science," sometimes called "scientism," that increasing numbers of people turn in their search for practical guidance in living. Let us be specific. According to this scheme of values, one of the most important things for man to achieve is to have a strong and healthy body. Contemporary man's wish for a healthy body is thus truly the successor to medieval man's wish for a virtuous soul, deserving of everlasting salvation. A healthy body is similarly regarded as useful, not, it is true, for salvation, but for comfort, sex appeal, happiness, and a long life. Efforts expended in pursuit of this goal —that is, of having a healthy (and this has of late included *attractive*) body —are truly colossal. Finally, having a healthy "mind" has been added to this value-scheme by regarding the "mind" as though it were simply another part of the human organism. According to this view, the human being is endowed with a skeletal system, digestive system, circulatory system, nervous system, etc.—and a "mind." Or, as the Romans had put it, *Mens sana in corpora sano:* "In a healthy body, a healthy mind." Strangely enough, much of modern psychiatry has been devoted to this ancient proposition. Psychiatrists who search for biological (genetic, biochemical, etc.) abnormalities as the causes of "mental illness" are, whether they know it or not, committed to this frame of reference and its covert values.

Even if we do not believe in the reducibility of psychiatry to biochemistry, the notion of mental illness implies (1) the positive value of "mental health," and (2) certain criteria according to which states of mental health and illness can be "diagnosed." In the name of this value, then, the same sorts of actions may be undertaken as were carried out by medieval man marching under the banner of God and Christ. What are some of these actions?

First, those who are considered especially strong and healthy—or who contribute to these values—are rewarded. The athletes, the beauty queens, and the movie stars are the modern-day "saints"—and the cosmetics manufacturers, doctors, psychiatrists, and so forth, their assistants. They are honored, admired, and rewarded. This is well known and should occasion little surprise. Who are the people who fall in the class of the witches and sorcerers? Who are the people who are persecuted and victimized in the name of "health" and "happiness?" There are many. In their front ranks are the mentally ill, and especially those who are so defined by others rather than by themselves (Szasz, 1960d). The involuntarily hospitalized mentally ill are regarded as "bad" and efforts are made to make them "better." Words like "good" and "bad" are used here in accordance with the value system in force. Though this is an ostensibly medical system of values, it is nonetheless an ethical scheme.[5] In addition to the mentally ill, elderly persons and people who are especially ugly or deformed find themselves in a class analogous to the defunct category of witches and sorcerers.

The reason why individuals displaying such characteristics are considered "bad" is inherent in the rules of the medical game. Just as witchcraft was an inverted theological game, so much of general psychiatry—especially the so-called care of the involuntary mental patient—is a kind of inverted medical game. The ethics of the medical game lay down health—defined, among other things, as a well-functioning body—as a positive value. Happiness is another such value. Their opposites are an ill-functioning body and unhappiness or depression. Hysteria, as we have seen, is a dramatized representation of the message: "My body is not functioning well." In this light, the "mental illness" called "depression" means: "I am unhappy."

Insofar as there is adherence to the ethics of the medical game, sick people will be disliked, at least to an extent. This tends to be mitigated by the sick person's submission to those who attempt to make him well and by his own efforts to recover. In many ways, however, patients with hysteria, and with mental illnesses generally, do not make "appropriate" efforts to get well. To that extent, they forfeit the average person's (and the physician's) disposition to behave kindly toward them and invite more-or-less thinly disguised sadism. In brief, it could be said that in the framework of medical ethics, the patient

[5] Both witchcraft and mental illness focus on patterns of deviation from social norms or rules of conduct. The notion of illness, of course, refers to the human body as an animal-machine rather than to the human being as a theological or social entity. Hence, the term "illness" implies that we deal with phenomena not primarily related to social factors.

is deserving of kindness only insofar as he is potentially healthy. This is wholly analogous to the medieval theological position according to which the witch or the heretic was worthy of human attention only insofar as he was a potential "true believer." In the one case, man is accepted as human—and thus deserving of humane treatment—only because he might be healthy; in the other, only because he might be a good Christian. Thus, neither sickness nor religious disbelief was given the kind of humane recognition it deserved.

It is easy, of course, to accord recognition for disbelief in regard to a subject that no longer commands general adherence. Thus with the rise of the rational-scientific spirit in Western culture, religious disbelief was accorded increasing recognition. Today, however, it is the medical world view that pervades our contemporary life. In line with this, there is insufficient general recognition that illness is as much a part of life as health. The possibility that bodily disabilities of various types—and human behaviors of all sorts—may be appropriate ways-of-life or modes of existence thus tends to be obscured and disallowed.

Coincident with the spread of medical scientism and the tendency to disallow the genuine existence of problems in human relationships, there is a rebirth, particularly in the United States, of an increasing antagonism to religious disbelief (Blanshard, 1960). Partly, this may be the result of a socially prevalent equation between agnosticism and communism. This simple rationalization, however, may merely hide a generalized dread of more openly confronting problems in human living. Thus, the very popularity of psychoanalysis and of various techniques of psychotherapy may be attributed to this pervasive wish to deny, alter, or avoid facing up to well-defined conflicts of human interests, whether these be interpersonal, social, economic, or ethical (Szasz, 1960c).

PART V | *Game-Model Analysis of Behavior*

"The game is then an illustration of the situation out of which an organized personality arises." George H. Mead (1934, p. 159)

CHAPTER 13

The Game-Playing

Model

of Human Behavior

Almost everything in this book thus far has presupposed what in effect is the game model of human behavior, first clearly formulated by George H. Mead (1934). Mead's thesis was that mind and self are generated in a social process and that linguistic communication is the single most important feature responsible for the differences between the behavior of animals and men. The details of Mead's theory of action (Mead, 1934, 1936, 1938) need not concern us here. It shall suffice for us to consider his ideas concerning games and their bearing on the problem of hysteria and mental illness.

The Social Nature and Development of Games

GEORGE H. MEAD ON GAMES, MINDS, AND HUMAN ACTIONS

Mead considered games as paradigmatic of social situations. Accordingly, they were of the greatest significance in his theory of human behavior which regarded man as essentially a role-taking animal. Playing a game presupposes that each player is able to take the role of all the other players. Mead also emphasized that rules of the game are of great interest to children and are crucial to the social development of the human being. Let us recall that the specific patterns of help-seeking and help-giving which develop during childhood were interpreted as a prototypal game. Thus, we have been concerned first with specific rules, having discussed them in Part IV, and will now turn our attention to a more general and abstract consideration of games.

The spirit of the game—that is, the belief that the social game (of living) is worth playing—Mead (1934) described as the "generalized other." Although this is not a particularly well-chosen term, the idea to which it refers is significant.

> The organized community or social group which gives to the individual his unity of self may be called "the generalized other." The attitude of the generalized other is the attitude of the whole community. Thus, for example, in the case of such a social group as a ball team, the team is the generalized other in so far as it enters—as an organized process or social activity—into the experience of any one of the individual members of it (pp. 153-154).

The social situation in which a person lives constitutes the team on which he plays and is, accordingly, of the utmost importance in determining *who he is* and *how he acts*. Thus, a psychiatric patient's behavior—as contrasted with a medical patient's illness—must be regarded as the product of biological and psychosocial determinants. In other words, man's so-called instinctual needs are shaped—and this may include inhibiting, fostering, or even creating "needs"—by the social game prevalent in his milieu. The conception of a dual, biosocial (Murphy, 1947) determination of behavior has become integrated into psychonanalytic theory by means of increasing emphasis on ego-psychology and object relationships. Useful as these modifications of classical psychoanalytic theory have been, explanations in terms of so-called ego-functions do not seem as adequate for either theory or therapy as those couched in terms of rules, roles, and games.

In this connection, let us briefly consider a problem illustrative of the connections between psychoanalysis and game theory (in the sense used here). The concepts of primary and secondary gain, although originating from the period of the classical theory, have been retained by almost all contemporary psychoanalytic authors. Gains derived from playing a game profitably—say, by being more kindly treated for an hysterical illness—are regarded as secondary. Thus as the term betrays, these gains are considered less significant as reasons (or motives) for the behavior in question than primary gains, which are derived from the alleged gratifications of unconscious instinctual needs.

Reinterpreting these phenomena in terms of a consistently rule-following, role-taking, and game-playing model of behavior, the need to distinguish between primary and secondary gains and the corresponding necessity to estimate the relative significance of alleged physiological needs and dammed-up impulses on the one hand and of social and interpersonal factors on the other hand disappears. Since needs and impulses cannot be said to exist in human social life without specified rules for dealing with them, instinctual needs cannot be considered solely in terms of biological rules (*cf.* Chapter 10). Instead, instinctual needs, too, must be viewed in terms of their psychosocial significance—that is, as parts of the game.

It follows that notions such as hysteria or mental illness can be properly understood only in the context of a specified social setting. In other words, while such diseases as syphilis and tuberculosis are in the nature of events or happenings, and hence can be described without taking cognizance of how men conduct themselves in their social affairs, hysteria, and all other phenomena now popularly called mental illnesses, are in the nature of actions. They are thus made to happen by sentient, intelligent human beings and can be understood best, in my opinion, in the framework of games. "Mental illnesses" thus differ fundamentally from ordinary diseases and are similar, rather, to certain moves or techniques in playing games. Suffering from hysteria is thus far from being sick and could more accurately be thought of as playing a game, correctly or incorrectly, skillfully or clumsily, successfully or unsuccessfully, as the case might be.

JEAN PIAGET ON THE DEVELOPMENT OF GAMES

I have used the notion of games as though it were familiar to most people. I believe this is justified, because everyone is familiar with how to play some game. Accordingly, games serve admirably as models for the clarification of other, less well-understood, social-psychological phenomena. Yet, the ability to follow rules, play games, and construct new games is a faculty not equally shared by all persons. It will thus be necessary to consider the child's development in regard to his ability to play games. In this connection, the distinctions among various types of games will also be briefly examined.

The evolution of games during childhood has been exhaustively studied by Piaget. His work (1928, 1932, 1951) will form the basis for the following comments. It is significant that Piaget (1932) regarded moral behavior simply as a certain type of rule-following: "All morality consists in a system of rules, and the essence of all morality is to be sought for in the respect which the individual acquires for these rules" (p. 1). Piaget thus equated the nature of morality, or ethical feeling and conduct, with the individual's attitude toward and practice of various rules. This point of view has much to recommend it, since it affords a scientific-rational basis for the analysis of moral schemes (games) and moral behavior (the players' actual behavior).

In his studies of game-rules, Piaget distinguished two more or less distinct features of rule-following behavior. One is the practice of rules, that is, the precise ways in which children of different ages apply rules. The other feature pertains to what he called consciousness of rules. By this Piaget meant self-reflection concerning rules or role-taking behavior (Mead, 1934). Piaget, however, carried this concept much farther than Mead, for he observed and described a hierarchy of role-taking attitudes. In other words, children of varying ages have different ideas concerning the character of the game-rules. In general, younger children regard them as obligatory, externally imposed, and "sacred," whereas older children gradually learn to regard rules as socially defined and, in a sense, self-imposed. Piaget (1932) thus traced rule-following and game-playing behavior from early childhood stages of egocentrism, imitation, and heteronomy to the later (mature) stage of cooperation, rational rule-following, and autonomy (pp. 86-95). Since for our purpose the details of the development of rule-following behavior are not relevant, only a brief summary of Piaget's scheme will be presented.

First, in regard to the practice or application of rules, Piaget distinguished four stages. The earliest stage is characterized by the automatic imitation of certain behavior-patterns on the part of the preverbal child. Piaget called these motor rules which later merge into habits. The second stage begins usually some time after the second year of life, "when the child receives from the outside the example of codified rules" (p. 16). The child's play during this phase is purely egocentric. He plays in the presence of others, but not with them. This type of rule-application is characterized by a combination of imitation[1] of others with a purely individual use of the examples received. For example, everyone can win at once. This stage usually ends at about the age of seven or eight years.

During the third stage, designated as the stage of incipient cooperation, children "begin to concern themselves with the question of mutual control and of the unification of rules" (p. 17). Nevertheless, play remains relatively idiosyncratic. When during this period children are questioned about the rules of the game in which they are engaged, they often give entirely contradictory accounts of them.

The fourth stage appears between the ages of eleven and twelve years and is characterized by the codification of rules. The rules of the game are now well understood; there is a correspondingly high degree of consensus

[1] Note that Piaget (1932) characterized this stage as consisting of the "imitation of seniors with egocentrism" (p. 41). It is no accident that the notion of imitation recurs here once again. Using imitation as a key concept, denoting by it processes of individual development on the one hand and social concepts (such as rules, roles, and games) on the other, an attempt will be made to demonstrate that an analysis of hysteria in terms of the game model and the interpretations offered previously (in terms of communication and rule-following) converge to form a single theory.

among children as to what they are. The game-rules are now explicit, public, and conventional.

So much for Piaget's description of the practice of rules. This scheme must be supplemented by the development of the consciousness of rules. By this was meant the child's (or adult's) experience in regard to the origin and nature of the rules, and especially his feeling, perception, and conception of how they obligate him to obey the rules.

Piaget (1932) described three stages in the development of rule-consciousness. During the first stage "rules are not yet coercive in character, either because they are purely motor, or else (at the beginning of the egocentric stage) because they are received, as it were, unconsciously, and as interesting examples rather than as obligatory realities" (p. 18). During the second stage, which does not begin until after the age of five years, rules are regarded as sacred and untouchable. Games composed of such rules are called heteronomous. Rules (and games) emanate from the adults and are experienced as lasting forever. "Every suggested alteration strikes the child as a transgression" (p. 18).

The third and final stage begins when the child regards rules as acquiring their obligatory character because of mutual consent. Such rules must be obeyed because loyalty to the group, or to the game, demands it. Undesirable rules, however, can be altered. It is this attitude toward games that we usually associate with and expect of an adult in a democratic society. Such a person is expected to know and feel that just as the rules of games are man-made, so are the laws of one's country. This may be contrasted with the rules of the game of a theocratic nation, in which the citizen is expected to believe that the laws are God-given. So-called autonomous games, in contrast to heteronomous ones, can be played only by individuals who have reached the last stages in the foregoing two developmental schemes.

The evolution of the child's concept of games and rules parallels, of course, the development of his intelligence (Piaget, 1952a&b, 1953, 1954). The ability to distinguish biological from social rules (Chapter 10) thus depends on a certain degree of intellectual and moral development. This makes it readily understandable that it is usually during adolescence that children begin to have doubts concerning the "rationality" of Biblical rules. It seems to me that what has been labeled adolescent rebelliousness in psychological and sociological writings may, in large part, be attributed to the fact that it is only at this time that children have enough sense, so to speak, to be able intelligently to scrutinize parental, religious, and social demands as systems of rules. The Bible lends itself especially well to demolition by the growing logic of the adolescent, for in it biological and social rules are often undifferentiated, or perhaps deliberately confused.[2] In Piaget's terms, all rules are treated as though they were parts of heteronomous games. This type of game fits best into the world of a less than ten-year-old child.

Since children, especially very young children, are utterly dependent on their parents, their relative inability to comprehend other than externally imposed, coercive rules is not very surprising. Similarly, the more adult persons depend, or are made to depend, on others (whether on individuals or groups), the more their game-playing attitudes will approximate those of children (e.g., Johnson, 1960).

A close parallel may be drawn among several parameters, each undergoing characteristic changes during childhood and each requiring that properly supporting human relationships be available to the growing child. The psychoanalytic construct "ego," Mead's "mind" and "self," intelligence (learning), and the development of moral sensibility and behavior all appear to be dependent—perhaps each in its own way—on the introjection of, and identification with, so-called "good objects" (Szasz, 1957c, 1958d). I shall let this matter rest here, for if pursued it would carry us too far afield. Keeping these considerations in mind will assist us, however, in giving an operational meaning to the otherwise largely pejorative use of the psychiatric and psychoanalytic notion of immaturity. By using a developmental scheme such as provided by Piaget—which rests, as Piaget himself duly noted, on certain preferential values of a given society—it is possible to speak meaningfully of relatively more or less mature types of game-playing. Later, we shall apply these concepts to an interpretation of hysteria and will show that the behavior so designated represents a relatively immature type of rule-following—that is, one based largely on heteronomy and coercion rather than on autonomy and reciprocity.

Personality Development and Moral Values

According to Piaget, the evolution of children's games proceeds from heteronomy to autonomy. In terms of interpersonal processes aimed at mastery, this corresponds to a movement from coercion and self-help toward intelligent, reciprocal cooperation among equals. Although Piaget described these psychological and social phenomena with great fidelity, I believe that he

[2] It would be idle to believe or pretend that religious teachings—and revolts against them—do not continue to play a significant role in contemporary American life. Indeed, several major contemporary ethical movements seem to share common ground in repudiating traditional religious doctrines. Thus (American) Humanism, (French) Existentialism, and (Russian) Communism have in common a rational atheism. This common feature, although noteworthy, should not obscure the vast differences among these radically different ethical movements.

did not stress sufficiently the ethical choices implicit in them. In other words, what Piaget described reflects, it seems to me, mainly the kind of development which some members of the middle and upper classes of contemporary Western nations would want for their own children, or for themselves. Autonomy, integrity, and mutually respectful cooperation are the prime values and developmental goals toward which this process of socialization aims. But are these the values for which the lower classes strive or which some of the organized religions uphold? It does not seem to me that they are. Lower-class persons—meaning men and women with little education, and perhaps in dire economic straits—tend to aspire to power and dominance rather than to equality.[3]

DOMINATION-SUBMISSION VERSUS EQUALITY AND RECIPROCITY

The fundamental human conflict between domination-submission and equality may be seen, though in somewhat different forms, in virtually all human affairs (e.g., Fromm, 1941). The French Revolution affords a classic example. The fight was waged in the names of *Liberté, égalité, et fraternité*. Two of these values—equality and fraternity—imply cooperation rather than oppression. Yet the cooperative value-ideals of the philosophers who provided the original impetus for the revolution gave way to the pragmatically held values of the masses. These values, in turn, did not differ greatly from the values by which the oppressed masses had been ruled by sovereign royalty. Power, coercion, and oppression thus took the place of equality, fraternity, and cooperation.

It is not surprising that in the next major European revolution, the ethical values of the lower classes received a more explicit formulation. The Marxist revolution promised a dictatorship of the proletariat: the oppressed shall become the oppressors! This was rather similar to the scriptural program according to which "the last shall be the first." The main differences between the two programs lay in their respective means of implementation.

"NATURAL SUPERIORITY" VERSUS POSTNATAL EXPERIENCE

I should like to make explicit here that I do not believe in the "natural superiority" or "inferiority" of any group of human beings. I hold, rather, that given a physically healthy baby, the effects of postnatal experiences generally far outweigh the role of biological characteristics in determining

---

[3] The aspiration for power, dominance, and exploitation of others is, of course, not limited to members of any single class in society. The extent to which these are the guiding values of people in all walks of life in the United States today is demonstrated and discussed in Sorokin and Lunden's *Power and Morality* (1959), and in many of the references cited therein.

the final shape which a human being takes. The total impact of education, broadly conceived, is still one of the most underrated phenomena in the modern world. I wish, therefore, emphatically to repudiate the traditional belief in the natural superiority of men—or of white men, "civilized" men, etc.—as well as the amusing reaction-formation to it which has proclaimed the "natural superiority" of women (Montagu, 1953). This does not mean that I do not consider well-educated men to be vastly different from uneducated ones. The difference, however, seems to be rather like the difference between people speaking different languages, say English and French. Since uneducated men cannot compete on equal footing in the game of life with their better educated brothers, they tend to become chronic losers. Players who always lose cannot be expected to harbor affectionate feelings toward either the game or their opponents.

PERSONALITY AS A NORMATIVE PSYCHOSOCIAL CONCEPTION

The conception of a distinctive "human" or well-functioning personality is rooted in psychosocial and ethical criteria. It is not biologically given, nor are biological determinants especially significant for it.

The view developed here is an attempt to formulate a systematic theory of personal conduct free of all references to so-called primary or biologically given needs.[4] This is not to deny that man is an animal with a genetically determined biological equipment which sets the upper and lower limits, as it were, within which he must function. We accept the limits, or the general range, and focus on the development of specific patterns of operation within them. Hence, our theory strives to eschew biological considerations as explanations, and instead attempts to construct a consistently psychosocial explanatory scheme. It was emphasized that not only is so-called psychological growth learned but so are childishness, immaturity, and mental illness. Two sets of phenomena were singled out as especially significant in this regard. They were the rules of helplessness and helpfulness learned in childhood, and the Bible as a paradigm of religious teachings. Charity, or charitableness, as a virtue forms a bridge between the childhood rules and the Biblical rules. As a general ethical ideal, it constitutes a powerful incentive toward fostering patterns of disability.

CONFLICTING VALUES IN PERSONALITY DEVELOPMENT

It is evident that there is a considerable range of values among different societies (Kluckhohn, 1949). Even within most single societies, adults and

---

[4] This attempt, of course, is hardly novel. A. Adler (1907-1937), Horney (1950), and Kardiner (1939) have made significant contributions in this direction. I have learned and borrowed from each of them.

growing children have some choices as to which values to teach and which to follow. In contemporary Western societies, the principal alternatives are between autonomy and heteronomy—or between "risky" freedom and "secure" slavery. (This is an oversimplification, but it is offered mainly for purposes of further orientation.)

Piaget (1932) wrote:

> *In our societies the child, as he grows up, frees himself more and more from adult authority; whereas in the lower grades of civilization puberty marks the beginning of an increasingly marked subjection of the individual to the elders and to the traditions of his tribe.* And this is why collective responsibility seems to us to be missing from the moral make-up of the child, whereas it is a notion that is fundamental in the code of primitive ethics ([ITALICS ADDED] p. 250).

We have seen (Chapter 11), however, that encouragement to strive toward adult integrity by emancipation from the unilateral authority of others is not the only force active in our society. Piaget has also discussed some of the forces that foster coercive, power-dependent, heteronomous behavior:

> It looks as though, in many ways, *the adult did everything in his power to encourage the child to persevere in its specific tendencies, and to do so precisely in so far as these tendencies stand in the way of social development.* Whereas, given sufficient liberty of action, the child will spontaneously emerge from his egocentrism and tend with his whole being towards cooperation, *the adult most of the time acts in such a way as to strengthen egocentrism in its double aspect, intellectual and moral* ([ITALICS ADDED] p. 188).

Although I fully agree with Piaget that some types of adult behavior foster the child's egocentrism, I rather doubt that the child would emerge from this stage and move toward autonomy spontaneously. Reciprocity and autonomy are complex values concerning human relationships and must also be taught (Gouldner, 1960). Naturally, they cannot be taught coercively, but rather must be practiced and thus be made examples for the child to emulate.

Piaget singled out the adult's coercive or autocratic attitude toward the child as a cause for his persistent subservience in later life. Although this factor may be subsumed under the rules of helplessness described earlier, it merits re-emphasis. Such infantilizing-oppressive influences are, of course, not limited to the family situation. On the contrary, they are ubiquitous and may be found in educational, religious, medical, and other settings. It was noted previously that egocentrism, rather than cooperation and autonomy, is fostered by certain religious teachings. The techniques by which submission, dependency, and infantilism are fostered in medicine and psychiatry have been repeatedly discussed (e.g., Meerloo, 1955; Szasz and Hollender, 1956). Important as this subject is for all of medicine, it is especially significant for psychiatry, because psychiatric patients are particularly uncertain of their social and moral behavior. Since social conduct has a more specific, as well as a more powerful, impact on one's sense of identity than does bodily illness, limitations or restrictions of such conduct have more far-reaching psychological effects. This is merely another way of saying that interpersonally or socially imposed limitations on freedom are even more crippling, as a rule, than those due to physical disability.

It has long been known that bodily disability predisposes to hysterical illness. Freud (Breuer and Freud, 1893-1895, p. 40) spoke of this as "somatic compliance" and Ferenczi (1916-1917) as "pathoneurosis." I would formulate this rather by saying that bodily illness teaches the person how to be ill. One's own illness—and, of course, the responses of others to it, with which it is inextricably intermingled—thus becomes a model, or a rule, which one may later choose to follow or not follow. In this light, the concept of "somatic compliance" becomes more general and could logically be called "psychosocial compliance." This expression is offered to denote the learning and following of rules which foster dependency, coercion, and mastery by exhibiting signs of helplessness.

Religious, medical, and educational situations abound in such rules. Consequently, those exposed to them are subjected to pressures to adapt by assuming the required *postures of helplessness* (e.g., patients committed to state hospitals, candidates in psychoanalytic institutes, etc.). This leads to behavior judged appropriate ("normal") within the system, but potentially at variance with criteria used outside of it. Resistance to the rules may be tolerated to varying degrees in different systems, but in any event tends to bring the individual into conflict with the group. Therefore, most persons seek to conform rather than to rebel. Another possibility for adaptation lies in becoming aware of the rules themselves and of their limited, situational relevance. This makes the necessary adaptation to the situation possible with relatively little social friction, while at the same time it insures the maintenance of a large measure of inner freedom. To do this, however, requires learning in a rather complex sense (that is, learning *about* learning), as well as resistance against being pressed into a role, despite the fact that role-acceptance may be richly rewarded.

At this point, the question may arise as to what connections, if any, there are between the foregoing considerations and the problems posed by hysteria and mental illness? I believe that there is an intimate connection between political history, ethics, and psychiatry, for each of these disciplines is concerned with the problem of what men value. Political history is meaningless unless human preferences in regard to social affairs are taken into account. This raises such issues as, for example, whether men place value on their belief that their rulers have a kinship relation to God or whether they prefer to be ruled by a personally powerful king or by an electorate, and so forth.

Ethics, of course, is directly concerned with the study of values, both in an empirical and normative sense (e.g., Perry, 1954; Pepper, 1958). The relation of psychiatry to ethics and politics has, until recently, been somewhat obscured. Yet, if we conceive of psychiatry as the study of human behavior, it is evident that it has a most intimate relationship to both ethics and politics. Indeed, this relationship was illustrated by means of different examples in each of the five Parts of this book. In relation to the problem of hysteria and mental illness, the connections between ethics and psychiatry may be highlighted by asking these questions: *What kind of human relationships and patterns of mastery does the so-called hysteric value?* Or, phrased somewhat differently: *What kind of (social) game does such a person want to play? And what sort of behavior does he regard as playing the game well and winning?*

Before these questions can be answered, it will be necessary to inquire further into the nature of games. This, in turn, will require a logical classification of games, similar to that used for languages. Such a classification will now be presented.

A Logical Hierarchy of Games

In speaking of games it has been assumed until now that they are all more or less of the same kind. This point of view will no longer suffice. To assume such a similarity among games would be as unserviceable as to assume that all statements made in English are essentially similar. Yet, from a linguistic or philological point of view, this position is well justified. It is unjustified only from a logical or semiotical point of view. Without making use of the distinction between object language and metalanguage, no scientific understanding of communicational processes is possible. To deepen our understanding of game-playing behavior, it will be necessary to construct a similar logical hierarchy of games.

Since games are composed, among other things, of bits of communicative action, it is not surprising that a hierarchy of games analogous to a hierarchy of languages is easily constructed. Words, or linguistic signs, point to referents. These may be physical objects, other words, or complex systems of signs. In a similar fashion, games are composed of systems of rules which point to certain acts. The rules stand in the same relationship to the acts as do words to referents in the case of languages. Accordingly, games with rules that point to the simplest possible set of coherent (or patterned) acts may be defined as object games. Games composed of rules which themselves point or refer to other rules may be called metagames. Typical examples of object games are patterns of so-called instinctive behavior. The goals of these games are physical survival, release of urinary, anal, or sexual tension, and so forth. Accordingly, playing object games is not limited to human beings. In the medical setting, the reflex immobilization of an injured extremity illustrates a move in an object game.

It is evident that the learned and distinctively human elements of behavior are entirely on the level of metagames. Examples of first-level metagames are the rules determining where to urinate and where not to, when to eat and when not to, and so forth. So-called ordinary or conventional games— such as bridge, tennis, or chess—constitute mixtures of (more or less complex) metagames. Some ordinary games will be examined as a preliminary to a game-model analysis of hysteria.

THE STRUCTURE OF ORDINARY GAMES

Let us apply the concepts of game-hierarchy to the analysis of an ordinary game, say tennis. This game, along with many others, is characterized, first of all, by a set of basic rules. The basic rules of tennis specify such things as the number of players, the layout of the court, the nature and use of rackets and balls, and so forth. Although these rules are basic to tennis, they could themselves be said to be metarules. In other words, the basic rules of tennis codify a metagame with respect to certain (logically) simpler games pertaining to laying out courts, setting up nets, using rackets, etc. When we play tennis, however, games lying on levels lower than the basic game do not usually come into consideration. These infra-tennis games are significant only to those who aspire to play tennis but are prevented from doing so, say, by not having enough money to buy the necessary equipment. For them, the rules of the game of living necessary to enable a person to play tennis may be of great significance.

Beginning at the level of the basic rules—assuming, that is, the presence of players, equipment, and so forth—it is evident that there is much more to an actual, true-to-life tennis game than could be subsumed under the basic rules. This is simply because there is more than one way to play tennis while still adhering to the basic rules. The basic rules merely provide a minimal framework or structure within which there is considerable latitude. For example, one player might want to win at any cost; another might consider that playing according to a certain style is desirable; and a third might consider playing fairly as most important (Dawkins, 1960). Each of these techniques imply rules specifying (1) that in order to play tennis one must follow rules A, B, and C and (2) how one should conduct oneself while following these rules. The latter could be said to constitute the rules of "metatennis"—although it must be remembered that in everyday language, the term "tennis" is used to denote all of the rules of the game (as it is played according to the expectations of a particular social group). The fact that ordinary games can be played in more than one way—that is, that they contain games at different logical levels—is well known and leads to conflict whenever different types of players meet.

When two wildly competitive youngsters play tennis, the game is so constituted that both players regard winning as their sole aim. Considerations of style, fair play, one's state of health, and everything else may become subordinated to this goal. In other words, they play to win at any cost. The players pursue this goal by adhering to the appropriate basic rules of the game, such as placing shots within the prescribed area of the court, serving from the proper position, etc. They avoid violating rules for which there are prescribed penalties, for this would jeopardize their chances of winning. This situation may be considered the first level of this game.

A next higher level of tennis may be distinguished—a "metatennis game," as it were—which, in addition to the basic rules, contains a new set of rules which refer to the basic rules. These might include rules concerning style, the tempo of the game, and others. Even more complex rules may be specified, such as those pertaining to courtesy toward one's opponent or to attitudes toward the umpire and the spectators. Playing according to higher level rules (metarules) implies two things. First, that the players will orient themselves to and follow a new set of rules, these being additional to, rather than in place of, the old set. Second, adopting new rules implies adopting new goals as well. In tennis, the principal new goal might be to play fairly, or perhaps elegantly, rather than merely to win at any cost. It is important to note now that the goals of the basic game and of the higher level game may come into conflict, although they need not necessarily do so. Adherence to the rules and aims ("ethics") of the higher level game usually imply that its rules and goals take precedence over those of the basic game. In other words, for a properly socialized Englishman, it is better—that is, more rewarding in relation to both the spectators and his own self-image—to be a "fair loser" than an "ugly winner." But if this is true, as indeed it is, then our everyday use of the words "loser" and "winner" *no longer do justice to what we want to say*. For when we speak of James as a "fair loser," especially if he is contrasted with an opponent considered an "ugly winner," what we mean is that James lost the basic game (of, say, tennis or boxing) but has won the metagame. But we cannot say anything like this in ordinary language—except by circumlocution (e.g., "James played a good game but lost")—for the word "game" blurs this distinction.

EVERYDAY LIFE AS A MIXTURE OF METAGAMES

Everyday life and human relations abound in situations essentially similar to the example sketched above. *Men are constantly engaged in behavior involving complicated mixtures of various logical levels of games.* Unless the precise games which men play are clarified—and further, whether they play well, badly, or indifferently—there is little chance to understand what "is going on" or to alter it.

In this analysis of game-playing behavior, use has already been made of some ideas first advanced by Russell in his analysis of logical types. Before presenting a brief exposition of Russell's theory, the problems that make his analysis indispensable to us, as psychiatrists or students of human behavior, will be indicated.

Let us begin once more with the question: What rules does man follow in his daily life? The metaphorical net which this question throws out falls so wide that it engulfs nearly everything. Let us assume, therefore, that this question is asked of a simple man. We aim merely at the basic rules of living, or at least at one version of them. According to this "simple" view of life, man was manufactured, as it were, by God. His behavior is governed by the moral (religious) teachings of his faith. Thus, the Biblical rules could be said to embody (at least one version of) the basic rules of the game of social living. From this point of view, the Ten Commandments may be likened to the directions one receives when purchasing a new appliance. These inform the buyer of the rules he must follow if he wishes to derive the benefits that the machine has to offer. If he fails to follow the directions, he will have to suffer the consequences. In the case of breakdowns, for example, the manufacturer's warranty is honored only if the machine has not been misused. Here is a perfect analogy for legitimate illness (manufacturing defect), as contrasted to sin or other types of unallowed illness (misuse of the machine). The Ten Commandments—and Biblical teachings generally— provide the rules that man must follow if he wishes to obtain the benefits which the manufacturer of the game of life (God) has to offer. The precise nature of the rewards are relevant only in connection with choosing among various games. Once a person is engaged in playing a game, one is justified in assuming that he is striving to maximize his gains and minimize his losses, in accordance with the rules.

In the case of real-life games, however, the situation is somewhat more complicated. It often happens that the game-rules instruct the player that in order to "win" it is necessary that he "lose." Does he henceforth lose when he wins and vice versa? This question is of the same type as the classic paradox of Epimenides, the Cretan, who asserted that "All Cretans are liars." Was he lying or telling the truth? This problem was first clarified by Russell (1908).

In this connection, let us recall some of the Biblical rules discussed in Chapter 11. Consider, for example, the following two rules for "good living": (1) "Blessed *are* the meek: for they shall inherit the earth" (Matthew 5:5); (2) "Blessed *are* they which are persecuted for righteousness' sake: for theirs is the kingdom of heaven" (Matthew 5:10).

I submit that a basic assumption underlies these rules—namely, that it *happens* that some people are meek and that others are persecuted. A logically correct analogy would be with, say, driving an overlong shot in a tennis game. Being meek and hitting a losing ball are tacitly assumed to be occurrences not deliberately sought! But are they not? Or might they not be? What if you should decide that you will reward the loser of a certain tennis match? Should one of the players become aware of this, it would be only rational for him to try to "lose." But can this still be called "losing the game?"

The situation is similar in regard to meekness. In the days of Jesus Christ, much as today, aggressive men often tended to get the better of their less aggressive neighbors. Ethical rules came into being, apparently, in an effort to provide for the sort of thing which the British call fair play. This, however, complicated matters considerably, for games of increasingly higher orders were thus created.

These considerations have brought us back to a topic considered in connection with the example of the tennis game. They underscore the observation that in religious rules, games, impersonations, and in innumerable occurrences of everyday life, phenomena confront us that cannot be understood without analyzing them in terms of a hierarchy of games. To further clarify the logic of game hierarchies, Russell's theory of logical types will now be presented.

RUSSELL'S THEORY OF LOGICAL TYPES

The basic ideas of this theory were first formulated by Bertrand Russell in 1908, in a paper entitled "Mathematical Logic as Based on the Theory of

Types." They were set in broader context in the first volume of Whitehead and Russell's *Principia Mathematica* (1910). Russell's fundamental insight consisted in asserting that *there is always a (logical) difference between things which make up a class and the class itself.* Stated differently, there is a *logical discontinuity between a class and its members.* This logical rule derives from and presupposes what Russell (1908) called the "hierarchy of types." A *type* is defined "as the range of significance of a propositional function, i.e., as the collection of arguments for which the said function has values. . . . The division of objects into types is necessitated by the *reflexive* fallacies which otherwise arise" (p. 75).

By "reflexive fallacies," Russell referred to the same sorts of problems in logic which are everyday occurrences in regard to rule-following. Since man is characteristically a sign-using and self-reflective animal, it follows that not only is he able to denote objects with signs but that he can also denote signs with other signs of higher levels. Likewise, he has the mental capacity not only to make rules but also to make rules about rules and rules about rules about rules and so on potentially *ad infinitum.* Hence, it is necessary to distinguish various *levels* within given *hierarchies* (of languages, rules, games). It was not until 1922, however, that Russell explicitly applied the principles of the theory of types to the logic of languages. This led to establishing hitherto unexpected connections between mathematics, logic, linguistics, philosophy, and finally psychiatry and the study of social behavior.[5]

The classic paradox of Epimenides is typical of the kind of problem encountered whenever we unwittingly switch from one logical level of language to another. Russell himself used this example repeatedly in his discussions of the theory of types. His clearest analysis of this dilemma was set forth in "The Philosophy of Logical Atomism" (1918):

> There is one other of these contradictions that I may as well mention, the most ancient, the saying of Epimenides that "all Cretans are liars." Epimenides was a man who slept for sixty years without stopping, and I believe that it was at the end of that nap that he made the remark that all Cretans were liars. It can be put more simply in the form: If a man makes the statement "I am lying," is

[5] I believe Bateson (Ruesch and Bateson, 1951) was the first to call attention to the significance of Russell's theory of types for psychiatry. Defining psychiatry as the study of (human) communicative behavior, he emphasized the need to distinguish various levels of communications (i.e., communication and metacommunication). In a recent essay, Bateson *et al.* (1956) again made use of Russell's theory of logical types, applying it to the elucidation of the communications which the schizophrenic patient and his significant objects characteristically exchange with one another.

he lying or not? If he is, that is what he said he was doing, so he is speaking the truth and not lying. If, on the other hand, he is not lying, then plainly he is speaking the truth in saying that he is lying, and therefore he is lying, since he says truly that that is what he is doing. . . . *The man who says "I am lying" is really asserting "There is a proposition which I am asserting and which is false." That is presumably what you mean by lying. . . . It follows that the word "proposition," in the sense in which we ordinarily try to use it, is a meaningless one, and that we have got to divide propositions up into sets and can make statements about all propositions in a given set, but those propositions will not themselves be members of the set* ([ITALICS ADDED] pp. 262-63).

Another way of phrasing Russell's thesis would be as follows: When we assert that "Mr. A. is lying," unless we specify the assertion which Mr. A. has made and which we consider a lie, we have made an incomplete statement. Incomplete statements are frequently encountered in everyday speech. They are often considered more meaningful or sensible than they are. Black (1951) suggested that the "leading principle of the theory of types," so far as it applies to ordinary language, "consists in the assertion that *grammatically* impeccable sentences often prove to be crypto-nonsense generated by the propensity for substituting in the same context words which agree in grammatical while differing in logical form" (p. 234). The distinguishing feature of such statements is that the speaker makes a tacit assumption as to how his incomplete utterance ought to be completed, and the listener is expected to supply the correct closure. Good examples of incomplete statements are contemporary advertisements of the type: "Buicks are Better!" We are not told better than *what*, since it is expected that we shall complete the statement by supplying the names of competing automobile manufacturers.

Similarly, it often happens that participants in a given communicational situation or game know, or correctly assume, what the rules of the game are. For instance, when psychiatrists speak of, say, an "hysterical paralysis," they take for granted that other psychiatrists adhere to certain basic rules governing the use of limbs. Confusion arises whenever different actors in the real-life drama play by different sets of rules, all the while assuming that they adhere to the same script. This, I think, is the basic discovery which Freud made when he noted what he called "transference." He observed that patients behaved as though they were interacting as children with their fathers, whereas in fact they were confronted as adults with their physicians

(Berne, 1957, 1958). Accordingly, it was as though they had been called on to act in one play, say, written by Shakespeare, and started to recite lines from another play, authored perhaps by Sophocles. And all the while the patients (actors) were unaware that this was not the play the lines of which they had been asked to recite (Grinker, 1959).

Looking at problems in living from this point of view, it seems apparent that much of what goes by the names of "growing up," "being sophisticated," getting "treated by psychoanalysis" (and other methods as well) are processes having one significant feature in common: The person learns, and is taught, that the rules of the game—and the very game itself—by which he has been playing are not necessarily the same as those used by others around him. He thus learns that others may not be interested in playing the game which he has been so avidly pursuing. Or, if they do have some interest in the game, they prefer some modifications of the rules. Thus, unless a person finds others to play his own game, according to his own rules—or wishes and is able to coerce others to accept life on his terms[6]— he has a choice among three basic alternatives.

One is to submit to the other person's coercive rules and accept the masochistic-submissive posture offered (Bieber, 1953).

The second alternative is increasingly to renounce socially shared activities and to withdraw into certain relatively idiosyncratic games. Such activities may be labeled scientific, artistic, religious, neurotic, or psychotic, depending on various, generally poorly defined criteria. The nature of these criteria need not concern us here, but we should note that the issue of *social utility* seems to play a significant role in it. In turn, this raises further questions: For whom (i.e., for what persons), and at what time (in history), is a particular game useful?

The third alternative to the basic life-problem sketched above lies in becoming aware of one's own games, as well as those of others, and in trying to make compromises among them. This is an arduous undertaking which often can be, at best, only partially successful. Its main reward lies in guaranteeing the integrity and dignity of one's own self and of all others with whom one interacts. Yet its hardships are such that it need not surprise us if many prefer easier means leading to what must appear, to them, as more glorious ends.

[6] This point of view makes the significant connections between mental illness and social class very clear, especially as it relates to the issue of power. In other words, persons who wield vast power have the opportunity, by and large, to coerce others to play their own games. And as long as they can do this, they cannot become "mentally ill" in a social sense (Szasz, 1958f, 1960c).

"Even if each woman dresses in conformity with her status, a game is still being played: artifice, like art, belongs to the realm of the imaginary. It is not only that girdle, brassiere, hair-dye, make-up disguise body and face; but that the least sophisticated of women, once she is 'dressed,' does not present herself to observation; she is, like the picture or the statue, or the actor on the stage, an agent through whom is suggested someone not there—that is, the character she represents, but is not." Simone de Beauvoir (1953, p. 533)

CHAPTER 14

The Codification

of Game-Rules:

Problems of Impersonation

and Cheating

Having considered the phenomenology and logical structure of games as paradigms of organized patterns of social intercourse, the problem of cheating may now be re-examined. It should be recalled that this study was begun by considering malingering and hysteria, however provisionally, as special kinds of cheating. This thesis can now be refined and extended.

Let us begin by raising these questions: What happens when someone claims to be playing a game but fails to obey its rules? Or, stated more precisely, what happens when a person maintains that he is playing game A, but on observation it is discovered that he is following the rules of game B? In this event, there are two distinct possibilities. The first is that the player really believes that he is playing game A, even though he is not. This may result from failure properly to distinguish game A from game B. The second possibility is that he is deliberately cheating. By this is meant that the person knows the rules of game A perfectly well but has chosen to disregard them, hoping to enhance his chances to win. It is significant that this player has not given up playing game A, for he continues to be committed to its end-goal, namely, winning. He has simply modified the rules, but has kept this rule-changing private (or secret)! *This noncodification of new rules is perhaps the most distinguishing characteristic of cheating.* These considerations underscore the cardinal significance of publicity in regard to game-rules.

Briefly, games are characterized by the following features: (1) A set of rules which impart a special identity to the game; (2) An expectation that the players adhere, voluntarily or otherwise, to the rules; and (3) The fact that games are interpersonal or social events. To start a game, two or more players are required.[1] It may be noted, therefore, that the common-sense view which regards games—and especially competitive games or sports— as aggressive and socially disjunctive is false. Without denying the aggressive (in the sense of "competitive") features of certain game-playing activities, I wish to emphasize the overriding significance of games as means of uniting people in common endeavor. Playing a game earnestly, implies that one's partners, opponents, and team-mates will be taken seriously. Games are therefore paradigms of human engagement or commitment. Disengagements from human relationships could thus be analyzed in terms of not playing a game or as taking the role of a spectator who merely watches the human drama of life but does not participate in it. This maneuver is of considerable significance in our contemporary culture. Others have spoken of it in terms of man's alienation from himself and those around him (Fromm, 1947; Horney, 1950), or as the borderline state (Knight, 1953; Schmideberg, 1959), or as problems or crises of identity (Erikson, 1956).

The occurrences to be discussed in this chapter could be conceptualized several ways—e.g., as cheating, sickness, stupidity, or sin. By analyzing the phenomena in terms of a game model of behavior, it will be possible to bring order and harmony to such apparently diverse and unrelated phenomena as lying, erring, cheating, malingering, the Ganser syndrome, and imposturing.

The Concept of Impersonation

Since man is a role-taking and rule-following animal, it is hardly surprising that so much in human behavior lends itself to analysis along the model of game-playing behavior. This is not a discovery. Rather, it is one of our

---

[1] Games that can be played alone, such as solitaire, will not be considered. Such games constitute special modifications of two- or multiperson games. In solitaire, for example, one could be said to be playing against the deck. Other players are present, as "internal objects" (in psychoanalytic terms) projected onto the rules, or as the "generalized other" (in Mead's terms) contained in the game.

basic postulates. My aim has been to apply this conceptual model to observations of psychiatric interest and to demonstrate its usefulness.

In examining specifically the issue of *game-violation*, it is logical to take impersonation as the starting point. Impersonation refers to a large class of events characterized by the assumption of another person's character or social role. It is evident that impersonation is a ubiquitous occurrence. As such, it is not specifically a psychiatric problem but is of concern to people in varied walks of life. This is reflected in the fact that everyday language (English, in our case) has numerous words to designate different kinds of impersonation. As nouns, denoting the impersonator, we have the charlatan, the confidence-man, the counterfeiter, the forger, the impostor, the spy, the traitor, and many others. Only two types of impersonators—namely, the malingerer and the hysteric—have been of special interest to psychiatrists. Organizing our observations in this way highlights once more that malingering and hysteria, and other so-called psychiatric phenomena, need not be viewed as diseases, but may be much more fruitfully regarded as special instances of impersonation.

A definition of impersonation is now in order. According to Webster, to impersonate is "to assume or act the person or character of. . . ." This definition immediately results in certain interesting difficulties for, if role-taking behavior is universal, how do we distinguish role-taking (say, in Mead's sense) from impersonation (in common-sense usage)? Although a general answer to this question is not nearly as informative as one aimed at a specific situation, the main difference between these two concepts lies in this: *Role-taking refers to consistent or "honest" role-playing, within the limits of the specific game*, whereas *impersonation refers to the pretended assumption of the role, manifested by inconsistent or "dishonest" role-playing*. For example: Taking the role of "seller" and approaching another person as a prospective "buyer" implies that the seller either owns the goods offered for sale, or is authorized to act in the owner's name. When a person sells something he does not own, he impersonates the role of the honest businessman and is called a "swindler."

Since role-taking is one of the universal characteristics of human behavior, it is evident that practically any given form of action can be "interpreted" as a form of impersonation. For example, the so-called Don Juan character may be said to impersonate (his idea of) acrobatic virility; the transvestite impersonates the social role and sexual functions of a member of the opposite sex; in a transference neurosis, the patient impersonates himself as a child; the list could be expanded *ad infinitum*.

IMPERSONATION IN CHILDHOOD

A large part of childhood is spent in impersonating other people. Children play at being fireman, doctor, nurse, mother, father, and so forth. Inasmuch as the child's identity is defined in predominantly negative terms—that is, as being prohibited from acting, or as being unable to perform, in certain ways—it is inevitable that he should seek role-fulfillment through impersonation. A child's real identity or social role is, of course, being a child. But in an instrumentally and scientifically oriented culture, as opposed to a tradition and kinship-oriented one, being a child tends to mean mostly that one is unable to act in certain ways. Thus, childhood itself may be viewed as a form of "disability."[2] That growing children may feel exactly this way about their status might be inferred from the increasing trend on the part of children—especially from the early teens onward—to imitate the external trappings of adult roles. Teenagers thus earnestly impersonate adults and in the process often convince themselves of the genuineness of their assumed roles.

Let us return to impersonation in younger children, say, between the ages of four and ten. In these childhood activities the observers (i.e., the grown-ups) have no difficulty recognizing the pretended, or impersonated, character of the child's act. This is because a child playing doctor or nurse presents a cognitive task of such utter simplicity that any adult who is not an imbecile could not help but master it. It is mainly the child's size, of course, which helps so decisively to give him an identity: he is small. Contrast this with an example taken from the adult world. Consider, for instance, the case of a psychologist practicing psychotherapy. For many people, such a person is indistinguishable from a "doctor." The point I want to make here is simply that to distinguish between medical and nonmedical psychotherapists, one must have a relatively large store of information. We cannot here rely on the person's size, skin color, or other equally easily ascertainable characteristics to aid us in differentiating between category A and category B.

Impersonation, then, is a constant feature of childhood. The notions of imitation, identification, and learning refer either to the same thing as impersonation or to what may be regarded as component parts of it. The purpose of this brief discussion of impersonation in childhood was merely to call attention to its ubiquity and to note the ease with which the child's

---

[2] Similar considerations hold for the aged. As old persons become unemployed and unproductive, and particularly if they are economically and physically disabled, their main role becomes being old.

basic role-identity (as viewed by others!) is established. The latter makes role-differentiation on the part of adult observers exceedingly easy. The problem of successful impersonation thus does not arise until after puberty and the attainment of physiological maturity.

Psychiatric and psychoanalytic authors (e.g., Abraham, 1925) have failed to distinguish between the general class of events, called impersonations, and certain members of this class, for example imposturing. Helene Deutsch (1942, 1955) in particular, has confused or equated the impostor and the impersonator. Some of her observations apply to imposturing, others to impersonating. The following quotation (H. Deutsch, 1955) is illustrative:

> The world is crowded with "as-if" personalities, and even more so with impostors and pretenders. Ever since I became interested in the impostor, he pursues me everywhere. I find him among my friends and acquaintances, as well as in myself. Little Nancy, a fine three-and-a-half-year-old daughter of one of my friends, goes around with an air of dignity, holding her hands together tightly. Asked about this attitude she explains: "I am Nancy's guardian angel, and I'm taking care of little Nancy." Her father asked her about the angel's name. "Nancy" was the proud answer of this little impostor (p. 503).

I believe that Deutsch correctly observed that the world is full of people who act "as if" they were someone else. Alfred Adler (1914) also emphasized this phenomenon and called it the "life-lie." In this connection, we should also recall Vaihinger's important work, *The Philosophy of "As If"* (1911), which significantly influenced both Freud's and Adler's psychological theories.

The point to be emphasized is that not all impersonators are impostors, although all impostors are impersonators. In illustrating impersonation, which she erroneously called imposturing, Deutsch cited examples of the behavior of children. To impersonate others is inevitable for children, since socially they are defined as *nobodies*. In her conclusion, Deutsch (1955) considered the essence of imposturing to lie in "pretending that we actually are what we would like to be" (p. 504). This is merely a restatement of the common human wish to appear better than one actually is. It is not a correct formulation, however, of imposturing, which implies deceitful role-taking for personal gain. Impersonation is an ethically more neutral term; as a class, it contains both ethically objectionable and unobjectionable types of role-pretensions.

The desire to be better or more important than one is, is likely to be strongest, of course, among children, or among persons who are, or consider themselves to be, in inferior, oppressed, or frustrating circumstances.[3] These are the persons who are most prone to resort to various methods of impersonation (Crichton, 1959a & b). Contrariwise, those who have been successful in realizing their aspirations—or, in other words, who are relatively well satisfied with their actual role achievements and definitions—will show little disposition to pretend to be anyone but themselves. They are satisfied with who they are and hence have no need to lie about it. They can afford the luxury of telling the truth about themselves.

Varieties of Impersonation

LYING

The simplest and best understood example of impersonation is lying. This term is used usually in relation to verbal or written communication. It comes into play only when the assumption is made that the communicants have pledged themselves to truthfulness. Thus, the term "lying" can be used meaningfully only in situations in which the rules of the game prescribe truthfulness. This is often assumed in everyday human relationships, and especially in those which are emotionally close, such as in marriage and friendship. Perjury is a special kind of lying, committed in a court of law by a person giving testimony. Here the rules of the game are explicitly formulated; lying (perjury) is punishable by legally enforced sanctions.

MAKING A MISTAKE

To make a mistake, or to err, is a very special kind of impersonation. It will be considered briefly because of its important relationship to lying on the one hand and to the issue of whether one's motives are conscious or unconscious on the other hand. We shall forego a general discussion of this subject and limit ourselves to the most clear-cut instance of making a mistake—namely, that which occurs in experimental science. In some ways this is a counterpart of the legal situation in which untruth equals lying, and which, in turn, is considered perjury. In a typical scientific experiment, the aim is to ascertain whether the result will be X (what has been predicted) or Y (some other result). The scientist does not claim to know what the result will be. On the contrary, he explicitly admits to uncertainty, and merely offers a

---

[3] I do not wish to imply that children are invariably oppressed or that their lack of a firm inner identity is due to "oppression." Indeed, the role of being oppressed can itself be the core of one's identity. The lack of firm personal identity in childhood is a reflection mainly of the child's insufficient social and psychological development.

prediction. The trial-and-error character of experimentation implies that if the prediction comes true it is said to be verified. If the observed result differs from the prediction, we speak of "error" and of "falsification" of the theory. Error here simply means that the result was not intended or anticipated. This is similar to a "mistake" in everyday life. The antonym of error or mistake is success or correct prediction, not truth! The notions of truth-and-lie on the one hand, and success-and-error on the other, pertain to two different games.

CHEATING

Cheating describes deviance from the rules in situations explicitly codified as games. Cheating usually serves the purpose of unfairly increasing the chances of winning. In addition to this strict usage, referring to card games, board games, and so forth, the word "cheating" is also used to describe acts of deceit or imposture of various kinds. A person may be "cheated" in a business venture or a husband may be "cheated" by his wife. These situations are characterized by the fact that the rules of the game are either explicitly stated and hence known to all concerned, or, if they are not stated, they are nevertheless relatively unambiguous. They could be readily stated should anyone wish to do so. The significant issue here is knowing the rules of the game. The maxim, "Ignorance of the law is no excuse," affords an excellent illustration. This ground-rule of Anglo-American law asserts that *it is the responsibility of every adult person to know what kind of games the State requires him to play.* Accordingly, to be ignorant of the law is tantamount to not being a fully socialized person.

When knowledge of the rules of the game might be lacking, or when its status is uncertain—for example, in relation to sickness or politics—we do not usually speak of cheating, but instead use such words and concepts as "hysteria" or "patriotism." Since a wide variety of human behavior can be regarded as though it were a kind of game, the scope of the word "cheating" can be greatly extended. Conceptualizing some of our traditional psychiatric problems in this way, it becomes apparent, I think, that many of these have little, if anything, in common with bodily illnesses. At the same time, their similarity to other forms of cheating becomes clear.

MALINGERING

Cheating is impersonating the correct player. Malingering is impersonating the correctly sick person. What constitutes correct sickness depends, of course, on the rules of the particular *illness game*. Since this has been discussed earlier, there is no need to be concerned now with what these rules might be.

It is the element of rule-awareness that needs to be emphasized. A person who knows nothing about the rules of the sickness game cannot malinger. This is a truism, and is much like asserting that someone who did not know that Picasso's canvasses were valuable could not, and hence would not, try to sell a forged Picasso for a large sum of money. This still leaves us with the problem of self-deception and error.

For instance, a person might truly believe that he was bodily ill when in fact he was not, and might then represent himself as sick. This is similar to, say, a person who has unknowingly purchased a good imitation of a Picasso, believing it to be an original, and who subsequently represents it and tries to sell it as a Picasso. Obviously, there is a difference between this man and the one who actually paints the imitation and then misrepresents it. Malingering has generally been used to describe such deliberate cheating, whereas hysteria and hypochondriasis have been conceptualized as unwitting or unintentional cheating. My aim here is to describe both malingering and hysteria as instances of impersonation. Whether the impersonation is conscious and deliberate or otherwise can be ascertained in two ways. First, by communicating with the person; second, by making inferences from his general behavior.

HYSTERIA, HYPOCHONDRIASIS, AND BODILY DELUSIONS

Special instances of impersonation are encountered in hysteria, hypochondriasis, and severe cases of bodily delusions (e.g., in schizophrenia). In hysteria, the patient impersonates the role of a sick person, partly by identifying with his symptom. Allegedly, however, he does not know that he has done so. When it is said that the hysteric cannot afford to be aware of what he is doing—for if he were, he could no longer do it—what is asserted in effect is that he cannot afford to tell himself the truth. By the same token, he also cannot afford to know that he is lying. He must lie both to himself and to others. This formulation underscores the significance of what has been said earlier concerning the relationship between oppression and helplessness on the one hand, and the use of hysterical and other types of indirect communications on the other hand. To be able to speak the truth is a kind of luxury which few people can afford. This we often forget. *To be able to be truthful one must be more or less grown up and personally secure, and one must live in a social situation which encourages, or at least permits, truthfulness.* We tend to take it for granted that truthful communications are everywhere fostered and rewarded and that lying and cheating are everywhere penalized. But this is far from the actual situation. I have endeavored to set forth and document some of the conditions that favor cheating of the type called hysteria.

In addition to conversion hysteria, hypochondriasis and schizophrenic bodily delusions also constitute examples of consciously unrecognized impersonations of bodily illness. For example, a person's conviction that he is dying, or that he is dead, would perhaps best be regarded as an impersonation of the dead role. In general, the less publicly supported the impersonation, the less self-reflective the person must be to maintain it. Indeed, the loosely used concept of psychosis could be defined as the label that is pinned on those who stubbornly cling to, and loudly proclaim, publicly unsupported role-definitions.

THE GANSER SYNDROME

This phenomenon (Ganser, 1898), to be examined in detail presently, typically consists of an impersonation of the "crazy role," by a prisoner, presumably for the purpose of securing a better life than one of penal servitude. There is a great deal of psychiatric controversy regarding the nature of this alleged illness and whether it is akin to malingering, hysteria, or psychosis (Arieti and Meth, 1959). I suggest that this problem be cast in the framework of the prison plus sickness games and that it be considered a special, strikingly transparent, form of cheating.

THE CONFIDENCE MAN

The confidence man impersonates a role that usually inspires some confidence. In the long run, whoever trusts him will have made a mistake. The impersonation is for selfish gain and is not openly acknowledged to the victim, although it may be acknowledged to the self and to others (Mann, 1954; Maurer, 1950). The impostor and the swindler belong essentially in the same class as the confidence man. "Confidence games" are so played that the immediate gains to the impersonator, and the equally immediate losses to those around him, are evident, at least in retrospect.

THEATRICAL IMPERSONATION

Finally, a few words must be said concerning theatrical impersonation. Here, impersonation occurs in a special social setting which explicitly identifies role-taking as impersonation. Thus, if an actor plays the role of Abraham Lincoln, the audience is informed, by means of appropriate messages, that the man who looks and talks like Lincoln is only taking his role for the purposes of the drama. This is a very special type of impersonation in that all the communicants are explicitly aware that it *is* impersonation. Nevertheless, it has much in common with the other types discussed.

This is not intended as a complete list of all known types of impersonations. It is impossible to prepare such a list, for there are as many impersonations as there are roles.[4] We touch here also on the much discussed subject of identity (e.g., Wheelis, 1958; Stein *et al.*, 1960), and its underlying psychological mechanism, identification (Greenson, 1954 a and b; Szasz, 1957c). In the existential analytic conceptions of *authentic* and *inauthentic existences* we encounter a similar concern—that is, with whether a state of being is genuine or impersonated (Ellenberger, 1958, pp. 118-119). Authentic existence is life-role consciously and responsibly assumed, while inauthentic existence is role foisted on the person and only passively—that is, without commitment—accepted by him. It is clear, therefore, that the notions of existence, role, and game are closely related. Current psychoanalytic studies concerned with identity, existential-analytic interest in authentic life patterns, and semiotical and game-analytic inquiry into behavior all point to certain common problems and similar attempts to solve them.

The Ganser Syndrome

The Ganser syndrome, which usually is considered to be a variant of either malingering or hysteria, provides an excellent illustration of the need to abandon the medical-pathological frame of reference in psychiatry and to substitute a communicational and game-playing model for it.

WHAT IS THE GANSER SYNDROME?

In 1898 a German psychiatrist, S. Ganser, described what he called a "specific hysterical twilight state," the chief symptom of which he identified as *Vorbeireden*. This was subsequently named *paralogia*, or the syndrome of approximate answers. According to Noyes (1956) this alleged syndrome is characterized by the following features:

> An interesting type of *mental disorder* sometimes occurring in the case of prisoners under detention awaiting trial was described by Ganser. It develops only after commission of a crime and, therefore, tells nothing about the patient's mental state when he committed the offense. In this *syndrome*, the *patient*, being under charges from which he would be exonerated were he *irresponsible*, begins, *without being aware of the fact*, to appear *irresponsible*. He appears stupid and unable to comprehend questions or instructions accurately. His replies are vaguely relevant to the query but absurd in content. He performs various uncomplicated, familiar tasks in an absurd manner, or gives approximate replies to

[4] In this connection, see Goffman's (1959) excellent discussion of human behavior as *performance*, and especially his comments on misrepresentation (pp. 58-66).

simple questions. The patient, for example, may attempt to write with the blunt end of his pencil, or will give 11 as the product of 4 x 3. *The purpose of the patient's behavior is so obviously to appear irresponsible that the inexperienced observer frequently believes that he is malingering. The dynamics is probably that of a dissociative process* ([ITALICS ADDED] pp. 505-506).

It should be noted that the person exhibiting this sort of conduct is immediately labeled a "patient," and his behavior a "mental disorder." But has it been shown that he is "sick?" Wertham (1949), for example, classified this phenomenon as malingering. He wrote:

A Ganser reaction is a hysterical pseudo-stupidity which occurs almost exclusively in jails and in old-fashioned German textbooks. It is now *known* to be almost always due more to *conscious malingering* than to unconscious stupefaction ([ITALICS ADDED] p. 191).

If the Ganser "patient" impersonates what he thinks is the behavior of the mentally sick—to plead irresponsibility and avoid punishment—how does his behavior differ from that of a person who cheats on his income tax return? As the former feigns stupidity, so the latter feigns relative poverty. It seems to be logically completely unjustified to consider this type of behavior as a form of illness (Weiner and Braiman, 1955). By so considering it, it is made to appear similar to phenomena such as pneumonia or cancer, and unlike phenomena such as income tax evasion or cheating in a game.

THE GANSER SYNDROME AS A FORM OF ROLE-TAKING AND CHEATING

I shall not dwell on a criticism of the medical (psychopathological) interpretation of these phenomena because much of what was said in criticism of a similar view of malingering (Chapter 2) is equally pertinent here. Instead, let us examine the sort of impersonation encountered here and its similarity to other types of role-taking.

It is astonishing how well persons exhibiting the typical features of the Ganser syndrome—and so-called malingerers and hysterics, too—have succeeded in convincing both themselves and those around them that they are, in fact, *sick* (meaning by this, disabled, not-responsible, perhaps even bodily ill). Their success in this regard is corroborated by the fact that according to both professional and popular opinion these forms of human conduct have increasingly come to be regarded as instances of illness or disability. This, of course, is exactly the message and the impression which those who act in this way wish to communicate and create. But in so doing, perhaps both they and we are misled and confused.

An excellent analogy from the world of the theater and motion pictures presents itself which might help to clarify this situation. The terms "type-casting" and "becoming typed" describe how an actor or actress who has frequently appeared in the same type of role will, in due time, create the impression in the public that he or she is "really" like the character type that they have repeatedly portrayed. Think of the actors who have been type-cast as "bad men" or of the actresses who have been publicly defined as "girls-next-door" or as "sexy babes." For Americans, the Frankenstein monster is Boris Karloff, Abraham Lincoln is Raymond Massey, and soon F.D.R. will be Ralph Bellamy. The actors' assumed identities may prove convincing not only to their audiences but finally to themselves as well. They may then begin to act off-stage much like they do on it.

The crux of this analogy between type-casting and the impersonation of the sick role in hysteria and allied "disorders" is that, psychiatric arguments to the contrary, I maintain that it does make a difference whether a role is assumed and impersonated or whether it is genuine. This statement requires explanation along two lines. First, it might be argued that if a person does not know that he is playing an assumed role, then his role must be regarded as genuine. It will be shown, however, that there are other bases than self-awareness for judging this matter. Second, it must constantly be kept in mind that the actor and the audience (i.e., patient and physician, or relatives) occupy two different, albeit complementary, sectors of a larger field. Impersonation and genuine role are defined sometimes by the actor, sometimes by the audience, and most often by a consensus of both. The two definitions may coincide or clash.

Roles: Assumed, Impersonated, and Genuine

THE ASSUMED ROLE BECOMES BELIEVABLE AND IS ACCEPTED

When the so-called malingerer or hysteric or Ganser syndrome patient becomes codified as "sick"—even if mentally sick—he has succeeded in making his assumed role believable and accepted. This phenomenon, which is encountered in many human relationships, characterizes most cases of so-called mental illness. It should be regarded in the same way as the "typing" of an actor. There is nothing especially unusual about this. It is known and accepted that our knowledge and image of the world around us is built up on the basis of our actual experiences. As the proverb has it, "Seeing is believing." Yet, it is also known that sense impressions or crude experiences cannot be taken at face value. They require critical scrutiny, checking, validation, comparison with the experiences of others, and so forth. This, then, raises the issue of complementary channels of information. It is evident that one can be critical of his impressions or information only if there is more than one way to find out about something. For example, by listening alone it may be impossible to distinguish between the actual singing of a person and a recording. Listening *and* looking resolves the problem.

In the case of the Ganser syndrome, psychiatrists, having defined this type of behavior as a form of mental illness, have confirmed or verified the sufferer's definition of himself as sick. The patient's "offer," as Balint (1957) has put it, was accepted by the physician and the community. *Instead of clarifying and repudiating the game, they have recodified and, in a sense, deepened it.* It is as though the theater audience accepted Raymond Massey as Abraham Lincoln and began to treat him as President of the United States. Obviously, this sort of response feeds back to the actor (patient), for whom it means, in effect, that he can no longer rely on his audience for another, more realistic, definition of his identity. I submit that this is an outcome with which few persons who start to impersonate the sick role reckon.

In general, persons assuming impersonated roles count on some form of resistance against their role-taking. The resistance may be put up by various persons or agencies. Malingerers, for instance, will be opposed by physicians; actors by drama critics and audiences; swindlers by those whom they have swindled and by the legal machinery of society; and so forth (J. Spiegel, 1954). As I have emphasized, the "audience's" resistance to the "actor's" taking an impersonated role is strongest at the beginning of a "performance." After an initial phase, the impersonated role is either repudiated or accepted. Once it has been accepted, it is scrutinized much less than it had been at the beginning. This is a familiar phenomenon. Once a schoolboy is regarded as a "good student," the teachers will scrutinize his performance much less strictly than the "bad student's." Similarly, actors, athletes, financiers, and others of *proved ability* can get away with much more than those not so defined.

In taking a role, then, the main task to be mastered is to put on a good performance. If the performance pertains to an instrumentally defined task —that is, to a genuine role—mastery of the task will mean successful role-taking, while failure in task-mastery will mean unsuccessful role-taking. If, however, the performance involves impersonation, the possibilities for failure are doubled. This is because the person may fail, first, by putting on an inadequate performance and having his role-pretension repudiated, and, second, by putting on too good a show and succeeding in making his impersonated role fully accepted.

It was mentioned how this may happen to some actors. In general, this hazard threatens only the successful performer, or one who has been well accepted in a particular role. Similarly, being called a malingerer and having one's sick-role aspirations repudiated is a danger facing only the beginner in this game. The person who has impersonated the sick role and whose impersonation has succeeded corresponds to the actor who has been so convincing in his theatrical performances that his role is mistaken for his real identity. I submit that this is the status of most persons whom today we call the "mentally ill." By and large, persons called "mentally ill" impersonate[5] the roles of helplessness, hopelessness, weakness, and often of bodily illness—when, in fact, their actual roles pertain to frustrations, unhappinesses, and perplexities due to interpersonal, social, and ethical conflicts.

I have tried to point out the dangers which threaten the impersonators (i.e., the mentally ill), as well as those who have accepted the impersonation (i.e., psychiatrists, the general public, etc.). The main danger, of course, is that a culturally shared *folie*, or myth, is thus brought into being and perpetuated.

FROM REPUDIATION OF "MENTAL ILLNESS" AS ILLNESS TO ITS ACCEPTANCE

In many ways, contemporary psychiatric orientations reflect the dangers characteristic of this later stage in the mental illness game. It was not always thus. During the early stages of this game—that is, in the days of Charcot, Breuer, and Freud—psychiatrists were violently opposed to impersonations of the sick role. At heart, most psychiatrists were neurologists and neuropathologists. Hence, they liked to see only "really" (i.e., neurologically) sick patients. They believed that all actors (i.e., mental patients) were imitators and frauds.

In contrast, at present psychiatrists have swung to the opposite extreme. They seemingly refuse to distinguish impersonations (cheating) from genuine roles (playing honestly). In refusing to exercise their critical faculties in these regards, psychiatrists have acted like the art expert, mentioned earlier (Chapter 2), who decided that a fine imitation was really just as good as an original masterpiece. This conviction may be and in fact often is implemented by refusing to attach pragmatic distinguishing marks to the two types of art work, or the two types of behavior, as the case may be. In art, this would mean that a forgery would be as highly valued as an original. In psychiatry, implementing the nondistinction between the categories of "original" and "imitation" consisted of the following. Having conceptualized psychiatric illness and treatment on the model of medical illness and treatment, psychiatrists left themselves no choice but to define psychiatric treatment as some-

---

[5] I do not wish to imply that this impersonation is a consciously planned strategy, arrived at by deliberate choice among several alternatives.

thing which could be "given" only to persons who "had" a psychiatric illness! This led not only to impossible complications in attempting to conceptualize the essential operations of so-called psychiatric illness and treatment (Szasz, 1956c, 1957c, 1958c), but also to a peculiar dilemma with regard to persons who impersonated the role of the "mentally sick patient."

Once a role is socially established and defined, it follows logically that it must, at least in principle, be possible to imitate or impersonate it. The question thus arises: How shall persons who imitate the mentally sick role be regarded? In other words, should those who "malinger insanity" be considered "ill" too? Clearly, they could not be given psychiatric treatment—and all that it implied for the aggrandizement of psychiatrists and the "cheating gains" of patients—unless they too were conceptualized and defined as "sick." Hence, the impersonators too were so defined.

The boundaries between the medical-psychiatric game and the real-life game became increasingly blurred as the former steadily encroached on areas previously occupied by the latter. All this, however, came about without anyone realizing what was happening. For the lonely, romantic movie fan falling in love with his idol, the unknown actress may become, by imperceptibly small steps, a close, likelife, and intimate figure. What are needed for this are a convincing performance plus a recipient who needs someone like the actress in her assumed role. But just as surely as men seem to need a Marilyn Monroe, or women a Clark Gable, *physicians need sick people!* I submit, therefore, that *anyone who acts sick—impersonating, as it were, this role—and does so vis-à-vis persons who are therapeutically inclined, runs the risk of being accepted in his impersonated role.* In being so accepted, he endangers himself in certain, often unexpected, ways. Although ostensibly he is requesting and receiving help, what is called "help" might be forthcoming only if he accepts the sick role and all that it may imply for his therapist.

The principal alternative to this dilemma lies, as suggested before, in abolishing the categories of ill and healthy behavior, and the prerequisite of mental sickness for so-called psychotherapy. This implies candid recognition that we "treat" people by psychoanalysis or psychotherapy not because they are "sick" but rather because: (1) They desire this type of assistance; (2) They have problems in living for which they seek mastery through understanding of the kinds of games which they, and those around them, have been in the habit of playing; and (3) We want and are able to participate in their "education" because this is our professional role.

SOME DIFFERENCES BETWEEN IMPERSONATED AND GENUINE ROLES

The notion of an impersonated role has meaning only insofar as it can be contrasted with a genuine role. One presupposes the other. The clue to differentiating impersonated or false roles or identities from genuine or real ones lies basically in the process of *verification*. This may be a social process, consisting of the comparison of opinions from various observers (Goffman, 1959, pp. 60-65). Or it may be a more subtle and scientifically more distinctive operation, consisting essentially of testing assertions or hypotheses against observations or experiments. In its simplest forms, verification involves no more than the use of complementary channels of information (e.g., sight and hearing, checking the patient's statements against certain official documents, etc.). Consider, for example, a patient who claims to be Jesus Christ. If you ask such a patient for evidence to support his claim, he may answer that he suffers and soon expects to die. Or he may say that his mother is the Virgin Mary. We may choose to disbelieve him, basing our opinion on the contrary evidence of his birth certificate or on information gained from his father or mother.

Of course, this is a trivial example. It fails to confront us with certain more subtle and difficult problems in validating roles, such as occur characteristically with patients complaining of pain. Here the question, if framed in these terms, is: Does the patient "really" have pain—that is, *is he a genuine occupant of the sick role?* Or is his pain "hysterical"—that is, due, for example, to identification with someone who had a similar complaint—and hence *does he impersonate the sick role?* In such a case we cannot rely on asking other people whether they believe that the patient is "sick" or "malingers." The criterion for differentiating between the two roles must be scientific-technical rather than social. In other words, it will be necessary to perform certain "operations" to secure more information on which to base further inferences. In the case of differentiating bodily from mental illness, the principal technique for gathering further information is the physical, laboratory, and psychological examinations of the patient.

Other examples, more akin to problems of role-playing encountered in psychiatric situations, are the mathematician who has tousled hair like Einstein's or the college student who always wears a tweed jacket and is never without his pipe. In these instances, our task is to distinguish appearance from performance. Is the Einstein-haired man really a gifted mathematician or does he try to make up in looks for what he lacks in mathematical skills? Similarly, an effort must be made to ascertain whether the hypothetical college student is a scholar or only tries to look like one.

Viewing impersonation and genuine role-playing in terms of games, they could be said to represent moves in two essentially different and distinct games. Both games, moreover, are on the level of complex metagames, since their respective rules refer to other rules on lower logical levels. The aims

as well as the rules of the two games differ markedly. *The goal of imperson-*
ation is to look like the person or role-performance that is imitated. The aim,
therefore, is to effect some type of outward ("superficial") similarity between self and object. This may be achieved by dress, manner of speech,
symptom, and so forth.[6]

Undergoing unnecessary surgical operations—"unnecessary," that is, from
the point of view of pathophysiology—often fulfils this function. The patient
here plays the illness game and seeks validation of the sick role from the
expert. The surgeon who consents to operate in such cases performs a psychologically and socially "useful" function, albeit his usefulness cannot be
justified on surgical grounds. His action consists essentially of legitimizing
the patient's claim to the sick role. By operating, then, he enables the patient
to "win." The surgical scar is official proof of illness. It is the diploma, the
trophy, the prize that goes to the winner!

Genuine role-playing, on the other hand, implies a game whose purpose,
usually consciously entertained, is to acquire certain skills or knowledge.
Here, too, a desire for a certain type of similarity to another person—say, an
actor or scientist—may be operative. But the aims as well as the rules of this
game require that the similarity be substantive rather than superficial. The
goal is learning, and hence an alteration of the "inner personality" rather
than a mere "outer change" such as occurs in impersonation.

The distinction between genuine and impersonated roles may be formulated in still another way by making use of the concepts of instrumental
and institutional groups and the criteria for membership in the group. *Instru-*
mental groups are those based on shared skills. Membership in such a
group, say in a Davis Cup team, implies that the person possesses a special
skill. This is considered to be a genuine role, because such a person "really
knows" how to play tennis. *Institutional groups,* on the other hand, are based
on kinship, status, and other noninstrumental criteria. These criteria do not
pertain to knowledge or skills and are, in this sense, more superficial. Consider, for example, the role of king in an hereditary dynasty. Upon the death
of the king, the crown prince becomes the new king. This transformation
from nonking to king role implies no change in knowledge or skills. It implies only a change in status.

The psychology of impersonation could be summed up in one sentence,
as a technique of behavior based on the model of hereditary monarchies.

[6] The *reasons* that prompt some persons to seek role-imitation rather than technical
competence and task-mastery need not concern us here. This subject is crucial, of course,
for psychological and sociological theory as well as for the practice of psychotherapy.

Implicit in this scheme is the belief that instrumental skills are unimportant.[7] Accordingly, all that is needed to succeed in the game of life is to "play a role" and gain social approval for it. Many parents still hold out this empty model as an ideal for their children to follow. When followed successfully, it leads to an "empty" life. When the child or young adult fails in this game, the outcome is often called "neurosis" or "delinquency." But perhaps it is really only an attempt on the part of the struggling self to fill the void and become genuinely engaged in a game—in any "real" game. Being "mentally ill" or "psychotic" may be the only game left to play for such a person.

[7] This is a significant feature in the psychology of the impostor and charlatan. Illustrative is the medical quack (Carson, 1960) masquerading as, say, someone specially skilled in rejuvenating people. Such a person may use his medical qualifications not instrumentally but only for the purpose of deceiving others.

"Lies—there you have the religion of slaves and taskmasters."

Maxim Gorky (1902, p. 78)

CHAPTER 15 | *Hysteria as a Game*

Our task now is to answer the question: What sort of game does a person said to have hysteria play? Following a general discussion of the type of game to which the term "hysteria" is usually applied, I shall present two illustrations. The first is from Sullivan, the second from my own clinical experience. The former will portray the outstanding characteristics of hysterical game-playing strategies. The latter will focus on the maneuver of lying as a specific characteristic of this game. Finally, the relationship of lying to interpersonal control and predictability will be discussed briefly.

General Outline of Hysteria as a Game

Using a slightly modified version of Piaget's (1932, 1951) scheme of the development of the capacity to follow rules and to be aware of them, I propose to distinguish *three stages or types of mastery (or control) of interpersonal processes*. They are: coercion, self-help, and cooperation. This series constitutes a developmental sequence. Coercion represents the simplest or easiest rule to follow, or game to play, self-help the next most difficult, while cooperation is the most complex and demanding of the three.

COERCION, SELF-HELP, AND COOPERATION IN HYSTERIA

The hysteric plays a game in which there is an unequal mixture of coercive, self-helping, and cooperative strategies. While coercive maneuvers predominate, elements of self-help and cooperation are not completely lacking. Another general characteristic of the hysteric is that he rarely plays well at his own game. At the same time, a distinct achievement of this type of behavior (or game-playing) is that it effects a synthesis of sorts among three distinct and to some extent conflicting games, values, and styles of life. Hysteria will thus be regarded as a composite of, and a compromise among, heterogeneous values and games. In this lies its strength and usefulness as well as its weakness.

I have said that the hysteric fails to play well at any one of three games. By this I meant that a person exhibiting so-called hysterical symptoms fails to master fully, or adequately, the task he has set for himself. To begin with, the hysteric places a strongly positive value on *coercive strategies*. True, he may not be aware that he has made a choice between coercion and other human values. His wish to coerce others may, in other words, be unconscious. Usually, however, it is not so much unconscious as it is inexplicit. In psychotherapy, it is generally easily recognized by the therapist and readily acknowledged by the patient. The main point to be emphasized here is that although the hysteric may espouse the value of coercion and domination, he cannot play this game in a skillful and uninhibited manner. To do so requires two qualities he often lacks. The first is a relatively complete and indiscriminating identification with the aggressor (A. Freud, 1936). This is required, generally, for anyone wishing to be ruthlessly domineering and destructive. A fusion of one's own ego or self with that of the previously powerful and oppressive person probably contributes to the second factor, namely, to a large measure of insensitivity to the needs and feelings of one's partner(s). The hysteric is too human to be so calloused, and hence is inhibited in playing the game of domination without disguise and with success. *He can coerce and dominate with suffering, but not with "selfish" will.*

Persons may change, of course, in the direction of increasingly uninhibited domination of others. Initially they may be able to coerce only by means of symptoms and suffering, but with the passage of time they may relinquish this disguise and adopt more direct methods of domination. The life of Mary Baker Eddy offers a dramatic illustration of this thesis (Dakin, 1929; Zweig, 1931). For many years her main technique of interpersonal mastery lay in hysterical strategies. She used a variety of bodily symptoms for this purpose, many of them verging on what we would call "schizophrenic bodily feelings" and their communications. In her middle years she gradually abandoned these maneuvers and substituted techniques of control by means of religious domination.

To play the game of self-help well requires *committing* one's self to it. This involves the person in a so-called schizoid orientation to life, leading to a large measure of isolation from other people. Human relationships are not especially sought; both their number and intensity are kept at a minimum. At the same time, special skills are heavily invested with interest. Religious, artistic, or other work-investments pre-empt the interest in personal relationships. Playing well at this game is highly rewarded in our culture. Preoccupation with one's body or with suffering and helplessness, however, tend to inhibit the ability to concentrate on the technical tasks that must be mastered to play this game skillfully. Too, the tendency to dominate others by exhibiting helplessness cannot be maintained unmodified in the face of a high degree of demonstrable competence in certain specific areas of life. The aim of coercing others by exhibiting helplessness may still be retained but the techniques subserving it must be modified. Consider, for example, the proverbial absentminded professor. Here is a composite picture of the famous scientist, highly skilled in his complex work-performance, say mathematics, who is at the same time as helpless as a child when it comes to feeding himself, putting on his galoshes, or paying his income tax. Exhibitions of helplessness in these areas invite help in exactly the same manner in which various complaints invite medical attention.

The game of cooperation, finally, requires the espousal of a value which the person exhibiting hysterical symptoms may not share at all. I believe that we are confronted here with a genuine *clash of values, namely, between equality and cooperativeness on the one hand, and inequality and domination-submission on the other*. This conflict of values actually takes place in two distinct spheres: in the intrapersonal system of the patient and in the interpersonal system of therapy.

In psychiatry, this problem is rarely formulated in these terms. Psychiatrists seem to operate with the tacit assumption that whatever their values are, they are the same values that their patients hold and their colleagues share! This, of course, cannot always be the case. If, however, value conflicts of the type mentioned are as important in psychiatry as has been suggested, why have they not been made more explicit? Would this not help in mastering the problems they pose? It seems to me that one reason, perhaps the main one, for not making value problems of this type more explicit is that whenever this is done *it threatens the cohesion of the group* which, until then, has kept its values officially undefined.[1] More will be said concerning the interrelations of hysteria, psychoanalysis, and problems of value presently.

[1] Many examples come to mind which illustrate this thesis. Consider, for instance, the moral problem of segregation, especially as it has been rekindled during the past few years by an explicit ruling of the United States Supreme Court. Until this ruling was handed down affirming that segregation was unconstitutional (and hence pragmatically unlawful), a mixture of potentially conflicting values concerning Negroes, equality, democracy, etc., could exist side by side without causing very much overt social tension. After the Supreme Court explicitly reasserted the ethical value of the Negro's equality with the white (specifically in regard to education), spokesmen for opposing values stiffened their positions. I do not want to be misunderstood as decrying this outcome. My intention is only to suggest that taking an explicit stand on matters of value might be, at least temporarily, socially divisive.

HYSTERIA AS A MIXTURE OF CONFLICTING VALUES AND DISPARATE GAMES

The notion that hysterical (or other neurotic) symptoms are compromises is a cornerstone of psychoanalytic theory. At the beginning of his work, Freud thought in terms of compromise-formations between (instinctual) drive and (social) defense, or between selfish needs and the requirements of social living. Still later, neurosis was conceptualized as being due to conflicts between id and ego, or id and superego.

Let us now describe hysteria as still another compromise, this time among three different types of games. Or, instead of compromise-formation, one could speak of a mixture of three different games. Hysteria is a mixture of the three patterns of human relationship and mastery described earlier (i.e., coercion, self-help, and cooperation). The typical features of each of these games shall now be briefly described.

The *coercive game* is characterized by the powerful promotive impact of iconic body signs on those to whom they are addressed. The patient's relatives, for example, tend to be deeply impressed by such communications, often much more deeply than they would be by equivalent statements framed in ordinary language. The display of sickness or suffering can thus be used to coerce others. As emphasized previously (Chapters 7 and 8), this feature of hysteria, more than any other, accounts for its immediate pragmatic value to the patient.

The *game of self-help* is also evident in most cases of hysteria. Classically, hysterical patients were said to exhibit an attitude of indifference toward their suffering. This manifest indifference signifies, first, a denial that the patient has in fact made a coercive communication and, second, that the patient aspires to a measure of self-sufficiency. Clinical and everyday observation discloses that hysterics are not wholly coercive in their relationship to others but are, to some extent, self-reliant and self-sufficient. To the extent to which they are, they play the game of self-help. They can attend to this, however, only halfheartedly, being ready to coerce by means of symptoms should other techniques of mastery fail. Learning new techniques of self-help or cooperation is relatively unfamiliar to them, and is usually not encouraged in the social setting in which they live.

Hysterics play the *cooperative game* very imperfectly. This is to be expected, since this game requires and presupposes a feeling of relative equality among the players. Persons employing hysterical techniques of communication feel—and often are—inferior and oppressed. In turn they aspire to feel superior to others and to oppress them. Equality of sorts, and some measure of cooperation, however, are inevitably sought as potential alternatives to the oppressed status.

Hysteria is thus regarded as mainly a coercive game, with small elements of self-help and still smaller elements of cooperation blended in. This view also implies that the hysteric is unclear, first, about what sort of things he values in human relationships and, second, about the relationship of his values to his actions. In other words, he is unconscious (unaware) of his values and their relation to his behavior. Illustrative of this contention is the case of the young woman who "falls ill" while nursing her sick father.

In this connection, it should be recalled that several of the patients reported in the early psychoanalytic literature were young women who became "ill" with hysteria while nursing—that is, taking care of—a sick, usually older relative. This was true in the case of Breuer's (Breuer and Freud, 1893-1895) famous patient, Anna O.:

> In July, 1880, the patient's father, of whom she was passionately fond, fell ill of a peripleuritic abscess which failed to clear up and to which he succumbed in April, 1881. During the first months of the illness Anna devoted her whole energy to nursing her father, and no one was much surprised when by degrees her own health greatly deteriorated. No one, perhaps not even the patient herself, knew what was happening to her; but eventually the state of weakness, anaemia and distaste for food became so bad that *to her great sorrow she was no longer allowed to continue nursing the patient* ([ITALICS ADDED] pp. 22-23).

Freud had repeatedly called attention to the precipitating circumstances of hysteria but attached a somewhat different interpretation and significance to them than I do here. In the "Five Lectures on Psycho-Analysis" (1910a), he wrote:

> And here we may quote from the report of the patient's illness the further fact that it made its appearance at a time when she was nursing her father, of whom she was devotedly fond, through the grave illness which led to his death, and that, *as a result of her own illness, she was obliged* to give up nursing him ([ITALICS ADDED] p. 11).

Anna O. thus started to play the hysterical game from a position of distasteful submission: she functioned as an oppressed, unpaid, sick-nurse, *who was coerced to be helpful by the very helplessness of a (bodily) sick patient.* The women in Anna O.'s position were—as are their counterparts today, who feel similarly entrapped by their small children—insufficiently aware of what they valued in life and of how their own ideas of what they valued affected their conduct. For example, young middle-class women in Freud's day considered it their duty to take care of their sick fathers. They treasured the value that it was their role to take care of father when he was sick. Hiring a professional servant or nurse for this job would have created a conflict for them, because it would have symbolized to them as well as to others that they did not love ("care for") their fathers. Notice how similar this is to the dilemma in which many contemporary American women find themselves, not, however, in relation to their fathers, but rather in relation to their young children. Today, married women are generally expected to take care of their children; they are not supposed to delegate this task to others. The "old folks" can be placed in a home; it is all right to delegate their care to hired help. This is an exact reversal of the social situation which prevailed in upper middle-class European circles until the First World War and even after it. Then, children were often cared for by hired help, while parents were taken care of by their children, now fully grown.

In both situations, the *obligatory* nature of the care required stimulates a feeling of helplessness in the person from whom help is sought. If a person cannot, in good conscience, refuse to provide help—and cannot even stipulate the terms on which he will supply it—then truly he becomes the captive of the help-seeker. Similar considerations apply to the relationship between patients and physicians. If physicians cannot define their own rules—that is, when to help and in what ways—then they, too, are threatened with becoming the hostages of patients (or their representatives).

The typical cases of hysteria cited by Freud involved a *value conflict*— and, hence, also a *game conflict*—concerning what the young women in question wished to do with themselves. Did they wish to prove that they were good daughters by taking care of their sick fathers? Or did they aspire to become independent of their elders, say, by having a family of their own, or in some other way? I submit that the conflict between these two aspirations was the crucial issue in these cases. The sexual problem—say, of the daughter's incestuous cravings for her father—I would regard as having been stimulated, at least in part, by the interpersonal situation in which the former had to attend to the latter's body. It may have been easier, moreover, to admit the sexual problem to consciousness and to deal with it than to cope with the ethical problem indicated. In the final analysis, the latter is a vast problem in living. As such, it cannot be solved by any particular maneuver but requires rather decision-making concerning goals and values toward which one desires to move and, having made the decisions, dedicated efforts to attain them.

SOME REMARKS ON PSYCHOANALYSIS AND ETHICS

How do these considerations apply to psychiatry and psychoanalysis? Certain values have been incorporated into these disciplines and are now contained in them. The question is: What are they? This question is especially significant for psychiatry and psychoanalysis as applied techniques, that is, as therapies. All psychiatric therapies have as their aim the alteration of human behavior, a subject of traditional interest for the ethicist.

The empirically held values of psychiatry and psychoanalysis can be ascertained only by inferring them from how psychotherapists actually practice (e.g., Burton, 1959). This is an important subject, but discussing it would divert us from the mainstream of our present inquiry. I shall limit myself, therefore, to indicating briefly the sources of some major value conflicts within psychoanalysis itself.

The ethical values embodied in psychoanalysis derive from a number of sources: from the spirit of nineteenth-century science, from medicine, from certain philosophers (particularly Schopenhauer and Nietzsche), from Judaism and Catholicism, and last but not least from Freud himself (Bakan, 1959; Rieff, 1959). What, then, are some of these values? The chief value, probably, is that knowledge, and specifically self-knowledge, is good. This is the ethics of science applied to the self as a part of nature. An implicit corollary of it is that knowledge should be widely publicized and freely available. It must not be held secret by a small group and used as a source of power on its own behalf. Although psychoanalysis clearly espoused the value of knowledge, its position in regard to the publicity of this knowledge became ambiguous as soon as psychoanalytic groups became organized.

Another, perhaps even more significant source of ethical dilemma lies in this question: What is the psychoanalytic concept of a good human relationship, whether in marriage, friendship, business, or elsewhere? We would search in vain in Freud's writings for an explicit answer to this question. One reason for this is that he tended to frame his investigations as though they were empirical, "naturalistic" studies. It was thus implied that he accepted things as they were and not as he wished them to be. But it should be apparent by now that in the social (or human) sciences it is virtually impossible to conduct empirical studies wholly devoid of valuations. This sort of imitation of physics is foredoomed to failure (Scriven, 1956). Furthermore, it is easy to demonstrate that Freud and other psychiatrists espoused certain values and condemned others. For instance, Freud not only "discovered" infantile sexuality; he also advocated the sexual enlightenment of children. Similarly, he not only studied the effects of sexual seductions on children but also took a clear stand against this practice, because of its alleged harmfulness for the future adult. Many other examples could be cited to illustrate Freud's preferences in regard to alternative patterns of human actions (Szasz, 1959a).

In regard to paired human relations, *Freud's position was that they are*

*always based on the dominance of one partner and the submission of the
other.* The notions of democracy, equality, reciprocity, and cooperation were
never discussed in his writings. His sociopolitical ideas and values followed in
the Platonic tradition, envisioning an intellectual and moral elite which dicta-
torially governed the masses. Freud's misogynous utterances are well known
(Freud, 1932). Probably less well appreciated is his insistence that the psychoanalytic relationship between analyst and analysand must be that of "a
superior and a subordinate" (Freud, 1914, p. 49). Although he admired many
things English, British political institutions apparently made little impression
on him. He did not seem to regard genuine cooperation between equals as
a positive value. To Freud, cooperation meant rather the imperfect person's
wisdom to follow the leadership of a more accomplished superior.

In contrast to Freud, Adler (A. Adler, 1925; Ansbacher and Ansbacher,
1956) freely expressed his concept of the morally desirable or "mentally
healthy" human relationship. It was characterized by a high degree of *social
interest* and *cooperativeness.* Adler also stressed the values of truthfulness
and competence while, at the same time, he placed much lesser emphasis on
self-knowledge than Freud. More recently, Fromm (1955) and Rogers (1942,
1951) also explicitly acknowledged and dealt with the nature and significance of the psychotherapist's ethical values.

Freud thus disguised and obscured, whereas Adler openly acknowledged
and discussed, the moral values inherent in their respective psychological observations and theories. It seems probable that this is one of the significant
reasons for the different receptions that Freudian and Adlerian psychologies
received. Freud's work bore the stamp of the impartial, cool-headed natural
scientist. The work of several scholars (Bakan, 1959; La Pierre, 1959; Rieff,
1959) was required to make explicit the values inherent in Freudian psychology and psychotherapy. Adler, in contrast, did not hide his values. Thus,
his work early diverged from medicine, theoretical psychology, and even
from psychotherapy and became closely associated with child-rearing, education, and the spirit of social reform.

Adler's work has been generally considered less serious and significant
scientifically than Freud's. This despite the fact that his views were much
more sociopsychologically oriented than Freud's and have, in fact, anticipated a great deal of later psychoanalytic ego-psychology. The point that I
wish to make is that I believe Adler was ahead of his time in openly acknowledging the role of values—and moral problems, generally—in human psychology and psychotherapy. At the beginning of this century, it was bad
enough to study sexual behavior. The scientific study of ethical behavior
was completely impossible. Only during the past several decades—and only

because of the rapid growth of the social sciences—has it become possible to undertake a scientifically respectable study of moral problems as an integral part of human behavior.

I have discussed elsewhere (1957b) how certain aspects of the psychoanalytic procedure require a high degree of mutual cooperation between two relatively equal participants. By this it was meant that although analyst and patient might be highly unequal in regard to the possession of certain skills and the knowledge of how to apply them, they are, or should be, relatively equal in terms of power over each other.

From the evidence available—that is, from what psychoanalysts do and say—one could infer two almost antithetical ethical positons in regard to psychoanalysis. One would be that psychoanalysis favors a leader-follower type of human relationship. The other would be that the ethical value inherent in psychoanalysis, both as theory and therapy, is cooperation among equals. The aim of therapy (somewhat oversimplified) is to maximize the patient's choices in the conduct of his life. This value must be entertained explicitly and must be espoused not only for him but potentially for everyone else as well. Hence, it is not the indiscriminate maximization of the patient's choices that is encouraged, for this could also be achieved by reducing the choices of others with whom he interacts (that is, by enslaving them). This, however, would run counter to the ethic of psychoanalysis (as I view it), which permits the maximization of choices only through the enhancement of skills, in the broadest sense of this word. In sum, our world must be enriched through our own efforts, and not merely made to appear enriched by interfering with the skills of our neighbor or by infringing on his opportunities.

An Illustration of the Hysterical Game:
Sullivan's "Hysterical Dynamism"

Although Sullivan persisted in using many traditional psychiatric concepts, he employed the game model of behavior in the actual description of his observations and interventions. In discussing hysteria (Sullivan, 1956), one of his first statements was:

> The hysteric might be said in principle to be a person who has a happy thought as to a way by which he can be *respectable* even though not living up to his *standards*. That way of describing the hysteric, however, is very misleading, for of course the hysteric never does have that thought. At least, it is practically *impossible to prove* that he has had that thought ([ITALICS ADDED] p. 203).

Sullivan thus asserted that the hysteric is a person who impersonates respectability, and who cheats. In the tradition of psychoanalysis, he added that the hysteric never does this in a consciously deliberate fashion. Although I cannot disagree with this—for it does not appear to be correct to assert that the hysteric carefully plans his strategy—I believe it is a mistake to place too much emphasis on the unwitting quality of this behavior. The riddle of precisely how conscious a given mental act is, has plagued psychoanalysis from its earliest days. I suspect that it is largely a pseudo problem, for it seems that the quality of consciousness—or, self-reflective awareness—depends, in large part, on the situation in which a person finds himself. In other words, it is partly a social characteristic, rather than simply a personal or psychological (cognitive) one.

The following passage provides a good example of hysteria viewed as game-playing behavior:

To illustrate how the hysteric dynamism comes into operation, let us say that a man with a strong hysterical predisposition has married, perhaps for money, and that his wife, thanks to his rather dramatic and exaggerated way of doing and saying things, cannot long remain in doubt that there was a very practical consideration in this marriage and cannot completely blind herself to a certain lack of importance that she has in her husband's eyes. *So she begins to get even.* She may for example, like someone I recently saw, develop a never-failing vaginismus, so that there is no more intercourse for him. And he will not ruminate on whether this vaginismus that is cutting off his satisfaction is directed against him, for the very simple reason that *if you view interpersonal phenomena with that degree of objectivity, you can't use an hysterical process to get rid of your own troubles.* So he won't consider that; but he will suffer terribly from privation and will go to rather extravagant lengths to overcome the vaginismus that is depriving him of satisfaction, the lengths being characterized by a certain rather theatrical attention to detail rather than deep scrutiny of his wife. But he fails again and again. Then one night when he is worn out, and perhaps has had a precocious ejaculation in his newest adventure in practical psychotherapy, he has the idea, "My God, this thing is driving me crazy," and goes to sleep. . . .

Now the idea, "This thing is driving me crazy," is the *happy idea that I say the hysteric has.* He wakes up at some early hour in the morning, probably at the time when his wife is notoriously most soundly asleep, and he has a frightful attack of some kind. It could be literally almost anything, but it will be very impressive to anyone around. His wife will be awakened, very much frightened, and will call the doctor. But before the doctor gets there, the husband, with a fine sense of dramatic values, will let her know, in some indirect way that he's terribly afraid he is losing his mind. She is reduced to a really agitated state by that. So when the doctor comes, the wife is in enough distress—in part because of whatever led to her vaginismus—to wonder if she might lose her own mind, and the husband is showing a good many odd symptoms ([ITALICS ADDED] pp. 204-06).

Sullivan's magnificent gift for seeing and portraying psychiatric "diseases" as problems in living is beautifully demonstrated here. The mutually coercive relationship between husband and wife is especially noteworthy; and so is the patient's impersonating or taking the role of the mentally ill person. These reactions are achieved, moreover, by means of nonverbal communications (e.g., vaginismus, the nocturnal "attack," and other symptoms).

Sullivan then proceeded to describe the hysterical dynamism as a form of unconscious or inexplicit malingering without, however, using this term. He spoke of hysteria rather as a form of "inverted sublimation." By this he meant that the patient "finds a way of satisfying unacceptable impulses in a personally satisfactory way which exempts him from social blame and which thereby approaches sublimation. But the activity, if recognized, would not receive anything but social condemnation" (pp. 207-08). These statements illustrate once again the use and function of nonverbal or indirect communications in hysteria, and also the close connection between hysteria and malingering. Phrased in terms of game-playing, the hysteric was here described as someone who would gladly take advantage of cheating if he thought he could get away with it. His cheating was so staged, moreover, as to lead those around him to interpret it not as a selfish stratagem but rather as unavoidable suffering.

Another aspect of the game the hysteric plays, or, more precisely, of the sort of player he is (and this, after all, is one of the determinants of the game he plays), may be discerned from the following passage:

The hysteric has a rather deep contempt for other people. I mean by this that he regards other people as comparatively shadowy figures that move around, I sometimes think, *as audience for his own performance.* How does this show? Well,—hysterics may be said to be the *greatest liars* to no purpose in the whole range of human per-

sonalities—nothing is good enough as it is. It always undergoes im-
provement in the telling; the hysteric simply has to exaggerate
everything a little.— . . . when they talk about their living—their
interests, their fun, their sorrows and so on—only superlative terms
will suffice them. And that, in a way, is a statement of the inade-
quacy of reality—which is what I mean when I say that hysterics
are rather contemptuous of mere events and mere people. *They act
as if they were accustomed to something better, and they are*
([ITALICS ADDED] pp. 209-210).

This touches on the fact that the hysterical game is relatively unsophisticated. It is well suited to children, uneducated people, the oppressed, and
the fearful; in brief, to those who feel that their chances for self-realization
and success on their own are poor. Thus, impersonation in general and lying
in particular are employed as strategies for self-advancement. Most of the
"dynamisms" mentioned by Sullivan thus far illustrate the use of coercive
maneuvers. This is consistent with my thesis that hysteria is predominantly
a coercive type of game.

Concerning hysterical conversion (i.e., the use of iconic body signs), Sullivan stated:

Now, when there is this conversion, it performs a useful function;
and that function occurs principally within the self-system. . . .
There one discovers sometimes the almost juvenilely simple type of
operation set up to profit from the disabling system. The patient
will often tell you in the most transparent fashion: "If it were not
for this malady then I could do—" and what follows is really quite
a grandiose appraisal of one's possibilities. The disability functions
as a convenient tool of security operations (p. 216).

This, of course, is only one aspect of conversion, albeit certainly a significant one. Sullivan's formulation is another way of saying that the hysteric
plays at being sick because he is afraid that, if he played in certain areas of
real-life activity, he would fail. Yet, by adopting this strategy, he also invites and assures his own defeat.

These considerations highlight the fact that the hysteric is not necessarily
disengaged from the aspiration and hope of playing other, socially shared
games. Whether and to what extent he may be influenced by psychotherapeutic methods is best assessed by estimating his interest in other games.

In this connection, it is noteworthy that Sullivan's therapeutic recommendations for hysteria centered around the theme of "making the symp-

toms unpleasant" (pp. 219-220). He apparently took the position that the best course was to battle it out, as it were, with the patient, and to frustrate his symptom-gratifications, thus forcing him to adopt newly acquired and more sophisticated techniques of communication and mastery. Although this approach has merit, I am not entirely in favor of it.[2] I mentioned it here only because it underscores the essential unity of the concepts of hysteria and malingering.

Sullivan's concluding remarks concerning hysteria strongly support the thesis that persons who tend to play this sort of game do so because they are impoverished in their game repertoire.

> The presence of the hysteric dynamism as the outstanding way of meeting difficulties in living seems to me to imply that the patient has missed a good deal of life which should have been undergone if he was to have a well-rounded personality with a rather impressively good prospect for the future. *Because hysterics learn so early to get out of awkwardnesses and difficulties with a minimum of elaborate process,* life has been just as they sound: singularly, extravagantly simple. And so, even if one could brush aside the pathogenic or pathologic mechanisms, one would have persons who are not at all well-suited to complex interpersonal environment. There they just haven't had the experience; *they have missed out on an education that many other people have undergone* ([ITALICS ADDED] p. 228).

What a person considers worth doing or worth living for will depend on what he has learned. Whether coercive or cooperative games are preferred will necessarily vary with the person's attitude or taste. Accordingly, there may be those for whom playing the hysterical (or any other "psychopathological") game is perfectly acceptable. There has been a persistent tendency in modern psychiatric theories to disallow this possibility.[3] Yet, the facts and reflections, at least as they are assembled here, require that explicit allowance be made for a much greater diversity of human behavior.

[2] Insofar as *the therapist elects to play the patient's game*, he may successfully outwit him and thus achieve dramatic symptom cures. This, however, does not usually help the patient either to understand better his own game-playing behavior, or to enlarge his game repertoire.

[3] There is a striking resemblance in this regard between the psychoanalytic and classical Christian attitudes toward humanity. Neither accepts *people as people!* Psychoanalysis accepts people as generally "sick" (i.e., "neurotic" or "psychotic"), whereas Christianity accepts them as generally "sinful."

Lying: A Specific Strategy in the Hysterical Game

REMARKS ON PSYCHIATRIC ATTITUDES TOWARD LYING

For the contemporary psychiatrist to speak of lying in connection with so-called mental illness is anathema. Once a person is called a "patient" his psychiatrist is no longer even permitted to consider such a thing as lying. The prohibition placed on this term and all it connotes has been at least as strong as that on sex in Victorian society, and perhaps even greater. Anyone who speaks of lying in connection with psychiatric problems, tends *ipso facto* to be identified as "antipsychiatric" or "antihumanitarian," meaning thereby that he is both wrong and bad. I believe this is most regrettable, and merely signifies the contemporary psychiatrist's (and lay person's) sentimentalizing attitude toward the so-called mentally ill. Such an attitude toward mental illness is harmful to science and has no place in it.

It has long been my impression that lying is one of the most significant occurrences, mechanisms, or communications—depending on how we choose to look at it—in the field of psychiatry. In a sense, I am simply restating one of Freud's earliest observations, namely, that *social hypocrisy is one of psychiatry's core problems*. He emphasized, for example, that both patients and physicians were in the habit of lying—if I may be permitted to re-introduce this useful word—when they spoke to each other (as well as to most other people) about matters of sex and money. How else are we to interpret Freud's story of his encounter with Chrobak in the case of the woman patient who was still a virgin after eighteen years of marriage? In relating this experience, Freud (1914, p. 296) stated that, as Chrobak saw it, the physician's social role and "ethical obligation" was to lie about the patient's condition, to protect the husband and the marriage. Whether to lie or not to lie were important issues in psychoanalysis, from its very inception. Indeed, many aspects of the psychoanalytic situation came into being in response to Freud's effort to be forthright with his patients.

It should be recalled that Adler, too, considered lying a significant subject for psychological investigation. This illustrates, I believe, that analysts were more forthright in the early days of psychoanalysis in recognizing that people—including physicians and patients—often lied to each other. Evidently, it is easier for a person to be observant concerning dishonesty if he feels that he has nothing to hide. Furthermore, the early psychoanalysts tended to avoid infantilizing patients. This is a most pertinent issue, since the prototypal interaction in which one person lies to another is the parent-child situation: the parent does not tell the child the truth, but communicates rather what he considers to be "good" for the child to hear. This parent-child model of helpfulness by lying has had a powerful impact on human relationships.

In seventeenth-century Europe, for example, it was considered a compliment to be told that one could lie "like a physician" (Fletcher, 1954, p. 42). Physicians were expected to deal with patients as adults deal with children. Hence, it was not only justifiable but indeed required that one lie, since to tell painful truths to patients was viewed as being unnecessarily cruel. This view is, of course, still prevalent. Since psychoanalysis has gained respectability and power as a medical specialty, psychoanalysts too have turned away from scrutinizing the role of deceit in interpersonal relationships. I submit that the contemporary psychiatric attitude toward lying borders on denial. Lying is either ignored or treated as something else—say, as amnesia, dissociative reaction, or as something called by some other more elegant term.

Closely related to lying but not quite identical with it is the phenomenon of not making something explicit. For example, if a physician avoids discussing the fee with a patient, he does not lie. Rather he leaves something unclear, unexplained, and uncertain. The main difference between lying and non-codification is that in the case of the latter the speaker does not actively misinform. The distinction is the same as between being misinformed and uninformed. However, by withholding information from a person who needs it, we may jeopardize his position just as effectively as if we were to lie to him. Perhaps in some ways this may be even worse, for it is now more difficult for the information-seeker to blame his informant! Accordingly, keeping a person in the dark concerning matters of importance might be regarded as potentially even more harmful than actively misinforming him.

A CLINICAL ILLUSTRATION

The following observations are from the context of the psychoanalytic treatment of a young woman. I shall say nothing concerning why she came for help or what sort of person she was. Let us focus on only one aspect of her behavior—namely, her lying. That she lied—in the sense that she communicated statement A to someone when she knew perfectly well that statement B was the truth—became apparent early in the analysis and remained a crucial theme throughout the treatment. The main reason why she lied was that she conceived of herself as a trapped child confronted by an overbearing, unreasonable, and intrusive mother. The simplest and most effective way in which she could cope with her mother was by lying. Finding that her mother would accept her lies without openly challenging them encouraged use of the maneuver and firmly established lying as a characteristic feature of her personality. In her adult life, many of her friends and especially her husband ostensibly accepted her lies, much as her mother had. Her own expectation in regard to untruthful communications was revealing. On the one hand, she hoped that her statements would be taken as the truth. On the other hand, she wished that her lies would be openly challenged and unmasked. She realized that the price she paid for getting away with lying was *persistent psychological subservience* to those to whom she lied. I might add that this woman led a socially well-compensated (i.e., "normal") life and did not lie "indiscriminately." She tended to lie only to people on whom she felt dependent or toward whom she was angry. The more she valued a relationship, the more strongly convinced was she that she could not risk an open expression of personal differences, such as might result from a forthright exchange of conflicting needs or opinions.

In these situations of feeling trapped, lying became for this patient an indirect communication, similar to hysterical conversion (i.e., the use of iconic body signs) or dream communication. As both she and I familiarized ourselves with the type of game she was playing, it became increasingly evident that the people to whom she lied knew, most of the time, that she was lying. And, of course, she did too. This did not in the least diminish the usefulness of the maneuver, the main value of which lay in *controlling the behavior* (or response) of the other player(s). Stated in terms of game-playing behavior, it was as though she could not afford to take the chance to *play honestly*. This would have meant that she simply had to make her move and was then required to wait to see what her "opponent's" move would be. The very thought of this made her unbearably anxious, especially when serious conflicts of interests were at stake. In contrast to this type of "open" game, therefore, she preferred to lie, *which meant making a communication the effect of which she could foretell*. This saved her from feeling anxious concerning what would happen. She knew, or thought that she knew, what her "opponent" would do, and in this she was, indeed, correct most of the time. Her marriage consisted of an exceedingly complicated game of lies. It was characterized by the fact that her husband ostensibly accepted her lies as the truth, but then used his knowledge that they were falsehoods to manipulate her in his own interests.

Uncertainty and Control in Game-playing Behavior

One of the characteristics of honest game-playing is that the activities of the other player(s) are predictable only within certain limits. For instance, in a game of chess or tennis, one cannot foretell exactly—unless the players are very unevenly matched, in which case we can hardly speak of a "game" at all—what one's opponent's move will be. To play a game, therefore, it is necessary to tolerate a measure of uncertainty. In the games of real-life social relationships, similar considerations hold true. In other words, if one plays honestly—for instance, by doing the best he knows how in a given task-oriented situation—he may not be able to predict very successfully how others will react to his efforts.[4] Suppose, then, that for some reason it becomes exceedingly important to know, to be able accurately to foretell, how another person will react to one's behavior. This is the situation, *par excellence*, which is conducive to lying—or, more generally, to cheating—of a certain type. *The aim of the game has now been changed from task-orientation and task-mastery to the control of the other player's moves.* To be successful in this, *information about the personality* of the other player(s) is essential. This might be contrasted with the need for skills, as the chief requirement for task-mastery.

These considerations have far-reaching implications for all situations in which those in authority are concerned with subordinates' *personalities*, rather than *performances*. Psychiatric or psychologic reports on employees furnished to employers or the psychoanalytic training system are illustrative examples (Szasz, 1958e). In these and numerous other situations, the subordinate person's inadequate task-performance is often tolerated—indeed, it is covertly fostered—because the superior person has relinquished the value and goal of proficiency in a practical task and has adopted in its place the value of manipulating (e.g., "treating") those under him.

In the case of chronic lying—for example, in a marriage relationship—it is clear that this arrangement, if acceptable to both parties, provides a large measure of rather cheaply earned security for them. How is this security achieved? The crux of the matter lies in the *metacommunicative meanings* of the lie and its acceptance. By communicating a lie, the liar informs his partner that he is afraid of him and wishes to please him. This implies that the latter has a hold on the former and, accordingly, need not be anxious about losing him. Conversely, the person who accepts a lie, by this act informs the liar that he, too, has a strong need for the relationship. By accepting the bribe, as it were, of flattery, cajolery, or sheer subservience implicit in being lied to, the recipient of the lie states, in effect, that he is willing to barter these items for the truth. Hence, the liar too is assured that he need not fear the loss of

---

[4] This is not true in ongoing adult-to-adult relationships based on reciprocally adequate task performances. Examples of this may be found in well-functioning (or perhaps ideal) employer-employee relationships.

his object. In this way, both parties gain a measure—often a very large measure—of security.

In contrast to this comfortable, albeit rather degrading arrangement, a human relationship based on the exchange of larger amounts of unmitigated truth might be more vulnerable to dissolution. I think herein lies one of the reasons for the fact that some "bad" marriages are much more stable, in the sense that they last longer, than many relatively "good" ones. The terms "bad" and "good" refer here to a particular kind of marriage-game, characterized by such rules as honesty, mutual trust, dignity, and so forth. In contrast, the continuation of a marriage or its dissolution by divorce, as mere facts, codify only the legal status of the relationship. They tell us nothing about the rules of the marriage-game. This is the main reason why, from a sociopsychological point of view, it is completely false to regard an ongoing marriage as a sign of success in game-playing (e.g., "mental health" or "maturity"), and divorce as a sign of failure in it (e.g., "mental illness" or "immaturity"). On the contrary, some marriages, as is well known, are defunct games. At the same time, divorce—which, in any case, forms an integral part of the marriage-game—may represent the players' active participation in the game rather than their withdrawal from it.

CHEATING TO LOSE

Inasmuch as lying—and more generally, cheating—has coercive, manipulative implications and uses, it should not surprise us to find that deception as a basic communicative maneuver has broad relevance to numerous situations outside of psychiatry. The hysteric or the mentally ill are not the only ones prone to resort to coercive tactics. We merely chose to study and illuminate these operations in their behavior. Similar observations may be made in a variety of interpersonal, social, and political situations.

In the relationship between adults and children, for example, the same mechanism is encountered in the phenomenon of "cheating to lose." This may sound like a contradiction in terms, for how can one cheat to lose? There is no contradiction, however, if the term "cheating" is used simply to describe the deliberate violation of the rules of the game. In common parlance, the further assumption is made that cheating is motivated by the wish to win. However, this need not always be the case. Cheating may also be motivated by the wish to lose. A good example is the situation of an adult playing with a child, say father and son playing a game of chess. Assuming that the father is the better player—as he is bound to be, at least until his son catches up with him—he might get the idea that to lose at least some of the games would encourage his son. He might implement this idea by cheating against himself, thereby letting his son win. This, of course, is a common occurrence in games or competitive sports in which adults and children play together. I submit that this is a good model for what psychiatrists call "supportive therapy" (e.g., Goldfarb, 1955, p. 183). Both these situations may be characterized as games so played that the *superior person (adult, therapist, etc.) benevolently permits his inferior partner (child, patient, etc.) to maximize his skills, without, at the same time, penalizing his shortcomings.* The entire arrangement is based, however, on a tacit definition of the child or patient as persons occupying inferior roles. The support or encouragement that the child (or patient) receives in this situation tends to be undone by the role-definition implicit in it. I am rather skeptical of the value of these maneuvers for the person whom they are supposed to help. Their value for the helper, on the other hand, is undeniable.

The role and significance of lying and of cheating to lose may be illustrated by several examples drawn from contemporary life: for example, the famous Russian purge-trials, in which accused persons testified against themselves and confessed to acts they had not committed (Meerloo, 1956), and the predicament of American prisoners of war in China, who apparently were forced to incriminate themselves, and confess to acts they had not committed (Lifton, 1956; Schein, 1951). If these occurrences are examined dispassionately—that is, without tacitly accepting current political and ethical value judgments as beyond scrutiny—it becomes evident that these "false confessions" are not as strange or unbelievable as they have been made out to appear. They have their counterparts in our culture, in two commonplace situations. Criminologists, psychiatrists, and even policemen and newspapermen know that when violent crimes are widely publicized, a number of people will give themselves up to the police and make false confessions. Another everyday Western counterpart of the totalitarian false confessions may be witnessed whenever a politically important person engages in a competitive sport with a professional athlete. This situation is a variant on the theme of the father cheating to lose to his son. Now it is a golfing champion who encourages the President of the United States to believe that he is a good golfer, or a tennis star who lets the King of Sweden score some points against him. These situations may be regarded as attempts to organize games involving very unevenly matched players. All of the participants know that in these circumstances no "real" (i.e., evenly matched) game is possible. There are two basic alternatives that permit bringing together such unevenly matched players in a game-playing situation. One is based on pretense: the better player pretends that he is not as good as he really is. The other alternative is based on the forthright recognition of the differences between the players. This difference is then counterbalanced by placing a handicap on the better player. I shall comment on handicapping presently, after concluding our discussion of cheating to lose.

The decision to cheat against one's self, or to assume the role of cheating to lose, may be self-determined or may be foisted on a person more or less against his will. The father may decide to "lose" to his son because he thinks this will please his son. The tennis star will "lose" to the king—at least some points or part-games—because this is regarded as the polite or correct thing to do. The innocent "bum" will confess to crimes he did not commit because he feels he has been defined as a criminal. By playing this role, he really pays homage to the oppressors who have stamped this identity on him. Similarly, Russian "spies" who confessed, or American prisoners of war in China admitting to things they had not done, played the game as they were led to play it. Their role—in the game constructed, arranged, and implemented by their superiors—was to act as if they were playing "telling the truth"; but "telling the truth" was further defined as self-incrimination. Thus, they could "win" only by "losing." Only by confessing did they play the game correctly. These considerations highlight—from a psychological rather than ethical viewpoint—the necessity for democratic law enforcement agencies to place very severe handicaps on themselves. Otherwise, they so far outclass in power the potentially accused citizen that the latter would have no chance to play a "good game" of criminality-or-innocence with them. This, indeed, is the case in totalitarian states.

In contrast to cheating to lose, which is based on pretense, handicapping is based on forthrightness and honesty. Handicapping, a term borrowed from the vocabulary of competitive games and sports, refers to a measure specifically designed to enable players of unequal strength to compete with each other in a "good game." A "good game" is one that is honestly played and to which each player is seriously committed. This is achieved by openly recognizing the differences between the players, and then minimizing the inequalities by placing a handicap on the stronger player—or, what is the same thing, by giving an advantage to the weaker one. The standard game-rules plus the handicap constitute a new game approaching as closely as possible the ideal game in which the players are evenly matched. The maneuver of handicapping, therefore, by honestly recognizing the differences among players, helps to maintain the integrity of the game, and of the players as well.

A SUMMING UP

Viewed as a game, hysteria is characterized by the goal of dominance and interpersonal control. The typical strategies employed in pursuing this goal are coercion by disability and illness. Deceitful gambits of various types, especially lies, also play a significant part in this game.

If we wish to address ourselves to the problem of the "treatment" of hysteria (and other "mental illnesses"), we must first clearly face the question: In what directions—that is, toward what types of games—should the behavior of the patient change? The word "therapy"—in contrast to the word "change"—implies that the patient's current behavioral state is "bad" and that the direction in which the therapist wishes the patient to move is "good," or at least "better." What is "bad," "better," and "good" are defined, of course, by the physician. Person-oriented psychotherapy requires, however, that patients be assisted in defining their own conceptions of psychosocial illness and health. This implies that a patient might set himself goals at variance with the values of his therapist. Accordingly, the patient may change in ways not specifically intended by the therapist and contrary to the latter's personal preferences. Surely, in an adequate theory of the psychotherapeutic interaction there should be room for this contingency.

Thus, descriptions of therapeutic interferences and of changes in the patient's life activities, to be of scientific value, might better be framed in terms of changes in the patient's game-orientations and strategies. For as we have seen, in the case of the hysteric, changes which might be labeled "improvements" or "cures" by some may occur in any one of the following directions: more effective coercion and domination of others; greater submission to others and increased preoccupation with suffering; withdrawal from the struggle over interpersonal control by progressive isolation from real-life relationships; and, finally, learning of the goals and strategies of certain other games in order to become invested in some of them.

> "Perfection of means and confusion of goals seem, in my opinion, to characterize our age. If we desire sincerely and passionately the safety, the welfare and the free development of the talents of men, we shall not be in want of the means to approach such a state."
>
> Albert Einstein (1941, p. 113)

CHAPTER 16

Object Relationships and the Game Model

Viewing the human personality or self in the framework of object relationships, its development may be said to consist of three principal features: (1) The acquisition or internalization of objects; (2) The assimilation of objects into the ego or self; and (3) Learning how to relinquish objects and acquire new ones (that is, forgetting and learning anew). All three of these, in various proportions, are necessary for the development of the personality in that particular way which we consider "human" in our culture. The synthesis of adequate internal objects into a harmonious whole is necessary in adult life for satisfactory living (Szasz, 1957c).

Objects, Rules, and Games

Much of the psychology of object relationships can be applied to our thesis concerning rules and games. For example, the handling of rules and games may be fruitfully analogized with the handling of objects. Or rules and games may be regarded as though they themselves functioned as objects. Since we are self-reflectively aware of rules and games, they do, in fact, function as objects. Hence, this formulation is accurate as a description of certain occurrences and also as a theoretical model.

In viewing object relationships, rule-following, and game-playing as different aspects of the fundamental human enterprise called *learning*, it becomes apparent that one of the main obstacles standing in the way of a more rational and less conflictful kind of social life is man's virtual *inability to forget what he has learned*. Perhaps "inability" is too strong a word. What I have in mind is merely that in our efforts to get together with our fellow man so that we can play the same game, we are hindered by two inter-related processes. One is the arduousness of learning something new. The other is the difficulty—which, however momentous it may be at times, is probably rarely insuperable—of forgetting, or modifying, what has been learned in the past. All this is merely another way of stating and expanding on Freud's (1910a) classic formulation that the hysteric suffers from reminiscences (p. 16). In terms of object relationships, this might be restated by asserting that the hysteric (and many others, too) suffers from the persistence of old (internal) objects and from his unmodified relationship to them. And, again, in terms of the game model, it could be said that the hysteric continues to play an old game, conducted in accordance with old rules. Moreover, he is unaware that he is doing so, and is, for this and other reasons, gravely handicapped from giving up the game he is playing and becoming invested in new games.

Diverse aspects of social life, whether they be regarded as normal or abnormal, may be clarified when scrutinized from this point of view.

OBJECT LOSS AND GAME LOSS: DEPRESSION AND ANOMIE

The idea is not novel that object loss and depression (or broadly, anxiety) and loss of social stability and anomie are similar and closely related phenomena and concepts. Heretofore, the association between them rested on the premise that groups are in some way similar to persons. As the latter needed supporting objects, and when they lost them became depressed, so, it was thought, groups needed firmly held goals and stable organizations. When these crumbled, the group lost its "spirit" and developed *anomie* (De Grazia, 1948). The latter term was made popular by Durkheim, who denoted by it the development of social apathy and disorganization which resulted from the loss of previously valued goals and aspirations. However much this view suffers from a rather simple personification of group life, it is not without merit. These ideas are widely discussed in sociological texts (for example, Merton, 1957a) and therefore are mentioned here only in passing.

Let us consider a somewhat different, although closely related, aspect of the relationship between individual and group psychology or, more precisely, between psychology and sociology. The weight of psychiatric and sociological writings reflects the tacit assumption that loss of object and its vicissitudes characterize the frame of reference of personal conduct; and similarly, that loss of norms and the vicissitudes of normlessness (anomie) characterize the frame of reference of social conduct. I now wish to suggest that it is relevant to consider also how norms and normlessness affect individuals. In other words, persons need not only human objects but also norms or rules —or, more generally—games that are worth playing! It is a matter of every-day observation that men suffer grievously when they can find no games worth playing, even though their object world might remain more or less intact. To account for this and similar events, it is necessary to consider the relationship of the ego or self to games. Otherwise, one is forced to reduce all manner of personal suffering to considerations of object relationships. To do so, however, does violence to the facts. At the same time, loss of game might be considered, in effect, another, more comprehensive aspect of what has traditionally been called loss of object. Conversely, since loss of a real or external object implies the loss of a player from the game—unless a substitute who fits exactly can be found—such loss inevitably results in at least some changes in the game. It is thus evident that the words "player" and "game" describe interdependent variables making up dynamic steady states—for example, persons, families, societies, and so forth.

Again, it may be profitable to make some connections between the fore-going formulations and the more traditional psychoanalytic view concerning the relationships between personality functioning and norms. In psychoanaly-sis, the *ego ideal* and the *superego* are the repositories of the rules and games that one has learned (or has made for himself). The ego ideal is the set of rules to which the ego tries to live up. The superego—a term often used interchangeably with ego ideal—functions classically chiefly as a censor: "This part (of the ego), which has the function (among others) of deciding which impulses are acceptable and which are not, is called the superego" (Fenichel, 1945, p. 18). Developmentally, the superego is said to be derived mainly from identification with the frustrating object. Thus, psychoanalysts speak of "fatherly" and "motherly" superegos (Fenichel, 1945, p. 104), depending on whether the father or mother was the frustrating object. It is a mistake, however, to regard the superego as though it were entirely a censor-ing, prohibiting agency. Identifications with all types of parental and cultural values contribute to the formation of the superego. Thus, prohibitions, per-missions, examples, and so forth are learned from persons. They become internal objects during personality development. Identifications with persons and roles, together with learning rules and games, make up the abstraction called "personality."

INTERDEPENDENCE OF OBJECT AND GAME

The connections between object and game mentioned above may be illustrated by the following examples. A child who has lost its mother not only has lost an object—that is, a human being invested with affection and other feelings—but also has been precipitated into a human situation that constitutes a new game. Living by the old rules, that is, playing the old game, is no longer possible. The mother's absence means that other persons will care for some of the child's needs, and, hence, he will have to adjust himself to the other persons.

Similar considerations hold for marriage. As traditionally conceived, this game was to endure for the lifetime of the players. Clearly, insofar as the players truly espoused this ideal, namely, that they were going to try to fulfill the marriage contract for as long as they lived, this provided them with a powerful protection against the trauma of game loss. Indeed, it seems to me that the institution of marriage must have evolved—and must have persisted as well as it has—not so much because it provides an ordered system of sexual relationships nor because it is necessary for child-rearing, but more fundamentally because it provides men and women with a stable human relationship, within the context of a relatively unchanging game. Marriage has attained this goal better probably than any other institution except the organized religions. Religious games tend to be exceedingly stable. This implies that having learned how to play these games, the person can relax, as it were, and stop learning and changing.

Loss of a parent in childhood, or loss of a spouse in adulthood, are situations in which loss of object and loss of game go hand in hand. There are some situations, however, in which loss of object and loss of game develop in such a manner that the two components are of relatively unequal magnitude. These situations are instructive, for in them are revealed certain otherwise hidden connections between individual life history, internal objects, values, and the social context in which a person lives.

VICISSITUDES OF CHANGING GAMES AND OBJECT RELATIONSHIPS

I shall briefly comment on two situations now in which changes in games and object relationships occur asynchronously. A good illustration of game loss without equally serious loss of significant external objects is afforded by the culture change—say, by immigration—of an entire family. Here, especially if the immigrants are accompanied by friends and servants, we have a situation in which people have lost certain games without necessarily having lost significant personal objects. Factors which need not concern us here influence this situation and may be conducive either to softening the blow of game loss or to magnifying it. In other words, such families either readily adapt themselves to new ways of living, a new language, etc., or go into prolonged mourning for the lost game. In the latter case, they will go on living as if they never left home. Little or no new learning will take place.

Instances in which object loss occurs without its being accompanied by equally serious game loss highlights the distinction between so-called real or external objects on the one hand and internal or fantasy objects (Szasz, 1957a, p. 118) on the other. Changes in relation to external objects will inevitably result in changes in the game situation. This is not equally true in the case of internal or fantasy objects. Consider, for instance, what happens when one's favorite fighter loses a championship bout. Or let us recall the death of President Roosevelt. Many persons who admired and loved him, but who did not actually "know" him, reacted to his death with grief and mourning. These two examples illustrate situations in which object loss of a certain type occurs without its being accompanied by significant changes in the person's game-playing activities, that is, his actual day-to-day life.

ON LEARNING NEW GAMES

The fundamental conception of learning may be applied to a whole range of phenomena including skills, relations to objects, rule-following, game-playing, and so forth. This would permit viewing certain key psychoanalytic conceptions in a broader light. Transference, for instance, could be viewed as a special instance of "playing an old game."[1] Although few workers today still believe that the occurrence of transference is limited to the context of the psychoanalytic situation, many still hold that it is a phenomenon pertaining essentially (or only) to object relationships. I submit that the characteristic features of this occurrence can be observed in other situations as well, particularly in the realm of learned skills. Thus, speaking a language with a foreign accent could be said to be similar to having a transference reaction to one's analyst. In the latter instance, a person will behave toward another as though the latter were someone else, previously familiar to him. The experiencing person, moreover, usually is unaware of the specific manifestations of this pattern of behavior. The same things are true for learning new languages. People who speak English or some other language with a foreign accent usually are unaware of their own distortions of the language.

---

[1] Casual references to the game as a model of real-life situations occur frequently in psychoanalytic writings. In a recent paper, Greenacre (1959), for example, wrote: "One thinks here of Fenichel's warning that *not joining in the game* is the principal task of handling the transference" ([ITALICS ADDED] p. 488). My aim has been to take this model much more seriously than it has been until now, and to base large parts of a theory of psychiatry and psychoanalysis on it.

In other words, to themselves they sound as if they were speaking correct English. It is only when they hear their recorded voice, or others point out—preferably by imitation—how they "really sound" that they can recognize their "linguistic transferences" from their mother tongue to English. The similarities here not only between the behavioral acts but also in the necessity for auxiliary channels of information (i.e., analyst, recording of one's voice) are striking. This view of transference derives from empirical observations concerning the human tendency to generalize experiences.[2]

The developmental phase during which learning occurs, or from which a specific pattern of transference derives, is of crucial significance for its later modifiability. It is necessary to conclude that there are real limitations to unlearning one's earliest experiences, whether these relate primarily to objects or to games. These are formed by massive, indiscriminating identifications and become an integral part of the personality. A thoroughgoing unlearning of these experiences may be virtually impossible. To aim for this goal may be unrealistic and, hence, harmful. This does not mean, of course, that nothing can be done about these early impressions and their effects on later personality functioning. On the contrary, only by adequate recognition of the relatively unmodifiable aspects of the personality is one able to know and come to terms with a part of the basic make-up of the "machine" that is man. To use a machine intelligently and effectively—whether the machine be an automobile, an electron microscope, or one's self—it is clearly as important to know what the machine cannot do as it is to know what it can do. For example, it is virtually impossible for an adult to relinquish completely his mother tongue. This task is more easily attained by children or adolescents. Similar considerations apply to interest in sports. European children who have acquired a liking for soccer may find it difficult to become interested in baseball as adults, even after living in the United States for many years. The same holds true, in reverse, for Americans living in Europe. This is noteworthy, since it can occur in spite of the immigrant's ready acquisition of other, more complex, games indigenous to the new cultural soil.

Experiences acquired in later life, on the other hand, are usually learned discriminatingly and with only partial identifications. Learning of this type is unlearned much more readily than are "motor rules" (Piaget, 1932), or so-called habits. Well-functioning new games may then replace older ones with hardly a trace of the past. If psychotherapists and patients fail to con-

---

[2] A remarkably perceptive early formulation of this phenomenon was provided by Mach (1885) who called it the "principle of continuity" (p. 57). See also Dollard and Miller (1950, Chap. XVII) and Szasz (1960a, p. 14).

sider these facts concerning the modifiability of man, they risk trying to change what cannot be changed and failing to change what can.

The Polarities: Interest–Apathy, Hope–Anomie

Further connections between our knowledge of object relationships and game-playing behavior may be sought by examining *attitudes* and *affects* from the point of view of the game model. From an object relationship viewpoint, the affect of "being interested in" someone or something must be considered fundamental. By this I refer to the same sort of thing as has been called "libidinal cathexis" or "investment," or simply "investment in objects." From the standpoint of the experiencing person, it could be said that objects exist only insofar as they are invested with interest. Although positively toned interest (e.g., "love") is generally considered preferable to negatively toned kinds (e.g., "hate"), both are preferred to a complete loss of interest. The latter signifies a far-reaching loss of objects and is a grave threat to the personality. The affects, attitudes, or "mental states" variously designated as apathy, disinterest, futility, hopelessness, emptiness, withdrawal, etc., all are pertinent in this connection.

There is, as a rule, a culturally given distinction among objects according to their suitability as items of sexual, work, and other interest. One of the things children learn, as they grow up in a given culture, is how to rank-order the use of objects in various activities on a scale of preferences and avoidances. Although many hierarchies of preference clearly depend, at least in part, on the biologically given needs of the human organism, the specific influences of oral, anal, and genital "needs" on their socially regulated expression allow for vast variations. Concerning this problem, I adhere to an essentially culturalistic position (e.g., Erikson, 1950). It remains to mention that a process of regression, or temporal degradation, tends to be set in motion when, for whatever reason, interest at some higher level (in the sense of a learning progression) of game-playing cannot be sustained. To stave off utter isolation and apathy, interest may be mobilized in one's body, ill health, reveries, and so forth.

A parallel series may be constructed by observing that to live, persons need to be interested in far more than just objects. *Man also needs games.* Interest in games—that is, in being alive and living—may be variously expressed. Its main features are feelings of zestfulness and hope and an attitude of curious and hopeful expectation. As a loving attitude implies orientation to objects, so a hopeful attitude implies a similar positively toned orientation to games (e.g., social relationships or contracts, social structures, games in the strict sense of the word, sports, etc.).

Hope, then, means the expectation of being successful in participating in the social interaction. This may imply winning, or playing well, or enjoying what one is doing, or any number of other things. The point is that a persistent interest or investment in playing various games is a *sine qua non* of social living, and of what is often thought of as "mental health." This is expressed well by the significance of work for the psychological integrity of modern man, especially when occupation is self-selected and considered socially important. For people who do not possess inherited wealth and who must therefore work to earn a livelihood, work situations furnish one of the more important sources of stable games. By remaining interested in working, men can play meaningfully and avoid boredom, apathy, and its dangers on the one hand, and reassessment of the self, its objects and games on the other. Both of these alternatives constitute sources of danger to most men. Thus, working people could be said to "play" the game of work, whereas the so-called idle rich "work" at the task of sustaining interest in play. For the latter, sports, travel, social gatherings, philanthropy, and other activities constitute outlets for their need for games.

The significance of hope has recently received new emphasis in psychiatry on the part of those who see in man's need for hope a contemporary justification for endorsing religious faith (e.g., Menninger, 1959). Of course, we all need to be hopeful about some things in life. But this hardly justifies, from a scientific point of view at least, a retreat to irrationalism and an endorsement of religion for mental health, as has been advocated by some. A game-analytic approach to problems in living makes it possible to describe more clearly what is common knowledge in this regard—that religious belief furnishes a stable game. Moreover, all religions—insofar as one can believe in them—engender hope. But, to some extent, this assertion is a tautology, for it is circular to argue that religious belief gives man hope, because it is also necessary to have hope that religion will be satisfying before he can believe in it.[3]

---

[3] These few comments merely offer a glimpse into the exceedingly complicated subject of the psychology of hope in relation to religious faith. The core of this problem is: What should man be *hopeful about?* In what should he *invest his hope?* Disregarding the broadly existential character of these questions, I wish to emphasize only that investing hope in religious faith is, psychoeconomically speaking, one of the best investments one can make. This is because by investing a small amount of hope in religion—especially in a Christian religion—one gets back a great deal of it. After all, let us remember that religions *promise* hope and gratifications of all sorts. Few other enterprises, other than fanatical nationalisms, promise as much. The rate of return on hope invested in religion is thus much higher than on hope invested in, say, rational work-a-day pursuits. Hence, those with small capitals of hope may do best by investing their "savings" in religion. From this point of view, religion could be said to be the *hope of the hopeless.* (In this connection, see Chapter 11, pp. 198-201.)

The dilemma of the circularity stemming from the fact that one must "give" hope before one can "get" any may perhaps be resolved. I believe that we are justified in maintaining that so long as a person lives and is not wholly unconscious, he has some sort of object relationships and is engaged in playing some types of games. Similarly, so long as man lives, he possesses some hope, however little. The Latin proverb, *Dum spiro, spero*—"As long as I live (breathe), I hope"—asserted precisely this. The completely, utterly hopeless man, just as the completely objectless man, is a psychological impossibility. Thus, no matter how apathetic, withdrawn, or schizophrenic a person might be, as scientists our task is to determine and describe the exact nature of his object world and game activities. Moreover, as humane therapists, our task is to help bring him to a developmentally and ethically higher level of object- and game-orientation, if it is possible to do so.

Indeed, we could go so far as to assert that psychoanalysis has always been concerned with the question: *What kind of game is the patient playing?* Although Freud might never have asked this question in quite this form, it seems justifiable to say that he regarded "neurosis" as one kind of game and "normality" as another. For example, masturbation was viewed as a childish game of sexual activity, whereas heterosexual intercourse was considered its adult version. These covert game-rules found expression in certain therapeutic attitudes. For instance, the need for the phobic patient to be confronted with the object she dreaded—to brave going out alone in the street, if that was what she feared—could be regarded as proving to her that she could play the game which she had insisted she could not play.

According to this view, specific "neuroses" or "psychoses"—for example, phobia, conversion hysteria, masochism, paranoia, etc.—constitute different games. The similarities and differences among them could be readily ascertained and tabulated. While this need not concern us here, it seems worth pointing out that in many of these games ("mental illnesses"), the chief aim of the player ("patient") is to control his opponent ("significant object") and/or to prove his superiority and omnipotence (A. Adler, 1907-1937; Silverberg, 1952).

REGRESSION IN OBJECT RELATIONSHIPS AND GAME-PLAYING

Different patterns of object relationships and of game-playing behavior can be ordered according to a scale of values ranging from simple to complex. In the case of object relationships, behavior may range from mutually satisfying human interactions of great social complexity toward the upper end of the scale, to object relationships making use of nonhuman (substitute or "part") objects toward the lower end of it. For game-playing behavior, the range extends from technically complex, equalitarian games to serious degradations of rule-following and severe anomie. Yet, even in states of relatively profound normlessness, certain patterns of norm-following can be discerned.

In his analysis of anomie, Merton (1957a) illustrated the development of this condition by showing what happens when men dishonor the rules of the game and resort to cheating:

> The working of this process eventuating in anomie can be easily glimpsed in a series of familiar and instructive, though perhaps trivial episodes. Thus, in competitive athletics, when the aim of victory is shorn of its institutional trappings and success becomes construed as "winning the game" rather than "winning under the rules of the game," a premium is implicitly set upon the use of illegitimate but technically efficient means. The star of the opposing football team is surreptitiously slugged; the wrestler incapacitates his opponent through ingenious but illicit techniques; university alumni covertly subsidize "students" whose talents are confined to the athletic field. The emphasis on the goal has so attenuated the satisfactions deriving from sheer participation in the competitive activity that only a successful outcome provides gratification. Through the same process, tension generated by the desire to win in a poker game is relieved by successfully dealing one's self four aces or, when the cult of success has truly flowered, by sagaciously shuffling the cards in a game of solitaire. The faint twinge of uneasiness in the last instance and the surreptitious nature of public delicts indicate clearly that the institutional rules of the game are known to those who evade them. But cultural (or idiosyncratic) *exaggeration of the success-goal leads men to withdraw emotional support from the rules* ([ITALICS ADDED] pp. 135-136).

From our point of view, it is important to emphasize that cheating in a game bespeaks of a measure of continued investment in and commitment to it. Evidently, men cheat, among other reasons, because this is one way in which they can maximize their gains. But the things gained themselves have relevance, meaning, and value only in the context of the game. Illustrative is runaway inflation induced by a bankrupt government resorting simply to printing more money. Once it becomes widely apparent that the government has become a monopolistic enterprise at counterfeiting, money—as paper money—loses its value. It then becomes worth literally only as much as the paper on which it is printed. Soon, of course, it ceases to be called "money." Similar considerations apply to social games, whether they involve cheating in poker, tennis, science, marriage, or everyday living.

What I wish to emphasize is that the degradations of game-rules in mental illnesses—e.g., hysteria, masochism, schizophrenia—can operate only so long as the patient's partner, and others around him, play the game according to rules other than those by which the patient plays. If game stability in the degraded rules is to occur—that is, if the mental illness game is to be stable even for a short time—the various players must *not* play the same game by the same rules. As a humorist requires a "straight man," so a schizophrenogenic parent requires a schizophrenic offspring, an agoraphobic wife requires a certain kind of "protective" (controlling) husband, and so forth. If the patient and the persons with whom he interacts were to play the same game by the same rules—that is, if they had symmetrical relationships among one another—the mental illness game could not come into being and flourish. This is merely another way of phrasing the psychoanalytically familiar notion that a patient's symptoms usually interlock—and form a complementary pattern—with the behavior of his significant objects.

These considerations are useful in formulating two basically dissimilar strategies toward changing certain kinds of game-playing activity (e.g., conversion hysteria, paranoia, etc.). One is to fight fire with fire, as it were, by adopting the same types of gambits as the patient has been using. This is what Sullivan has advocated with the "hysteric" (Chapter 15). Some of John Rosen's (1953) strategies seem likewise to be of this sort. In some situations, probably all psychotherapists—as well as persons in various walks of life—have resorted to this method, without its necessarily having been so understood. Using the example of inflation again, if enough "smart investors," having recognized the government as a massive counterfeiter, resorted to treating money as worthless, the inflation game could not last long. Gradual inflation requires that the "government" and the "people" play by somewhat different rules. It may be in the interest of the former that the "real" value of money gradually decrease; while it is usually in the interest of the latter that money retain its value undiminished over the years.

In sum, it may be stated that when all the players in a game throw the rules to the wind and devote themselves to cheating on a grand scale, the game—that is, the social situation—becomes *rapidly self-liquidating*. This is in contrast to honestly played, equalitarian games, which tend to be *self-perpetuating*. They are potentially endless and are terminated either by death or by mutual consent.

The human cost of self-liquidating games is, of course, vast. Runaway inflation can last only a few months. Soon, money is completely worthless and the game is finished. A new game must then be started. The economic, ethical, social—in brief, human—damage that has been wrought in this process of game-degradation and game-liquidation is staggering. Widespread unemployment, social anarchy, and revolution are its usual aftermath. The same sort of consequences, though on a smaller scale, follow when hysterical or masochistic strategies are answered in kind. The problem of "mental illness" might be liquidated, but only at the cost of destroying the productivity, integrity, and often the very humanity, of one, or often of all, of the participants in the game. The new game that is begun when the havoc is over often is on the level of a stereotyped living out of simple roles, awaiting release in death.

A fundamentally different strategy toward altering game-playing activities is that entailed in psychoanalysis and certain forms of psychotherapy. In particular, the psychoanalytic situation may be regarded as a new game that therapist and patient undertake to play. It is a game different from all other games which the patient has been playing. It is set up, in fact, to be expressly different from the patient's "real-life" game, since it is precisely this difference—codified in psychoanalysis as the contrast between "transference" and "reality"—that the patient is there to witness. In essence, the patient pays the analyst to have a firsthand experience with a kind of game diversity, and specifically to be able to learn from it without incurring the usual penalties associated with trying out dangerous games by actually playing them.

It is a crucial feature of psychoanalysis and psychoanalytic psychotherapy that they serve as learning situations in which an attempt is made to acquaint the player ("patient") more fully with the penalties of his own strategies ("neurosis"). Since he is usually not fully acquainted with these—and, on the contrary, tends to overrate the effectiveness of his game and underrate the games of others—such a learning experience is often effective in fostering his desire to modify his behavior. Once this desire is firmly established, the remainder—given a rational, searching, and intelligent effort at understanding and change on the part of both therapist and patient—is relatively easy. It is easy, provided of course that the patient shares certain ethical aspirations inherent in this kind of psychotherapy. If he does not, the game that he was playing might have been the best for him. The effort to change it is then not likely to be "therapeutic" for him, although it might help some persons around him. Whether this is, or is not, a proper psychiatric function, however, is a moot question which deserves further attention.

Psychiatry as Social Action

The thesis that psychiatric operations constitute types of social action has been well documented. Although more obvious in the case of such occurrences as involuntary hospitalization or commitment than in psychoanalysis, the idea that psychiatric activity of any sort is, among other things, a form of social action must be taken as our point of departure for what follows. I propose to distinguish three classes of action patterns, more or less distinct and separate from each other, according to the psychiatrist's position vis-à-vis the games which he encounters in his patients, their families, and the society in which they and he live.

The psychiatrist as theoretical scientist is an expert on game-playing behavior and shares his knowledge of this subject with those who hire him as expert, or who wish to learn from him as a scientist who makes his knowledge public.

The psychiatrist as applied scientist or social engineer sorts out players and assigns them to the games which they can, or ought to, play.

The psychiatrist as social manipulator of human material punishes, coerces, or otherwise influences people to induce them to play, or to cease to play, certain games.

The first type of psychiatric activity is such as to make the work of the psychiatrist virtually indistinguishable from the work of the anthropologist, the social psychologist, the sociologist, or the so-called behavioral scientist. Psychiatry, so conceived, is a branch of social science. It must, nevertheless, remain of interest and significance to medicine—even if it ceases to parade as a biological science—unless the scope of medical activities be restricted to confines much narrower than it presently occupies. Insofar as medicine must assist persons who are in distress—rather than merely repair biophysical bodies that are deranged—it seems inconceivable that it should be able to function without knowledge concerning man as a social being. The psychoanalytic therapist's social role, although not exactly that of theoretical scientist, comes close to it. This is because his direct social impact is restricted to those who are prepared to be exposed to it of their own volition. Psychoanalytic treatment, properly conceived, is not forced on anyone, any more than information or knowledge is forced on anyone in a democratic society.

The psychiatrist as social engineer, sorting out players for their "proper" games, is encountered in the military services, marriage counseling, psychiatric hospitals, courts, and elsewhere (Szasz, 1956b, 1957e, 1959b). In the military services, for example, the psychiatrist's role is to determine who can play being soldier and who cannot. Those who cannot are punished and/or released from the game. Similarly, the state hospital psychiatrist's job, perhaps a bit oversimplified, is to ascertain who must play the game of "mental illness." Those who cannot play the game of "social normality" are assigned to the game of "psychiatric illness." In effect this means that they must take the role of mental patient and all that it embraces. Moreover, they are deprived of the opportunity to change games, so to speak. They can get out of the mental illness game only if they are willing and able to play at being normal, or if they die.

The third type of psychiatric activity—the active manipulation of persons, families, groups, and so forth—is not clearly demarcated from the second type. The main distinction between the two is that in the former the psychiatrist's activity is limited, by and large, to sorting, classifying, or role-assigning, whereas in the latter it proceeds to molding the "patients" into the forms or roles that have been chosen for them. For instance, a psychiatrist who merely advises a married couple not to get a divorce has done a job of classifying or sorting. He decided to sort the two people into the class of marriage partners (to each other). If, however, he does not stop there but proceeds to "treat" both husband and wife, with the explicit aim of helping the marriage to succeed, then he is also acting as a source of influence to bring about the desired role-playing in the patients. Shock therapy, psychotherapy with children, and many other psychiatric interventions illustrate activities of this kind. The activities of the psychiatrist as social engineer, sorting people into the pigeonholes of "identity" in which they "belong" and making sure that they will fit by exerting the "right" kinds of influence on them, have not passed unnoticed by some astute literary and philosophical observers (Dennis, 1955; Russell, 1953, 1954). Needless to say, I think we ought to have serious reservations concerning psychiatric activities of the second and third types. My considerably greater satisfaction with the first type of psychiatric activity, however, must not be construed to mean that I believe all is well with it. It would be desirable to keep an open and critical mind toward it as well.

"The strain of civilization . . . *is created by the effort which life in an open and partially abstract society continually demands from us—by the endeavor to be rational, to forego at least some of our emotional social needs, to look after ourselves, and to accept responsibilities. We must, I believe, bear this strain as the price to be paid for every increase in knowledge, in reasonableness, in cooperation and in mutual help, and consequently in our chances of survival, and in the size of the population. It is the price we have to pay for being human."*

Karl R. Popper (1945, p. 172)

Summary and Conclusions

Hysteria as a typical example of mental illness was chosen as the starting point for our inquiry into the nature of self-experience and personal conduct. Charcot, Breuer, Freud, and many of their contemporaries observed that certain patterns of human behavior—or, more precisely, certain modes of nonverbal communication—resembled neurological illnesses, yet differed from them in crucial ways. For historical and social reasons, the phenomena in question were *defined* and *classified* as members of the class "disease." Thus, hysteria as a quasi-neurological illness formed the nucleus around which the vast structure of "psychopathology" gradually crystallized.

Origin of the Modern Concept of Mental Illness

HYSTERIA AND THE CONCEPT OF ILLNESS

The error of classifying hysteria as an illness, with emphasis on its similarities to known neurological diseases, is attributable mainly to the nineteenth-century reductionist conception of personal conduct. According to this view, all behavior was regarded as a problem in muscle and nerve physiology. As a tabetic ataxia was explained by certain nerve lesions, it was assumed that normal behavior too could be adequately explained by describing its neuroanatomical and neurophysiological correlates. This approach rested on the erroneous belief that there were no significant differences between complex items of learned behavior on the one hand, and the behavioral

294

manifestations of *defects of the body* on the other hand. It followed that whenever defective functioning of the body was encountered it was regarded as *prima facie* evidence of illness. In view of the practical task of the neurologist, it is easy to see why he should have been especially prone to make this mistake. It often happens that diseases of the nervous system (for example, multiple sclerosis, brain tumor) first manifest themselves by peculiarities in personal conduct. It was tempting to conclude from such occurrences that brain and behavior stand in a simple type of cause-and-effect relationship to each other.

This approach was consistent with the prevalent philosophical preconceptions of medical workers concerning the principles of their science. It allowed them to treat as medical problems all manner of complicated human situations that found overt expression in the patient's belief that he was ill. If known methods of physiochemical examination failed to reveal the presence of bodily disease, this was of no great concern. The late nineteenth-century physician's model of disease was derived from his experiences with tuberculosis, syphilis, and typhoid fever. As the causes of these illnesses had been discovered by medical science, so it would be with hysteria and mental illnesses.

Charcot succeeded in making hysteria acceptable to the medical profession. This achievement, however, was in the nature of a social reform, not a scientific discovery. Although some members of suffering humanity were promoted, as it were, to higher social rank, this was attained at the cost of obscuring the logical character of the observed phenomena.

Because of the conceptual make-up of late nineteenth-century psychiatry, hysteria was compared and contrasted with malingering on the one hand, and with "real illness" on the other. The persistent medical and psychiatric opinion that behavior which imitated illness was an effort to cheat or fool doctors made it necessary to condemn it. Hence, physicians who wished to prevent the condemnation of people exhibiting this type of behavior had to insist that such patients *were* "ill." In this way their behavior could still be described as essentially illness-imitating—and could be studied scientifically—while at the same time the pejorative diagnosis of malingering could be avoided. This strategy contained a hidden danger. The notion of illness, at first used mainly with a socially promotive aim in mind, rapidly became accepted as the correct description of "facts." The expression "mental illness" was not understood in a metaphorical sense as it should have been, but attained a high degree of concretization and began to lead a life of its own. Now it is a *panchreston* (Hardin, 1956), a word that is supposed to explain everything, whereas it explains nothing and serves only to hinder our critical understanding. In modern psychiatry this thesis is exemplified by the persistent denial that a person may *wish* to imitate sickness and *play the role* of a disabled person without necessarily being sick. The nosological categorization of every possible feature of malingering as a manifestation of mental illness is a result of this tendency.

SOCIOLOGY OF THE PHYSICIAN-PATIENT RELATIONSHIP

In late nineteenth-century Europe and America, medical care could be obtained by purchase and owned, much as private property. Private medical practice became an integral part of capitalistic, individualistic society. Those who could not afford to buy this commodity were forced to obtain it—as they did many other things in life—through the charity of others. The private practice type of relationship between physician and patient was a crucial antecedent of the psychoanalytic situation. In both, the therapist was the patient's agent, in contrast to being the agent of some other person or group.

Nineteenth-century medical practice may be profitably compared to contemporary Western practices. Today, medical practice is characterized by a mixture of *private* and *insured* situations. The insurance scheme introduces third (and fourth, etc.) parties into the transaction between sufferer and healer. Finally, in the Soviet system of medical practice the physician is an agent of the state. Depending on the type of disability the patient has, the Soviet medical system readily leads to various conflicts between physician, patient, and state. The concept of malingering is very much in vogue in Russia, whereas in Western countries it has largely been displaced by the concepts of hysteria, neurosis, and mental illness. None of these terms denotes or describes a "disease entity." Actually, they arise from and reflect characteristic features of the social matrix of the therapeutic situation. They point to covert preferences of individualistic or collectivistic ethics and their attendant notions concerning the duties and privileges of citizen and state in regard to each other.

WHAT IS PSYCHIATRY?

It is customary to define psychiatry as a medical specialty concerned with the study, diagnosis, and treatment of mental illnesses. This is a worthless and misleading definition. Mental illness is a myth. Psychiatrists are not concerned with mental illnesses and their treatments. In actual practice they deal with personal, social, and ethical problems in living.

I have argued that, today, the notion of a person "having mental illness" is scientifically crippling. It provides professional assent to a popular rationalization, namely, that problems in human living experienced and expressed in terms of bodily feelings or signs (or in terms of other "psychiatric symptoms") are significantly similar to *diseases of the body*. It also undermines the principle of personal responsibility, upon which a democratic political system is necessarily based, by assigning to an external source (i.e., the "illness") the blame for antisocial behavior. We know that for the individual patient this attitude precludes an inquiring, psychoanalytic approach to problems which "symptoms" at once hide and express. Codifying every type of occurrence that takes place in a medical setting as, *ipso facto,* a medical problem makes about as much sense as suggesting that when physicists quarrel their argument constitutes a problem in physics.

Although powerful institutional pressures lend massive weight to the tradition of keeping psychiatric problems within the conceptual fold of medicine, the scientific challenge seems clear. The task is to redefine the problem of mental illness so that it may be encompassed under the general category of the science of man. Medicine itself contributes to this enterprise, as do numerous other disciplines. The psychiatric and psychoanalytic approaches to this task, however, must be defined more clearly. It is inevitable that these disciplines must stand or fall with whatever value their special methods possess. Since their methods pertain to the analysis of communications, and since their concepts involve those of psychosocial structure and sign-using behavior, we should delay no longer in describing our work in terms appropriate to these methods and concepts. This, of course, would necessitate a thoroughgoing revision—and indeed, a scuttling—of many of our notions concerning both psychopathology and psychotherapy. The former should be conceived in terms of object relationships, sign-using, rule-following, social roles, and game-playing. As to psychotherapy, it should be systematized as a theory of human relationships, involving special social arrangements and fostering certain values and types of learning.

Semiotical Analysis of Behavior

The bodily signs of conversion hysteria—for example, an hysterical seizure or paralysis—were chosen as typical examples of at least one type of so-called psychiatric symptom. Our inquiry was focused on the following questions: (1) What type of language, or communication system, is employed by persons exhibiting this kind of behavior? (2) What type of object relationship is secured and maintained by means of hysterical communications? (3) What are the specific interpersonal functions of indirect communications in general, and of dreams and certain "psychiatric symptoms" in particular?

THE "PSYCHIATRIC SYMPTOM" AS A FORM OF PICTURE LANGUAGE

It was found that a sign relation of iconicity was the chief characteristic of signs typically encountered in hysterical symptom-communications. An iconic sign is defined as an object, X, which because of its similarity to another object, Y, is used to denote the latter. The relation of similarity (iconicity) is usually based on appearance, as for example in a photograph. It may also be based on function. Thus, animals may symbolize (represent) people, as in cartoons, because both exhibit manifestations of life.

The observation that hysterical symptoms depict certain occurrences was originally made by Freud. He asserted that hysteria was like a pantomime, or dumb-show, in which the patient expressed a message by means of non-verbal signs. Pseudocyesis is a good example. It is a pictorial representation of the idea "I am pregnant." Hysterical body language therefore consists essentially of pictures. As such, it is similar to other picture languages, such as *picture puzzles* or *charades*. In each of these, communication is achieved by means of pictures (iconic signs) instead of words (conventional signs). In a picture puzzle, the name "Forrestal" may be depicted by showing a picture of several trees to the right of which is placed a tall man. Given such a puzzle, the task is to translate from picture language to word language. Similarly, in the game of charades, a proverb, quotation, or almost anything "spelled out" in words must be so "acted out" by one of the players that his teammates shall recognize the message. In both of the examples cited, there is a two-way process of translation or sign-transformation. In charades, the person who acts out the message must translate from English (or some other ordinary language) to pantomime, while his teammates must reverse the process by transforming pantomime back into English. In hysteria, and in many other behavioral phenomena as well, the task of the psychiatrist is similar to that confronting a person who tries to unravel a picture puzzle. The meaning of hysteria—stated in the form of a picture language, or, more precisely, in the form of a language composed of iconic signs—must be rendered into everyday verbal language.

The logical character of communications composed of iconic body signs was then compared to other types of communications. Since hysterical body language constitutes a mode of communication logically inferior to that of object and metalanguages, it was designated a protolanguage. Ordinary object language stands in a meta relation to protolanguage.

THE FUNCTIONS OF PROTOLANGUAGE

Protolanguage may serve all the cognitive and instrumental uses of ordinary language. The differences in usefulness between an iconic sign language and a conventional symbol language lie in the degree to which the various language functions may be exercised by means of each. Thus, for purely cognitive purposes, protolanguage is greatly inferior to object and meta-languages. It is superior, however, for purposes of affective and promotive communication. Thus, the facial expression of grave suffering, perhaps accompanied by tears and groans, usually is more effective in imparting a mood and in inducing a wished-for action, than the simple statement "I am in pain."

Protolanguage is relatively nondiscursive. This is inherent in its being composed of iconic rather than conventional signs. The former mode of symbolization embodies a more idiosyncratic or private sign relationship than does the latter. The most public or impersonal language systems (for example, mathematics, the Morse code) are the most discursive, while the typically private or personal idioms (for example, an "hysterical" or "schizo-phrenic" symptom) are relatively nondiscursive. Because of the iconicity and nondiscursiveness of hysterical body language, it affords vast possibili-ties for mistakes and misunderstandings in cognitive communication. Ex-ploration of the cognitive or informative use of iconic body signs made it possible to ask whether such communication might be similar to mistakes and lies in everyday language. An analysis of this problem disclosed that there is a compelling parallelism between the concepts of malingering, hysteria, and (ordinary "organic") illness on the one hand and the concepts of lying, making a mistake, and telling the truth on the other.

Considerations of the uses of iconic body signs in a psychiatric context led, finally, to highlighting an hitherto unrecognized function of this mode of communicative behavior. The object-seeking and relationship-maintaining function of any type of communication was arrived at by a combined semiotical and object relations approach to problems of communication in psychiatry. This point of view lends special force to the interpretation of such things as the dance, religious ritual, and the representative arts. In each of these, the participant or the viewer is enabled *to enter into a significant human relationship by means of a particular system of communication.* The same is true, of course, for logically higher levels of language, such as mathematics. Scientists achieve and maintain object contact with their colleagues by means of special languages, just as members of primitive tribes may gratify similar needs by means of a ritual dance. It is significant, however, that the language of science has, in addition to its object-relations aspect, a cognitive facet as well, and that this is largely, although not entirely, absent in the more primitive communicative modes. Still, considerations of object contact are at least potentially relevant in connection with all sign-using functions.

THE USES OF INDIRECT COMMUNICATIONS

Hysteria or any mental illness may also be considered an indirect communication or language that is used ambiguously, usually in order to give the recipient of the message a choice between several alternative replies. Hints, allusions, and metaphorical expressions of all kinds are everyday examples of indirect communications. The need for this mode of communication arises typically in the family. The social conditions of this unit make it necessary that family members curb their wishes and hence also the explicit symbolic representations of them. This leads to the inhibition ("repression") of direct forms of communication and provides the stimulus for the development of relatively more devious, or indirect, forms of need-communicative behavior. The function of hinting was illustrated by an analysis of dream communication. The "hysterical symptom" may also be regarded as a hint addressed to the patient's significant objects or to physicians.

The chief advantages of hinting—and hence of hysteria—are the following: (1) It provides a mode of sending a message whose effect is feared, either because the communication pertains to the expression of an ego-alien wish or because it is an aggressive reproach against a loved but needed person. (2) It permits the expression of a communication without full commitment to it. In other words, it provides an escape route should the message misfire or backfire. (3) It makes it possible for a person to be granted what he desires without having to ask for it explicitly. It thus protects the help-seeking person from being humiliated should his request be denied. This is an exceedingly important mechanism, commonly used by children. It is also employed by adults, either because they have retained certain childish ideals (for example, "I should not need anything or anybody"), or because they find themselves in a situation in which they feel more strongly committed to a person than the "objective conditions" would warrant (for example, "love at first sight"). In these situations, hinting—whether by means of socially acceptable metaphors or "mental symptoms"—provides an exploratory mode of communication.

Situations of close personal interdependence favor indirect communications, whereas certain more impersonal, functional types of social relations foster direct communications. In the psychoanalytic situation, the hinting functions of hysteria, dreams, and other "mental symptoms" are subjected to persistent scrutiny. Indeed, it may be said that one of the aims of the analytic process is to induce the patient to relinquish his indirect ("symptomatic," "transference") communications and to substitute for them direct messages framed in the straightforward idiom of ordinary English. This is accomplished by placing him in a situation in which hinting is not rewarded, as it might be in ordinary life, but direct communication is. This is inherent in the conditions of the analytic situation, in which an explicit positive value is placed on direct communication (absolute truthfulness, privacy of the two-person situation, etc.). Thus, the interpersonal conditions of analysis are such as to favor a process of change in regard to the patient's (habitual) sign-using behavior.

In this regard, being in analysis could be compared to going to a foreign country for purposes of study. By means of this analogy, the double impact of psychoanalysis on the patient's sign-using behavior may be illustrated. First, it induces him to give up his habitual mode of communicating (mother tongue, symptom language) and to substitute for it a *new language* (foreign language, direct communication in ordinary language). To accomplish this alone, however, might be merely a "transference cure." Ideally, psychoanalysis accomplishes more than this, just as going abroad to study physics enables the student to learn a foreign language *and* physics. Similarly, in the psychoanalytic situation the analysand is not only induced to shift from symptom-language to ordinary verbal communication but is *also taught to examine and understand the particular patterns of object relationships which he has had and the communicative patterns to which these gave rise.* Thus, the basic aim of psychoanalytic treatment is to enable the patient to learn about his object relationships and communicative behavior. A shift from protolanguage to object and metalanguage must be successfully achieved before mastery of the more far-reaching task of self-knowledge can be attempted.

The chief purpose of iconic body language may be merely to make contact with objects. For some people, sometimes, no verbal language may be available with which legitimately to address their fellow man. If all else fails, there still remains the language of illness—a language that virtually everyone the world over knows how to speak and understand. This is the idiom which the lonely, the downcast, the poor, and the uneducated can still use and thereby hope to "get something" which they had failed to obtain in other ways. Thus, the language of illness—and of social deviance, too—constitutes the last, and perhaps the firmest, bastion on the grounds of which unsatisfied and "regressed" man can make a last stand and claim his share of human "love" (Szasz, 1957a). For the average layman, or for the therapeutically dedicated physician or psychiatrist, this message of non-specific help-seeking may, of course, be difficult to hear, since all labor under the assumption that what they see and hear are manifestations of "illness." This leaves them no choice but to endeavor to "cure" or at least "ameliorate" the "disease." Yet, it seems that this whole imagery is false. The spectacle that faces us is simply an aspect of the *human condition*— call it fate, destiny, life style, character, existence, or what you will—and what we hear and see are *the cries for help* and their *pictorial representations*.

The Rule-following Model of Behavior

"Social life," as Peters (1958) reminded us, "is never like the jungle life popularized by evolutionary theories, a matter of mere survival; it is a matter of surviving in a certain sort of way" (p. 127). To ask, then, "In what sort of way?" and to provide answers to this question, is the task of the sciences concerned with man as a social being. Since survival by means of exhibiting "hysteria" (or "mental illness") is one distinctively human form of survival, it is necessary to study the factors that contribute to this pattern of human existence.

CLASSIFICATION OF RULES

Three broad categories of rules may be distinguished. In the first group, designated as natural laws or biological rules, belong the regularities that must be obeyed lest sheer physical survival be jeopardized. Examples are the need to satisfy hunger or thirst and the prevention of injuries from falling, drowning, burning, and the like. Prescriptive laws constitute the next group. These are the rules—whether social, religious, or moral—that govern social life among particular groups of men. The Bible or the American Constitution and Bill of Rights are typical examples. They define the rules of the game by which social living in a given community shall be played. The third group, named "imitative or interpersonal rules," is composed of those patterns of action which must be copied by children, more or less accurately, from the behavior of the adults about them, if they are to partake of the social life of the group: for example, the learning of one's mother tongue, the use of household items, patterns of eating, and the like. Biological rules are of the utmost importance for the survival of the human (and animal) body and species. The exploration, the elucidation, and sometimes the alteration of these rules are the aims of the basic medical sciences (physiology, bio-chemistry, genetics, etc.) and of clinical medicine. Social and interpresonal rules, on the other hand, constitute the core-subject of the sciences of man (anthropology, psychiatry, psychoanalysis, psychology, sociology, etc.).

THE FAMILY SITUATION, RELIGION, AND THE RULES FOR GETTING AND GIVING HELP

Childhood patterns of help-seeking and help-getting form the core of a system of rules that in later life may foster the seeking or imitating of illness or disability in order to induce others to care for one. This communicative, coercive feature of disabilities of all sorts is often enhanced by Jewish and Christian religious teachings. In this connection, an examination of the Bible as a rule-book was undertaken. It was shown that the Judaeo-Christian religions contain numerous incentives to being ill or disabled. States of distress and failure—whether because of stupidity, poverty, sickness, or what not—may be interpreted as potentially desirable goals, for as the hungry infant is given the mother's breast, so the disabled human being is promised God's all-embracing helpfulness and benevolence. This pattern of human interaction and communication is regarded as the main source of a vast number of rules, all of which conspire, as it were, to foster man's infantilism and dependence. These may be contrasted with rules emphasizing the need for man's striving for mastery, responsibility, self-reliance, and mutually cooperative interdependence.

WITCHCRAFT AND HYSTERIA

The specific effects of certain Biblical rules on human conduct were illustrated by means of the social phenomenon of medieval witchcraft. The psychiatric and the rule-following theories of witchcraft were compared. According to the former, witches were misdiagnosed hysterics. According to the latter, they were persons sacrificed as scapegoats in a real-life game in which the activities of God and devil were taken too literally and too seriously.

Witchcraft existed as an integral part of the medieval Christian game of life. This game was theologically defined, and demanded that the players conduct themselves according to rules which were impossible to follow. Violation of the game-rules—that is, cheating—was thus unavoidable. Hence, virtually everyone was a cheat. In general, persons of high social status could cheat much more easily and safely than persons of low status. Poor old women were especially expendable and most of the witches were recruited from among their ranks. High officials of the Roman Catholic Church—who themselves disobeyed the rules of the game most flagrantly and whose activities sparked the Protestant Reformation—fostered the persecution of those who were alleged to cheat.

In the language of chess, the persecution of witches meant that poor, unimportant people (pawns) were sacrificed to insure the safety and well-being of the ruling classes (king and queen). By this maneuver, victory for God (the master player) was assured. In addition to insuring God's continued glory, this operation also served to preserve the social *status quo*. Witch-hunts and witch-trials were, accordingly, a safety valve of society. Some aspects of contemporary psychiatric practices—especially psychiatric operations involving involuntary patients and legal actions—appear to serve a function analogous to that served by the medieval witch-trials.

The contest between theological persecutor and witch is closely paralleled by the contest between institutional psychiatrist and involuntary mental patient. The former is always the victor, the latter forever the vanquished. The concept of mental illness and the social actions taken in its name serve the self-seeking interests of the medical and psychiatric professions, just as the notion of witchcraft served the interests of the theologians, acting in the name of God. As the theological game was the "opiate of the people" in past ages, so the medical-psychiatric game is the opiate of contemporary peoples. By draining interpersonal and group tensions, each game fulfills the function of social tranquilization.

The Game-playing Model of Behavior

DEVELOPMENTAL AND LOGICAL ASPECTS OF GAMES

The model of games was selected as offering the most comprehensive map by which to chart the social behavior of human beings. The models of sign-using and rule-following, used earlier, may be subsumed under this more general scheme.

Initially, games were considered as they are encountered in everyday experience, in familiar card and board games (bridge, checkers, chess, etc.). Children's attitudes toward game-rules show an interesting and exceedingly significant progression. Briefly summarized, preschool children are virtually unable to adhere to rules; they play games idiosyncratically, in the presence of other children but not with them. Subsequently, children learn to adhere to the rules of the game, but regard the rules—and the game as a whole —as "sacred." At this stage, rules are rather poorly understood and slavishly followed. Usually not before their early teens do children gain an appreciation of game-rules as conventional and cooperatively constructed. Relatively mature, autonomous game-playing behavior may thus be contrasted with immature, heteronomous game-playing behavior. In addition to the important developmental distinctions among different types of game-playing behaviors, a logical hierarchy of games similar to the logical hierarchy of languages may be constructed. The concept of game-hierarchies has important applications both in everyday life and in psychiatry. The familiar moral conflict that sometimes exists between ends and means is a conflict involving game-hierarchies. End-goals occupy a logically higher level than strategies used in pursuing them.

ETHICS, GAMES, AND PSYCHIATRY

As long as the socioethical values of psychiatric theories and therapies remain obscure and inexplicit, their scientific worth is bound to be rather limited. This is simply because human social behavior is fundamentally ethical behavior. It is difficult to see, therefore, how such behavior could be described, or how modifications of it could be advocated, without at the same time coming to grips with the issue of ethical values. Psychoanalytic descriptions of behavior and of therapy, for example, have emphasized instinctual forces, pathogenic occurrences, and mental mechanisms at the expense of explicitly specifying norms and values. The concept of genital primacy (Fenichel, 1945, p. 61) as a norm or value is a typical example of the psychiatric-psychoanalytic dilemma that must be resolved. In this concept, a norm of adult human functioning is described and covertly advocated without, however, specifying the socioethical context in which a person's "genital primacy" is supposed to occur. It is left open whether genital primacy in the social context of king and concubine, master and servant, soldier and prostitute, or husband and wife is considered the ideal goal. Thus, we have no provisions either for describing or for judging the variations in, say, marital relations in societies that are autocratic and democratic, or those that are patriarchal, matriarchal, and pediarchal (child-dominated).

In the theory of personal conduct which I have put forward—and implictly, in the theory of psychotherapy that may be based upon it—I have endeavored to correct this deficiency, emphasizing the urgent need to clearly specify norms and values first and techniques of behavior second. This approach was illustrated by emphasizing the end-goals of the hysterical game which were identified as domination or interpersonal control. It follows from this goal that coercing strategies may be employed in pursuit of it. In contrast, one might espouse the goals of self-reliant competence and dignified human interdependence. It is evident that these goals could not be secured by coercive techniques, for pursuing them in thi fashion would conflict with the very ends that are sought. Since the end determine, within a certain range, the means that may be used to attain them, failure to specify clearly and to bear in mind end-goals cannot be corrected by concentration on, or training in, specific techniques of living.

IMPERSONATION AND CHEATING

"Impersonation" refers to taking someone else's role under false pretenses; or, what is essentially the same, to claiming to play game A while, in fact, playing game B. The word "cheating" refers to a similar concept, but one that is more limited in scope. It is applied to the behavior of persons whose game-playing activity is judged to deviate from the correct or agreed-upon rules. For example, malingering, the Ganser syndrome, and hysteria all include elements of cheating, meaning thereby violation of the rules in order to maximize one's advantages.

The significance of impersonation as a theoretical-explanatory conception for psychiatry is considerable. This notion touches on the familiar psychoanalytic concepts of identification, ego-formation, ego-identity, self-system, etc., but expands on them by introducing considerations of social role and interpersonal strategy. In this light, the modern concept of "mental illness" and its "psychiatric treatment" presents us with a double impersonation. On the one hand so-called psychiatric patients impersonate the sick role: the hysteric acts as though he were bodily ill, and invites "treatment" in accordance with the rules of the medical game. Concomitantly, psychiatrists and psychoanalysts, by accepting the problems of their patients as manifestations of "illness," commit a complementary act of impersonation: they impersonate physicians and play the role of the medical therapist. This act of impersonation, however, also goes on independently of the machinations of patients. It is actively fostered by the present-day professional organizations of psychotherapeutic practitioners, as well as by the members as individuals.

I refer here to the *credo* of most contemporary psychiatrists, that psychiatry—including psychotherapy—is significantly similar to other branches of medicine, and belongs to it. It seems to me, however, that medical psychotherapists, having had a medical training, only look like other doctors —just as hysterics only look like organically sick persons. The difference between the purely communicational interventions of the psychotherapist and the physicochemical actions of the physician represents an instrumental gulf between the two groups that no institutional resemblance can convincingly close. It is common knowledge that when clinical psychologists press their claims to practice independent psychotherapy, they tend to be regarded (especially by physicians) as impersonators of the medical role of "taking care of sick people." But the same could be said for medically trained psychotherapists whose work also differs in crucial ways from that of the surgeon or internist.

Until now, this impersonation has served the apparent interests of both mental patients and psychiatrists. Thus, no one has really protested against this variation on the theme of the myth of the emperor's clothes. I think the time is now ripe to consider seriously the possibility that the medical aspects of psychotherapy are about as substantial as the legendary emperor's cloak which was so finely woven that only the wisest and most perspicacious men could perceive it. To claim that he was naked was, therefore, tantamount to self-confessed stupidity, as well as an affront against a powerful personage.

Analyses and arguments attempting to clarify the differences between medicine and psychiatry (or psychoanalysis) have been hampered by similar factors. It is almost as though medicine and psychiatry (psychotherapy) were husband and wife united in an unstable marriage. Those who emphasize what the couple have in common, hoping thereby to stabilize the relationship, are honored and rewarded as the doers of meritorious deeds. On the other hand, those who notice and comment on the differences between them are treated as though it were *they* who were breaking up an otherwise perfect union. As could be expected, marriage counseling to save the union—expressed partly as a propagandizing "psychosomatic medicine" and partly as a redefining of psychoanalysis as "psychoanalytic medicine" —has tended to flourish, whereas work clarifying the differences between medicine and psychiatry (irrespective of where this might lead) has been virtually nonexistent.

GAMES, OBJECTS, AND VALUES

In conclusion, some connections between the theories of object relationships and game-playing were presented. For adults (and probably also for children after the age of ten to twelve years), games and their constituent rules often function as objects. In other words, loss of game—that is, the inability to play a game, either because of the unavailability of other players or because of changes in one's own game-playing propensities—no less than loss of object, leads to serious disequilibrium within the personality, requiring adaptive, reparative measures. Indeed, objects and games are interdependent, since the players are of necessity *people*. Hence, psychology and sociology are interlocking and interdependent.

The game model of human behavior appears well suited for unifying psychology, sociology, and ethics. For example, the sociological concept of anomie—a state of social unrest resulting from the dissolution of established rules—could readily be integrated with the psychoanalytic concepts of object loss, anxiety-depression, and ego identity. Loss of a sense of satisfying personal identity is linked to *modern man's inevitable loss of the "games" learned early in life.* In other words, modern man, if he is at all educated, cannot play the same sorts of games which he played as a youngster, or which his parents played, and remain satisfied with them. Cultural conditions are changing so rapidly that everyone tends to share the problem of the immigrant who *must* change games because he has moved from one country to another. Even those who stay put geographically find themselves in a world other than that of their parents. Indeed, as they grow older they usually find themselves in a world other than that of their youth. In this dilemma, man is confronted by the imperative need to relinquish old games and to learn to play new ones. Failing this, he is forced to play new games by old rules, the old games being the only ones he knows how to play. *This fundamental game-conflict leads to various problems in living. It is these that the modern psychotherapist is usually called on to "treat."*

Three general types of game-conflict may be distinguished. One is characterized by the person's inability to forget the old rules, or by his outright unwillingness to relinquish playing the old game. This may result in a refusal to play any of the games that others play: It is a kind of "strike" against living. Various so-called disability states—malingering, hysteria, and "dependency reactions"—illustrate such a "strike" or revolt against the challenge to learn. A second type of game-conflict consists of the superimposition of old goals and rules upon new games. Illustrative is the "transference neurosis" or reaction, the "neurotic character structure," the foreign accent, and so on; in each of these, we are confronted by a pattern of behavior that is the result of mixing different, to some extent mutually incompatible, games. Finally, a third type of game-conflict, manifested in a general disappointment-reaction, develops from the realization that man can play no transcendentally valid (God-given) game. Many react to this insight with the feeling that, in this case, *no game is worth playing!* The significance of this condition—namely, *that no game is really worth playing*—appears to be especially great for contemporary Western man.

In Pirandello's play, *The Rules of the Game* (1919, p. 25), the following conversation takes place:

LEONE: Ah, Venanzi, it's a sad thing, when one has learnt every move in the game.
GUIDO: What game?
LEONE: Why . . . this one. The whole game—of life.
GUIDO: Have you learnt it?
LEONE: Yes, a long time ago.

Leone's despair and resignation come from believing that there is such a thing as *the* game of life. Indeed, if mastery of *the* game of life were the problem of human existence, having achieved this task, what would there be left to do? But there is no game of life, in the singular. The games are infinite.

Modern man seems to be faced with a choice between two basic alternatives. On the one hand, he may elect to despair over the lost usefulness or the rapid deterioration of games painfully learned. Skills acquired by diligent effort may prove to be inadequate for the task at hand almost as soon as one is ready to apply them. Many people cannot tolerate repeated disappointments of this kind. In desperation, they long for the security of stability—even if stability can be purchased only at the cost of personal enslavement. The other alternative is to rise to the challenge of the unceasing need to learn and relearn, and to try to meet this challenge successfully.

The momentous changes in contemporary social conditions clearly forewarn that—if man survives—his social relations, like his genetic constitution, will undergo increasingly rapid mutations. If this is true, it will be imperative that all people, rather than just a few, *learn how to learn*. I use the term "to learn" rather broadly. It refers, first, to the adaptations that man must make to his environment. More specifically, man must learn the rules that govern life in the family, the group, and the society in which he lives.

Further, there is the learning of technical skills, science, and learning to learn. Clearly, there is no "objective" limit to learning. The limiting factor is *in man*—not in the challenge to learn. Leone's dilemma is the dilemma of a man so far withdrawn from life that he fails to appreciate, and hence to participate in, the ever-changing game of life. The result is a shallow and constant life which may be encompassed and mastered with relative ease.

The common and pressing problem today is that, as social conditions undergo rapid change, men are called upon to alter their modes of living. Old games are constantly scrapped and new ones started. Most people are totally unprepared to shift from one type of game-playing to another. They learn one game or, at most, a few, and desire mainly the opportunity to live out life by playing the same game over and over again. But since human life is largely a social enterprise, social conditions may make it impossible to survive without greater flexibility in regard to patterns of personal conduct.

Perhaps the relationship between the modern psychotherapist and his patient is a beacon that ever-increasing numbers of men will find themselves forced to follow, lest they become spiritually enslaved or physically destroyed. By this I do not mean anything so naive as to suggest that "everyone needs to be psychoanalyzed." On the contrary, "being psychoanalyzed" —like *any* human experience—can itself constitute a form of enslavement and affords, especially in its contemporary institutionalized forms, no guarantee of enhanced self-knowledge and responsibility for either patient or therapist. By speaking of the modern psychotherapeutic relationship as a beacon, I refer to a simpler but more fundamental notion than that implied in "being psychoanalyzed." This is the notion of being a *student of human living*. Some require a personal instructor for this; others do not. Given the necessary wherewithal and ability to learn, success in this enterprise requires, above all else, the sincere desire to learn and to change. This incentive, in turn, is stimulated by hope of success. This is one of the main reasons why it is the scientist's and educator's solemn responsibility to clarify—never to obscure—problems and tasks.

I hope that I have been successful in avoiding the pitfalls of mysticism and obscurantism which, by beclouding the problems to be tackled and solved, foster feelings of discouragement and despair. We are all students in the school of life. In this metaphorical school, none of us can afford to become discouraged or despairing. And yet, in this school, religious cosmologies, nationalistic myths, and lately psychiatric theories have more often functioned as obscurantist teachers misleading the student, than as genuine clarifiers helping him to help himself. Bad teachers are, of course, worse than no teachers at all. Against them, skepticism is our sole weapon.

Bibliography

ABERNETHY, G. L. (ed.) (1959). *The Idea of Equality. An Anthology.* Richmond, Va.: John Knox Press, 1959.

ABRAHAM, K. (1925). "The History of an Impostor in the Light of Psychoanalytic Knowledge." In, R. Fliess (ed.). *The Psychoanalytic Reader.* Vol. I, pp. 353-368. New York: International Universities Press, 1948.

ADLER, A. (1907-1937). Selections from his writings. In, H. L. ANSBACHER and R. R. ANSBACHER (eds.). *The Individual Psychology of Alfred Adler.* New York: Basic Books, 1956.

ADLER, A. (1914). "Life-lie and Responsibility in Neurosis and Psychosis. A Contribution to Melancholia." In, A. Adler. *The Practice and Theory of Individual Psychology.* Translated by P. RADIN. (1925), pp. 235-245. Paterson, N. J.: Littlefield, Adams, 1959.

ADLER, A. (1925). *The Practice and Theory of Individual Psychology.* Translated by P. RADIN. Paterson, N. J.: Littlefield, Adams, 1959.

ADLER, A. (1931). *What Life Should Mean to You.* New York: Capricorn Books, 1958.

ADLER, M. J. (1937). *What Man Has Made of Man. A Study of the Consequences of Platonism and Positivism in Psychology.* New York: Frederick Ungar, 1957.

ALDRICH, V. C. (1932). Symbolization and similarity. *The Monist,* 42:564.

ALEXANDER, F. (1943). "Fundamental Concepts of Psychosomatic Research: Psychogenesis, Conversion, Specificity." In, F. Alexander, T. M. French, *et al. Studies in Psychosomatic Medicine,* pp. 3-13. New York: Ronald Press, 1948.

ALEXANDER, F. (1950). *Psychosomatic Medicine, Its Principles and Applications.* New York: W. W. Norton.

ALEXANDER, F., FRENCH, T. M., *et al.* (1948). *Studies in Psychosomatic Medicine. An Approach to the Cause and Treatment of Vegetative Disturbances.* New York: Ronald Press.

ALLPORT, G. W. (1955). *Becoming. Basic Considerations for a Psychology of Personality.* New Haven: Yale University Press.

ALTMAN, L. L. (1959). "West" as a symbol of death. *Psychoanalyt. Quart.*, *28*:236.

ANSBACHER, H. L., and ANSBACHER, R. R. (eds.) (1956). *The Individual Psychology of Alfred Adler. A Systematic Presentation in Selections from His Writings.* New York: Basic Books.

ARIETI, S. (1955). *Interpretation of Schizophrenia.* New York: Robert Brunner.

ARIETI, S. (1959). "Schizophrenia." In, S. Arieti *et al.* (eds.). *American Handbook of Psychiatry.* Vol. I, Chapters 23 and 24, pp. 454-507. New York: Basic Books.

ARIETI, S., and METH, J. M. (1959). "Rare, Unclassifiable, Collective, and Exotic Psychotic Syndromes." In, S. Arieti *et al.* (eds.) *American Handbook of Psychiatry.* Vol. I, Chapter 27, pp. 546-563. New York: Basic Books.

AUBERT, V., and MESSINGER, S. L. (1958). The criminal and the sick. *Inquiry, 1*:137.

BAKAN, D. (1959). *Sigmund Freud and The Jewish Mystical Tradition.* Princeton, N. J.: Van Nostrand.

BALINT, M. (1951). "On punishing offenders." In, G. B. Wilbur and W. Muensterberger (eds.). *Psychoanalysis and Culture*, pp. 254-279. New York: International Universities Press.

BALINT, M. (1957). *The Doctor, His Patient and The Illness.* New York: International Universities Press.

BARRETT, W. (1958). *Irrational Man. A Study in Existential Philosophy.* Garden City, N. Y.: Doubleday.

BATESON, G., JACKSON, D. D., HALEY, J., and WEAKLAND, J. (1956). Toward a theory of schizophrenia. *Behavioral Science, 1*:251.

BELLAK, L. (1959). "The Unconscious." In, L. Bellak (cons. ed.). *Conceptual and Methodological Problems in Psychoanalysis. Ann. N. Y. Acad. Sc.*, *76*:1066.

BERNE, E. (1957). Ego states in psychotherapy. *Am. J. Psychotherapy, 11*:293.

BERNE, E. (1958). Transactional analysis: A new and effective method of group therapy. *Amer. J. Psychotherapy, 12*:735.

BIEBER, I. (1953). The meaning of masochism. *Amer. J. Psychotherapy 7:433.*

BINSWANGER, L. (1956). "Existential Analysis and Psychotherapy." In, F. Fromm-Reichmann and J. L. Moreno (eds.). *Progress in Psychotherapy*, pp. 144-148. New York: Grune & Stratton.

BIRDWHISTELL, R. L. (1959). "Contribution of Linguistic-Kinesic Studies to the Understanding of Schizophrenia." In, A. Auerback (ed.). *Schizophrenia. An Integrated Approach*, Chapter 5, pp. 99-124. New York: Ronald Press.

BLACK, M. (1951). "Russell's Philosophy of Language." In, P. A. Schilpp (ed.). *The Philosophy of Bertrand Russell*, pp. 227-256. New York: Tudor.

BLANSHARD, P. (1953). *The Irish and Catholic Power. An American Interpretation.* Boston: Beacon Press.

BLANSHARD, P. (1960). *God and Man in Washington.* Boston: Beacon Press.

BLEULER, E. (1924). *A Textbook of Psychiatry.* Translated by A. A. BRILL. New York: Macmillan, 1944.

BOHANNAN, P. (1954). Translation—A problem in anthropology. *The Listener, 51*:815.

BOWMAN, K. M., and ROSE, M. (1954). Do our medical colleagues know what to expect from psychotherapy? *Am. J. Psychiat., 111*:401.

BRAITHWAITE, R. B. (1953). *Scientific Explanation. A Study of the Function of Theory, Probability and Law in Science.* Based Upon the Tarner Lectures, 1946. Cambridge: Cambridge University Press, 1955.

BRENNER, C. (1955). *An Elementary Textbook of Psychoanalysis.* New York: International Universities Press.

BREUER, J., and FREUD, S. (1893-95). "Studies on Hysteria." In, *The Standard Edition of the Complete Psychological Works of Sigmund Freud.* Vol. II. London: Hogarth Press, 1955.

BRIDGMAN, P. W. (1936). *The Nature of Physical Theory.* Princeton, N. J.: Princeton University Press.

BRIDGMAN, P. W. (1959). *The Way Things Are.* Cambridge, Mass.: Harvard University Press.

BRINTON, C. (1950). *Ideas and Men. The Story of Western Thought.* Englewood Cliffs, N. J.: Prentice-Hall.

BRINTON, C. (1959). *A History of Western Morals.* New York: Harcourt, Brace.

BROWN, R. W. (1956). "Language and categories." In, J. S. Bruner, J. J. Goodnow, and G. A. Austin. *A Study of Thinking*, pp. 247-312. New York: John Wiley & Sons.

BROWN, R. (1958). *Words and Things.* Glencoe, Ill.: The Free Press.

BRUNER, J. S., GOODNOW, J. J., and AUSTIN, G. A. (1956). *A Study of Thinking.* New York: John Wiley & Sons.

BURCHARD, E. M. L. (1960). Mystical and scientific aspects of the psychoanalytic theories of Freud, Adler and Jung. *Amer. J. Psychotherapy, 14:*289.

BURCKHARDT, J. (1868-71). *Force and Freedom.* New York: Meridian Books, 1955.

BURTON, A. (ed.) (1959). *Case Studies in Counseling and Psychotherapy.* Englewood Cliffs, N. J.: Prentice-Hall.

BUTLER, S. (1872). *Erewhon.* Harmondsworth, Middlesex: Penguin Books, 1954.

BUTLER, S. (1903). *The Way of All Flesh.* London: Penguin Books, 1953.

CARSON, G. (1960). *The Roguish World of Doctor Brinkley.* New York: Holt, Rinehart and Winston.

CHAPMAN, J. S.(1957). Peregrinating problem patients: Münchausen's syndrome. *J.A.M.A., 165:*927.

COHEN, E. A. (1954). *Human Behaviour in the Concentration Camp.* Translated by M. H. Braaksma. London: Jonathan Cape.

COLBY, K. M. (1955). *Energy and Structure in Psychoanalysis.* New York: Ronald Press.

COLLIE, J. (1913). *Malingering and Feigned Sickness.* London: Edward Arnold.

CRICHTON, R. (1959a). *The Great Impostor.* New York: Random House.

CRICHTON, R. (1959b). Uproarious trip with the master impostor. *Life*, July 6, 1959, pp. 96-104.

CRITCHLEY, M. (1939). *The Language of Gesture.* London: Edward Arnold.

DAKIN, E. F. (1929). *Mrs. Eddy. The Biography of a Virginal Mind.* New York: Scribner.

DAVIS, K. (1938). Mental hygiene and the class structure. *Psychiatry, 1:*55.

DAWKINS, P. M. (1960). We play to win, they play for fun. *New York Times Magazine*, April 24, 1960, p. 34.

DeBeauvoir, S. (1953). *The Second Sex.* Translated and Edited by H. M. Parshley. New York: Knopf.

DeGrazia, S. (1948). *The Political Community. A Study of Anomie.* Chicago: The University of Chicago Press.

Dennis, N. (1955). *Cards of Identity.* London: Weidenfeld and Nicolson.

Deutsch, F. (1922). Biologie und Psychologie der Krankheitsgenese. *Internat. Ztschr. Psychoanal., 8:*290.

Deutsch, F. (1939). Choice of organ in organ neuroses. *Internat. J. Psycho-Analysis, 20:*252.

Deutsch, F. (ed.) (1959). *On the Mysterious Leap from the Mind to the Body. A Workshop Study on the Theory of Conversion.* New York: International Universities Press.

Deutsch, H. (1942). Some forms of emotional disturbance and their relationship to schizophrenia. *Psychoanalyt. Quart., 11:*301.

Deutsch, H. (1955). The impostor. Contribution to ego psychology of a type of psychopath. *Psychoanalyt. Quart., 24:*483.

Dewey, J. (1922). *Human Nature and Conduct. An Introduction to Social Psychology.* New York: Henry Holt.

Dewey, J. (1938). "Unity of Science as a Social Problem." In, O. Neurath, R. Carnap, and C. Morris (eds.). *International Encyclopedia of Unified Science.* Vol. I, pp. 29-38. Chicago: The University of Chicago Press, 1955.

Dollard, J., and Miller, N. E. (1950). *Personality and Psychotherapy. An Analysis in Terms of Learning, Thinking, and Culture.* New York: McGraw-Hill.

Dostoevsky, F. M. (1861-62). *Memoirs from the House of the Dead.* Translated by Jessie Coulson. New York: Oxford University Press, 1956.

Drucker, P. F. (1949). *The New Society. The Anatomy of the Industrial Order.* New York: Harper.

Einstein, A. (1933). "On the Methods of Theoretical Physics." In, A. Einstein. *The World as I See It,* pp. 30-40. New York: Covici, Friede, 1934.

Einstein, A. (1941). "The Common Language of Science." In, A. Einstein. *Out of My Later Years,* pp. 111-113. New York: Philosophical Library, 1950.

Eissler, K. R. (1951). "Malingering." In, G. B. Wilbur and W. Muensterberger (eds.). *Psychoanalysis and Culture,* pp. 218-253. New York: International Universities Press.

Ellenberger, H. F. (1958). "A Clinical Introduction to Psychiatric Phenomenology and Existential Analysis." In, R. May, E. Angel, and H. F. Ellenberger (eds.). *Existence: A New Dimension in Psychiatry and Psychology,* pp. 92-124. New York: Basic Books.

Engels, F. (1877). *Anti-Dühring.* Selection quoted in G. L. Abernethy (ed.). *The Idea of Equality. An Anthology,* pp. 196-200. Richmond, Va.: John Knox Press, 1959.

Erikson, E. H. (1950). *Childhood and Society.* New York: W. W. Norton.

Erikson, E. H. (1956). The problem of ego identity. *J. Am. Psychoanalyt. A., 4:*56.

Fairbairn, W. R. D. (1952). *Psychoanalytic Studies of the Personality.* London: Travistock Publications.

FAIRBAIRN, W. R. D. (1954). Observations on the nature of hysterical states. *Brit. J. M. Psychol.,* 27:105.

FEIGL, H. and SELLARS, W. (eds.) (1949). *Readings in Philosophical Analysis.* New York: Appleton-Century-Crofts.

FELLOWS, L. (1960). Israeli police halt active hunt for boy, 8, hidden by zealots. *New York Times,* Sunday, May 15, 1960, p. 5.

FENICHEL, O. (1945). *The Psychoanalytic Theory of Neurosis.* New York, W. W. Norton.

FERENCZI, S. (1912). "To Whom Does One Relate One's Dreams?" In, S. Ferenczi. *Further Contributions to the Theory and Technique of Psycho-Analysis,* p. 349. London: Hogarth Press, 1950.

FERENCZI, S. (1913a). "The Symbolism of Bed-linen." In, S. Ferenczi. *Further Contributions to the Theory and Technique of Psycho-Analysis,* p. 359. London: Hogarth Press, 1950.

FERENCZI, S. (1931b). "The Kite as a Symbol of Erection." In, S. Ferenczi. *Further Contributions to the Theory and Technique of Psycho-Analysis,* pp. 359-360. London: Hogarth Press, 1950.

FERENCZI, S. (1914). "Vermin as a Symbol of Pregnancy." In, S. Ferenczi. *Further Contributions to the Theory and Technique of Psycho-Analysis,* p. 361. London: Hogarth Press, 1950.

FERENCZI, S. (1916-17). "Disease or Patho-neuroses." In, S. Ferenczi. *Further Contributions to the Theory and Technique of Psycho-Analysis,* pp. 78-89. London: Hogarth Press, 1950.

FERENCZI, S. (1919). "The Phenomena of Hysterical Materialization." In, S. Ferenczi. *Further Contributions to the Theory and Technique of Psycho-Analysis,* pp. 89-104. London: Hogarth Press, 1950.

FERENCZI, S. (1921). "The Symbolism of the Bridge." In, S. Ferenczi. *Further Contributions to the Theory and Technique of Psycho-Analysis,* pp. 352-356. London: Hogarth Press, 1950.

FERENCZI, S. (1923). " 'Materialization' in Globus Hystericus." In, S. Ferenczi. *Further Contributions to the Theory and Technique of Psycho-Analysis,* pp. 104-105. London: Hogarth Press, 1950.

FEUER, L. S. (ed.) (1959). *Basic Writings on Politics and Philosophy, by Karl Marx and Friedrich Engels.* Garden City, N. Y.: Doubleday.

FIELD, M. G. (1957). *Doctor and Patient in Soviet Russia.* Cambridge, Mass.: Harvard University Press.

FLETCHER, J. (1954). *Morals and Medicine. The Moral Problems of: The Patient's Right to Know the Truth, Contraception, Artificial Insemination, Sterilization, Euthanasia.* Princeton, N. J.: Princeton University Press.

FLIESS, R. (1959). "On the Nature of Human Thought. The Primary and the Secondary Processes as Exemplified by the Dream and other Psychic Productions." In, M. Levitt (ed.). *Readings in Psychoanalytic Psychology.* Chapter 15, pp. 213-220. New York: Appleton-Century-Crofts.

FRANK, P. (1941). *Modern Science and Its Philosophy.* New York: George Braziller, 1955.

FREUD, A. (1936). *The Ego and the Mechanisms of Defense.* New York: International Universities Press, 1946.

FREUD, S. (1893a). "Charcot." In, *Collected Papers*. Vol. I, pp. 9-23. London: Hogarth Press, 1948.

FREUD, S. (1893b). "Some Points in a Comparative Study of Organic and Hysterical Paralyses." In, *Collected Papers*. Vol. I, pp. 42-58. London: Hogarth Press, 1948.

FREUD, S. (1900). "The Interpretation of Dreams" (I & II). In, *The Standard Edition of the Complete Psychological Works of Sigmund Freud*. Vols. IV and V, pp. 1-621. London: Hogarth Press, 1953.

FREUD, S. (1901). "On Dreams." In, *The Standard Edition of the Complete Psychological Works of Sigmund Freud*, Vol. V, pp. 631-686. London: Hogarth Press, 1953. (Permission to reprint granted by W. W. Norton.)

FREUD, S. (1905a). "Fragment of an Analysis of a Case of Hysteria." In, *The Standard Edition of the Complete Psychological Works of Sigmund Freud*. Vol. VII, pp. 1-122. London: Hogarth Press, 1953.

FREUD, S. (1905b). "Three Essays on the Theory of Sexuality." In, *The Standard Edition of the Complete Psychological Works of Sigmund Freud*. Vol. VII, pp. 123-245. London: Hogarth Press, 1953.

FREUD, S. (1905c). "Wit and Its Relation to the Unconscious." In, *The Basic Writings of Sigmund Freud*, pp. 633-803. Translated and edited, with an Introduction by A. A. Brill. New York: Modern Library, 1938.

FREUD, S. (1909). "General Remarks on Hysterical Attacks." In, *Collected Papers*. Vol. I, pp. 100-104. London: Hogarth Press, 1948.

FREUD, S. (1910a). "Five Lectures on Psycho-Analysis." In, *The Standard Edition of the Complete Psychological Works of Sigmund Freud*. Vol. XI, pp. 1-55. London: Hogarth Press, 1957.

FREUD, S. (1910b). "The Antithetical Sense of Primal Words. A Review of a Pamphlet by Karl Abel, *Über den Gegensinn der Urworte* (1884)." In, *Collected Papers*. Vol. IV, pp. 184-191. London: Hogarth Press, 1948.

FREUD, S. (1913). "Further Recommendations in the Technique of Psycho-Analysis." In, *Collected Papers*. Vol. II, pp. 342-365. London: Hogarth Press, 1948.

FREUD, S. (1914). "On the History of the Psycho-Analytic Movement." In, *Collected Papers*. Vol. I, pp. 287-359. London: Hogarth Press, 1948.

FREUD, S. (1915). "The Unconscious." In, *The Standard Edition of the Complete Psychological Works of Sigmund Freud*. Vol. XIV, pp. 159-204. London: Hogarth Press, 1957.

FREUD, S. (1916-17). *A General Introduction to Psychoanalysis*. Garden City, N. Y.: Garden City, 1943.

FREUD, S. (1920). "Memorandum on the Electrical Treatment of War Neurotics." In, *The Standard Edition of the Complete Psychological Works of Sigmund Freud*. Vol. XVII, pp. 211-215. London: Hogarth Press, 1955.

FREUD, S. (1927). *The Future of an Illusion*. New York: Liveright, 1949.

FREUD, S. (1928). "Dostoevsky and Parricide." In, *Collected Papers*. Vol. V, pp. 222-242. London: Hogarth Press, 1950.

FREUD, S. (1930). *Civilization and Its Discontents*. London: Hogarth Press, 1946.

FREUD, S. (1932). *New Introductory Lectures on Psycho-Analysis*. New York: W. W. Norton, 1933.

FREUD, S. (1940). *An Outline of Psychoanalysis*. New York: W. W. Norton.

FROMM, E. (1941). *Escape from Freedom.* New York: Rinehart.

FROMM, E. (1947). *Man for Himself. An Inquiry into the Psychology of Ethics.* New York: Rinehart.

FROMM, E. (1951). *The Forgotten Language. An Introduction to the Understanding of Dreams, Fairy Tales and Myths.* New York: Rinehart.

FROMM, E. (1955). *The Sane Society.* New York: Rinehart.

FROMM, E. (1957). "Symbolic Language of Dreams." In, R. N. Anshen (ed.). *Language: An Enquiry into its Meaning and Function.* Chapter XII, pp. 188-200. New York: Harper.

FROMM, E. (1959). *Sigmund Freud's Mission: An Analysis of his Personality and Influence.* New York: Harper.

GALBRAITH, J. K. (1958). *The Affluent Society.* Boston: Houghton Mifflin.

GALLINEK, A. (1942). Psychogenic disorders and the civilization of the Middle Ages. *Am. J. Psychiat., 99:*42.

GANSER, S. (1898). Über einen eigenartigen Hysterischen Dämmerzustand. *Arch. Psychiat., 30:*633.

GITELSON, M. (1952). The emotional position of the analyst in the psychoanalytic situation. *Internat. J. Psycho-Analysis, 33:*1.

GLOVER, E. (1949). *Psychoanalysis.* London: Staples Press.

GOFFMAN, E. (1959). *The Presentation of Self in Everday Life.* Garden City, N. Y.: Doubleday.

GOLDFARB, A. I. (1955). Psychotherapy of aged persons. IV. One aspect of the psychodynamics of the therapeutic situation with aged patients. *Psychoanalyt. Rev., 42:*180.

GOLDSTEIN, K. (1948). *Language and Language Disturbances.* New York: Grune and Stratton.

GOLDSTEIN, K. (1951). *Human Nature in the Light of Psychopathology.* Cambridge, Mass.: Harvard University Press.

GOLDSTEIN, K., and SCHEERER, M. (1941). *Abstract and Concrete Behavior: An Experimental Study with Special Tests.* Psychological Monographs, Vol. 53, No. 2.

GORER, G. (1948). *The American People. A Study in National Character.* New York: W. W. Norton.

GORKY, M. (1902). *The Lower Depths. A Drama in Four Acts.* English Translation by Jenny Covan. New York: Brentanos, 1923. The line quoted as a motto is reprinted in a better translation in, C. MORLEY, and L. D. EVERETT (eds.) *Familiar Quotations,* p. 1201. Boston: Little, Brown.

GOULDNER, A. W. (1960). The norm of reciprocity: A preliminary statement. *Am. Sociol. Rev., 25:*161.

GREENACRE, P. (1959). Certain technical problems in the transference relationship. *J. Am. Psychoanalyt. A., 7:*484.

GREENSON, R. (1954a). Problems of identification: Introduction. *J. Am. Psychoanalyt. A., 2:*197.

GREENSON, R. (1954b). The struggle against identification. *J. Am. Psychoanalyt. A., 2:*200.

GREGORY, R. L. (1953). On physical model explanations in psychology. *Brit. J. Phil. Sc., 4:*192.

GRINKER, R. R. (1959). A transactional model for psychotherapy. *A.M.A. Arch. Gen. Psychiat.,* 1:132.

GRODDECK, G. (1927). *The Book of the It: Psychoanalytic Letters to a Friend.* London: C. W. Daniel, 1935.

GRODDECK, G. (1934). *The World of Man, As Reflected in Art, in Words and in Disease.* London: C. W. Daniel.

GUILLAIN, G. (1959). *J.-M. Charcot, 1825-1893. His Life—His Work.* Edited and Translated by Pearce Bailey. New York: Paul B. Hoeber.

HALL, C. S. (1953). A cognitive theory of dream symbols. *J. Gen. Psychol.,* 48:169.

HARDIN, G. (1956). The meaninglessness of the word protoplasm. *Scient. Month.,* 82:112.

HARDIN, G. (1959). *Nature and Man's Fate.* New York: Rinehart.

HARLOW, H. F., and ZIMMERMANN, R. R. (1959). Affectional responses in the infant monkey. *Science,* 130:421.

HAYEK, F. A. (1960). *The Constitution of Liberty.* Chicago: The University of Chicago Press.

HENDERSON, D., and GILLESPIE, R. D. (1950). *A Textbook of Psychiatry.* Seventh Edition. London: Oxford University Press.

HILGARD, E. R. (1956). *Theories of Learning.* Second Edition. New York: Appleton-Century-Crofts.

HOLLINGSHEAD, A. B. (1955). "Social Behavior and Social Rules." In, I. Galdston (ed.). *Ministry and Medicine in Human Relations,* pp. 71-80. New York: International Universities Press.

HOLLINGSHEAD, A. B., and REDLICH, F. C. (1958). *Social Class and Mental Illness. A Community Study.* New York: John Wiley.

HORNEY, K. (1939). *New Ways in Psychoanalysis.* New York: W. W. Norton.

HORNEY, K. (1950). *Neurosis and Human Growth.* New York: W. W. Norton.

HUIZINGA, J. (1927). *The Waning of the Middle Ages.* New York: Doubleday, 1956.

HUXLEY, A. (1952). *The Devils of Loudun.* New York: Harper.

INKELES, A., and BAUER, R. A. (1959). *The Soviet Citizen. Daily Life in a Totalitarian Society.* Cambridge, Mass.: Harvard University Press.

JAKOBSON, R. (1957). "The Cardinal Dichotomy in Language." In, R. N. Anshen (ed.). *Language: An Enquiry into its Meaning and Function.* Chap. IX, pp. 155-173. New York: Harper.

JESPERSON, O. (1905). *Growth and Structure of the English Language.* Ninth Edition. Garden City, N. Y.: Doubleday, 1955.

JOHNSON, D. L. (1960). The moral judgment of schizophrenics. *J. Nerv. & Ment. Dis.,* 130:278.

JONES, E. (1953, 1955, 1957). *The Life and Work of Sigmund Freud.* Vols. 1, 2, 3. New York: Basic Books.

JUNG, C. G. (1940). *The Integration of the Personality.* Translated by Stanley Dell. London: Routledge and Kegan Paul, 1952.

JUNG, C. G. (1945). *Psychological Reflections. An Anthology of the Writings of C. G. Jung.* Selected and edited by Jolande Jacobi. New York: Pantheon (Bollingen Series XXXI), 1953.

JUNG, C. G. (1952). *Symbols of Transformation. An Analysis of the Prelude to a Case of Schizophrenia.* Translated by R. F. C. HULL. New York: Pantheon (Bollingen Series XX), 1956.

KANZER, M. (1955). The communicative function of the dream. *Internat. J. Psycho-Analysis, 36*:260.

KARDINER, A. (1939). *The Individual and His Society. The Psychodynamic of Primitive Social Organization.* With a Foreword and Two Ethnological Reports by Ralph Linton. New York: Columbia University Press, 1949.

KASANIN, J. S. (1944). "The Disturbance of Conceptual Thinking in Schizophrenia." In, J. S. Kasanin (ed.). *Language and Thought in Schizophrenia, Collected Papers,* pp. 41-49. Berkeley and Los Angeles: University of California Press.

KAUFMANN, W. (1956). "Existentialism from Dostoevsky to Sartre." In, *Existentialism from Dostoevsky to Sartre,* pp. 11-51. Edited, with an Introduction, Prefaces, and New Translations by W. KAUFMANN. New York: Meridian, 1960.

KEMENY, J. G. (1959). *A Philosopher Looks at Science.* Princeton, N. J.: Van Nostrand.

KINBERG, O. (1958). Swedish psychiatry. *Am. J. Psychiat., 115*:505.

KLUCKHOHN, C. (1949). *Mirror For Man. A Survey of Human Behavior and Social Attitudes.* New York: Premier Books, 1959.

KNIGHT, R. P. (1953). Borderline states. *Bull. Menninger Clinic, 17*:1.

KRÄMER, H., and SPRENGER, J. (1486). *Malleus Malleficarum.* Translated, with an Introduction, Bibliography and Notes by the Rev. Montague Summers. London: Pushkin Press, 1948.

KROEBER, A. L. (1954). *Anthropology Today. An Encyclopedic Inventory.* Chicago: The University of Chicago Press.

KUHN, H. (1950). "Existentialism." In, V. Ferm (ed.). *A History of Philosophical Systems.* Chapter 32, pp. 405-417. New York: Philosophical Library.

LANGER, S. K. (1942). *Philosophy in a New Key.* Cambridge, Mass.: Harvard University Press. (Page references to Mentor Books edition, 1953.)

LAPIERRE, R. (1959). *The Freudian Ethic.* New York: Duell, Sloan and Pearce.

LAUGHLIN, H. P. (1960). European psychiatry: England, Denmark, Italy, Greece, Spain and Turkey. *Am. J. Psychiat., 116*:769.

LEBENSOHN, Z. (1958). Impressions of Soviet psychiatry. *A.M.A. Arch. Neurol. & Psychiat., 80*:735.

LECKY, W. E. H. (1894). *History of European Morals, From Augustus to Charlemagne.* 2 Vols. Third Edition, Revised. New York: Appleton.

LEWINSOHN, R. (1958). *A History of Sexual Customs.* Translated by Alexander Mayce. New York: Harper.

LEWIS, J. (1926). *The Bible Unmasked.* New York: Freethought Press, 1948.

LIFTON, R. J. (1956). "Thought reform" of Western civilians in Chinese communist prisons. *Psychiatry, 19*:173.

LINCOLN, A. (1858). From a letter. In, C. Morley and L. D. Everett (eds.). *Familiar Quotations,* p. 455. Boston: Little, Brown, 1951.

LINSKY, L. (ed.) (1952). *Semantics and the Philosophy of Language. A Collection of Readings.* Urbana, Ill.: University of Illinois Press.

LINTON, R. (1945). *The Cultural Background of Personality.* New York: Appleton-Century.

LINTON, R. (1957). *The Tree of Culture.* New York: Knopf.

MacINTYRE, A. C. (1958). *The Unconscious. A Conceptual Analysis.* London: Routledge & Kegan Paul.

M'KENDRICK, A. (1912). *Malingering and Its Detection. Under the Workmen's Compensation and Other Acts.* Edinburgh: E. & S. Livingstone.

MACH, E. (1885). *The Analysis of Sensations and the Relation of the Physical to the Psychical.* Translated by C. M. Williams. Revised and supplemented from the Fifth German Edition by Sydney Waterlow, with a new Introduction by Thomas S. Szasz. New York: Dover Publications, 1959.

MANN, T. (1954). *Confessions of Felix Krull: Confidence Man.* Translated by DENVER LINDLEY. New York: Knopf, 1955.

MARX, K. (1844). "A Critique of the Hegelian Philosophy of Right." In, K. Marx. *Selected Essays,* pp. 11-39. Translated by H. J. STENNING. New York: International Publishers, 1926.

MARX, K. (1890). *Capital. A Critique of Political Economy. The Process of Capitalist Production.* Translated from the Third German Edition by SAMUEL MOORE and EDWARD AVELING. Edited by Frederick Engels. Revised and Amplified According to the Fourth German Edition by Ernest Untermann. New York: Modern Library.

MAURER, D. W. (1940). *The Big Con, The Story of the Confidence Man and the Confidence Game.* Indianapolis: Bobbs-Merrill.

MAY, R. (1958). "The Origins and Significance of the Existential Movement in Psychology." In, R. May, E. Angel, and H. F. Ellenberger (eds.). *Existence: A New Dimension in Psychiatry and Psychology,* Chapter I, pp. 3-36. New York: Basic Books.

MAY, R., ANGEL, E., and ELLENBERGER, H. F. (eds.) (1958). *Existence: A New Dimension in Psychiatry and Psychology.* New York: Basic Books.

MEAD, G. H. (1934). *Mind, Self and Society. From the Standpoint of a Social Behaviorist.* Edited, with an Introduction, by CHARLES W. MORRIS. Chicago: The University of Chicago Press.

MEAD, G. H. (1936). *Movements of Thought in the Nineteenth Century.* Chicago: The University of Chicago Press.

MEAD, G. H. (1938). *The Philosophy of the Act.* Chicago: The University of Chicago Press.

MEERLOO, J. A. M. (1955). Medication into submission, the danger of therapeutic coercion. *J. Nerv. & Ment. Dis.,* 122:353.

MEERLOO, J. A. M. (1956). *The Rape of the Mind. The Psychology of Thought Control.* New York: World.

MENNINGER, K. A. (1938). *Man Against Himself.* New York: Harcourt, Brace.

MENNINGER, K. A. (1959). Hope. (The Academic Lecture.) *Am. J. Psychiat.,* 116:481.

MERTON, R. K. (1957a). *Social Theory and Social Structure.* Revised and enlarged edition. Glencoe, Ill.: The Free Press.

MERTON, R. K. (1957b). The role set. *Brit. J. Sociol.,* 8:106.

MILLER, N. E., and DOLLARD, J. (1941). *Social Learning and Imitation.* New Haven: Yale University Press.

MISES, R. von (1951). *Positivism. A Study in Human Understanding.* New York: George Braziller, 1956.

MONTAGU, A. (1953). *The Natural Superiority of Women.* New York: Macmillan.

MORLEY, C., and EVERETT, L. D. (eds.) (1951). *Familiar Quotations.* A Collection of Passages, Phrases, and Proverbs, traced to their sources in ancient and modern literature by JOHN BARTLETT. Twelfth Edition, Revised and Enlarged. Boston: Little, Brown.

MORRIS, C. W. (1946). *Signs, Language and Behavior.* New York: Prentice-Hall.

MORRIS, C. W. (1955). "Foundations of the Theory of Signs." In, O. Neurath, R. Carnap, and C. W. Morris (eds.). *International Encyclopedia of Unified Science.* Vol. I, pp. 77-137. Chicago: The University of Chicago Press.

MULLER, H. J. (1959). One hundred years without Darwinism are enough. *The Humanist, 19*:139.

MUNTHE, A. (1930). *The Story of San Michele.* New York: Dutton.

MURPHY, G. (1947). *Personality: A Bio-Social Approach to Origins and Structure.* New York: Harper.

MYRDAL, G., with the assistance of STERNER, R. and ROSE, A. (1944). *An American Dilemma. The Negro Problem and Modern Democracy.* New York: Harper.

NADEL, S. F. (1954). *Nupe Religion.* Glencoe, Ill.: The Free Press.

NARAYAN, R. K. (1959). New role for India's "holy men." *New York Times Magazine,* September 6, 1959, p. 9.

NEIMAN, L. J., and HUGHES, J. W. (1951). The problem of the concept of role— A re-survey of the literature. *Social Forces, 30*:141.

NEWCOMB, T. M. (1951). *Social Psychology.* New York: Dryden Press.

NIEBUHR, R. (1958). Thinkers and thought. *The New York Times Book Review,* July 13, 1958, p. 4.

NIETZSCHE, F. (1888). "The Twilight of the Idols; Or How to Philosophize with a Hammer." In, *The Works of Friedrich Nietzsche.* Vol. XI, pp. 198-199. New York: Macmillan, 1896.

NOGUCHI, H., and MOORE, J. W. (1913). A demonstration of Treponema Pallidum in the brain in cases of general paralysis. *J. Exper. Med., 17*:232.

NOYES, A. P. (1956). *Modern Clinical Psychiatry.* Fourth Edition. Philadelphia: W. B. Saunders.

OGDEN, C. K., and RICHARDS, I. A. (1930). *The Meaning of Meaning. A Study of the Influence of Language upon Thought and of the Science of Symbolism.* With Supplementary Essays by B. Malinowski and F. G. Crookshank. Third Revised Edition. New York: Harcourt, Brace.

OPPENHEIMER, J. R. (1957). Impossible choices. *Science, 125*:1021.

OSTOW, M. (1958). Biological basis of religious symbolism. *Internat. Record of Med., 171*:709.

PAINE, T. (1794). *The Age of Reason, Being An Investigation of True and Fabulous Theology.* New York: The Thomas Paine Foundation.

PARRINDER, G. (1958). *Witchcraft.* Harmondsworth, Middlesex: Penguin Books.

PARSONS, T. (1952). *The Social System.* Glencoe, Ill.: The Free Press.

PARSONS, T. (1958a). "Definitions of Health and Illness in the Light of American Values and Social Structure." In, E. G. Jaco (ed.). *Patients, Physicians and Illness.* Chapter 20, pp. 165-187. Glencoe, Ill.: The Free Press.

PARSONS, T. (1958b). Social structure and the development of the personality. Freud's contribution to the integration of psychology and sociology. *Psychiatry, 21*:321.

PAULING, L. (1956). The molecular basis of genetics. *Am. J. Psychiat., 113*:492.

PEPPER, S. C. (1958). *The Sources of Value.* Berkeley and Los Angeles: University of California Press.

PERRY, R. B. (1954). *Realms of Value. A Critique of Human Civilization.* Cambridge, Mass.: Harvard University Press.

PETERS, R. S. (1958). *The Concept of Motivation.* London: Routledge & Kegan Paul.

PIAGET, J. (1928). *Judgment and Reasoning in the Child.* Translated by MARJORIE WARDEN. London: Routledge & Kegan Paul, 1952.

PIAGET, J. (1932). *The Moral Judgment of the Child.* Translated by MARJORIE GABAIN. Glencoe, Ill.: The Free Press.

PIAGET, J. (1951). *Play, Dreams and Imitation in Childhood.* Translated by C. GATTEGNO and F. M. HODGSON. London: William Heinemann.

PIAGET, J. (1952a). *The Child's Conception of Number.* Translated by C. GATTEGNO and F. M. HODGSON. London: Routledge & Kegan Paul.

PIAGET, J. (1952b). *The Origins of Intelligence in Children.* Translated by MARGARET COOK. New York: International Universities Press.

PIAGET, J. (1953). *Logic and Psychology.* With an Introduction on Piaget's Logic by W. MAYS. Manchester: The University Press.

PIAGET, J. (1954). *The Construction of Reality in the Child.* Translated by MARGARET COOK. New York: Basic Books.

PIERS, G., and SINGER, M. G. (1953). *Shame and Guilt. A Psychoanalytic and a Cultural Study.* Springfield, Ill.: Charles C Thomas.

PIRANDELLO, L. (1919). "The Rules of the Game." Translated by ROBERT RIETTY. In, L. Pirandello: *Three Plays.* Introduced and Edited by E. MARTIN BROWNE. Harmondsworth, Middlesex: Penguin Books, 1959.

POLANYI, M. (1958a). *Personal Knowledge.* Chicago: The University of Chicago Press.

POLANYI, M. (1958b). *The Study of Man.* The Lindsay Memorial Lectures. Chicago: The University of Chicago Press, 1959.

POPPER, K. R. (1944-45). *The Poverty of Historicism.* Boston: Beacon Press, 1957.

POPPER, K. R. (1945). *The Open Society and Its Enemies.* Princeton, N. J.: Princeton University Press, 1950.

POPPER, K. R. (1957). "Philosophy of Science: A Personal Report." In, C. A. Mace (ed.). *British Philosophy in the Mid-Century,* pp. 153-191. New York: Macmillan.

PUMPIAN-MINDLIN, E. (1959). "Propositions Concerning Energetic-Economic Aspects of Libido Theory: Conceptual Models of Psychic Energy and Structure in Psychoanalysis." In, L. Bellak (cons. ed.). *Conceptual and Methodological Problems of Psychoanalysis. Ann. N. Y. Acad. Sc.,* 76:1038.

PURTELL, J. J., ROBINS, E., and COHEN, M. E. (1951). Observations on clinical aspects of hysteria. *J.A.M.A., 146*:902.

RAPOPORT, A. (1954). *Operational Philosophy: Integrating Knowledge and Action.* New York: Harper.

RAVEN, C. E. (1959). *Science, Medicine and Morals. A Survey and a Suggestion.* New York: Harper.

REICHARD, S. (1956). A re-examination of "Studies on Hysteria." *Psychoanalyt. Quart., 25:155.*

REICHENBACH, H. (1947). *Elements of Symbolic Logic.* New York: Macmillan.

REICHENBACH, H. (1951). *The Rise of Scientific Philosophy.* Berkeley: University of California Press.

RIEFF, P. (1959). *Freud, The Mind of the Moralist.* New York: Viking.

RIESE, W. (1953). *The Conception of Disease: Its History, Its Versions and Its Nature.* New York: Philosophical Library.

ROBINS, E., PURTELL, J. J., and COHEN, M. E. (1952). "Hysteria" in men. *New Eng. J. Med., 246:677.*

ROGERS, C. R. (1942). *Counseling and Psychotherapy. Newer Concepts in Practice.* Boston: Houghton Mifflin.

ROGERS, C. R. (1951). *Client-Centered Therapy: Its Current Practice, Implications, and Theory.* Boston: Houghton Mifflin.

ROHEIM, G. (1943). *The Origin and Function of Culture.* Nervous and Mental Disease Monograph No. 69. New York: Nervous and Mental Disease Monographs.

ROSEN, J. N. (1953). *Direct Analysis: Selected Papers.* New York: Grune & Stratton.

ROSTOW, W. W. (1952). *The Dynamics of Soviet Society.* New York: Mentor Books, 1954.

RUESCH, J. (1957). *Disturbed Communication. The Clinical Assessment of Normal and Pathological Communicative Behavior.* New York: W. W. Norton.

RUESCH, J. (1959). "General Theory of Communication in Psychiatry." In, S. Arieti *et al.* (eds.). *American Handbook of Psychiatry.* Vol. I, Chapter 45, pp. 895-908. New York: Basic Books.

RUESCH, J., and BATESON, G. (1951). *Communication. The Social Matrix of Psychiatry.* New York: W. W. Norton.

RUESCH, J., and KEES, W. (1956). *Nonverbal Communication.* Berkeley and Los Angeles: University of California Press.

RUSSELL, B. (1908). "Mathematical Logic as Based on the Theory of Types." In, B. Russell. *Logic and Knowledge. Essays, 1901-1950,* pp. 59-102. Edited by R. C. MARSH. New York: Macmillan, 1956.

RUSSELL, B. (1918). "The Philosophy of Logical Atomism." In, B. Russell. *Logic and Knowledge. Essays, 1901-1950,* pp. 177-281. Edited by R. C. MARSH. New York: Macmillan, 1956.

RUSSELL, B. (1922). Introduction to L. Wittgenstein's *Tractatus Logico-Philosophicus,* pp. 7-8. London: Routledᵉ & Kegan Paul.

RUSSELL, B. (1945). *A History of Western Philosophy.* New York: Simon and Schuster.

RUSSELL, B. (1948). *Human Knowledge: Its Scope and Limits.* New York: Simon and Schuster.

RUSSELL, B. (1953). "Satan in the Suburbs, or Horrors Manufactured Here." In, B. Russell. *Satan in the Suburbs and Other Stories,* pp. 1-59. New York: Simon and Schuster.

RUSSELL, B. (1954). "A Psychoanalyst's Nightmare: Adjustment—A Fugue." In, B. Russell. *Nightmares of Eminent Persons*, pp. 21-30. London: Bodley Head.

RUSSELL, B. (1955). "On the Importance of Logical Form." In, O. Neurath, R. Carnap, and C. Morris (eds.). *International Encyclopedia of Unified Science*. Vol. I, pp. 39-41. Chicago: University of Chicago Press.

RYLE, G. (1949). *The Concept of Mind*. London: Hutchinson's University Library.

RYLE, G. (1957). "The Theory of Meaning." In, C. A. Mace (ed.). *British Philosophy in the Mid-Century*, pp. 237-264. New York: Macmillan.

SAPIR, E. (1921). *Language. An Introduction to the Study of Speech*. New York: Harcourt, Brace.

SARBIN, T. R. (1943). The concept of role-taking. *Sociometry, 6*:273.

SARBIN, T. R. (1950). Contributions to role-taking theory. I. Hypnotic behavior. *Psychol. Rev., 57*:255

SARBIN, T. R. (1954). "Role Theory." In, G. Lindzey (ed.). *Handbook of Social Psychology*. Vol. I, Chapter 6, pp. 223-258. Cambridge, Mass.: Addison-Wesley.

SAUL, L. J. (1935). "A Note on the Psychogenesis of Organic Symptoms." In, F. Alexander, T. M. French, *et al. Studies in Psychosomatic Medicine*, pp. 85-90. New York: Ronald Press, 1948.

SCHACHTEL, E. G. (1959). *Metamorphosis. On the Development of Affect, Perception, Attention, and Memory*. New York: Basic Books.

SCHEIN, E. H. (1951). The Chinese indoctrination program for prisoners of war. *Psychiatry, 14*:171.

SCHILLER, J. C. F. (1798). "Der Ring des Polykrates." In, Schiller. *Werke*. Vol. I, pp. 176-179. 12 Vols. Mit Einleitung von Gotthilf Lachenmaier. Berlin-Leipzig: Th. Knaur Nacht, 1908.

SCHLAUCH, M. (1942). *The Gift of Language*. New York: Dover, 1955.

SCHLICK, M. (1932). "Causality in Everyday Life and in Recent Science." In, H. Feigl and W. Sellars (eds.). *Readings in Philosophical Analysis*, pp. 515-533. New York: Appleton-Century-Crofts, 1949.

SCHLICK, M. (1935). "On the Relation Between Psychological and Physical Concepts." In, H. Feigl and W. Sellars (eds.). *Readings in Philosophical Analysis*, pp. 393-407. New York: Appleton-Century-Crofts, 1949.

SCHMIDEBERG, M. (1959). "The Borderline Patient." In, S. Arieti *et al.* (eds.). *American Handbook of Psychiatry*. Vol. I, Chapter 21, pp. 398-416. New York: Basic Books.

SCRIVEN, M. (1956). "A Possible Distinction Between Traditional Scientific Disciplines and the Study of Human Behavior." In, H. Feigl and M. Scriven (eds.). *Minnesota Studies in the Philosophy of Science*. Vol. 1, pp. 330-339. Minneapolis: University of Minnesota Press.

SELLARS, W. (1954). Some reflections on language games. *Philosophy of Science, 21*:204.

SELLARS, W., and HOSPERS, J. (eds.) (1952). *Readings in Ethical Theory*. New York: Appleton-Century-Crofts.

SIGERIST, H. E. (1951). "Primitive and Archaic Medicine." In, *A History of Medicine*. Vol. I. New York: Oxford University Press.

SIGERIST, H. E. (1960). *Henry Sigerist on the Sociology of Medicine.* Edited by M. I. Roemer. Foreword by J. M. MACKINTOSH. New York: MD Publications.

SILVERBERG, W. V. (1952). *Childhood Experience and Personal Destiny. A Psychoanalytic Theory of Neurosis.* New York: Springer.

SOROKIN, P. A., and LUNDEN, W. A. (1959). *Power and Morality. Who Shall Guard the Guardians?* Boston: Porter Sargent.

SPENCER, H. (1884). *The Man Versus The State.* Boston: Beacon Press, 1950.

SPIEGEL, J. (1954). The social roles of doctor and patient in psychoanalysis and psychotherapy. *Psychiatry, 17:369.*

SPIEGEL, R. (1959). "Specific Problems of Communication in Psychiatric Conditions." In, S. Arieti *et al.* (eds.). *American Handbook of Psychiatry.* Vol. I, Chapter 46, pp. 909-949. New York: Basic Books.

STEIN, M. R., VIDICH, A. J., and WHITE, D. M. (eds.) (1960). *Identity and Anxiety. Survival of the Person in Mass Society.* Glencoe, Ill.: The Free Press.

STEVENSON, A. (1959). Adlai Stevenson on psychiatry in U.S.S.R. *Am. J. Psychotherapy, 13:530.*

STIERLIN, H. (1958). Contrasting attitudes toward the psychoses in Europe and in the United States. *Psychiatry, 21:141.*

STRACHEY, J. (1934). The nature of the therapeutic action of psycho-analysis. *Internat. J. Psycho-Analysis, 15:127.*

SULLIVAN, H. S. (1947). *Conceptions of Modern Psychiatry.* The First William Alanson White Memorial Lecture. Washington, D.C.: The William Alanson White Psychiatric Foundation.

SULLIVAN, H. S. (1953). *The Interpersonal Theory of Psychiatry.* Edited by H. S. PERRY and M. L. GAWEL. With an Introduction by M. B. COHEN. New York: W. W. Norton.

SULLIVAN, H. S. (1956). *Clinical Studies in Psychiatry.* Edited by H. S. PERRY, M. L. GAWEL, and M. GIBBON. With a Foreword by D. M. BULLARD. New York: W. W. Norton.

SULLOWAY, A. W. (1959). *Birth Control and Catholic Doctrine.* With an Introduction by ALDOUS HUXLEY. Boston: Beacon Press.

SZASZ, T. S. (1956a). Some observations on the relationship between psychiatry and the law. *A.M.A. Arch. Neurol. & Psychiat., 75:297.*

SZASZ, T. S. (1956b). Malingering: "Diagnosis" or social condemnation? Analysis of the meaning of "diagnosis" in the light of some interrelations of social structure, value judgment, and the physician's role. *A.M.A. Arch. Neurol. & Psychiat., 76:432.*

SZASZ, T. S. (1956c). On the experiences of the analyst in the psychoanalytic situation. A contribution to the theory of psychoanalytic treatment. *J. Am. Psychoanalyt. A., 4:197.*

SZASZ, T. S. (1957a). *Pain and Pleasure. A Study of Bodily Feelings.* New York: Basic Books.

SZASZ, T. S. (1957b). On the theory of psycho-analytic treatment. Internat. J. Psycho-Analysis, *38:166.*

SZASZ, T. S. (1957c). A contribution to the psychology of schizophrenia. *A.M.A. Arch. Neurol. & Psychiat., 77:420.*

Szasz, T. S. (1957d). Commitment of the mentally ill: "Treatment" or social restraint? *J. Nerv. & Ment. Dis., 125:293.*

Szasz, T. S. (1957e). Psychiatric expert testimony: Its covert meaning and social function. *Psychiatry, 20:313.*

Szasz, T. S. (1958a). Psychoanalysis as method and as theory. *Psychoanalyt. Quart., 27:89.*

Szasz, T. S. (1958b). Psychiatry, ethics, and the criminal law. *Columbia Law Review, 58:183.*

Szasz, T. S. (1958c). Scientific method and social role in medicine and psychiatry. *A.M.A. Arch. Int. Med., 101:228.*

Szasz, T. S. (1958d). Men and machines. *Brit. J. Phil. Sci., 8:310.*

Szasz, T. S. (1958e). Psycho-analytic training: A sociopsychological analysis of its history and present status. *Internat. J. Psycho-Analysis, 39:598.*

Szasz, T. S. (1958f). Politics and mental health: Some remarks apropos of the case of Mr. Ezra Pound. *Am. J. Psychiat. 115:508.*

Szasz, T. S. (1959a). "A Critical Analysis of Some Aspects of the Libido Theory: The Concepts of Libidinal Zones, Aims, and Modes of Gratification." In, L. Bellak (cons. ed.). *Conceptual and Methodological Problems in Psychoanalysis. Ann. N. Y. Acad. Sc., 76:975.*

Szasz, T. S. (1959b). The classification of "mental illness." A situational analysis of psychiatric operations. *Psychiat. Quart., 33:77.*

Szasz, T. S. (1959c). "Recollections of a Psychoanalytic Psychotherapy: The Case of the 'Prisoner K.'" In, A. Burton (ed.). *Case Studies in Counseling and Psychotherapy.* Chapter 4, pp. 75-110. Englewood Cliffs, N. J.: Prentice-Hall.

Szasz, T. S. (1959b). "Psychoanalysis and Medicine." In, M. Levitt (ed.). *Readings in Psychoanalytic Psychology.* Chapter 24, pp. 355-374. New York: Appleton-Century-Crofts.

Szasz, T. S. (1959e). "Language and Pain." In, S. Arieti et al. (eds.). *American Handbook of Psychiatry.* Vol. I, Chapter 49, pp. 982-999. New York: Basic Books.

Szasz, T. S. (1959f). The communication of distress between child and parent. *Brit. J. Med. Psychol., 32:161.*

Szasz, T. S. (1959g). Psychiatry, psychotherapy, and psychology. *A.M.A. Arch. Gen. Psychiat., 1:455.*

Szasz, T. S. (1960a). Mach and psychoanalysis. *J. Nerv. & Ment. Dis., 130:6.*

Szasz, T. S. (1960b). The myth of mental illness. *American Psychologist, 15:113.*

Szasz, T. S. (1960c). Moral conflict and psychiatry. *Yale Rev., 49:555.*

Szasz, T. S. (1960d). Civil liberties and the mentally ill. *Cleveland-Marshall Law Rev., 9:399.*

Szasz, T. S., and Hollender, M. H. (1956). A contribution to the philosophy of medicine. The basic models of the doctor-patient relationship. *A.M.A. Arch. Int. Med., 97:585.*

Szasz, T. S., Knoff, W. F., and Hollender, M. H. (1958). The doctor-patient relationship in its historical context. *Am. J. Psychiat., 115:522.*

Tarski, A. (1944). The semantic conception of truth. *Philosophy and Phenomenological Research, 4:341.*

TAUBER, E. S., and GREEN, M. R. (1959). *Prelogical Experience. An Inquiry into Dreams and Other Creative Processes.* New York: Basic Books.

VAIHINGER, H. (1911). *The Philosophy of "As If." A System of the Theoretical, Practical, and Religious Fictions of Mankind.* Translated by C. K. OGDEN. London: Routledge & Kegan Paul, 1952.

VON DOMARUS, E. (1944). "The Specific Laws of Logic in Schizophrenia." In, J. S. Kasanin (ed.). *Language and Thought in Schizophrenia,* pp. 104-114. Berkeley and Los Angeles: University of California Press.

WEINBERG, A. (Ed.) (1957). *Attorney for the Damned.* Foreword by Justice W. O. DOUGLAS. New York: Simon & Schuster.

WEINBERG, J. R. (1950). *An Examination of Logical Positivism.* London: Routledge & Kegan Paul.

WEINER, H., and BRAIMAN, A. (1955). The Ganser syndrome: A review and addition of some unusual cases. *Am. J. Psychiat., 111:*767.

WERTHAM, F. (1949). *The Show of Violence.* Garden City, N. Y.: Doubleday & Co.

WHARTON, E. (1911). *Ethan Frome.* New York: Charles Scribner's.

WHEELIS, A. (1958). *The Quest for Identity.* New York: W. W. Norton.

WHITE, R. W. (1941). "A Preface to the Theory of Hypnotism." In, S. S. Tomkins, (ed.). *Contemporary Psychopathology, A Source Book.* Chapter 36, pp. 479-502. Cambridge, Mass.: Harvard University Press, 1947.

WHITEHEAD, A. N., and RUSSELL, B. (1910). *Principia Mathematica.* Second Edition, Vol. I. Cambridge: Cambridge University Press, 1950.

WIENER, N. (1948). *Cybernetics. Or Control and Communication in the Animal and the Machine.* New York: John Wiley.

WIENER, N. (1950). *The Human Use of Human Beings. Cybernetics and Society.* Garden City, N. Y.: Doubleday Anchor, 1954.

WIENER, N. (1960). Some moral and technical consequences of automation. *Science, 131:*1355.

WOODGER, J. H. (1952). *Biology and Language. An Introduction to the Methodology of the Biological Sciences Including Medicine.* Cambridge: Cambridge University Press.

WOODGER, J. H. (1956). *Physics, Psychology and Medicine. A Methodological Essay.* Cambridge: Cambridge University Press.

WORTIS, J. B. (1950). *Soviet Psychiatry.* Baltimore: Williams & Wilkins.

YARNELL, H. (1957). An example of the psychopathology of religion: The Seventh-day Adventist denomination. *J. Nerv. & Ment. Dis., 125:*202.

ZIEGLER, F. J., IMBODEN, J. B., and MEYER, E. (1960). Contemporary conversion reactions: A clinical study. *Am. J. Psychiat., 116:*901.

ZILBOORG, G. (1935). *The Medical Man and the Witch During the Renaissance.* The Hideyo Nogushi Lectures. Baltimore: Johns Hopkins Press.

ZILBOORG, G. (1941). *A History of Medical Psychology.* In collaboration with G. W. Henry. New York: W. W. Norton.

ZILBOORG, G. (1943). *Mind, Medicine, and Man.* New York: Harcourt, Brace.

ZWEIG, S. (1931). *Mental Healers. Franz Anton Mesmer, Mary Baker Eddy, Sigmund Freud.* Translated by EDEN and CEDAR PAUL. New York: Viking, 1932.

Author Index